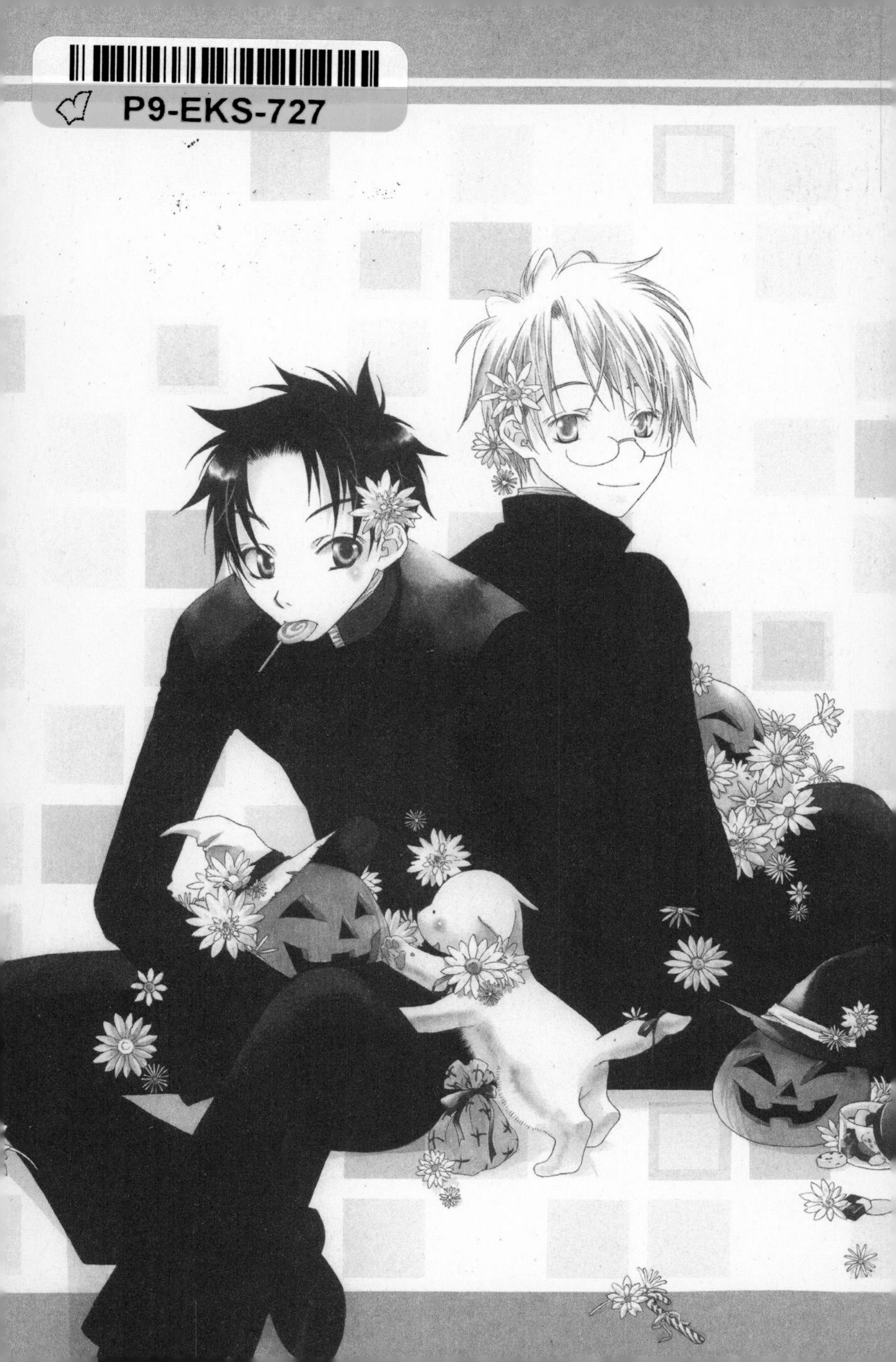

Translation – Christine Schilling
Adaptation – Mallory Reaves
Lettering – Jihye Hong
Production Manager – James Dashiell
Editor – Brynne Chandler

A Go! Comi manga

Published by Go! Media Entertainment, LLC

Black Sun Silver Moon Volume 3
© 2004 TOMO MAEDA
All rights reserved.
First published in Japan in 2004 by SHINSHOKAN Co., Ltd. Tokyo
English Version published by Go! Media Entertainment, LLC under license
from SHINSHOKAN Co., Ltd.

English Text © 2007 Go! Media Entertainment, LLC. All rights reserved.

Visit us online at www.gocomi.com
e-mail: info@gocomi.com

ISBN 978-1-933617-35-0

First printed in October 2007

1 2 3 4 5 6 7 8 9

Manufactured in the United States of America

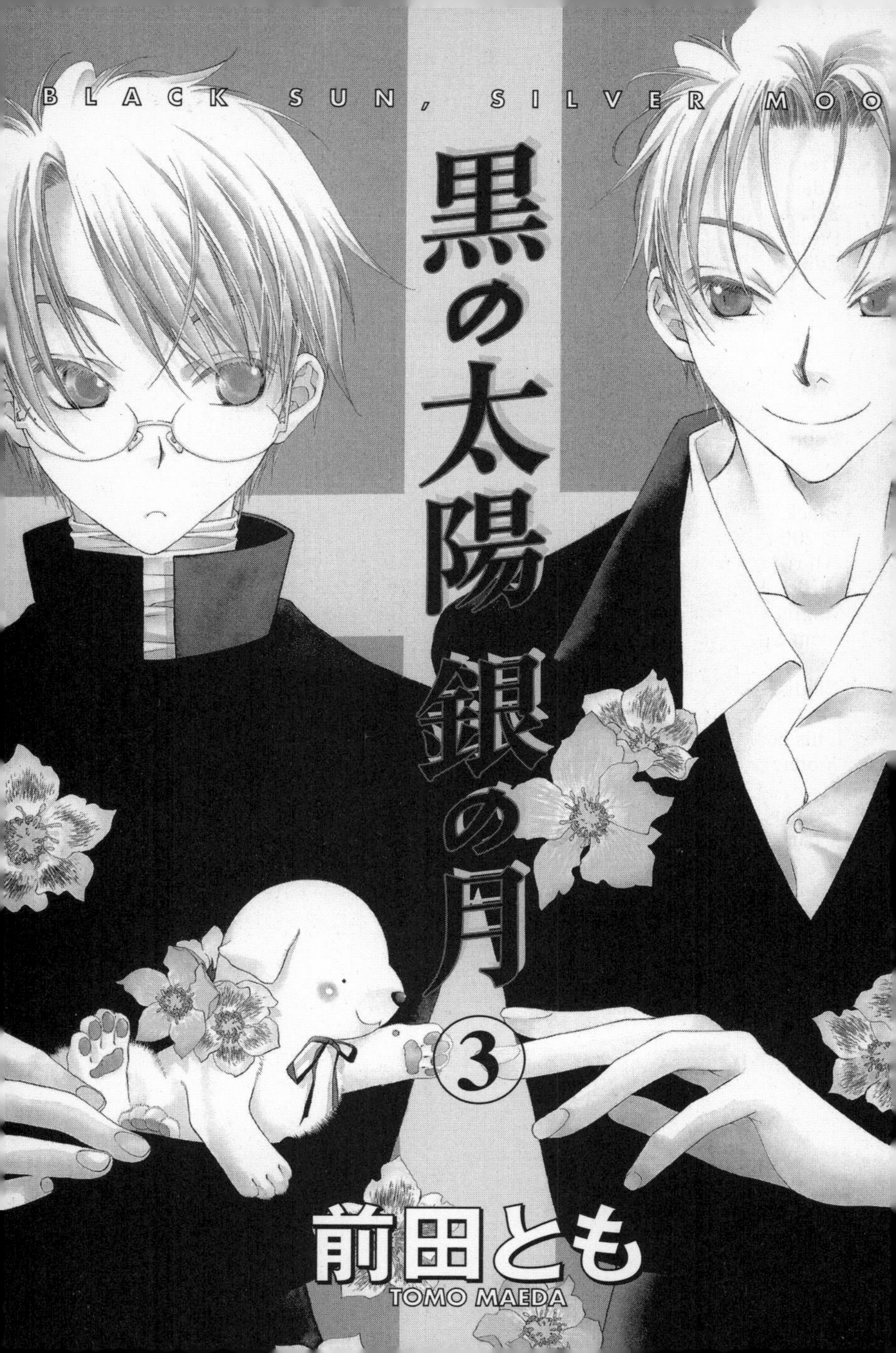
BLACK SUN, SILVER MOO
黒の太陽 銀の月
3
前田とも
TOMO MAEDA

CONTENTS

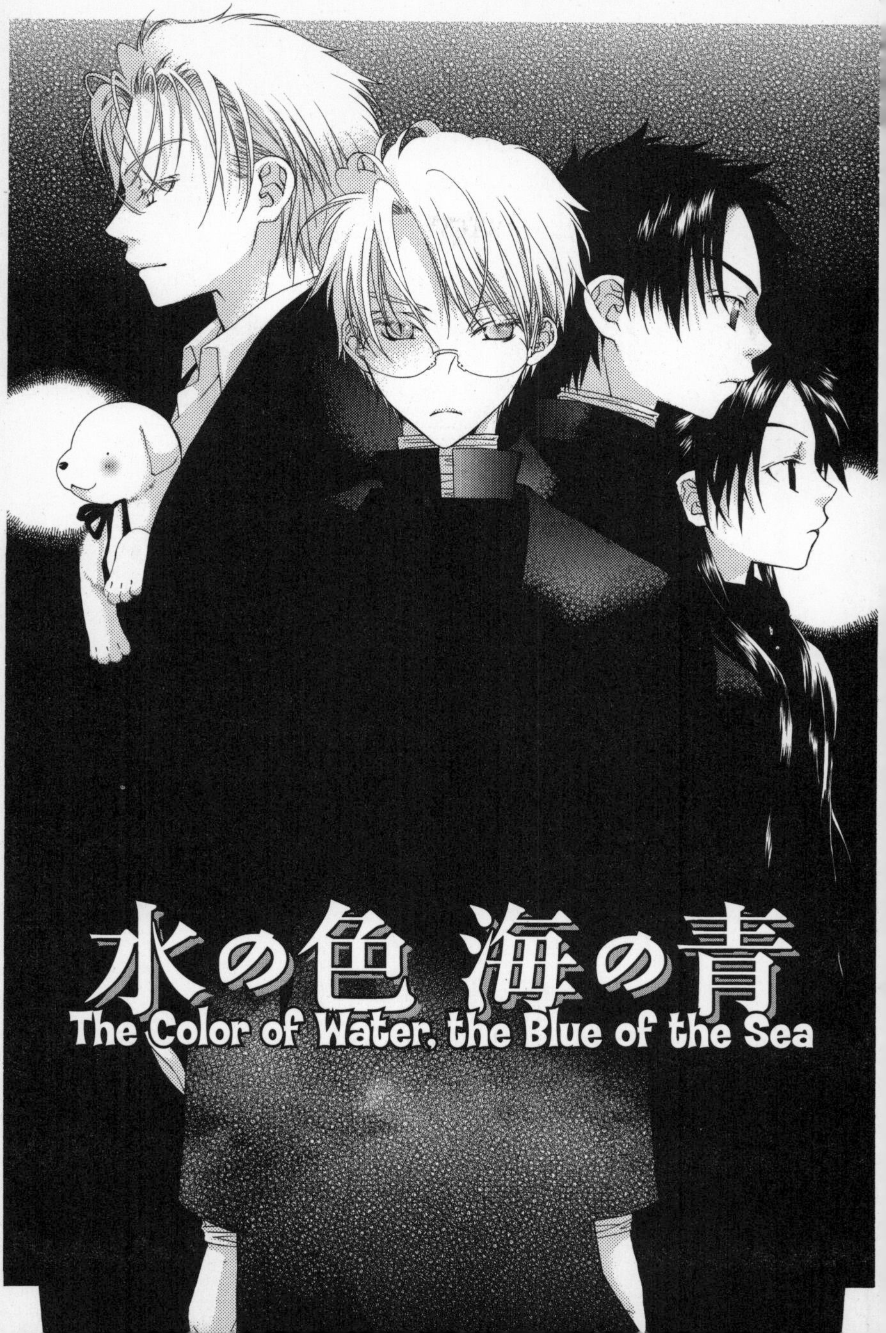
水の色 海の青
The Color of Water, the Blue of the Sea

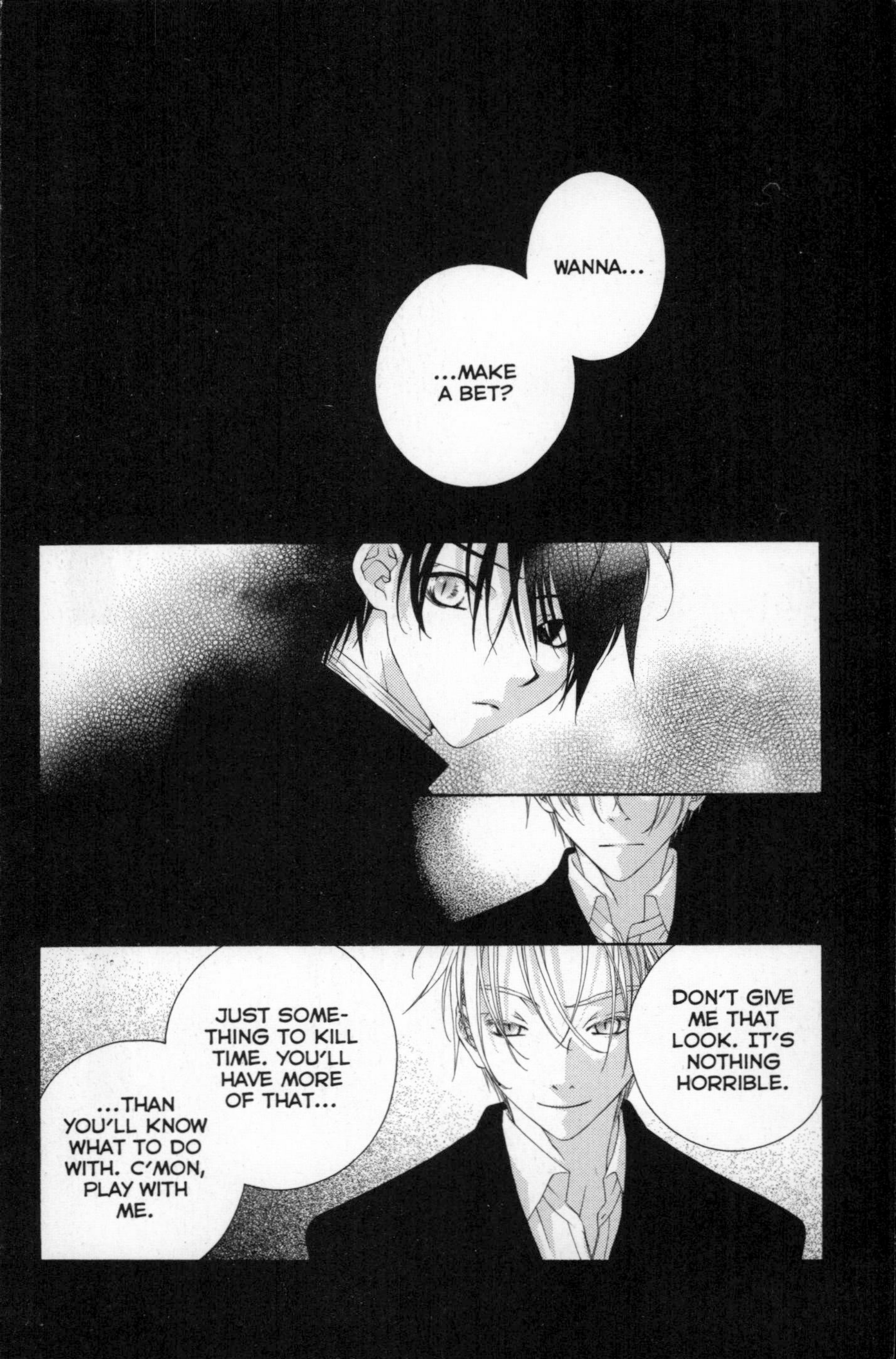
WANNA...
...MAKE A BET?
DON'T GIVE ME THAT LOOK. IT'S NOTHING HORRIBLE.
JUST SOME-THING TO KILL TIME. YOU'LL HAVE MORE OF THAT...
...THAN YOU'LL KNOW WHAT TO DO WITH. C'MON, PLAY WITH ME.

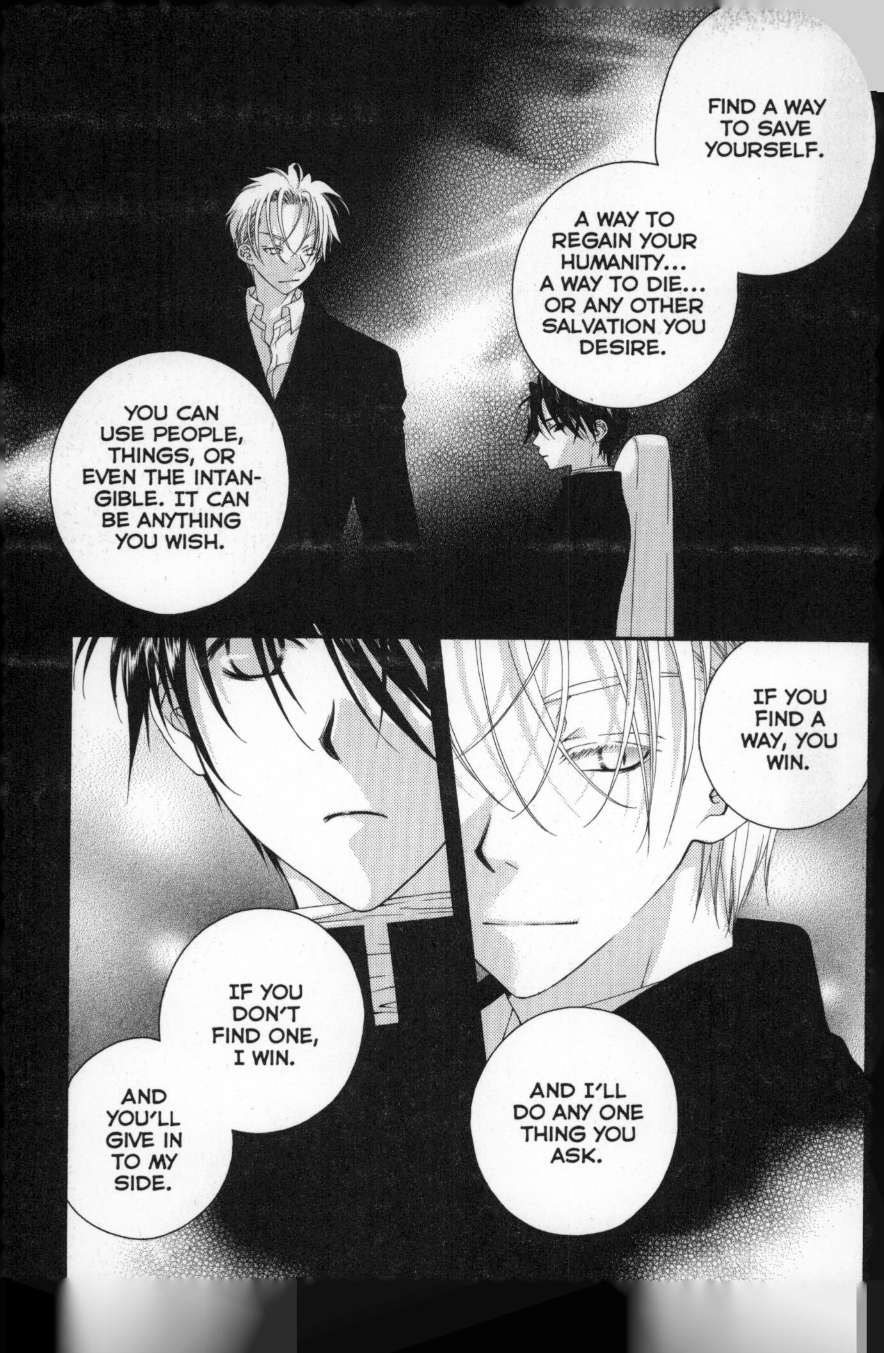
FIND A WAY TO SAVE YOURSELF.
A WAY TO REGAIN YOUR HUMANITY... A WAY TO DIE... OR ANY OTHER SALVATION YOU DESIRE.
YOU CAN USE PEOPLE, THINGS, OR EVEN THE INTAN-GIBLE. IT CAN BE ANYTHING YOU WISH.
IF YOU FIND A WAY, YOU WIN.
AND I'LL DO ANY ONE THING YOU ASK.
IF YOU DON'T FIND ONE, I WIN.
AND YOU'LL GIVE IN TO MY SIDE.

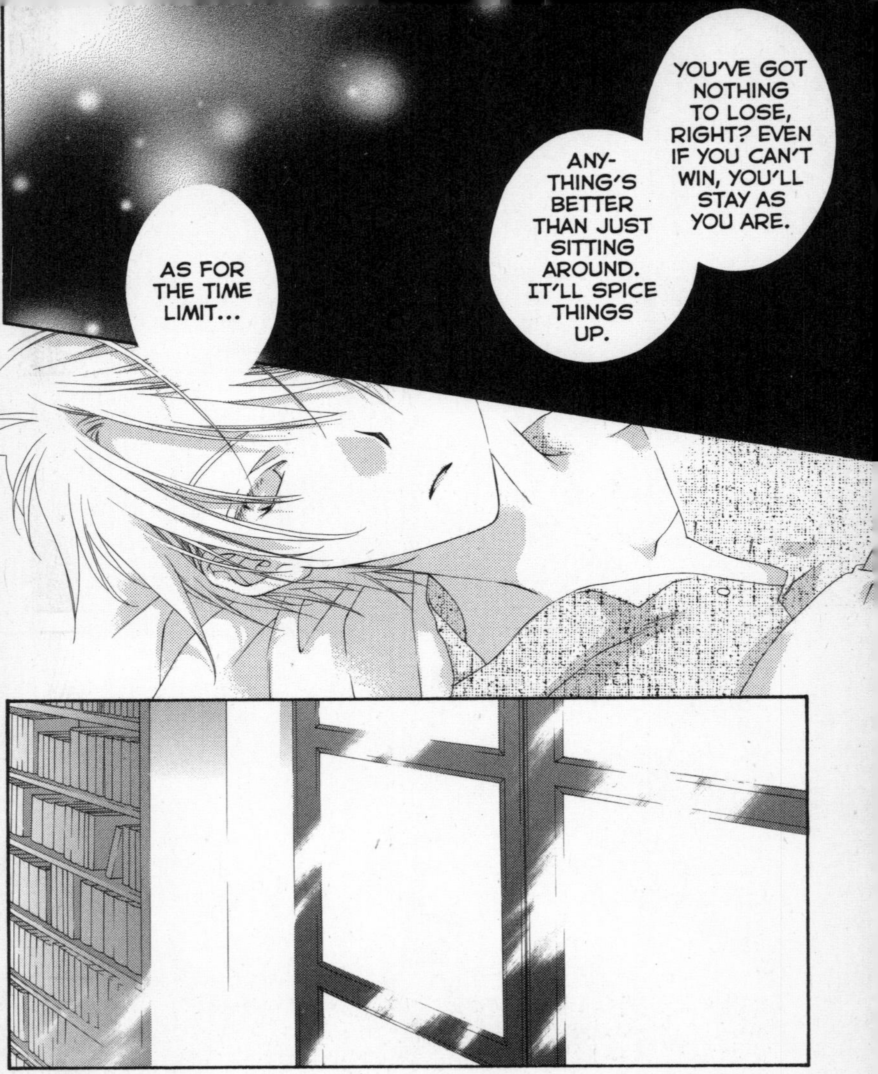
YOU'VE GOT NOTHING TO LOSE, RIGHT? EVEN IF YOU CAN'T WIN, YOU'LL STAY AS YOU ARE.
ANY-THING'S BETTER THAN JUST SITTING AROUND. IT'LL SPICE THINGS UP.
AS FOR THE TIME LIMIT...
YOU CAN DECIDE HOW LONG THIS WILL GO ON.
IT'S ALL UP TO YOU.

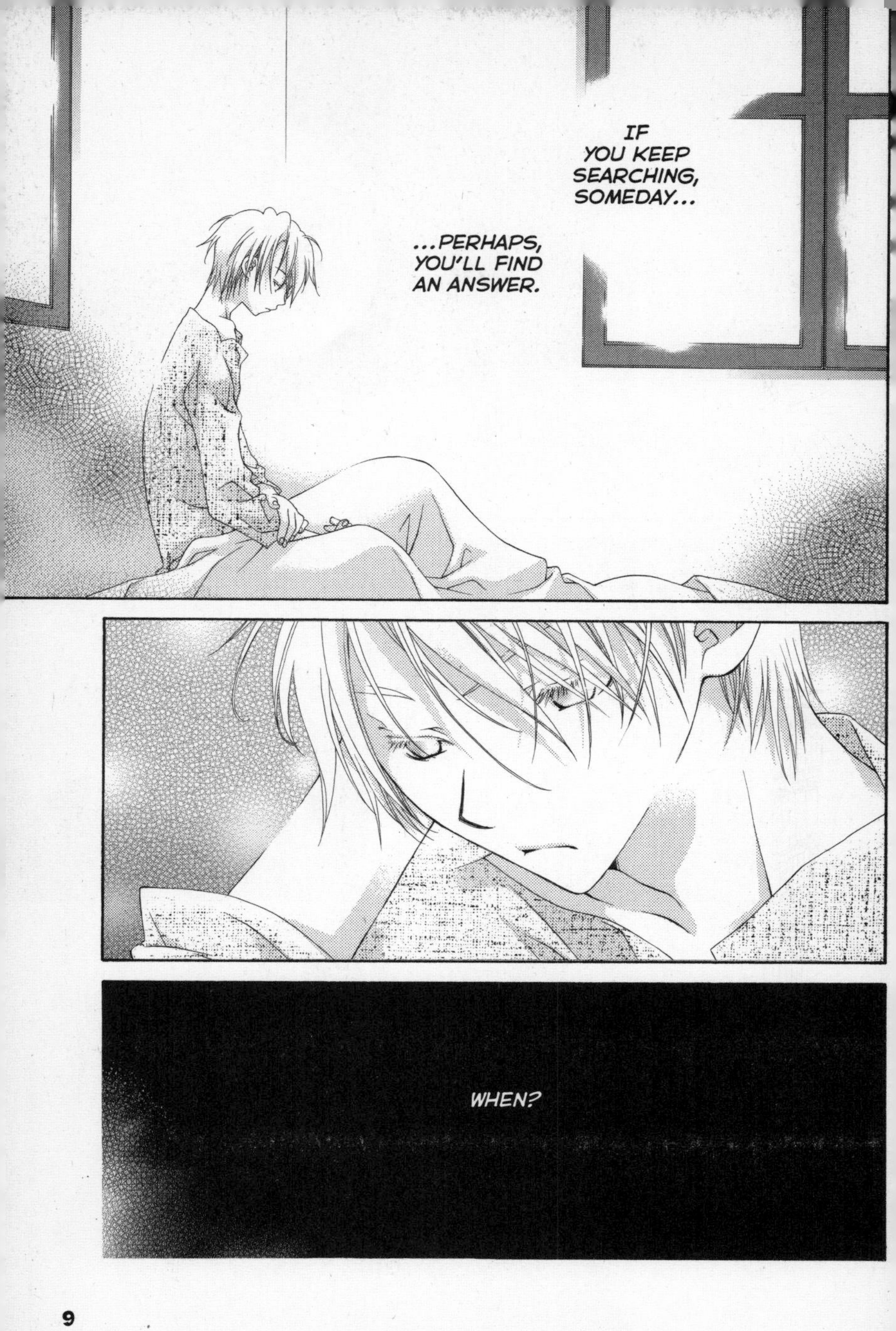
IF YOU KEEP SEARCHING, SOMEDAY...
...PERHAPS, YOU'LL FIND AN ANSWER.
WHEN?

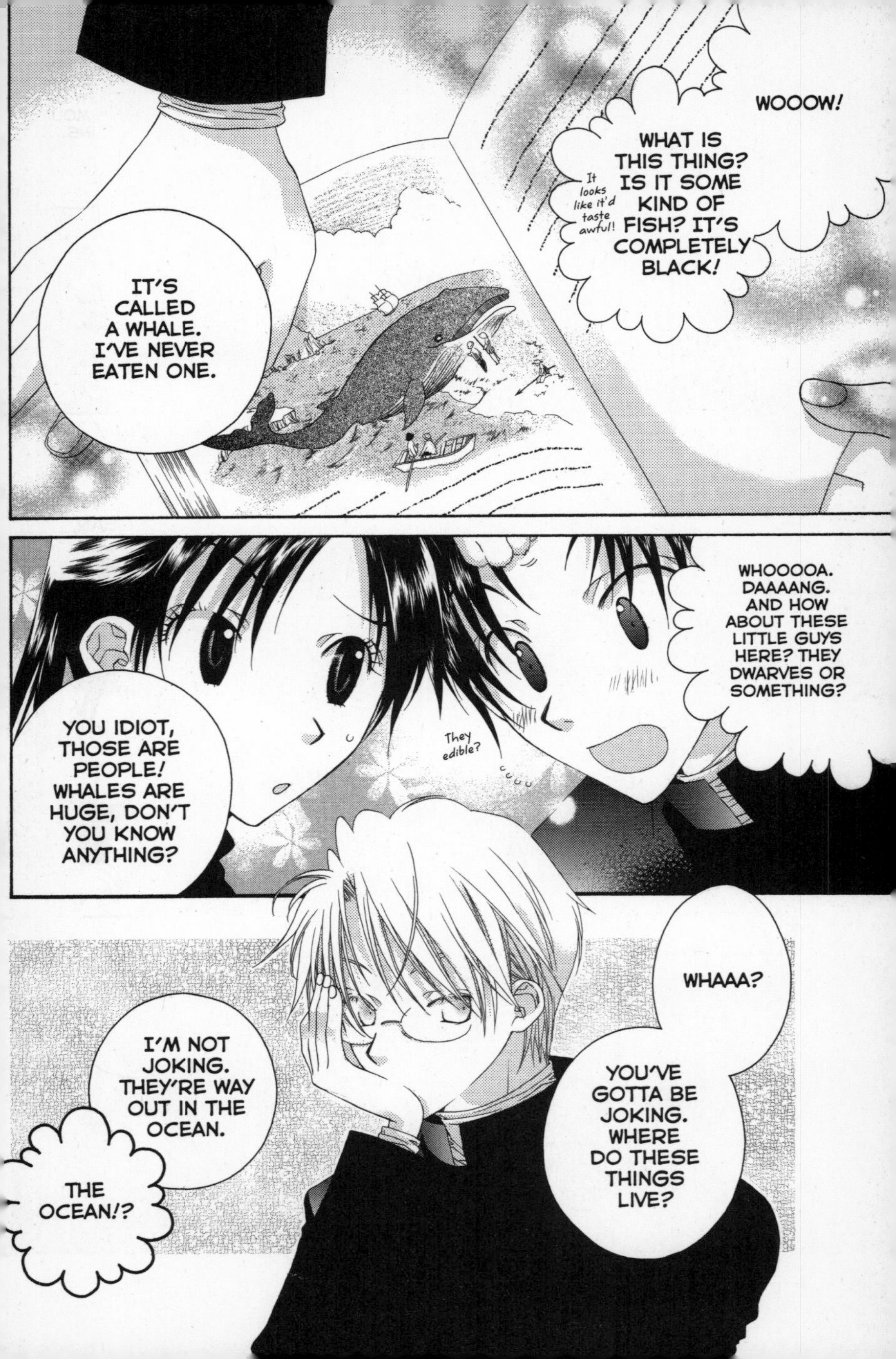
WOOOW!
WHAT IS THIS THING? IS IT SOME KIND OF FISH? IT'S COMPLETELY BLACK!
It looks like it'd taste awful!
IT'S CALLED A WHALE. I'VE NEVER EATEN ONE.
WHOOOOA. DAAAANG. AND HOW ABOUT THESE LITTLE GUYS HERE? THEY DWARVES OR SOMETHING?
They edible?
YOU IDIOT, THOSE ARE PEOPLE! WHALES ARE HUGE, DON'T YOU KNOW ANYTHING?
WHAAA?
YOU'VE GOTTA BE JOKING. WHERE DO THESE THINGS LIVE?
I'M NOT JOKING. THEY'RE WAY OUT IN THE OCEAN.
THE OCEAN!?

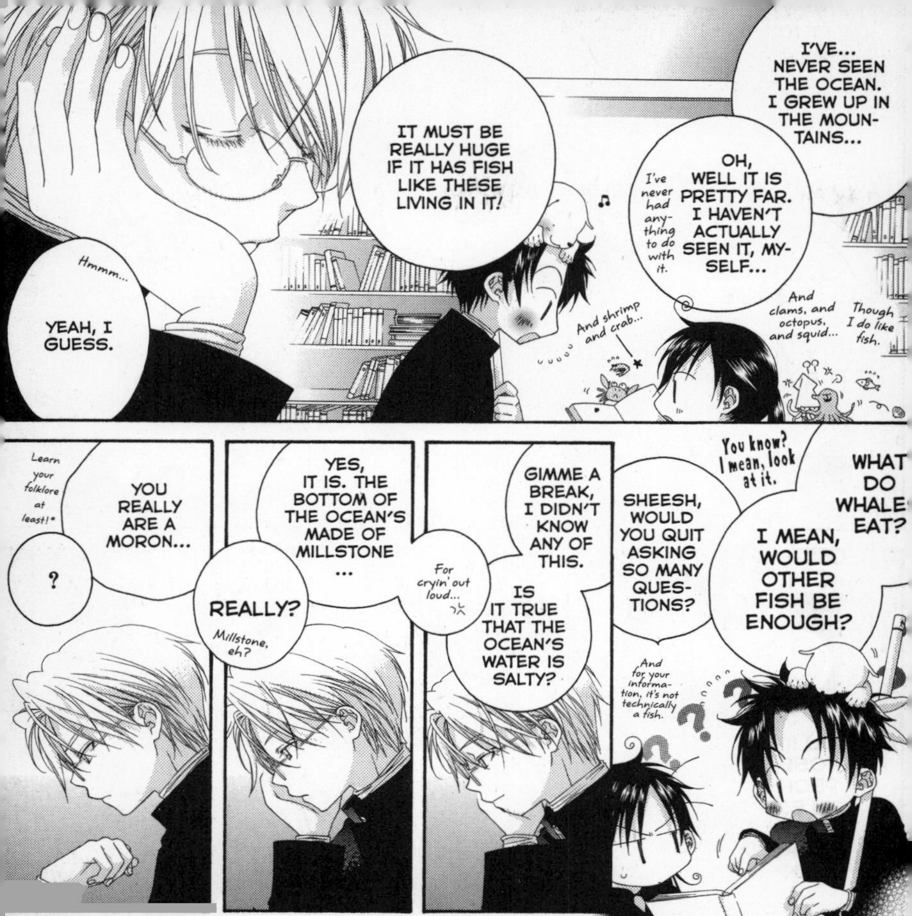
I'VE... NEVER SEEN THE OCEAN. I GREW UP IN THE MOUN-TAINS...
OH, WELL IT IS PRETTY FAR. I HAVEN'T ACTUALLY SEEN IT, MY-SELF...
I've never had any-thing to do with it.
Though I do like fish.
And clams, and octopus, and squid...
And shrimp and crab...
IT MUST BE REALLY HUGE IF IT HAS FISH LIKE THESE LIVING IN IT!
Hmmm...
YEAH, I GUESS.
WHAT DO WHALE EAT?
I MEAN, WOULD OTHER FISH BE ENOUGH?
You know? I mean, look at it.
SHEESH, WOULD YOU QUIT ASKING SO MANY QUES-TIONS?
And for your informa-tion, it's not technically a fish.
GIMME A BREAK, I DIDN'T KNOW ANY OF THIS.
IS IT TRUE THAT THE OCEAN'S WATER IS SALTY?
For cryin' out loud...
YES, IT IS. THE BOTTOM OF THE OCEAN'S MADE OF MILLSTONE...
REALLY?
Millstone, eh?
YOU REALLY ARE A MORON...
Learn your folklore at least!*
?

*SEE TRANSLATOR'S NOTES

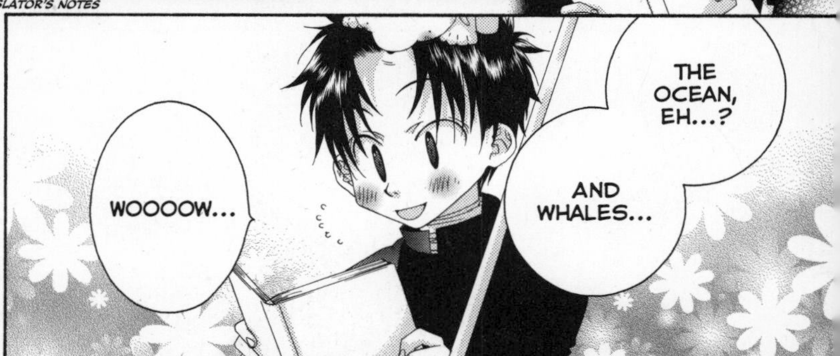
THE OCEAN, EH...?
AND WHALES...
WOOOOW...

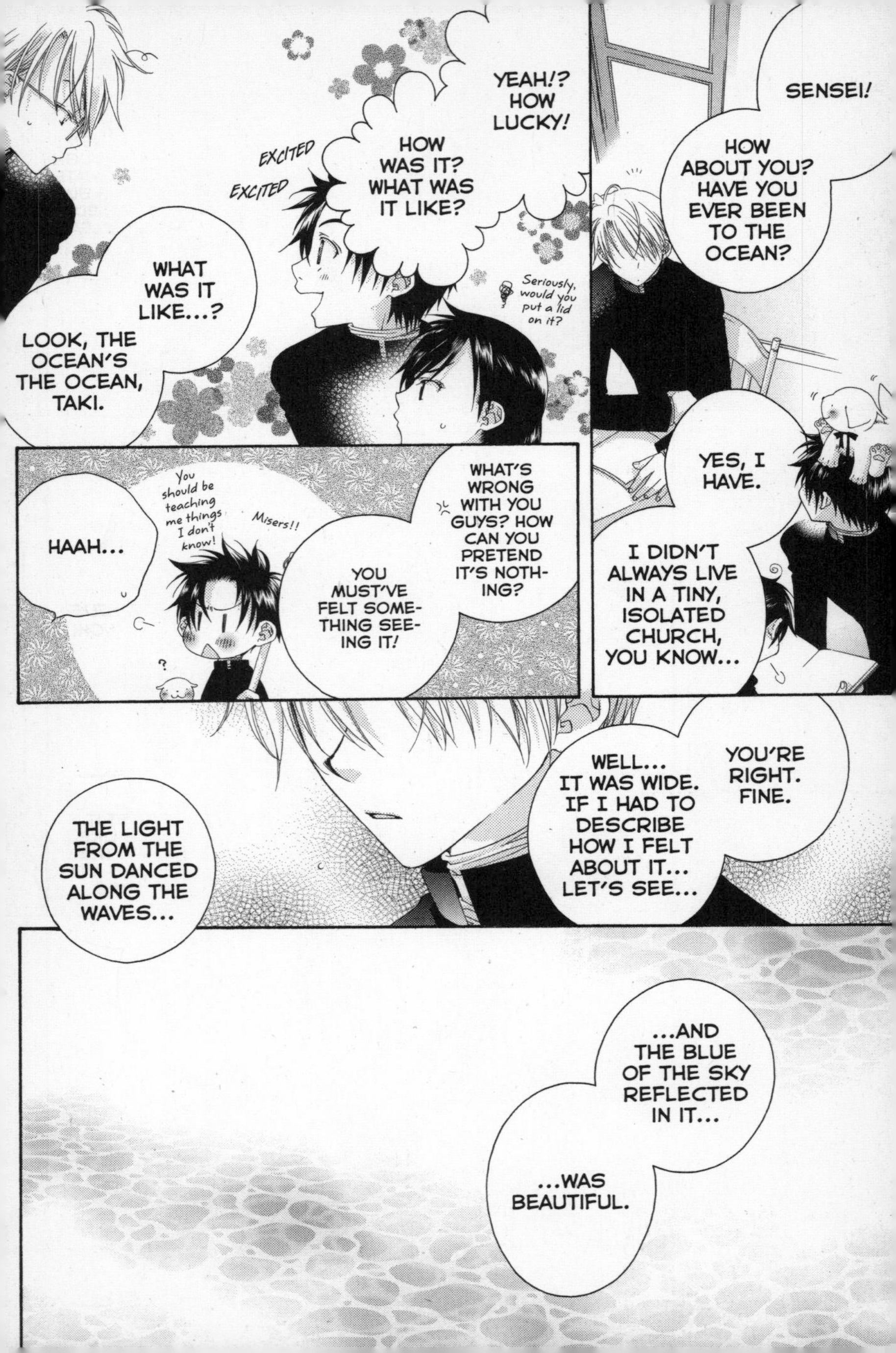
SENSEI!
HOW ABOUT YOU? HAVE YOU EVER BEEN TO THE OCEAN?
YES, I HAVE.
I DIDN'T ALWAYS LIVE IN A TINY, ISOLATED CHURCH, YOU KNOW...
YEAH!? HOW LUCKY!
HOW WAS IT? WHAT WAS IT LIKE?
EXCITED
EXCITED
Seriously, would you put a lid on it?
WHAT WAS IT LIKE...?
LOOK, THE OCEAN'S THE OCEAN, TAKI.
WHAT'S WRONG WITH YOU GUYS? HOW CAN YOU PRETEND IT'S NOTH-ING?
YOU MUST'VE FELT SOME-THING SEE-ING IT!
Misers!!
You should be teaching me things I don't know!
HAAH...
YOU'RE RIGHT. FINE.
WELL... IT WAS WIDE. IF I HAD TO DESCRIBE HOW I FELT ABOUT IT... LET'S SEE...
THE LIGHT FROM THE SUN DANCED ALONG THE WAVES...
...AND THE BLUE OF THE SKY REFLECTED IN IT...
...WAS BEAUTIFUL.

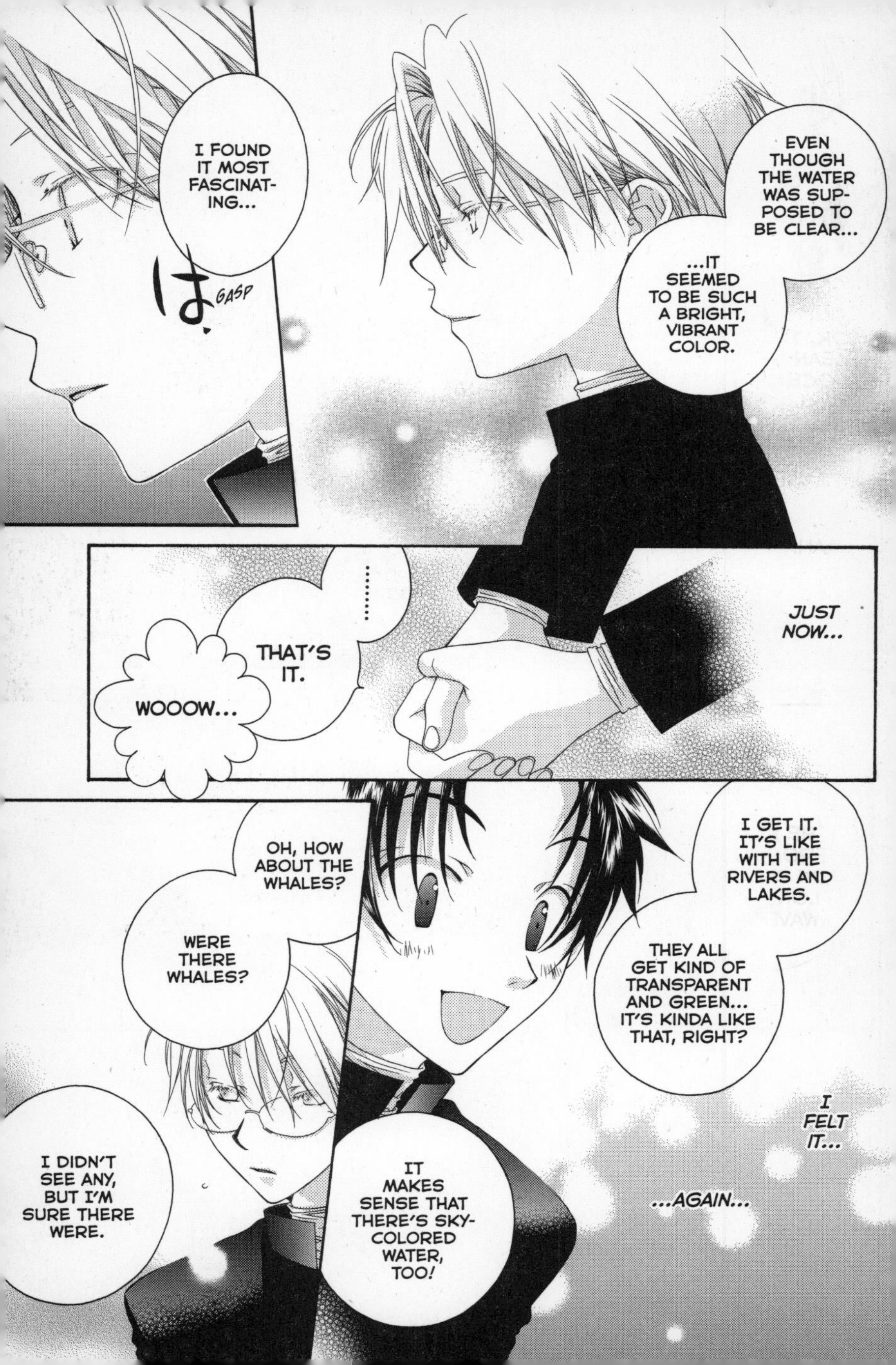
EVEN THOUGH THE WATER WAS SUPPOSED TO BE CLEAR...
...IT SEEMED TO BE SUCH A BRIGHT, VIBRANT COLOR.
I FOUND IT MOST FASCINATING...
は GASP
JUST NOW...
......
THAT'S IT.
WOOOW...
I GET IT. IT'S LIKE WITH THE RIVERS AND LAKES.
THEY ALL GET KIND OF TRANSPARENT AND GREEN... IT'S KINDA LIKE THAT, RIGHT?
I FELT IT...
...AGAIN...
IT MAKES SENSE THAT THERE'S SKY-COLORED WATER, TOO!
OH, HOW ABOUT THE WHALES?
WERE THERE WHALES?
I DIDN'T SEE ANY, BUT I'M SURE THERE WERE.

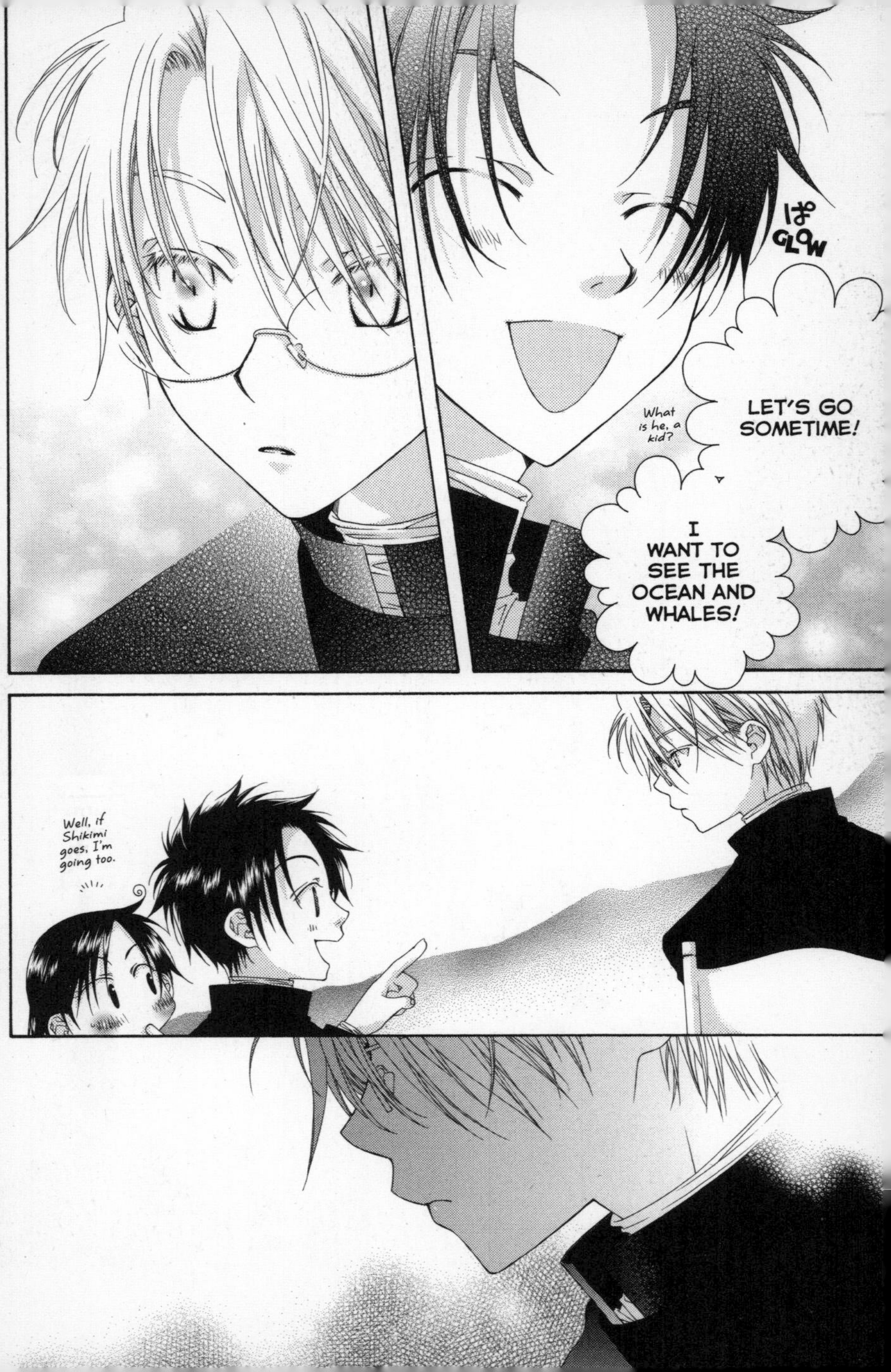
ぱ
GLOW
LET'S GO SOMETIME!
I WANT TO SEE THE OCEAN AND WHALES!
What is he, a kid?
Well, if Shikimi goes, I'm going too.

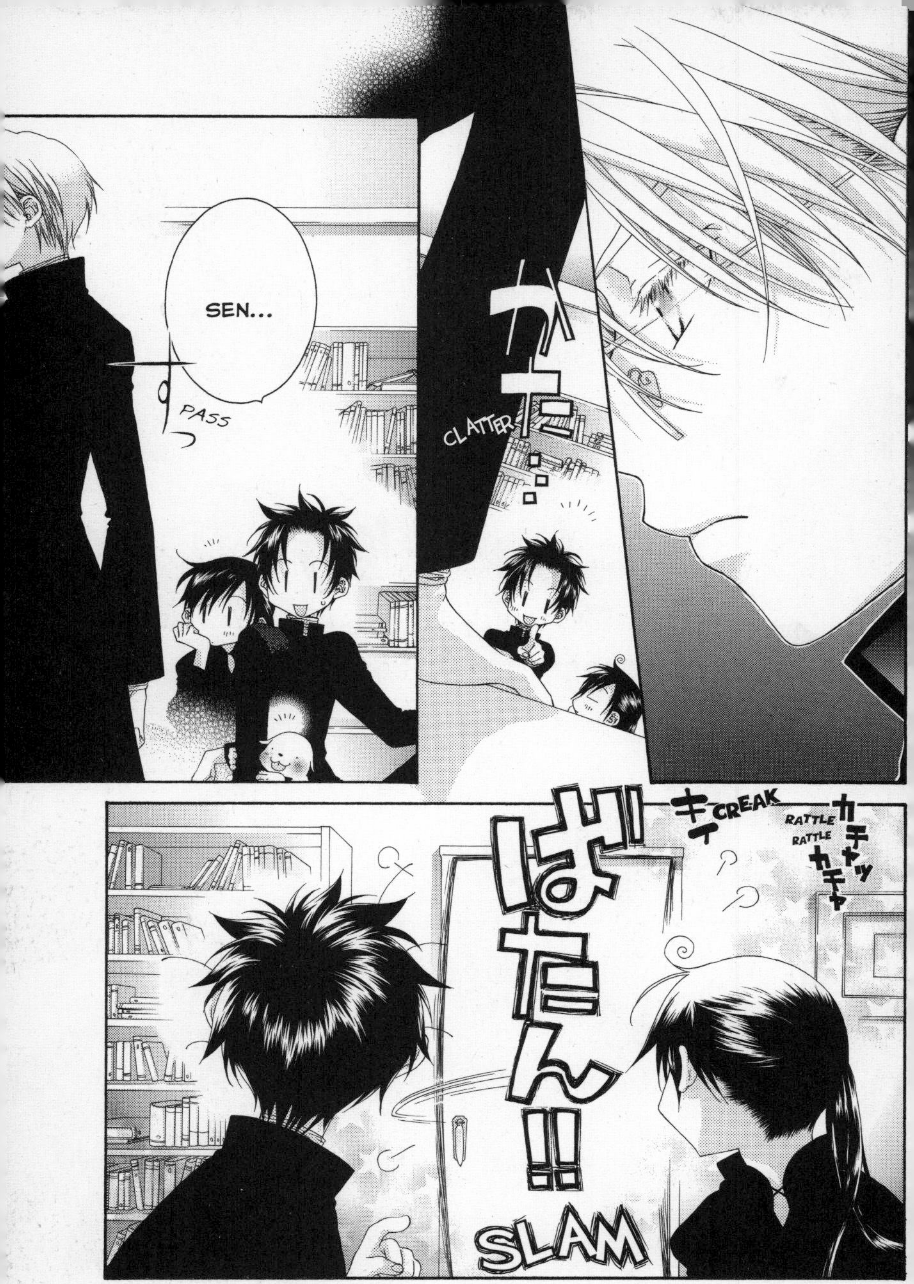

CLATTER
SEN...
PASS
キィ
CREAK
カチャッ カチャ
RATTLE RATTLE
ばたん!!
SLAM

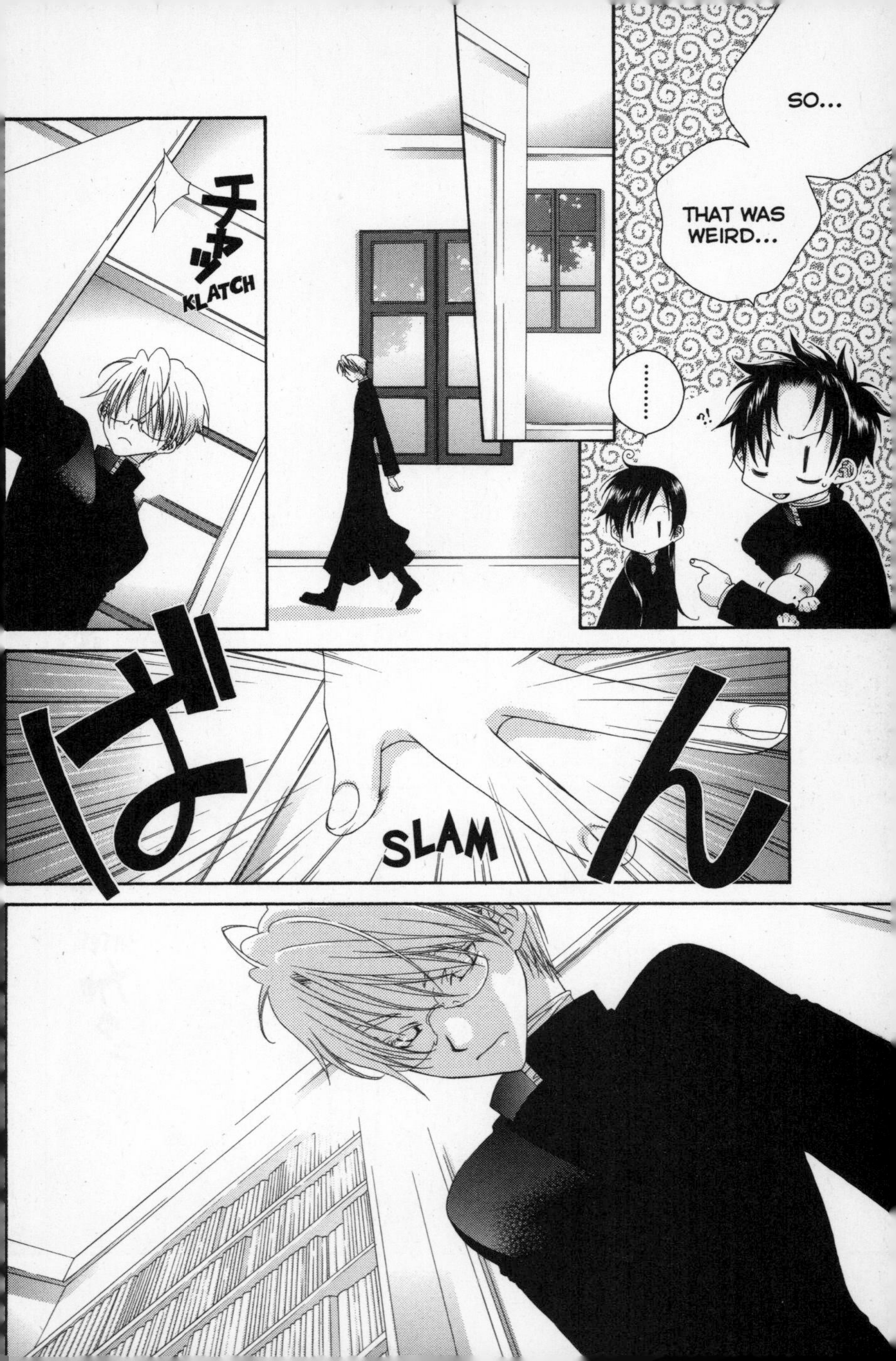
SO...
THAT WAS WEIRD...
......
?!
チャッ
KLATCH
ばん
SLAM

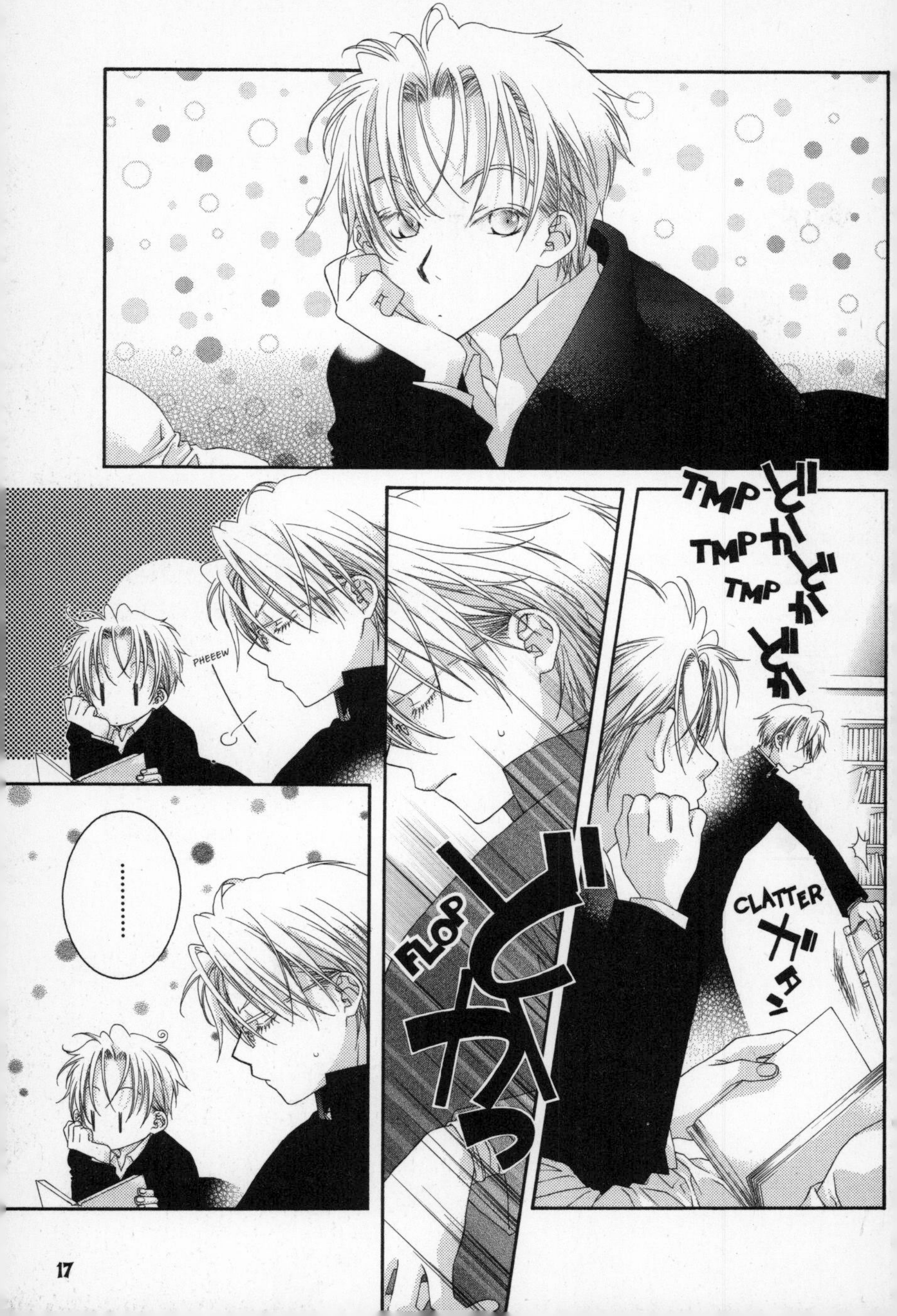
TMP
TMP
TMP
CLATTER
FLOP
PHEEEW
......

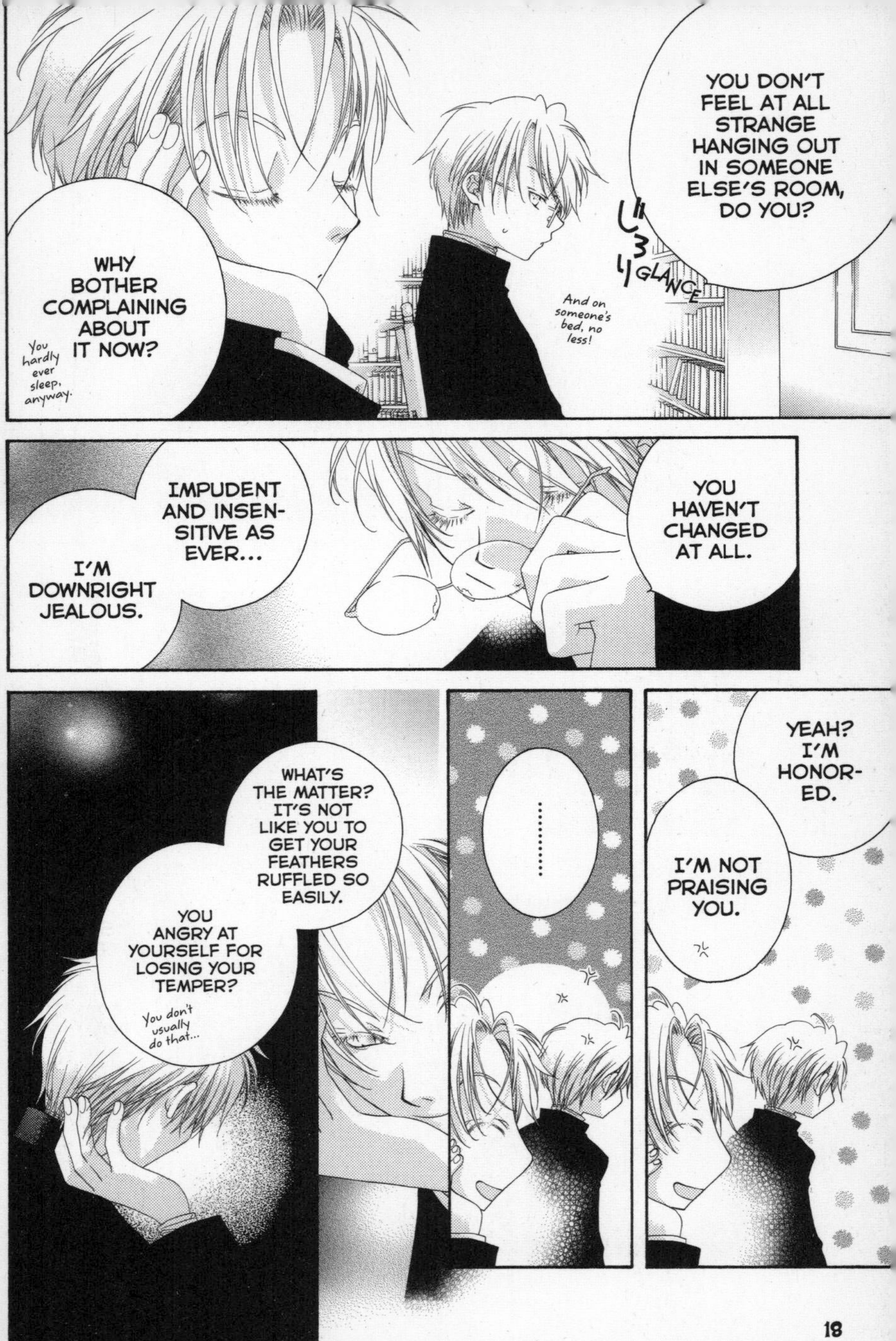

YOU DON'T FEEL AT ALL STRANGE HANGING OUT IN SOMEONE ELSE'S ROOM, DO YOU?
GLANCE
And on someone's bed, no less!
WHY BOTHER COMPLAINING ABOUT IT NOW?
You hardly ever sleep, anyway.
YOU HAVEN'T CHANGED AT ALL.
IMPUDENT AND INSEN-SITIVE AS EVER...
I'M DOWNRIGHT JEALOUS.
YEAH? I'M HONOR-ED.
I'M NOT PRAISING YOU.
......
WHAT'S THE MATTER? IT'S NOT LIKE YOU TO GET YOUR FEATHERS RUFFLED SO EASILY.
YOU ANGRY AT YOURSELF FOR LOSING YOUR TEMPER?
You don't usually do that...

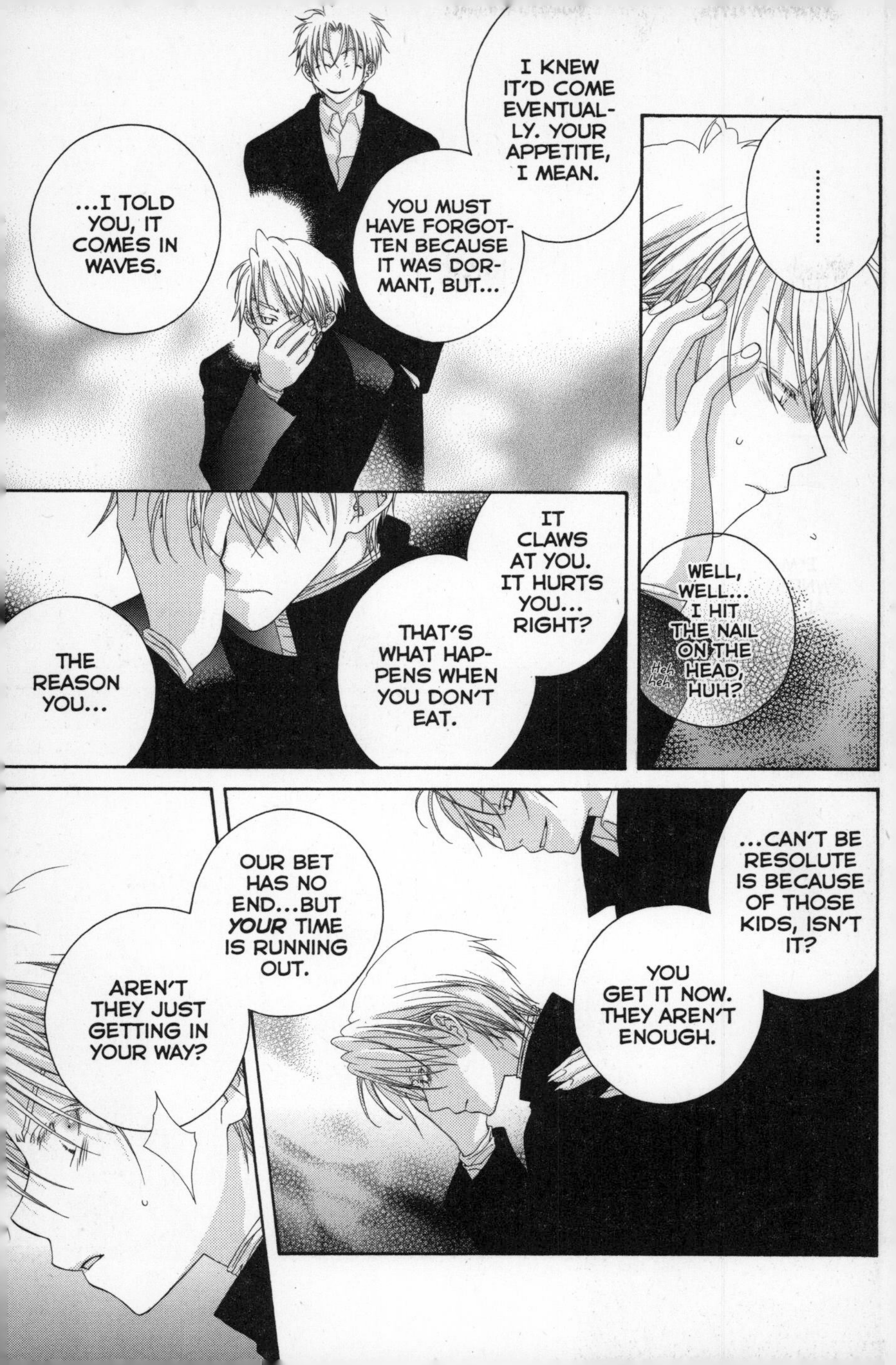
......
WELL, WELL... I HIT THE NAIL ON THE HEAD, HUH?
Heh heh.
I KNEW IT'D COME EVENTUAL-LY. YOUR APPETITE, I MEAN.
YOU MUST HAVE FORGOT-TEN BECAUSE IT WAS DOR-MANT, BUT...
...I TOLD YOU, IT COMES IN WAVES.
IT CLAWS AT YOU. IT HURTS YOU... RIGHT?
THAT'S WHAT HAP-PENS WHEN YOU DON'T EAT.
THE REASON YOU...
...CAN'T BE RESOLUTE IS BECAUSE OF THOSE KIDS, ISN'T IT?
YOU GET IT NOW. THEY AREN'T ENOUGH.
OUR BET HAS NO END...BUT *YOUR* TIME IS RUNNING OUT.
AREN'T THEY JUST GETTING IN YOUR WAY?

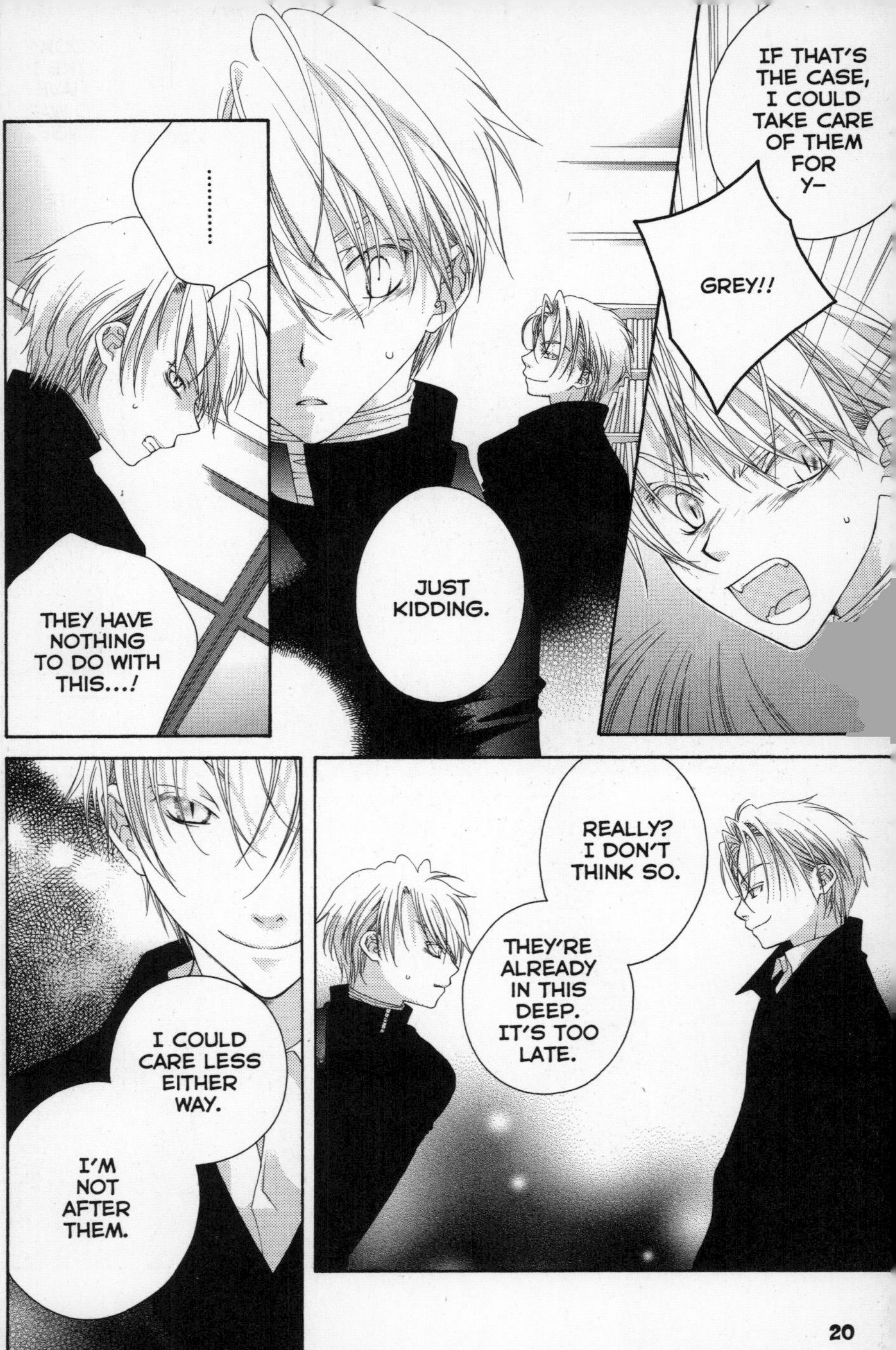
IF THAT'S THE CASE, I COULD TAKE CARE OF THEM FOR Y—
GREY!!
JUST KIDDING.
....
THEY HAVE NOTHING TO DO WITH THIS...!
REALLY? I DON'T THINK SO.
THEY'RE ALREADY IN THIS DEEP. IT'S TOO LATE.
I COULD CARE LESS EITHER WAY.
I'M NOT AFTER THEM.

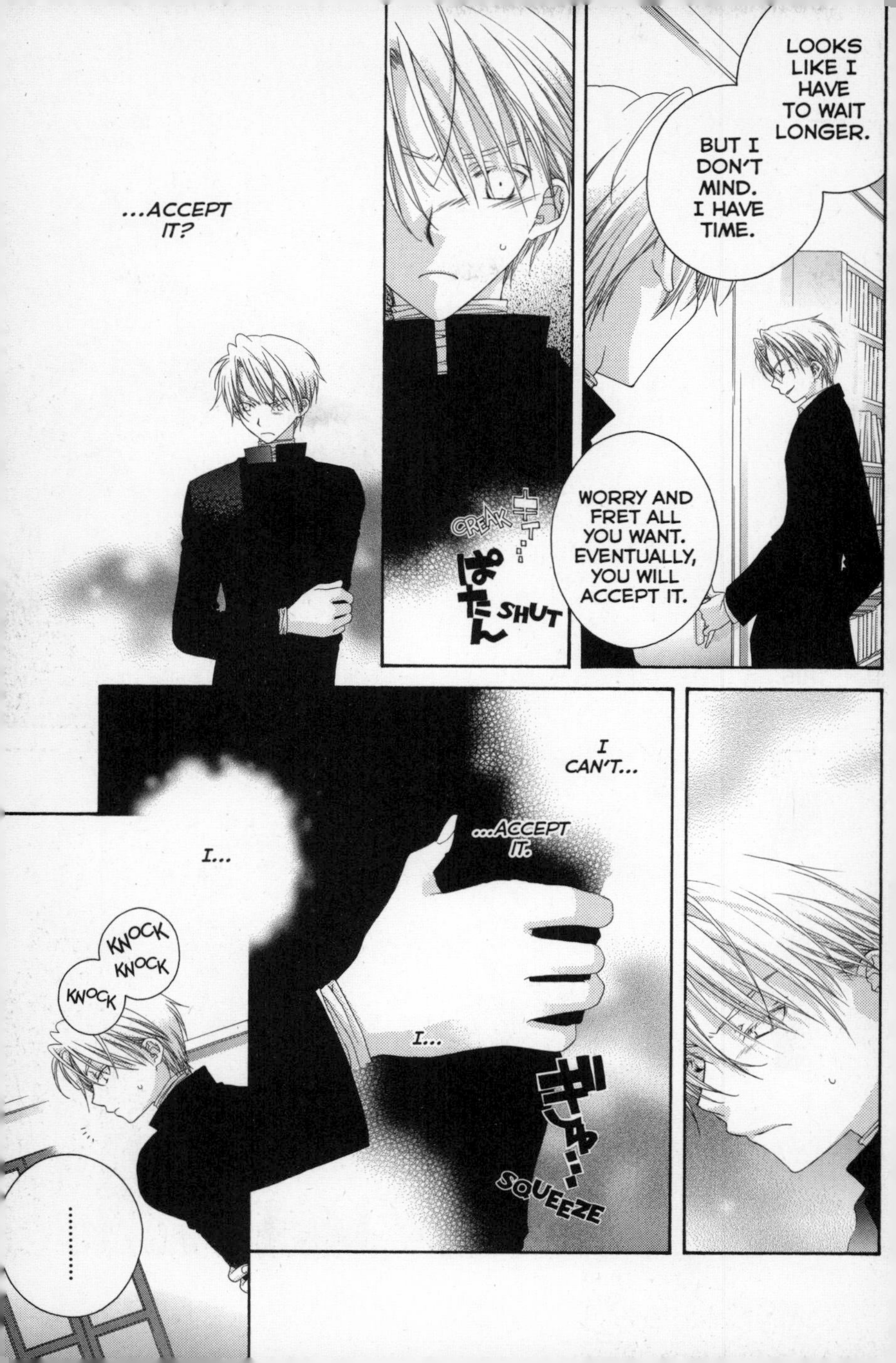
LOOKS LIKE I HAVE TO WAIT LONGER.
BUT I DON'T MIND. I HAVE TIME.
WORRY AND FRET ALL YOU WANT. EVENTUALLY, YOU WILL ACCEPT IT.
CREAK
ぱたん
SHUT
...ACCEPT IT?
I CAN'T...
...ACCEPT IT.
I...
SQUEEZE
I...
KNOCK KNOCK KNOCK
....

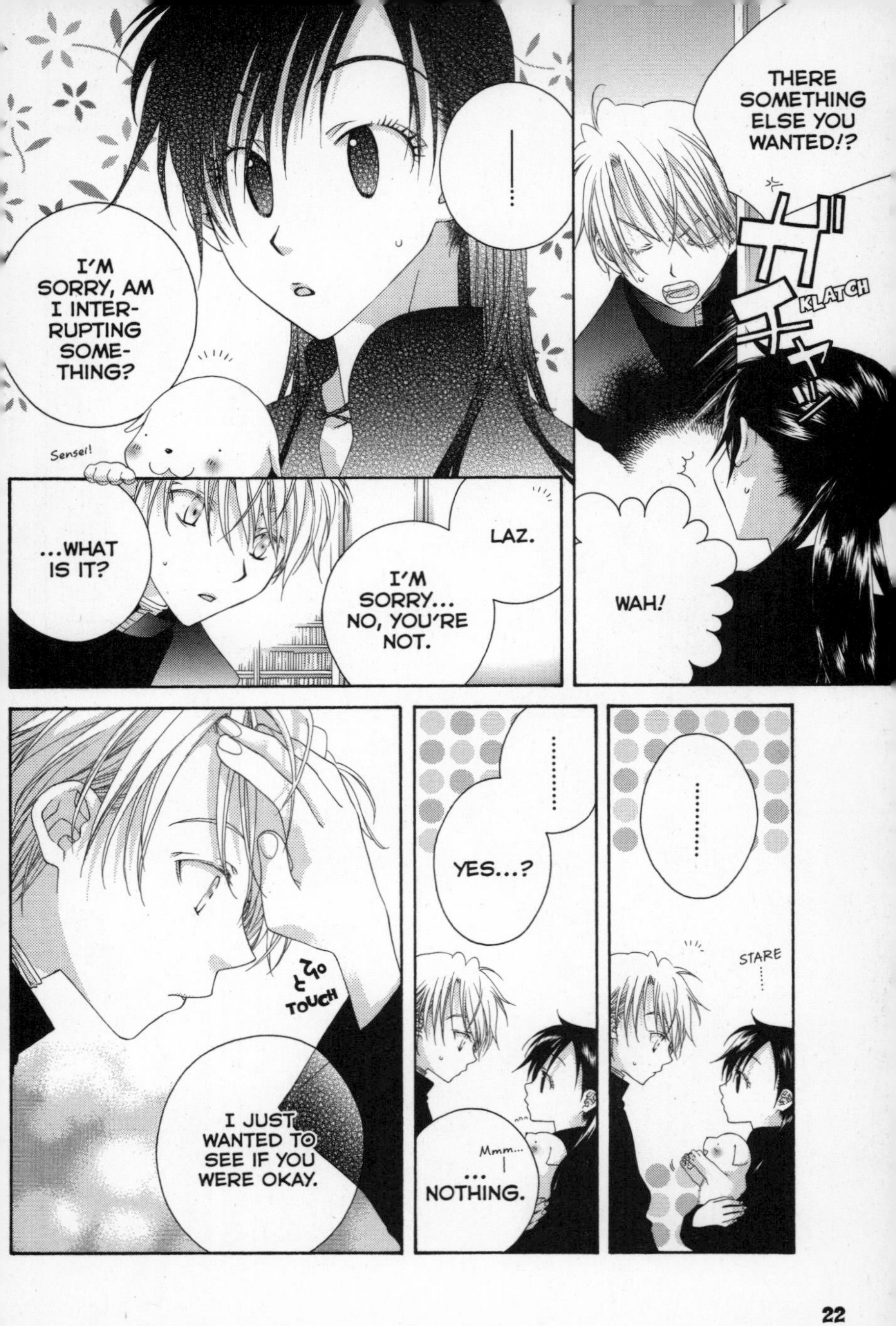
THERE SOMETHING ELSE YOU WANTED!?
KLATCH
WAH!
—......
I'M SORRY, AM I INTER-RUPTING SOME-THING?
Sensei!
LAZ.
I'M SORRY... NO, YOU'RE NOT.
...WHAT IS IT?
......
STARE......
......
YES...?
Mmm...
... NOTHING.
TOUCH
I JUST WANTED TO SEE IF YOU WERE OKAY.

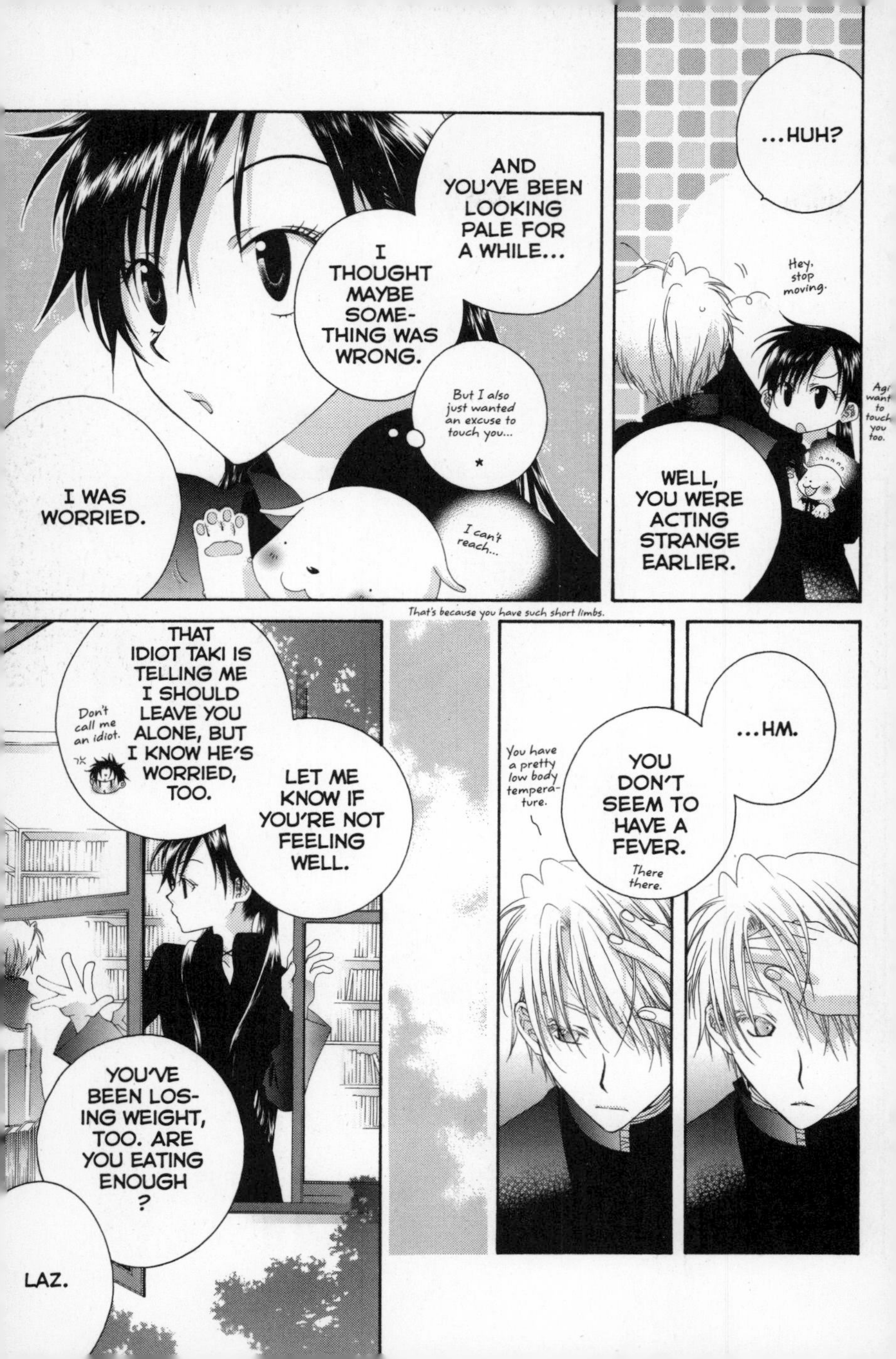
...HUH?
Hey, stop moving.
Agi want to touch you too.
WELL, YOU WERE ACTING STRANGE EARLIER.
AND YOU'VE BEEN LOOKING PALE FOR A WHILE...
I THOUGHT MAYBE SOME-THING WAS WRONG.
But I also just wanted an excuse to touch you... *
I WAS WORRIED.
I can't reach...
That's because you have such short limbs.
...HM.
YOU DON'T SEEM TO HAVE A FEVER.
There there.
You have a pretty low body tempera-ture.
THAT IDIOT TAKI IS TELLING ME I SHOULD LEAVE YOU ALONE, BUT I KNOW HE'S WORRIED, TOO.
Don't call me an idiot.
LET ME KNOW IF YOU'RE NOT FEELING WELL.
YOU'VE BEEN LOS-ING WEIGHT, TOO. ARE YOU EATING ENOUGH ?
LAZ.

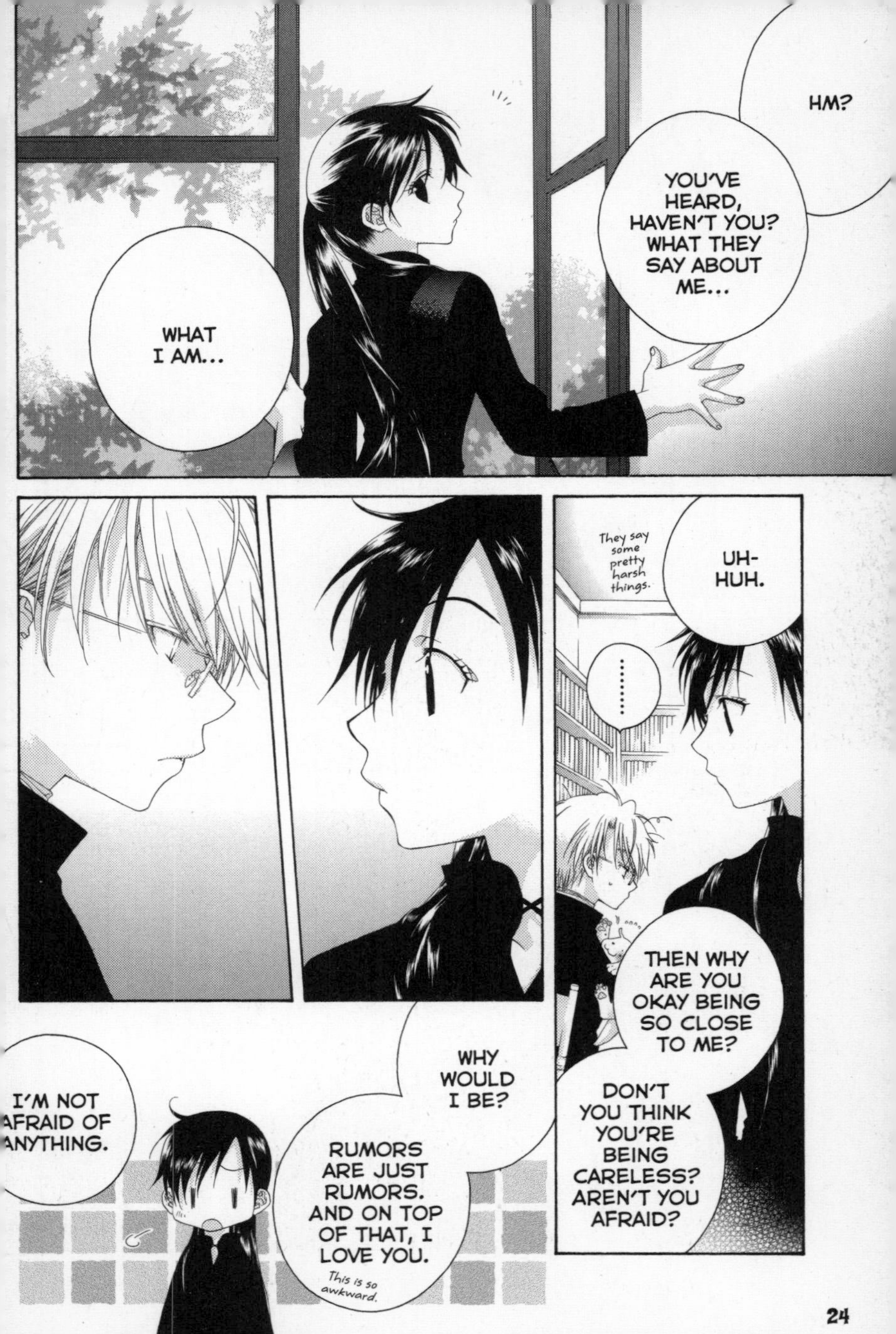
HM?
YOU'VE HEARD, HAVEN'T YOU? WHAT THEY SAY ABOUT ME...
WHAT I AM...
UH-HUH.
They say some pretty harsh things.
......
THEN WHY ARE YOU OKAY BEING SO CLOSE TO ME?
DON'T YOU THINK YOU'RE BEING CARELESS? AREN'T YOU AFRAID?
WHY WOULD I BE?
RUMORS ARE JUST RUMORS. AND ON TOP OF THAT, I LOVE YOU.
This is so awkward.
I'M NOT AFRAID OF ANYTHING.

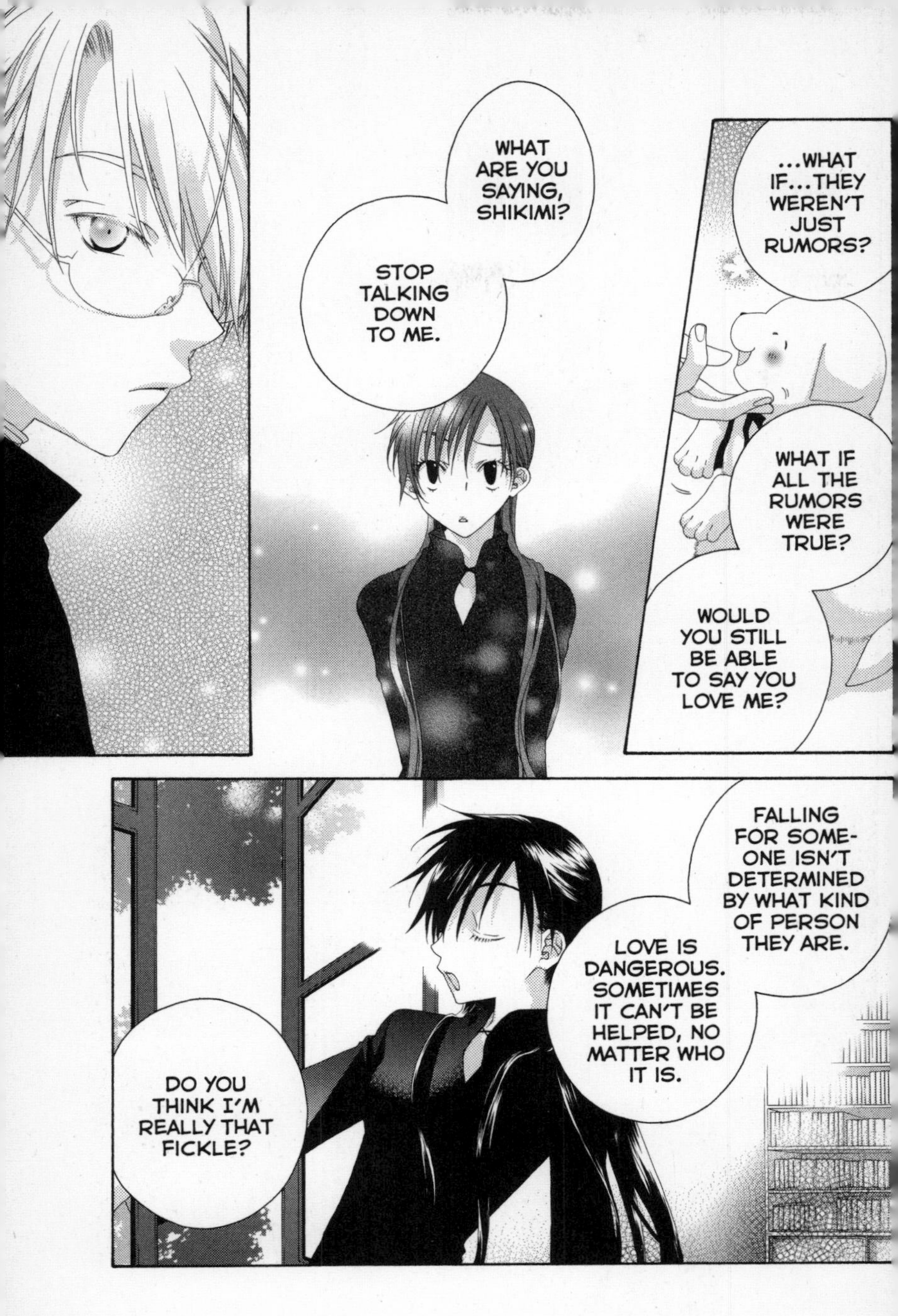
...WHAT IF...THEY WEREN'T JUST RUMORS?
WHAT IF ALL THE RUMORS WERE TRUE?
WOULD YOU STILL BE ABLE TO SAY YOU LOVE ME?
WHAT ARE YOU SAYING, SHIKIMI?
STOP TALKING DOWN TO ME.
FALLING FOR SOME-ONE ISN'T DETERMINED BY WHAT KIND OF PERSON THEY ARE.
LOVE IS DANGEROUS. SOMETIMES IT CAN'T BE HELPED, NO MATTER WHO IT IS.
DO YOU THINK I'M REALLY THAT FICKLE?

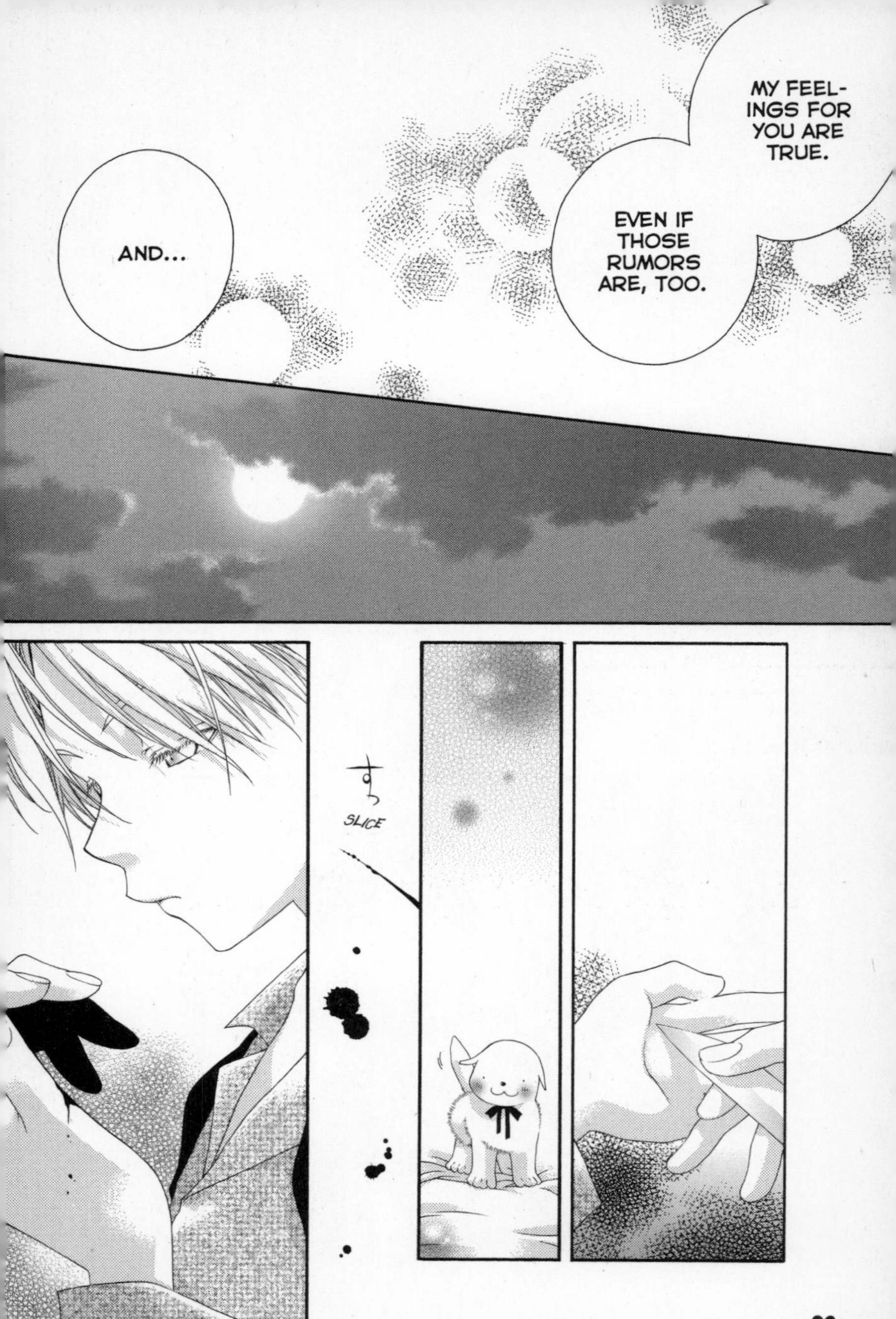
MY FEEL-
INGS FOR
YOU ARE
TRUE.
EVEN IF
THOSE
RUMORS
ARE, TOO.
AND...
すっ
SLICE

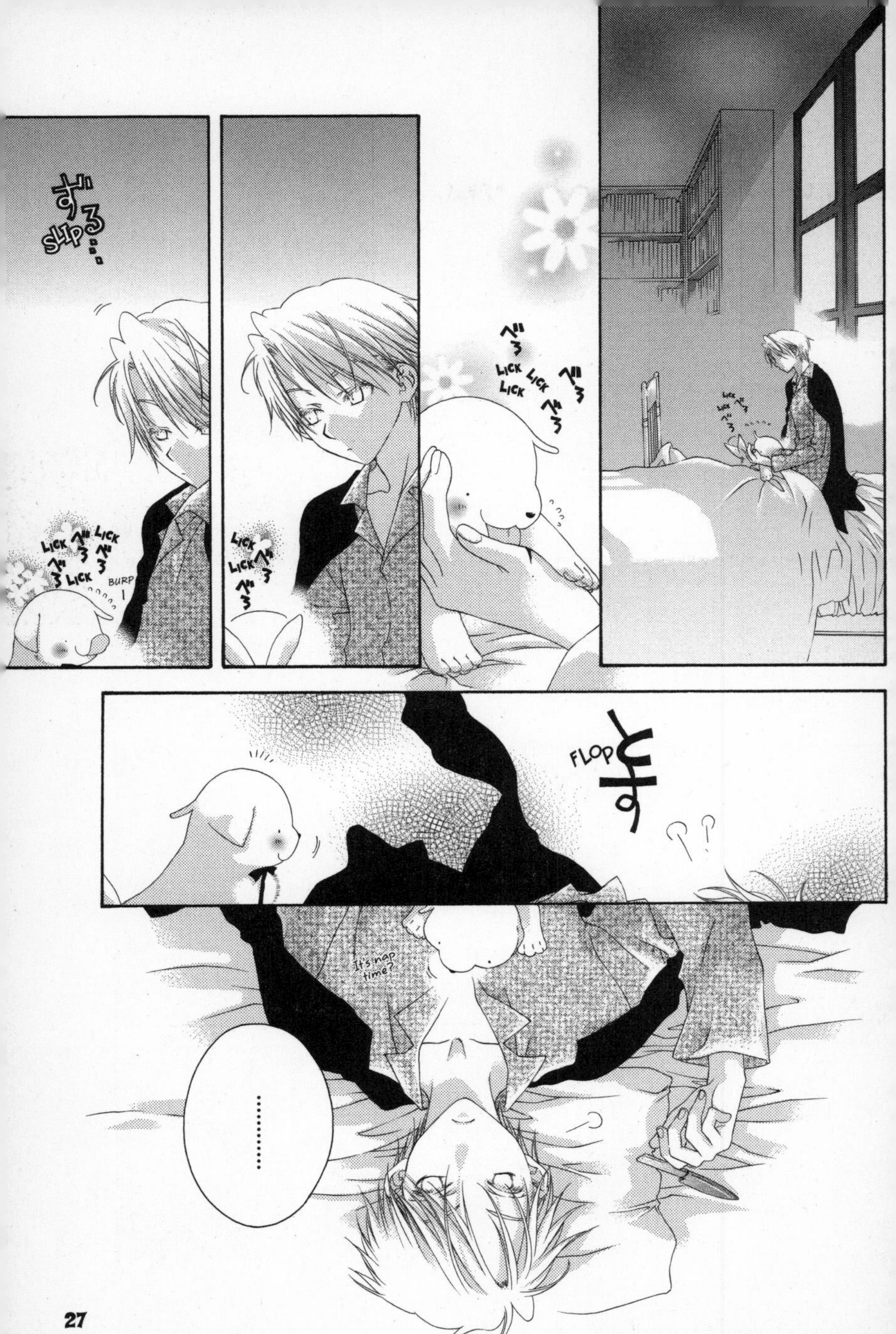
LICK べろ LICK べろ
べろ LICK LICK LICK べろ べろ
LICK LICK べろ べろ
ずる SLIP...
LICK べろ LICK べろ べろ LICK
BURP
FLOP とす
It's nap time?
....

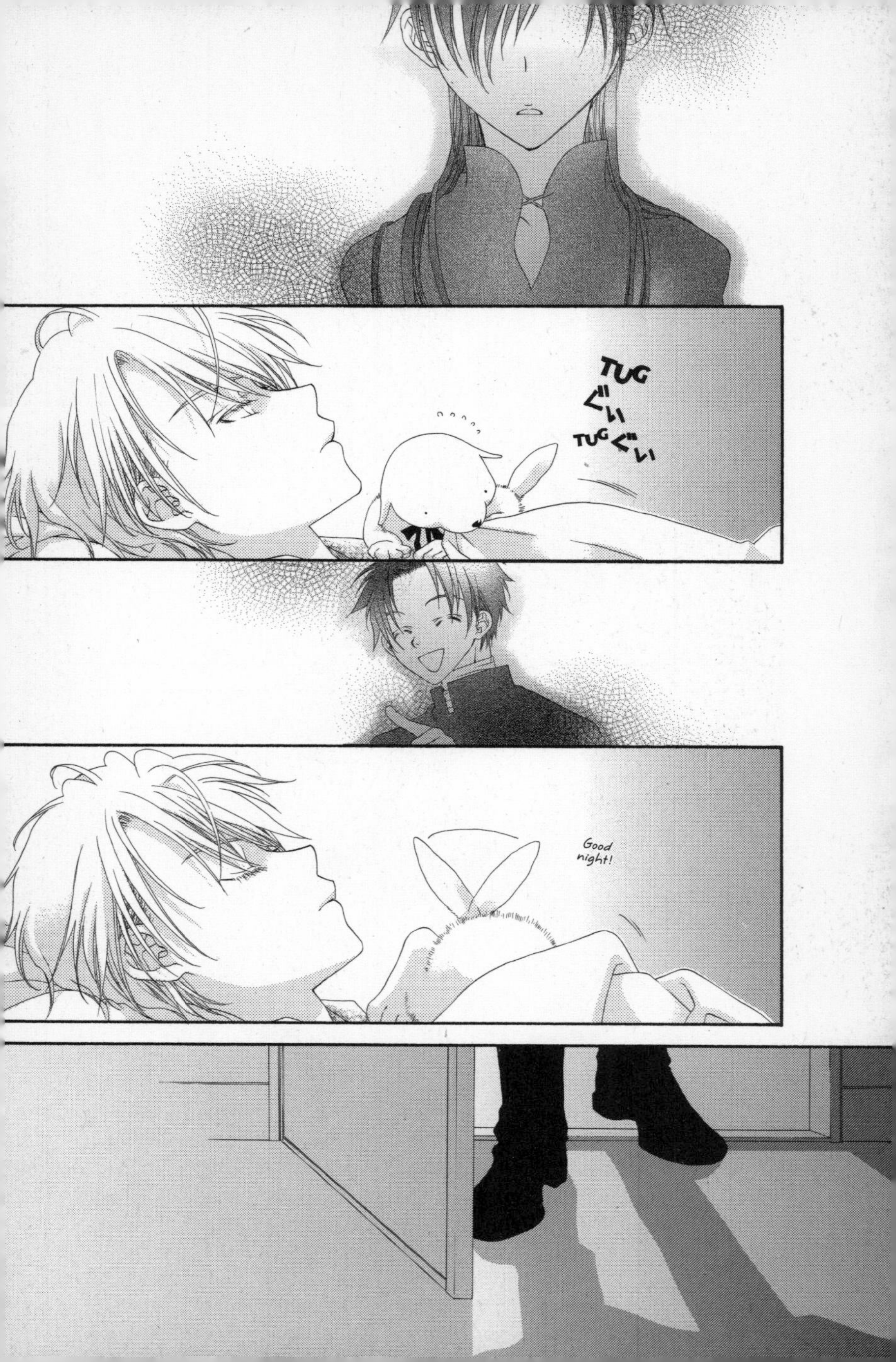
TUG
ぐい
TUG ぐい
Good night!

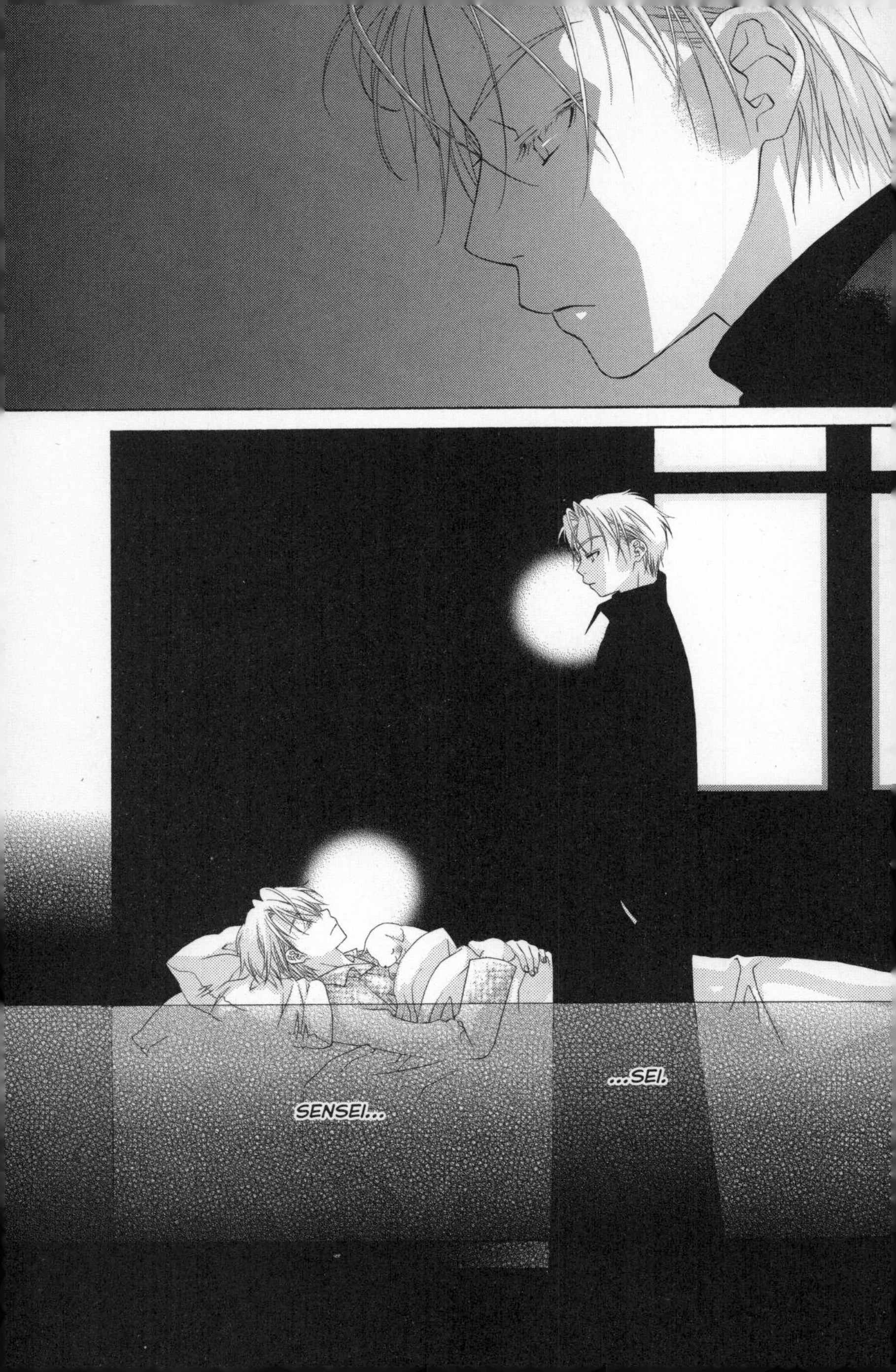
...SEI.
SENSEI...

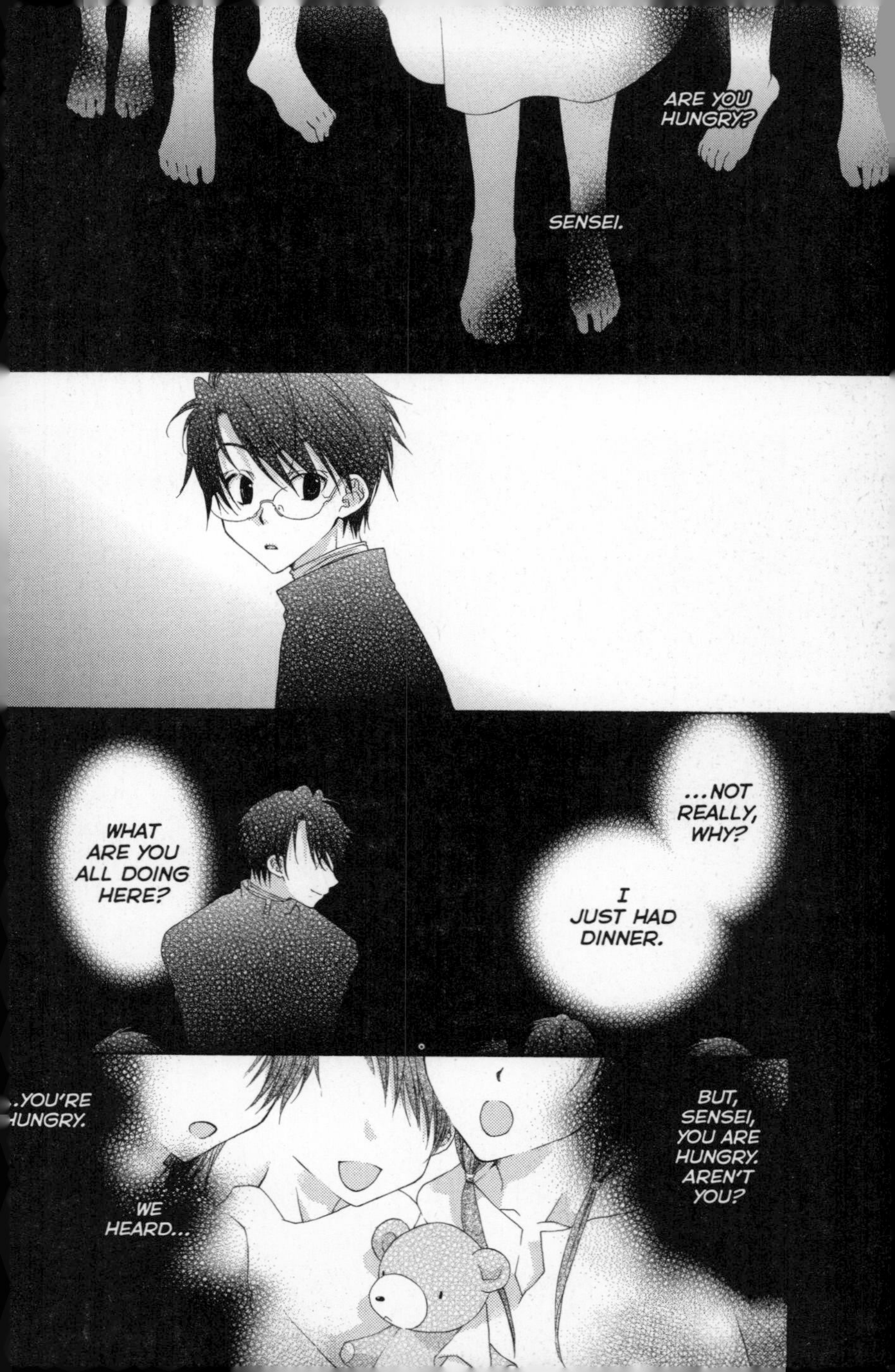
ARE YOU HUNGRY?
SENSEI.
...NOT REALLY, WHY?
I JUST HAD DINNER.
WHAT ARE YOU ALL DOING HERE?
BUT, SENSEI, YOU ARE HUNGRY. AREN'T YOU?
WE HEARD...
..YOU'RE HUNGRY.

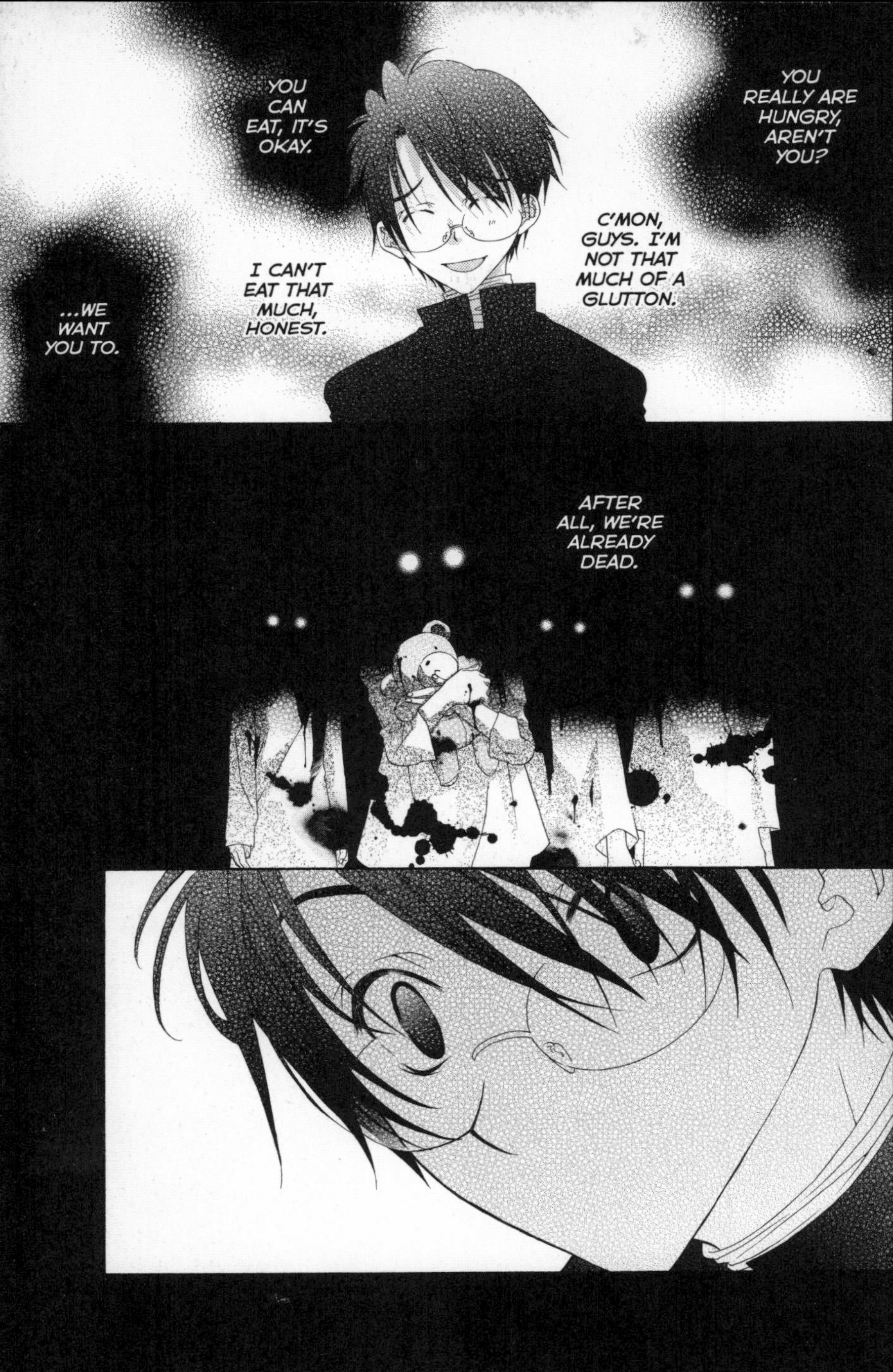
YOU REALLY ARE HUNGRY, AREN'T YOU?
C'MON, GUYS. I'M NOT THAT MUCH OF A GLUTTON.
YOU CAN EAT, IT'S OKAY.
I CAN'T EAT THAT MUCH, HONEST.
...WE WANT YOU TO.
AFTER ALL, WE'RE ALREADY DEAD.

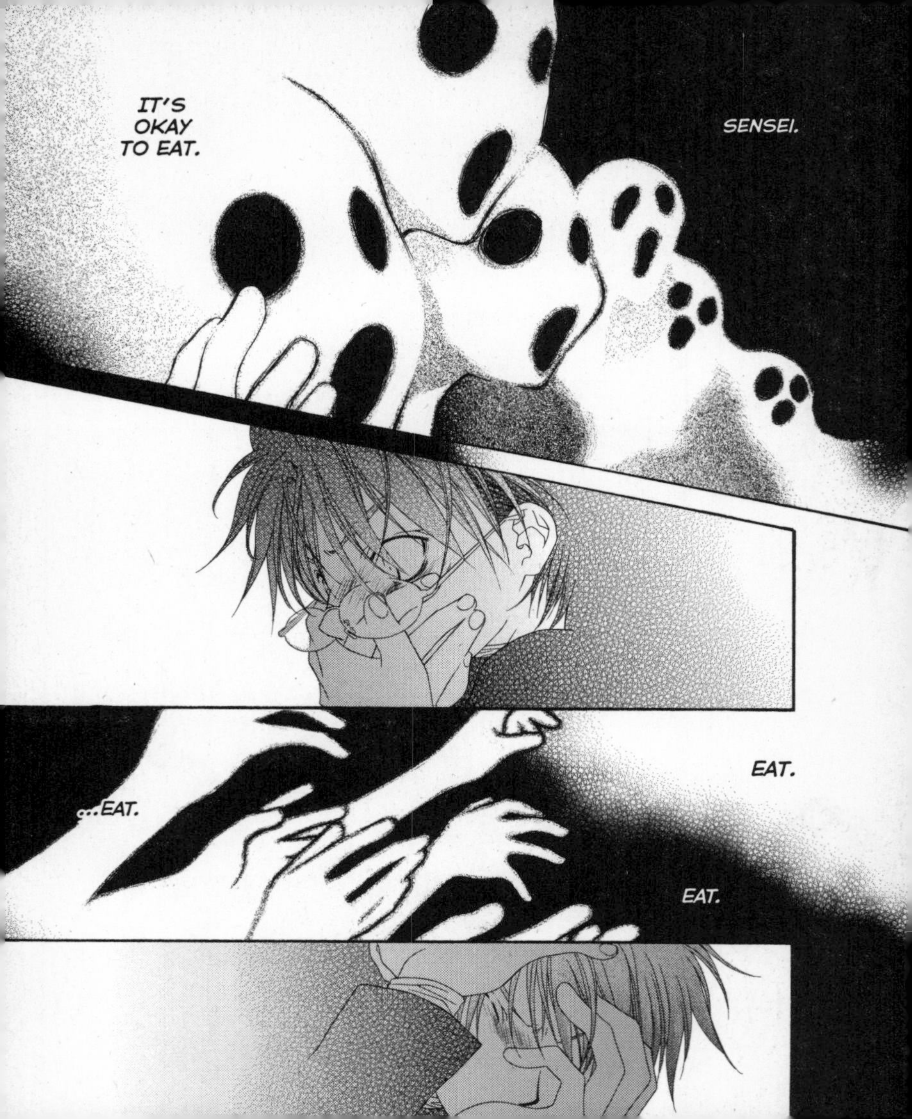
SENSEI.
IT'S OKAY TO EAT.
EAT.
...EAT.
EAT.

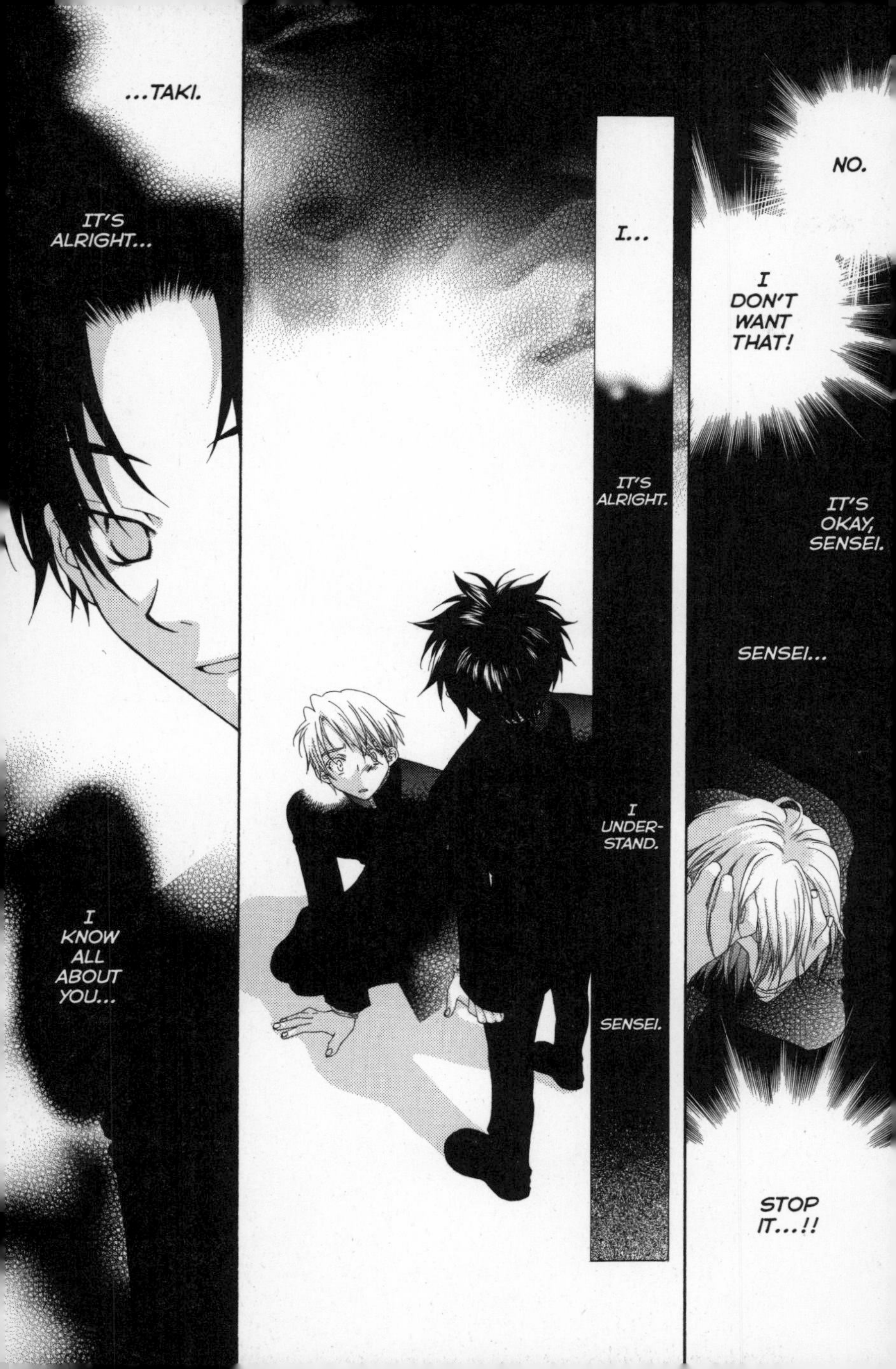
NO.
I DON'T WANT THAT!
IT'S OKAY, SENSEI.
SENSEI...
STOP IT...!!
I...
IT'S ALRIGHT.
I UNDER-STAND.
SENSEI.
...TAKI.
IT'S ALRIGHT...
I KNOW ALL ABOUT YOU...

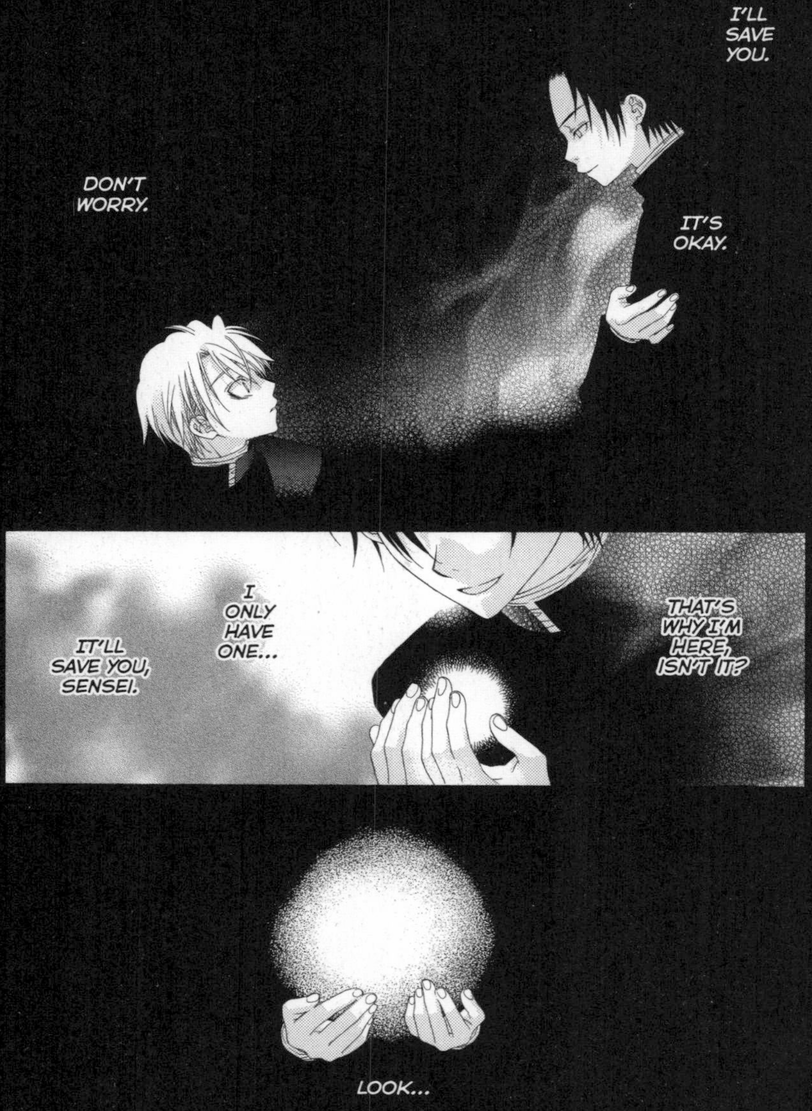
I'LL SAVE YOU.
IT'S OKAY.
DON'T WORRY.
THAT'S WHY I'M HERE, ISN'T IT?
I ONLY HAVE ONE...
IT'LL SAVE YOU, SENSEI.
LOOK...

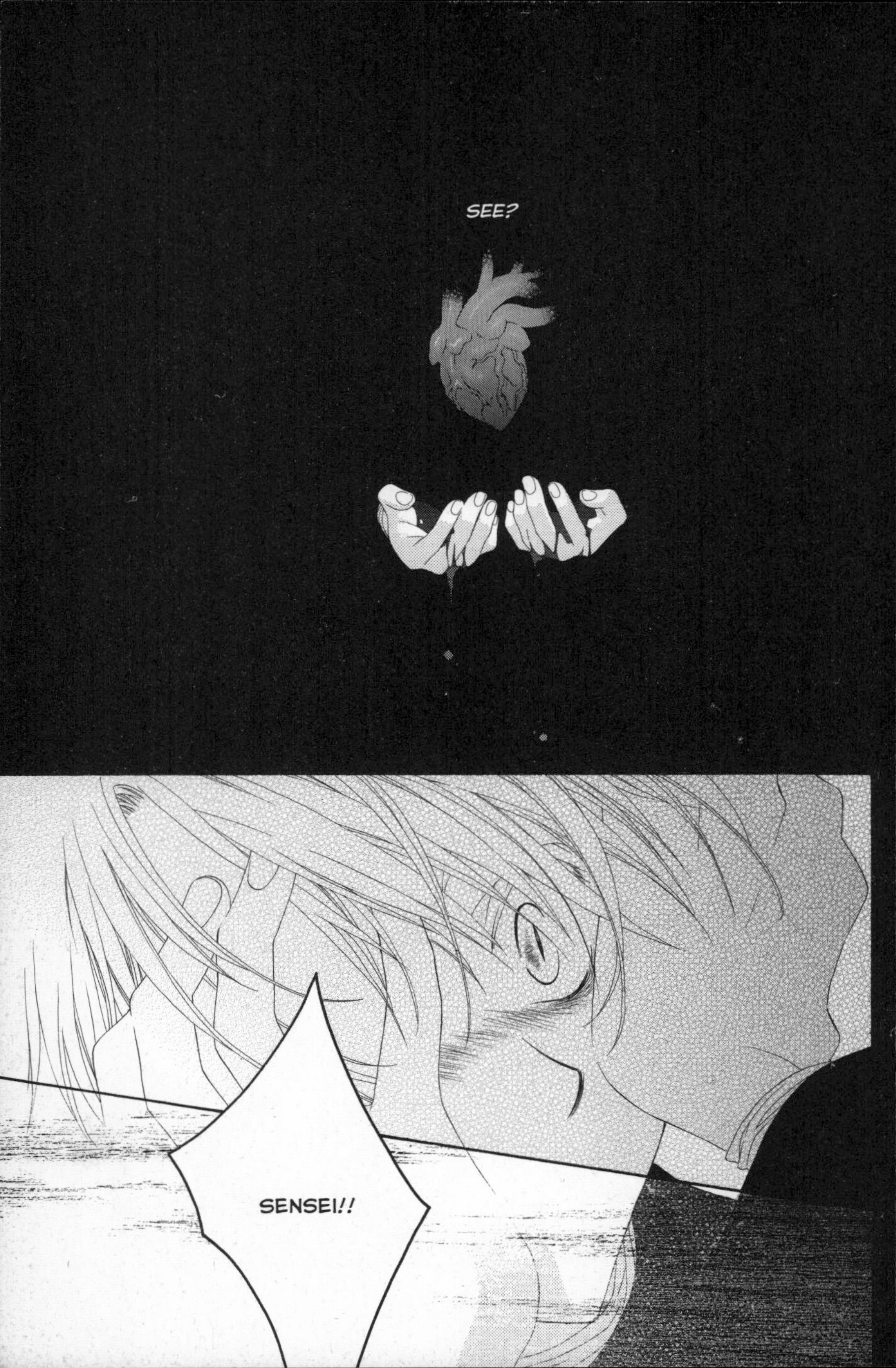
SEE?
SENSEI!!

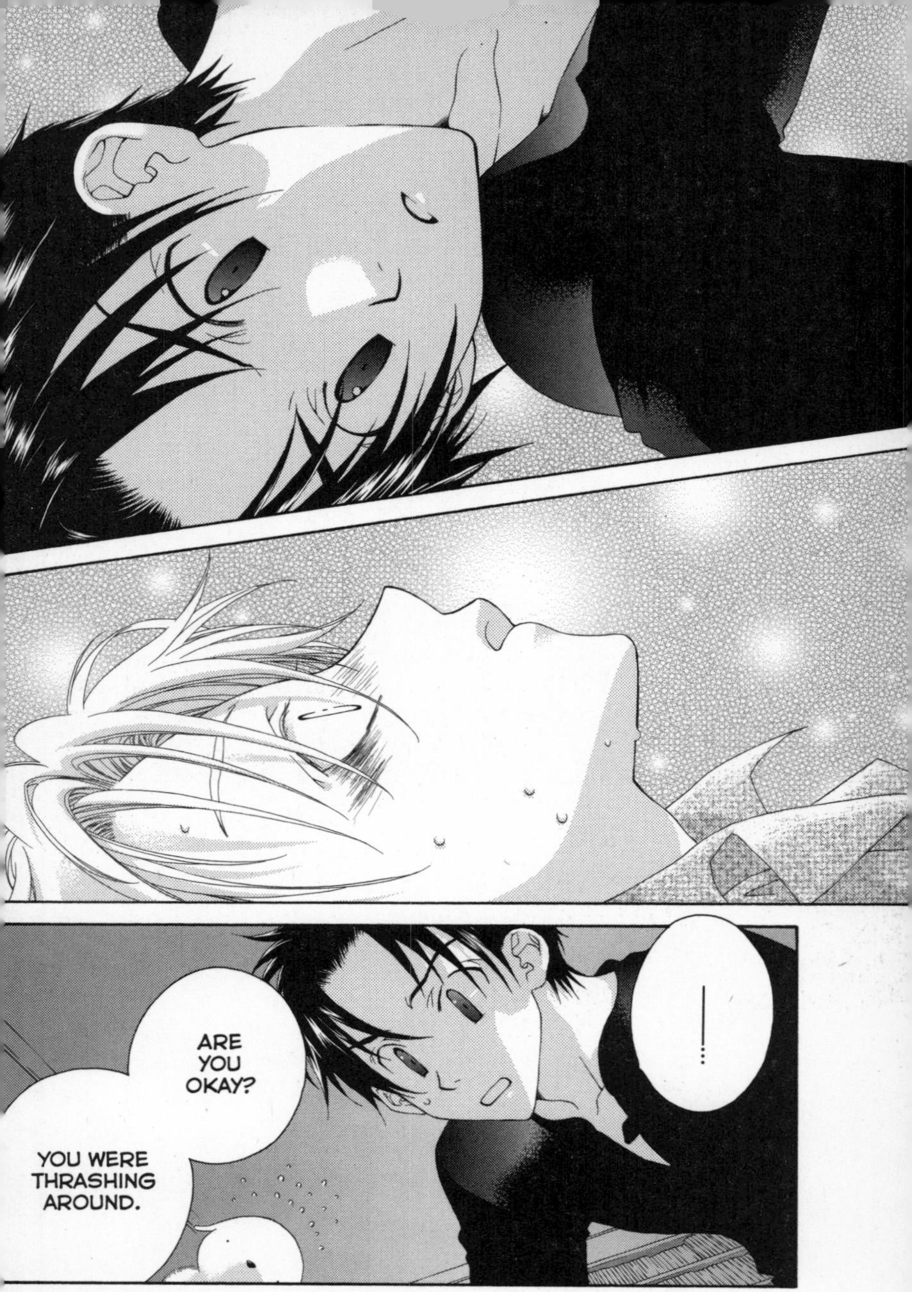
—…
ARE YOU OKAY?
YOU WERE THRASHING AROUND.

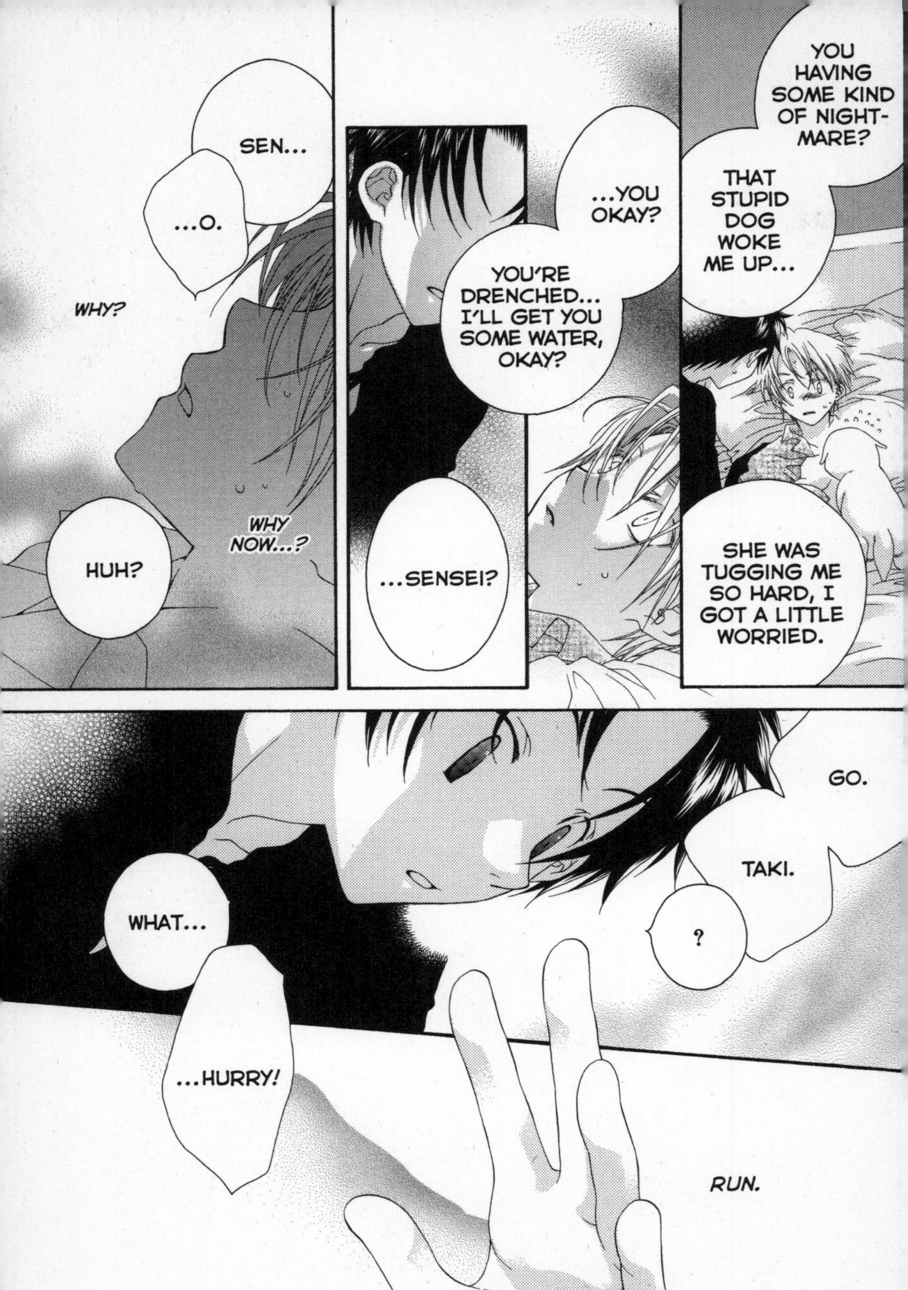
YOU HAVING SOME KIND OF NIGHT-MARE?
THAT STUPID DOG WOKE ME UP...
SHE WAS TUGGING ME SO HARD, I GOT A LITTLE WORRIED.
...YOU OKAY?
YOU'RE DRENCHED... I'LL GET YOU SOME WATER, OKAY?
...SENSEI?
SEN...
...O.
WHY?
WHY NOW...?
HUH?
GO.
TAKI.
?
WHAT...
...HURRY!
RUN.

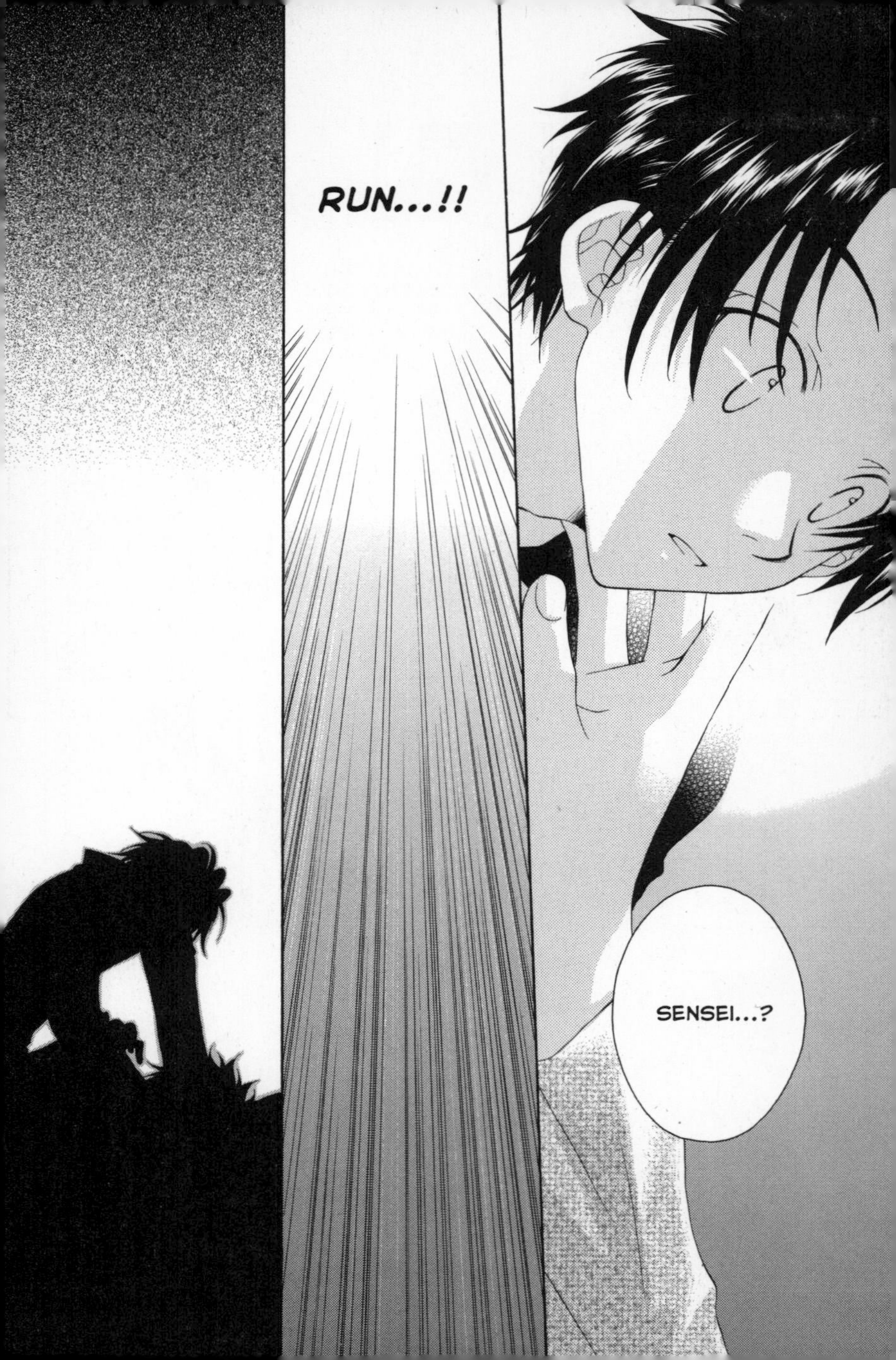
SENSEI...?
RUN...!!

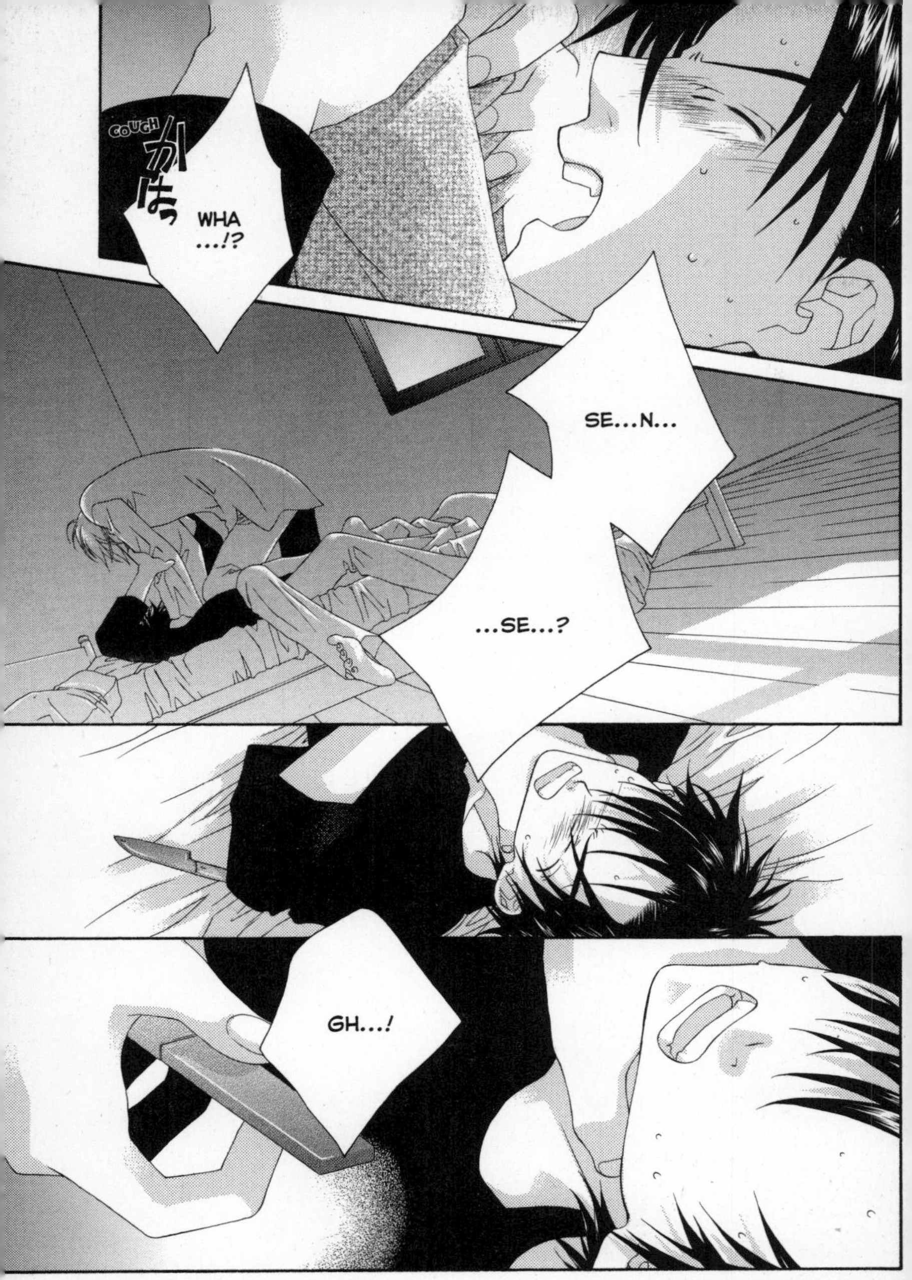
COUGH
かはっ
WHA ...!?
SE...N...
...SE...?
GH...!

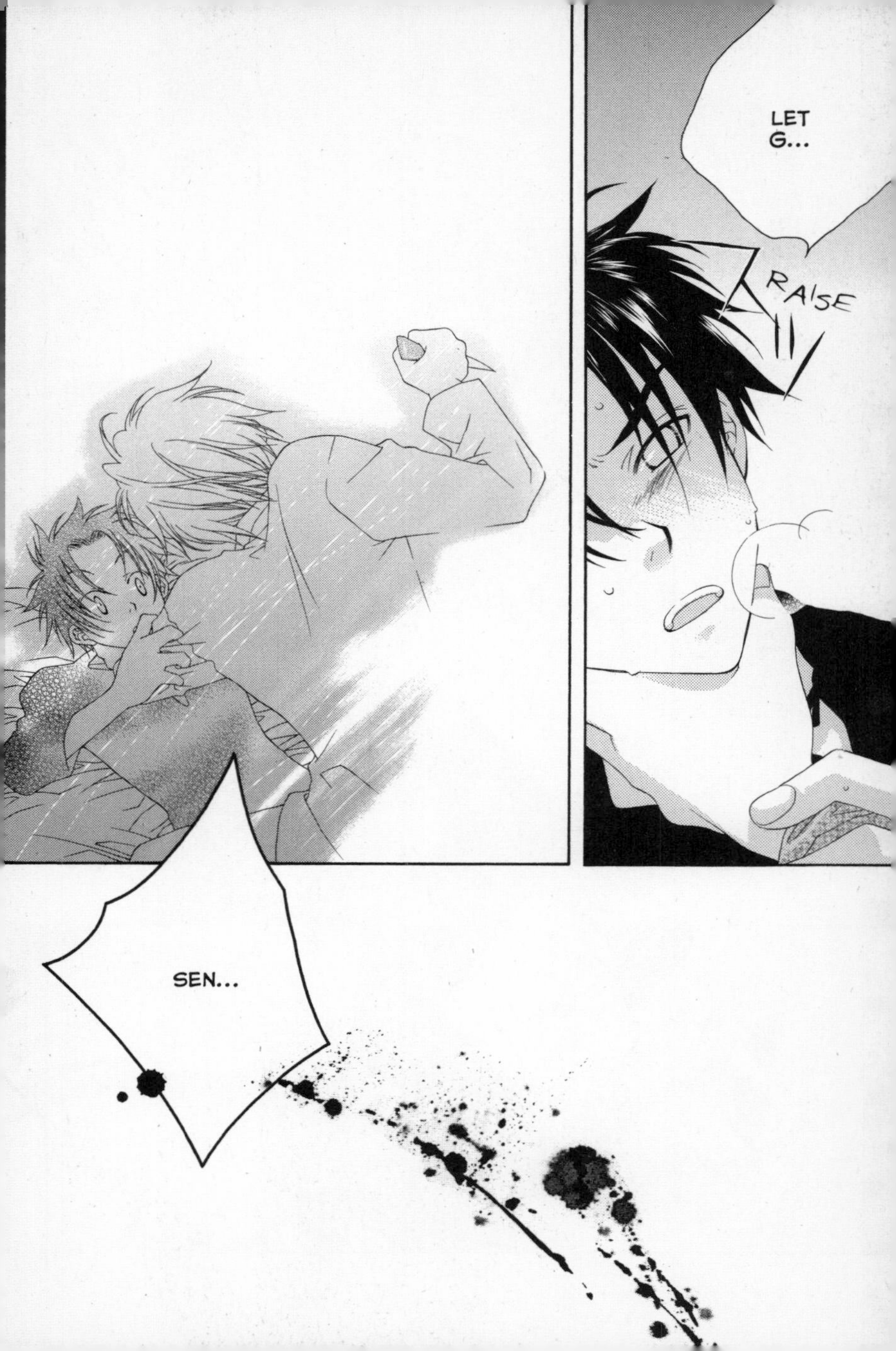
LET G...
RAISE
SEN...

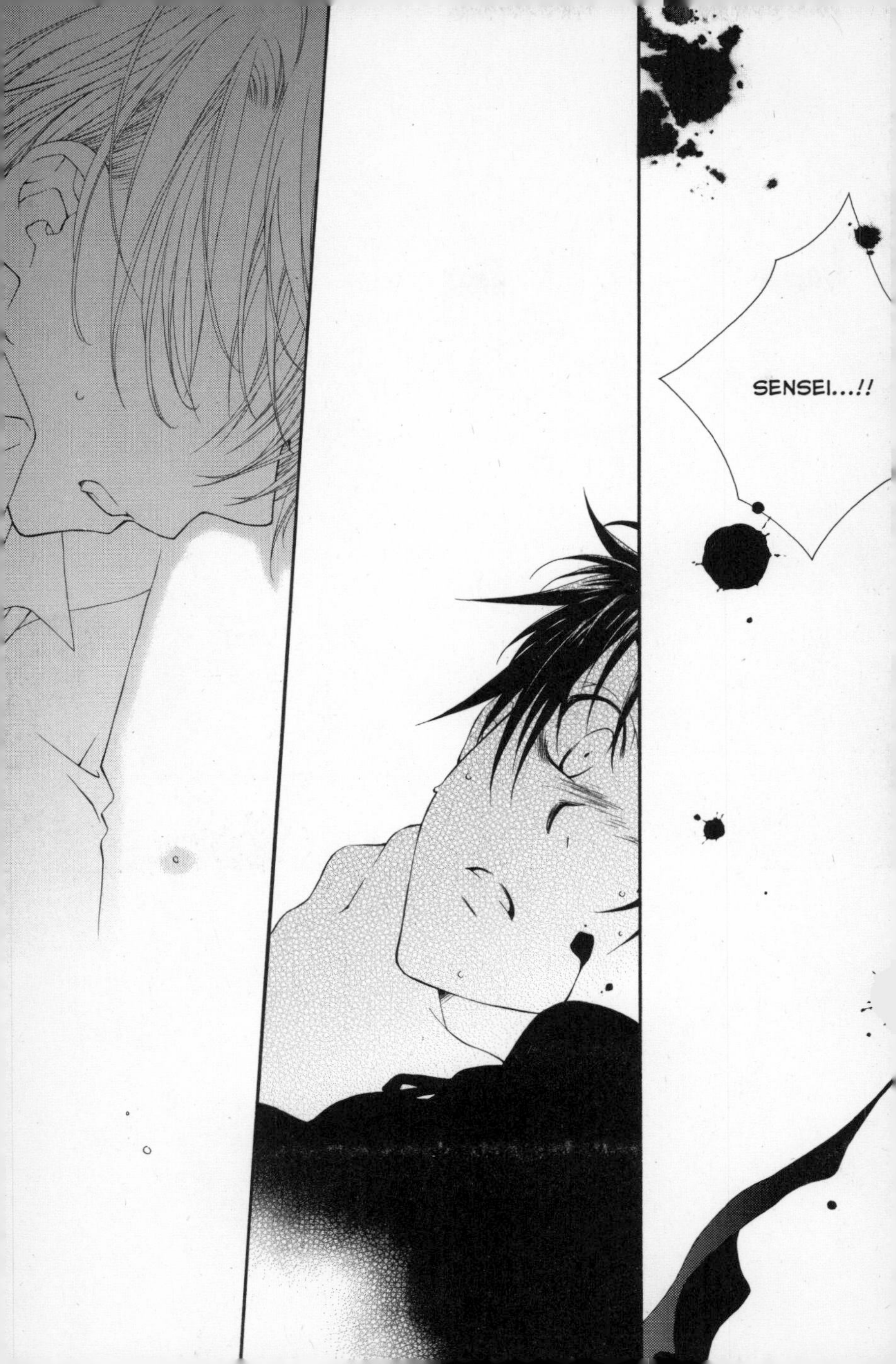
SENSEI...!!

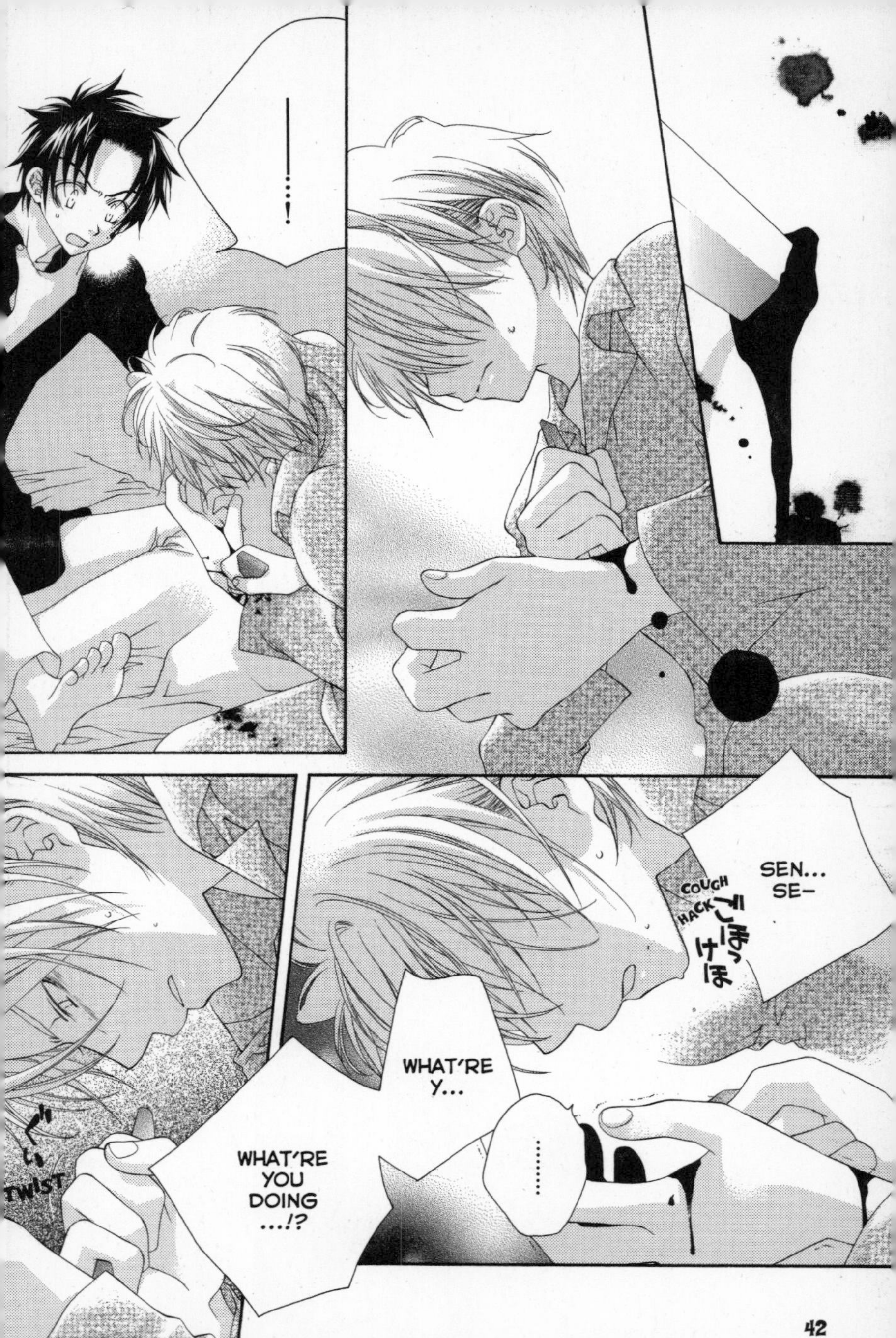
—...!
SEN... SE-
COUGH HACK
ごほっ けほ
WHAT'RE Y...
......
WHAT'RE YOU DOING ...!?
ぐい
TWIST

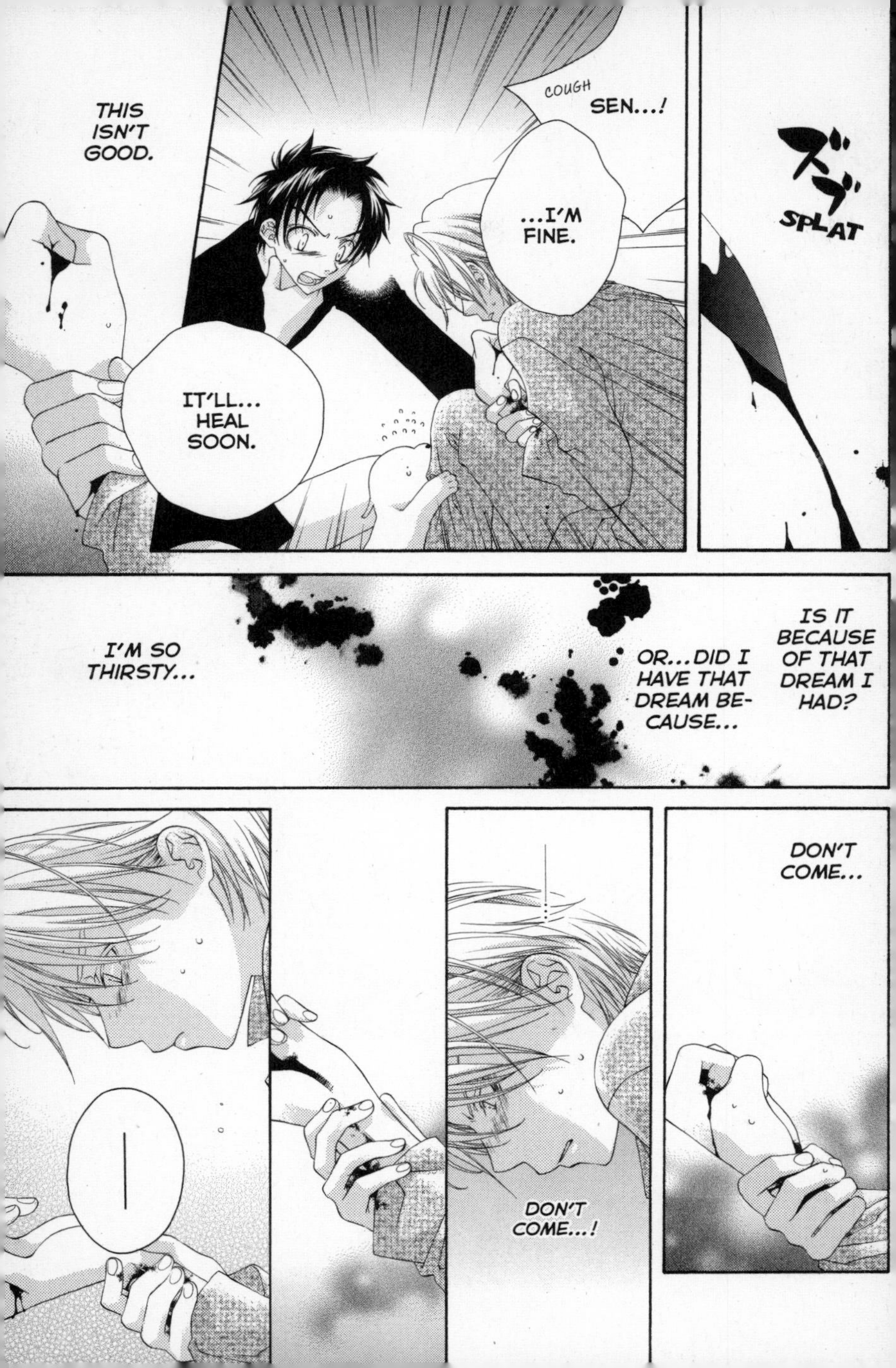
ズブ
SPLAT
COUGH
SEN...!
...I'M FINE.
THIS ISN'T GOOD.
IT'LL... HEAL SOON.
IS IT BECAUSE OF THAT DREAM I HAD?
OR...DID I HAVE THAT DREAM BE-CAUSE...
I'M SO THIRSTY...
DON'T COME...
...!
DON'T COME...!
—

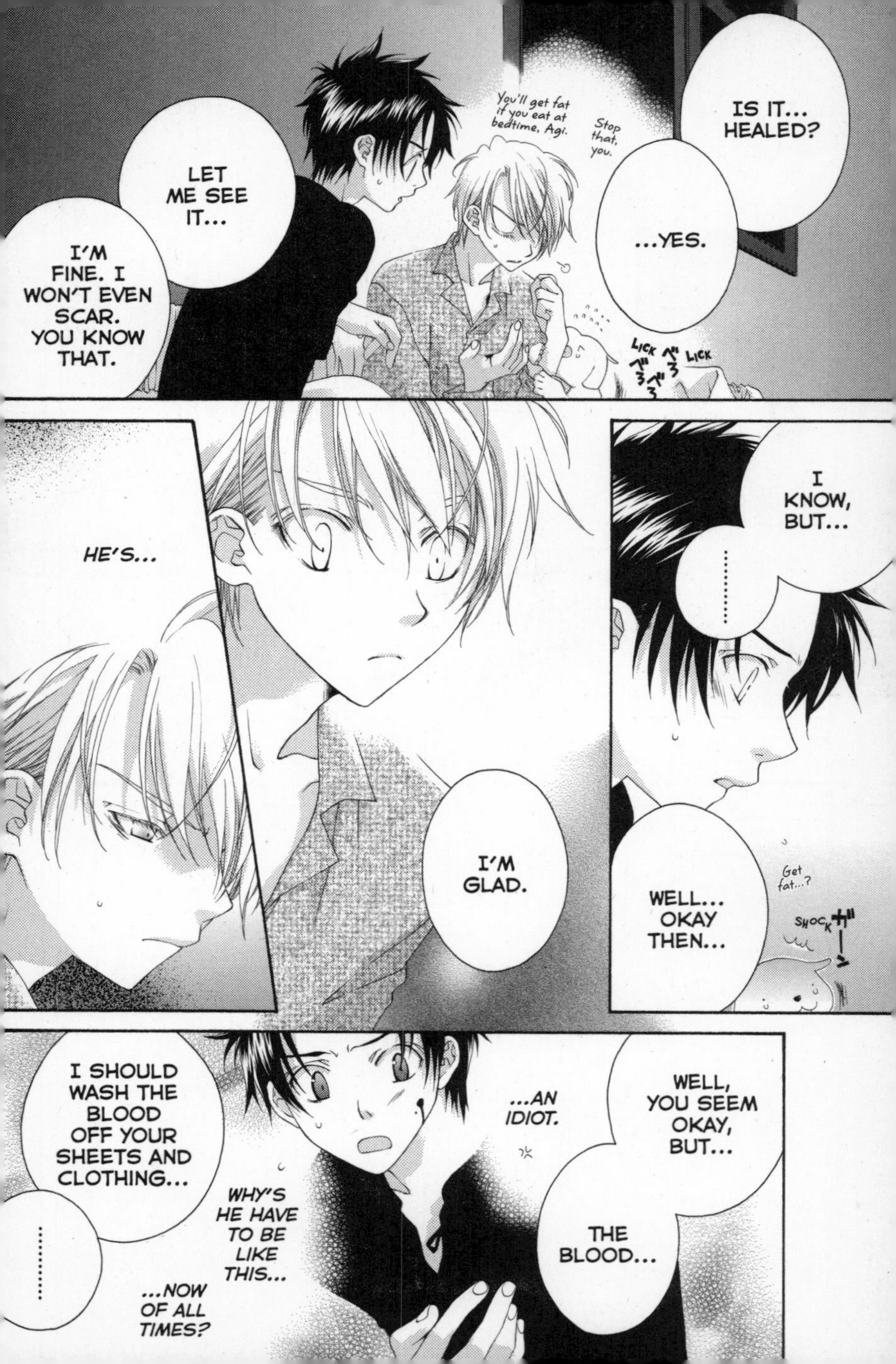
IS IT... HEALED?
...YES.
Stop that, you.
You'll get fat if you eat at bedtime, Agi.
LICK LICK
LET ME SEE IT...
I'M FINE. I WON'T EVEN SCAR. YOU KNOW THAT.
I KNOW, BUT...
......
WELL... OKAY THEN...
Get fat...?
SHOCK
I'M GLAD.
HE'S...
WELL, YOU SEEM OKAY, BUT...
THE BLOOD...
...AN IDIOT.
I SHOULD WASH THE BLOOD OFF YOUR SHEETS AND CLOTHING...
WHY'S HE HAVE TO BE LIKE THIS...
...NOW OF ALL TIMES?
......

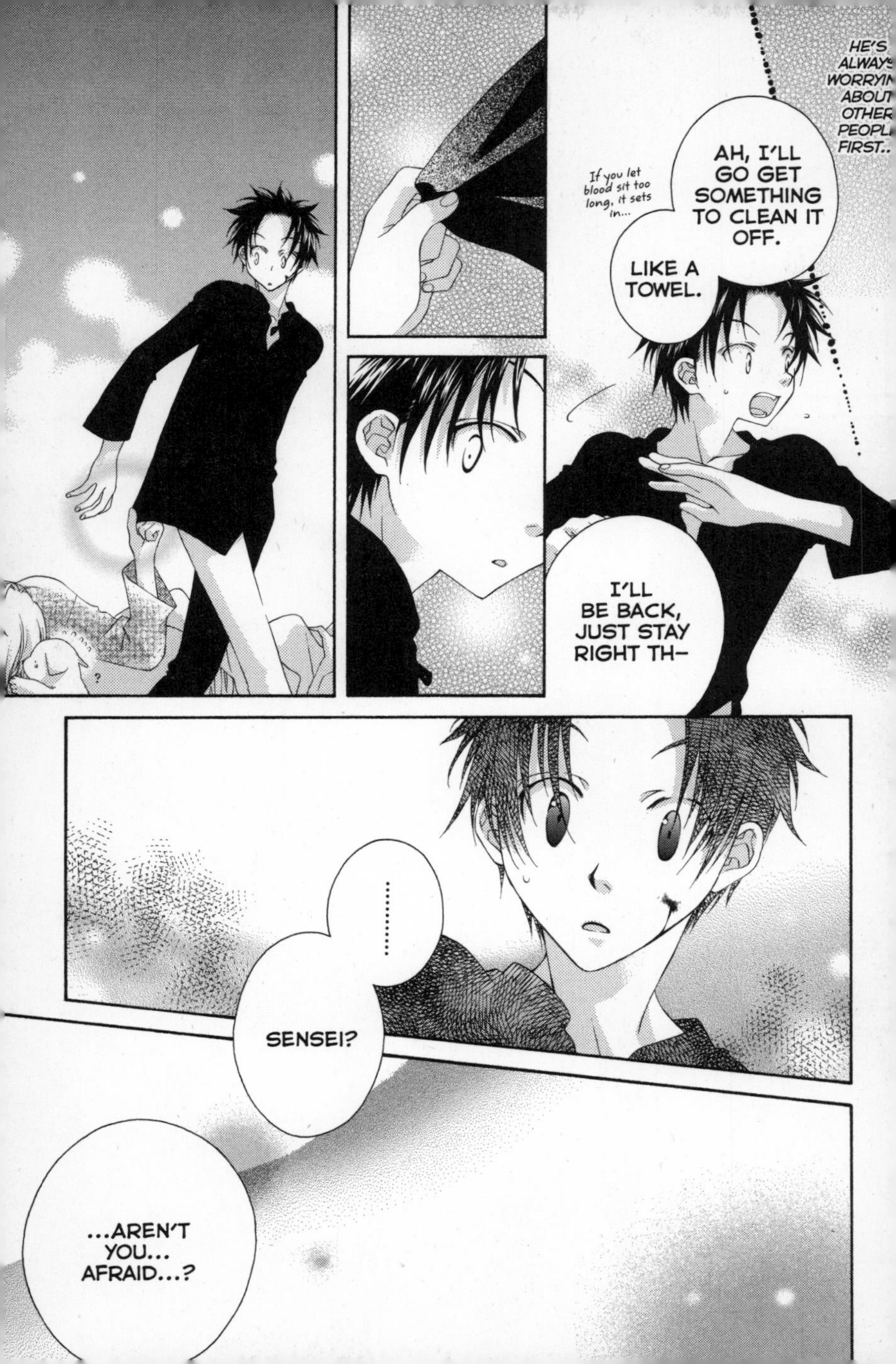
HE'S ALWAYS WORRYIN ABOUT OTHER PEOPL FIRST..
AH, I'LL GO GET SOMETHING TO CLEAN IT OFF.
LIKE A TOWEL.
If you let blood sit too long, it sets in...
I'LL BE BACK, JUST STAY RIGHT TH–
?
....
SENSEI?
...AREN'T YOU... AFRAID...?

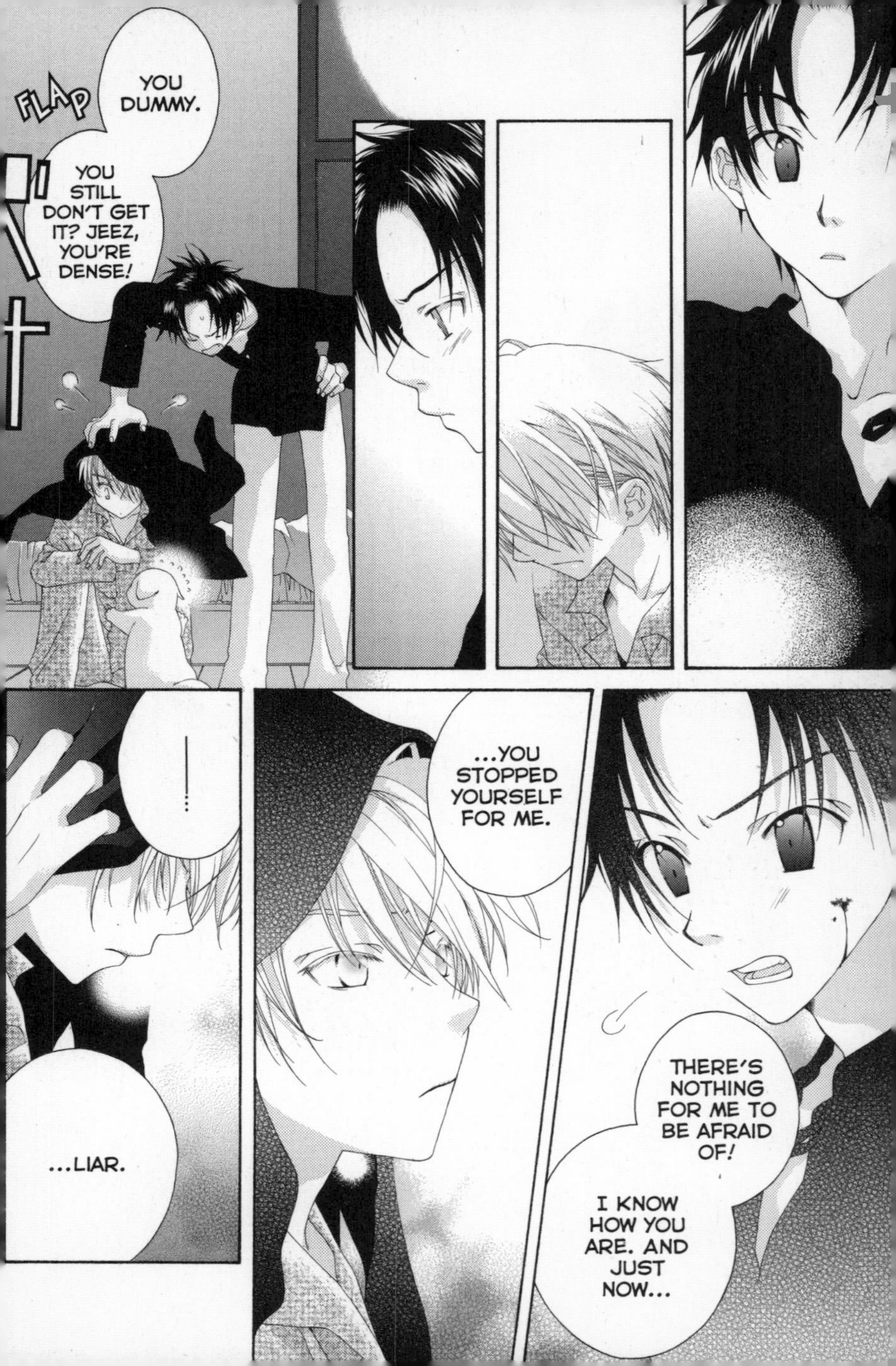

YOU DUMMY.
FLAP
YOU STILL DON'T GET IT? JEEZ, YOU'RE DENSE!
THERE'S NOTHING FOR ME TO BE AFRAID OF!
I KNOW HOW YOU ARE. AND JUST NOW...
...YOU STOPPED YOURSELF FOR ME.
...
...LIAR.

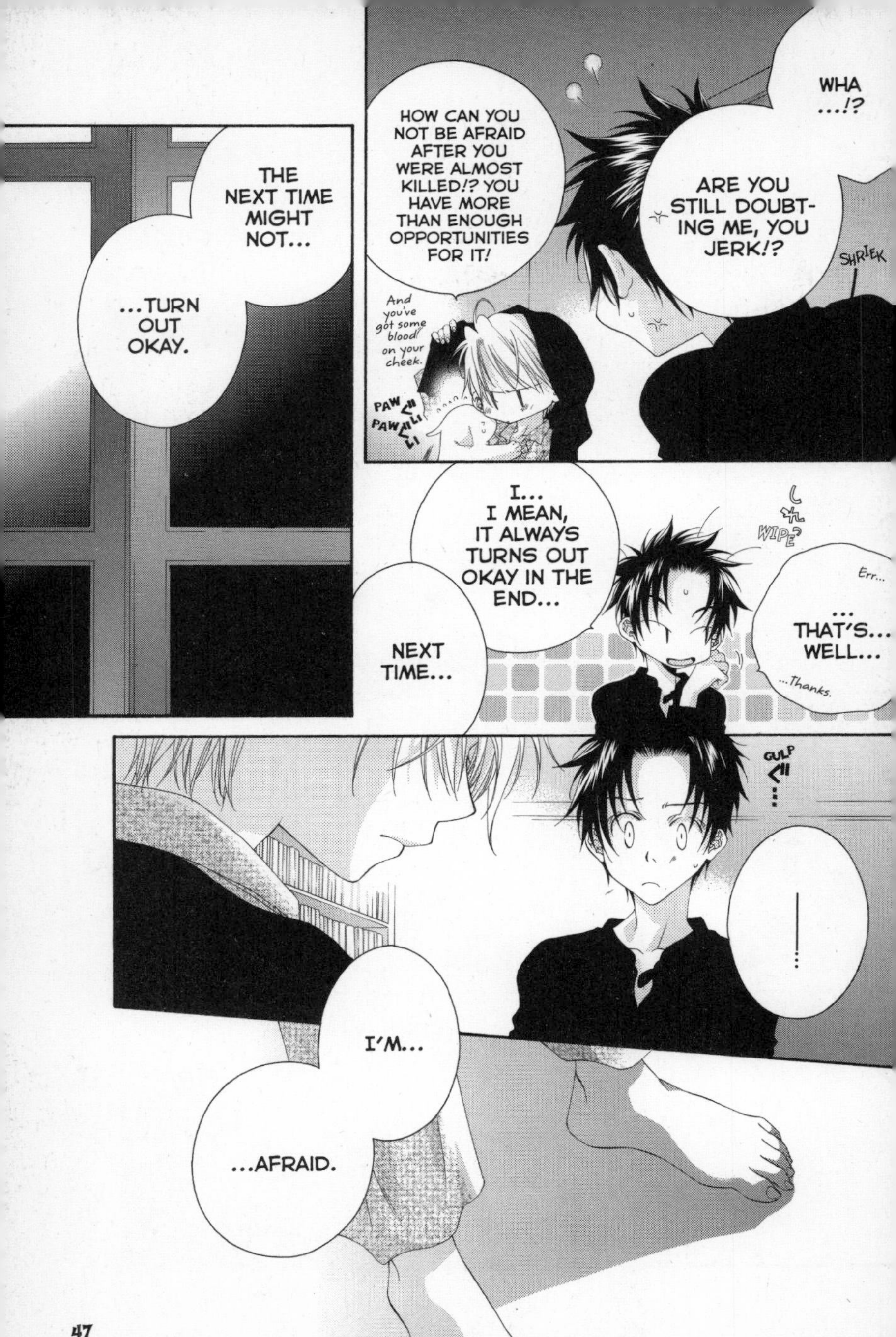
WHA ...!?
ARE YOU STILL DOUBTING ME, YOU JERK!?
SHRIEK
HOW CAN YOU NOT BE AFRAID AFTER YOU WERE ALMOST KILLED!? YOU HAVE MORE THAN ENOUGH OPPORTUNITIES FOR IT!
And you've got some blood on your cheek.
PAW PAW
WIPE
Err...
... THAT'S... WELL...
...Thanks.
I... I MEAN, IT ALWAYS TURNS OUT OKAY IN THE END...
NEXT TIME...
THE NEXT TIME MIGHT NOT...
...TURN OUT OKAY.
GULP
—...
I'M...
...AFRAID.

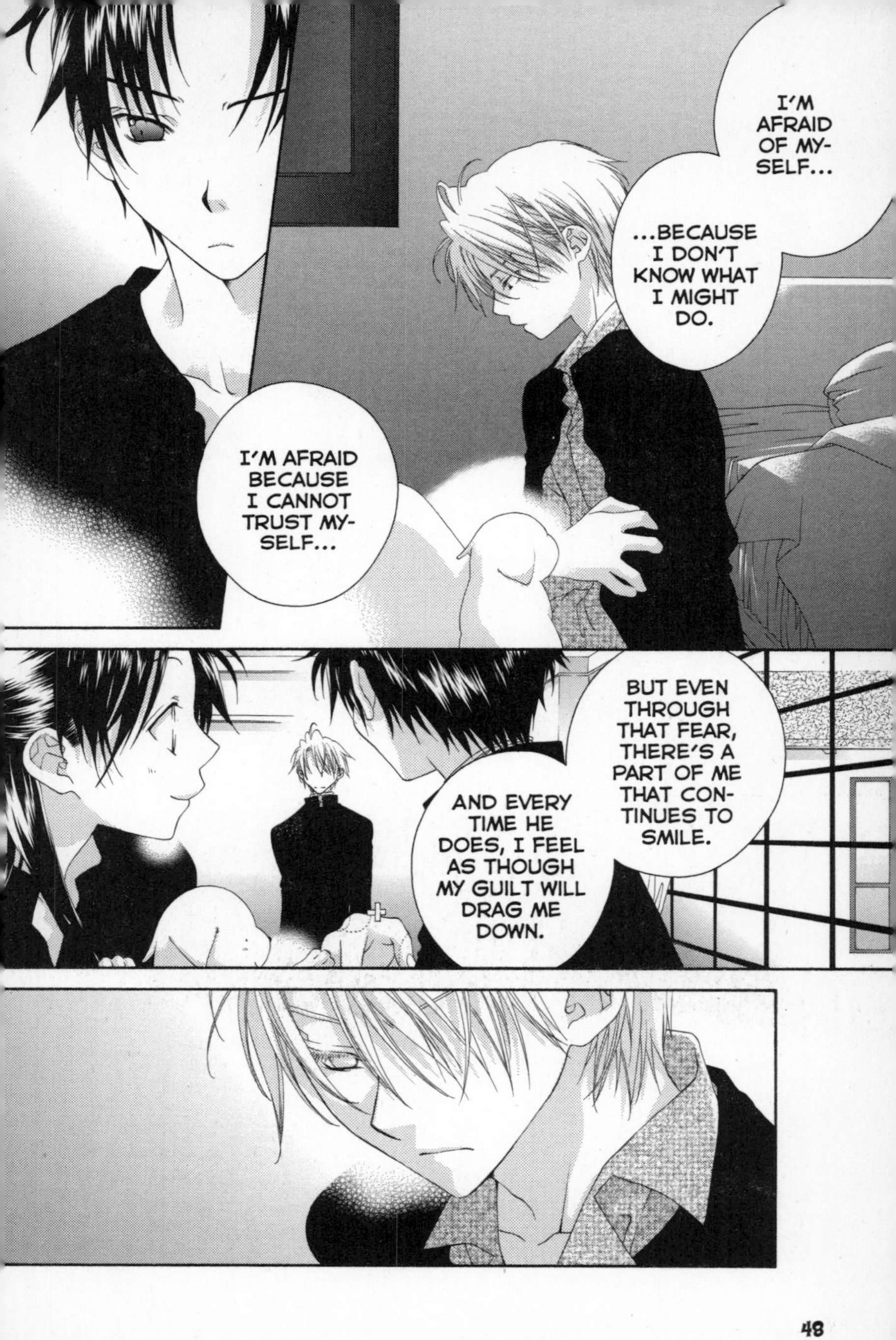
I'M AFRAID OF MY-SELF...
...BECAUSE I DON'T KNOW WHAT I MIGHT DO.
I'M AFRAID BECAUSE I CANNOT TRUST MY-SELF...
BUT EVEN THROUGH THAT FEAR, THERE'S A PART OF ME THAT CON-TINUES TO SMILE.
AND EVERY TIME HE DOES, I FEEL AS THOUGH MY GUILT WILL DRAG ME DOWN.

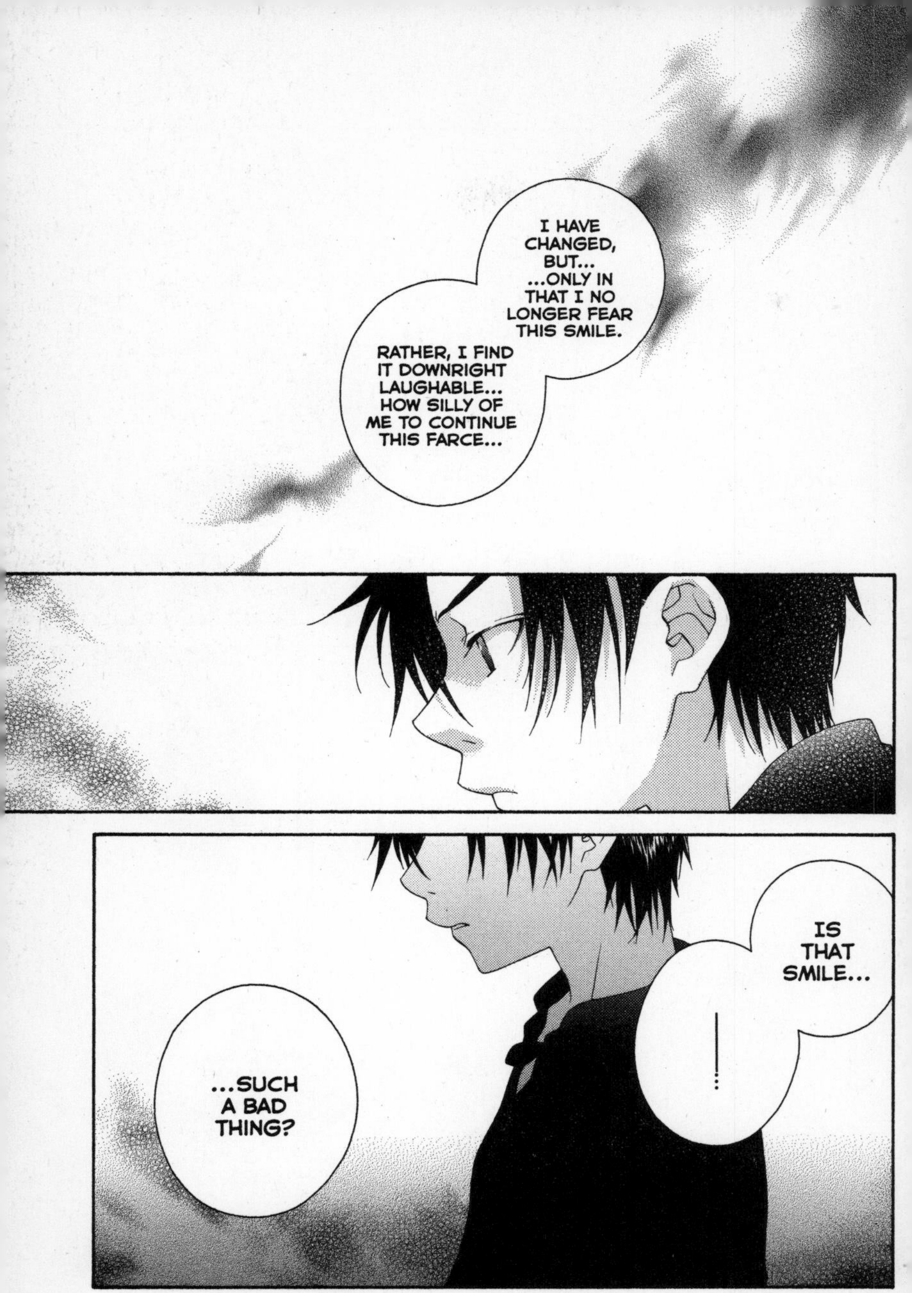
I HAVE CHANGED, BUT... ...ONLY IN THAT I NO LONGER FEAR THIS SMILE.
RATHER, I FIND IT DOWNRIGHT LAUGHABLE... HOW SILLY OF ME TO CONTINUE THIS FARCE...
IS THAT SMILE...
...SUCH A BAD THING?

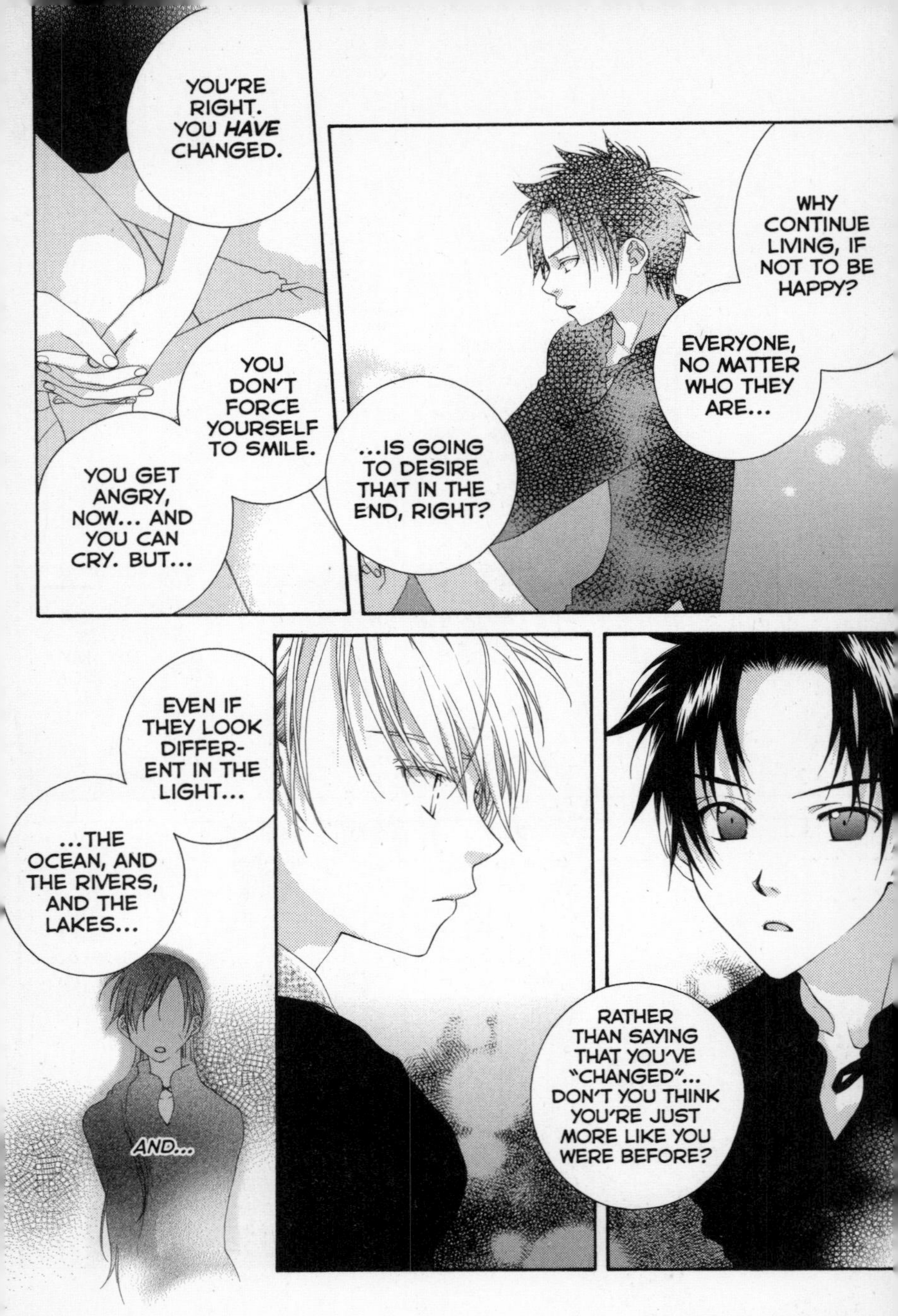
WHY CONTINUE LIVING, IF NOT TO BE HAPPY?
EVERYONE, NO MATTER WHO THEY ARE...
...IS GOING TO DESIRE THAT IN THE END, RIGHT?
YOU'RE RIGHT. YOU *HAVE* CHANGED.
YOU DON'T FORCE YOURSELF TO SMILE.
YOU GET ANGRY, NOW... AND YOU CAN CRY. BUT...
RATHER THAN SAYING THAT YOU'VE "CHANGED"... DON'T YOU THINK YOU'RE JUST MORE LIKE YOU WERE BEFORE?
EVEN IF THEY LOOK DIFFER-ENT IN THE LIGHT...
...THE OCEAN, AND THE RIVERS, AND THE LAKES...
AND...

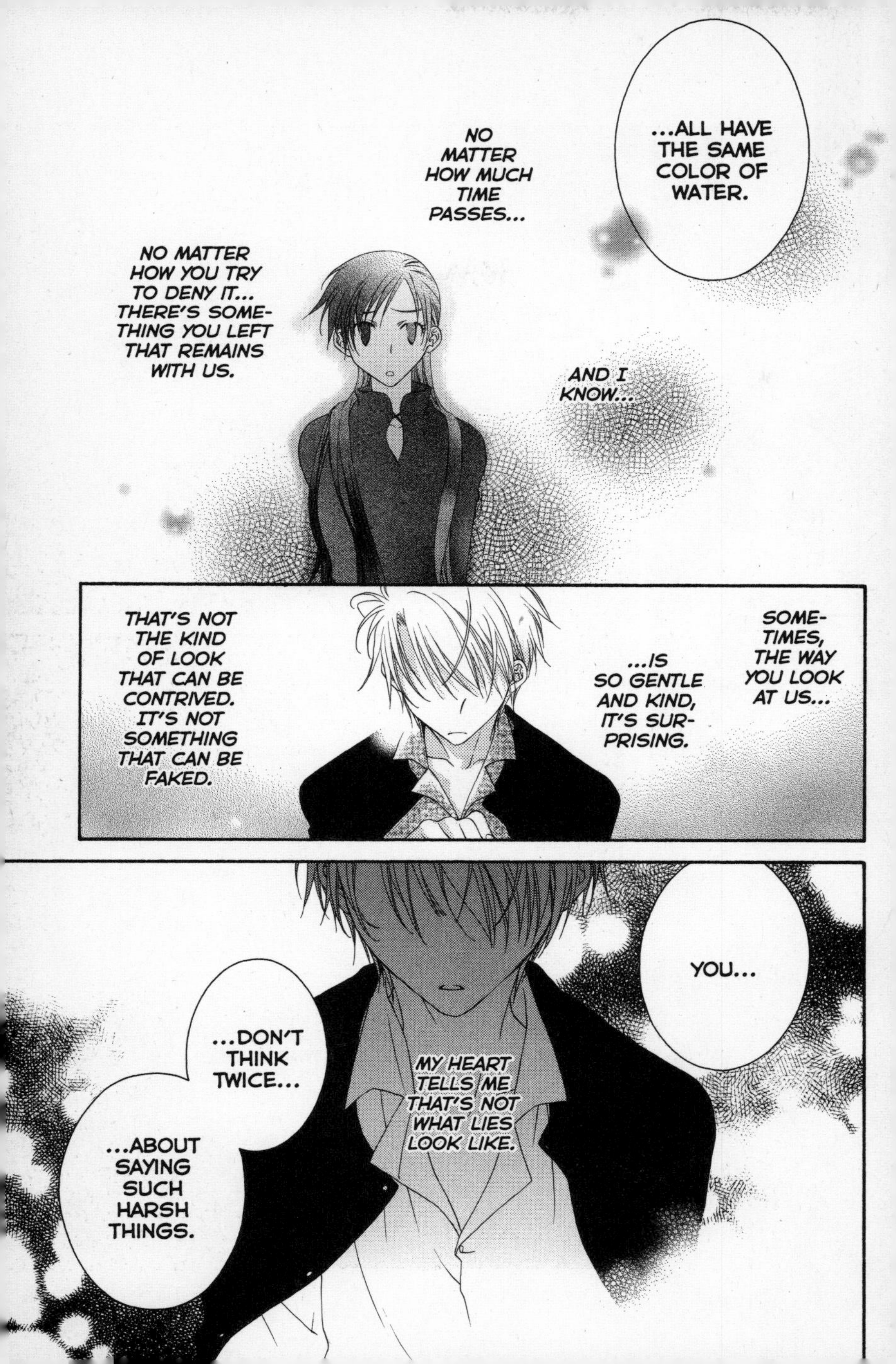
...ALL HAVE THE SAME COLOR OF WATER.
NO MATTER HOW MUCH TIME PASSES...
NO MATTER HOW YOU TRY TO DENY IT... THERE'S SOME-THING YOU LEFT THAT REMAINS WITH US.
AND I KNOW...
SOME-TIMES, THE WAY YOU LOOK AT US...
...IS SO GENTLE AND KIND, IT'S SUR-PRISING.
THAT'S NOT THE KIND OF LOOK THAT CAN BE CONTRIVED. IT'S NOT SOMETHING THAT CAN BE FAKED.
YOU...
...DON'T THINK TWICE...
...ABOUT SAYING SUCH HARSH THINGS.
MY HEART TELLS ME THAT'S NOT WHAT LIES LOOK LIKE.

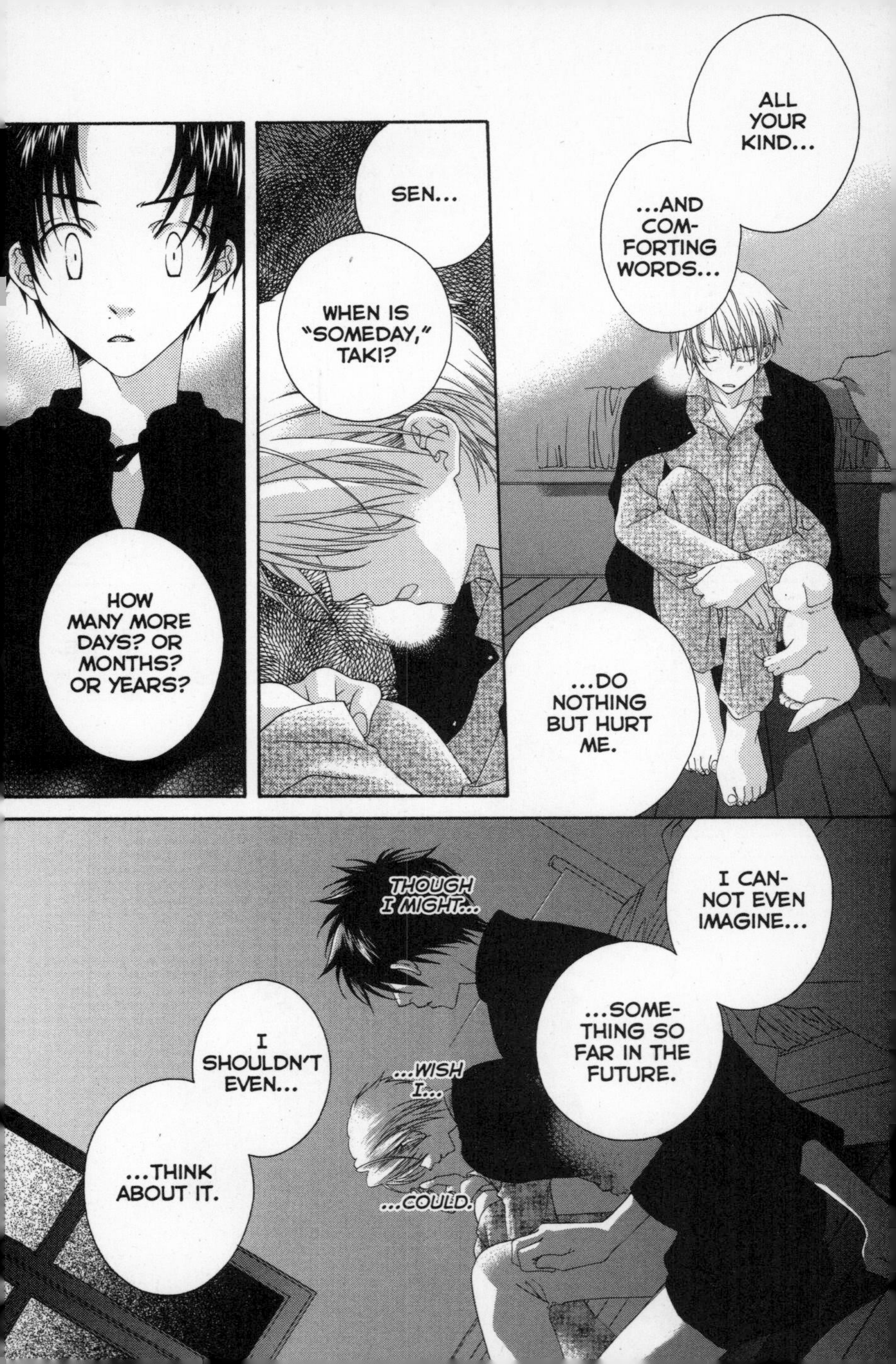
ALL YOUR KIND...
...AND COM-FORTING WORDS...
...DO NOTHING BUT HURT ME.
SEN...
WHEN IS "SOMEDAY," TAKI?
HOW MANY MORE DAYS? OR MONTHS? OR YEARS?
I CAN-NOT EVEN IMAGINE...
...SOME-THING SO FAR IN THE FUTURE.
THOUGH I MIGHT...
...WISH I...
...COULD.
I SHOULDN'T EVEN...
...THINK ABOUT IT.

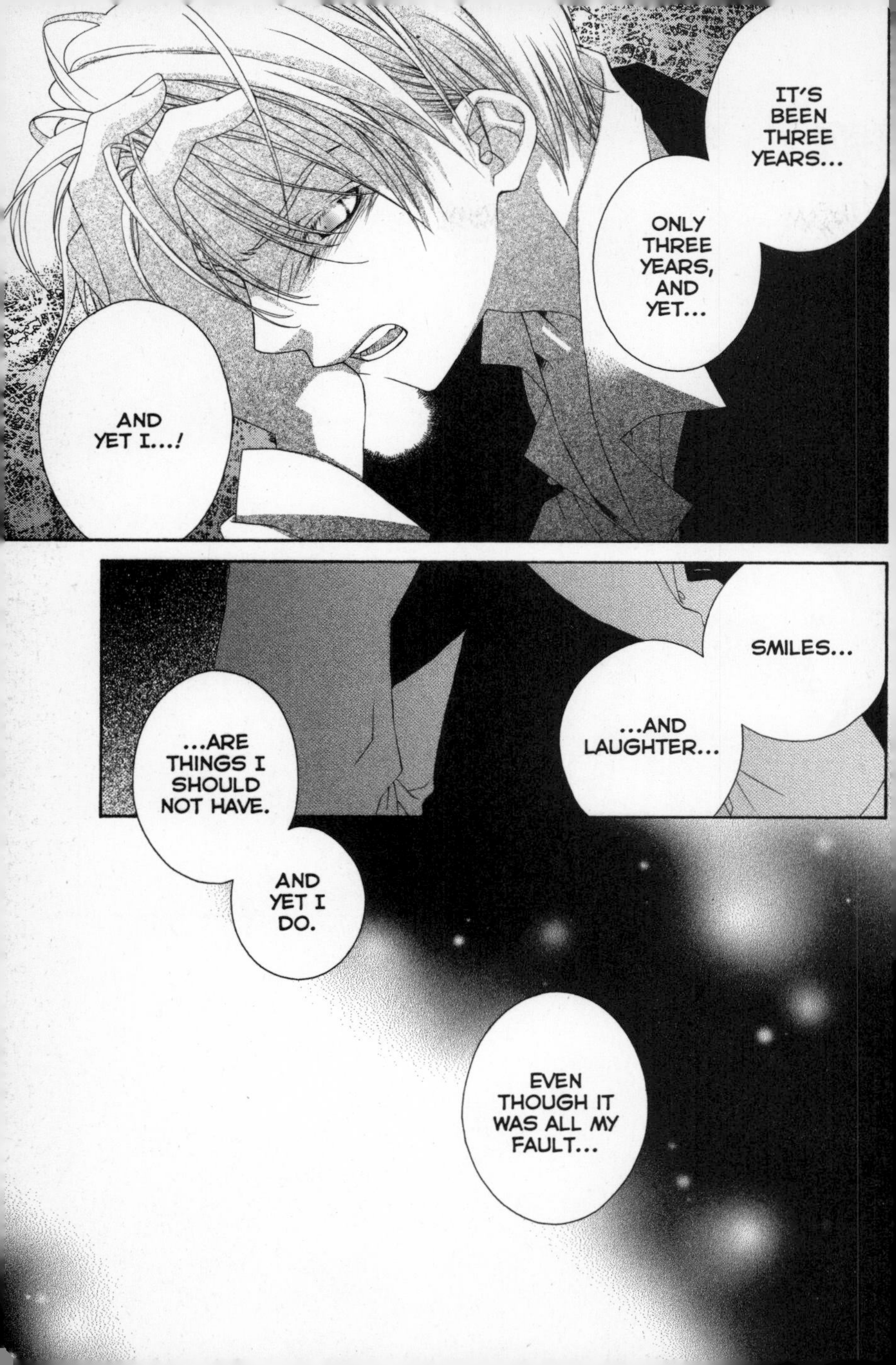
IT'S BEEN THREE YEARS...
ONLY THREE YEARS, AND YET...
AND YET I...!
SMILES...
...AND LAUGHTER...
...ARE THINGS I SHOULD NOT HAVE.
AND YET I DO.
EVEN THOUGH IT WAS ALL MY FAULT...

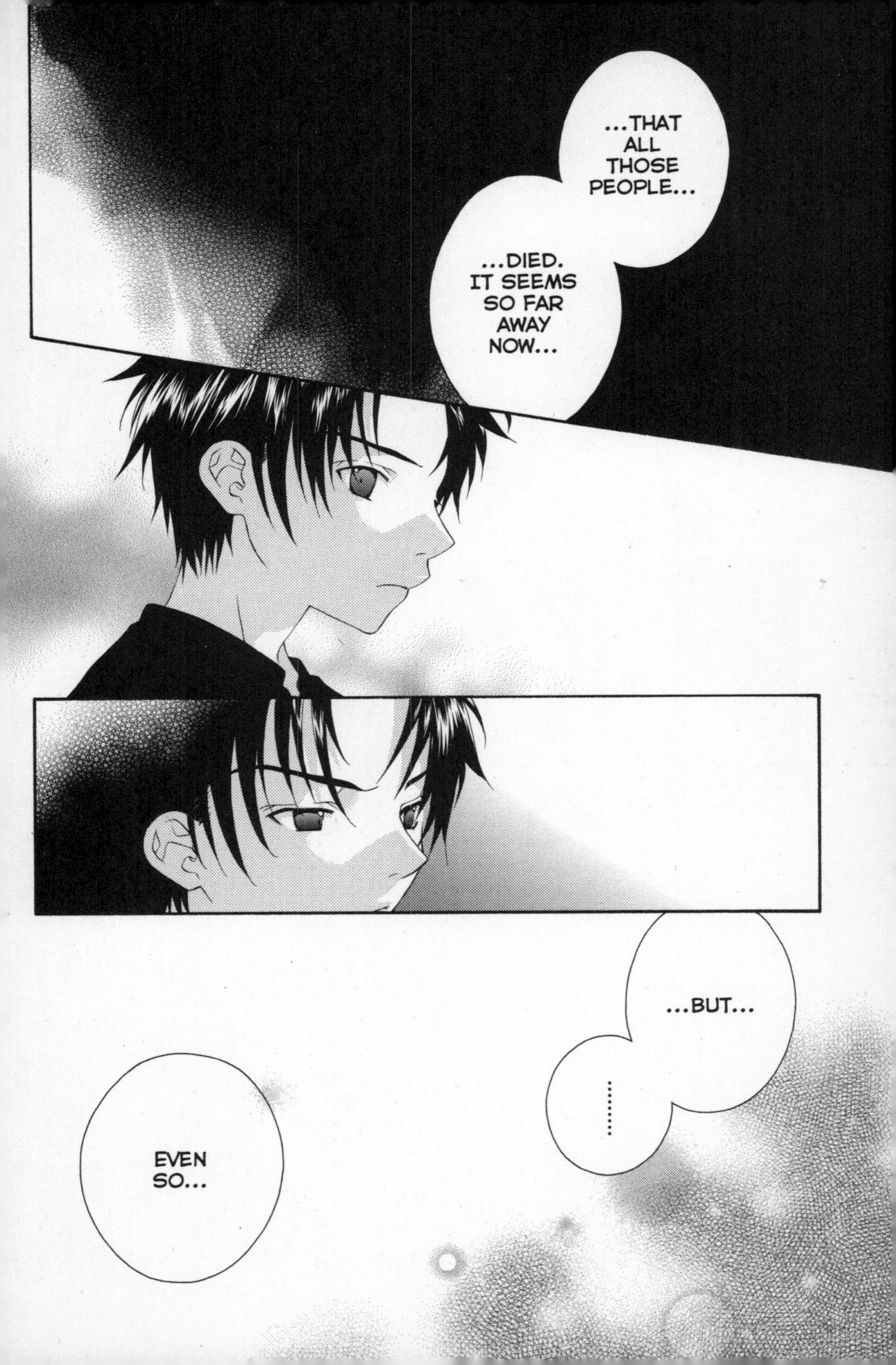
...THAT ALL THOSE PEOPLE...
...DIED. IT SEEMS SO FAR AWAY NOW...
...BUT...
......
EVEN SO...

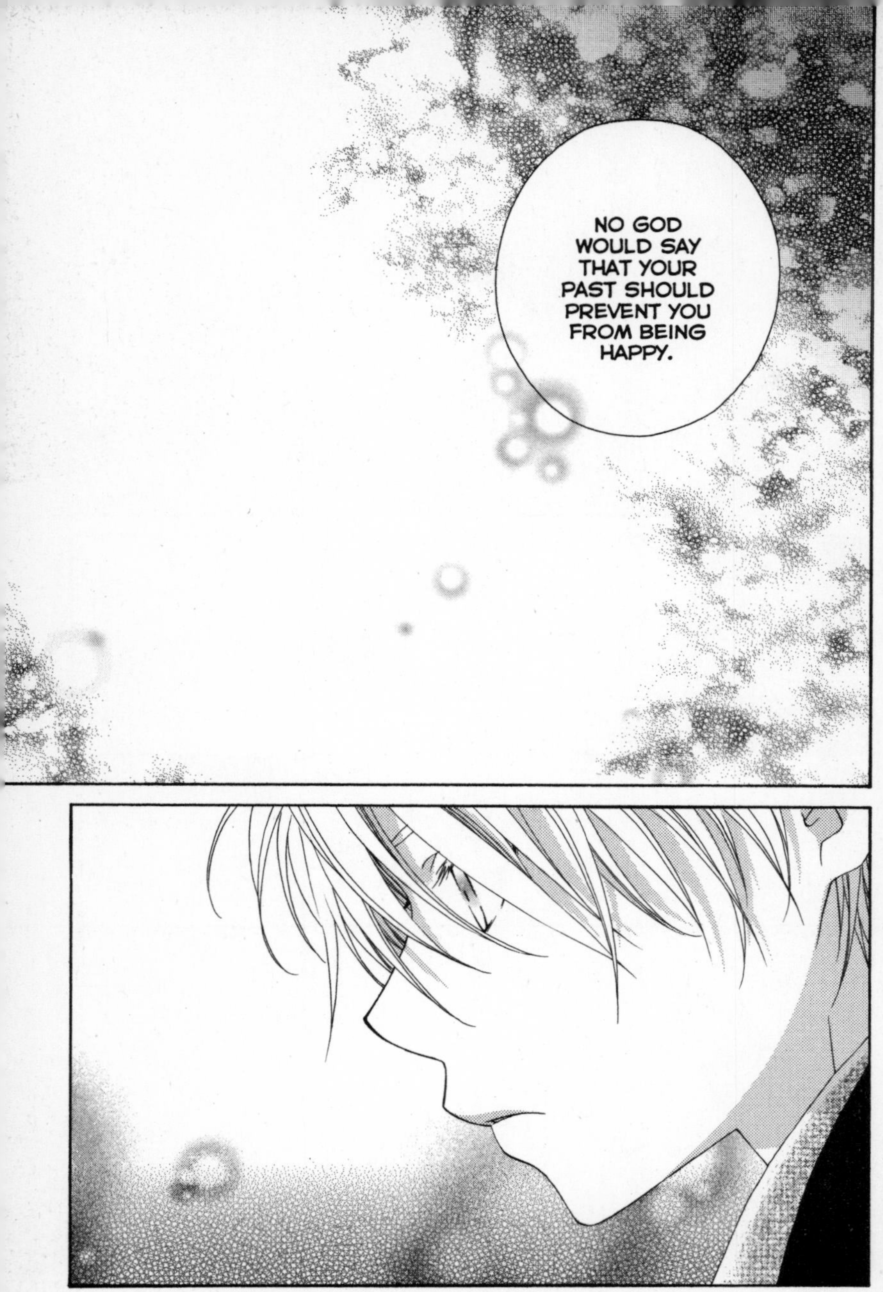
NO GOD WOULD SAY THAT YOUR PAST SHOULD PREVENT YOU FROM BEING HAPPY.

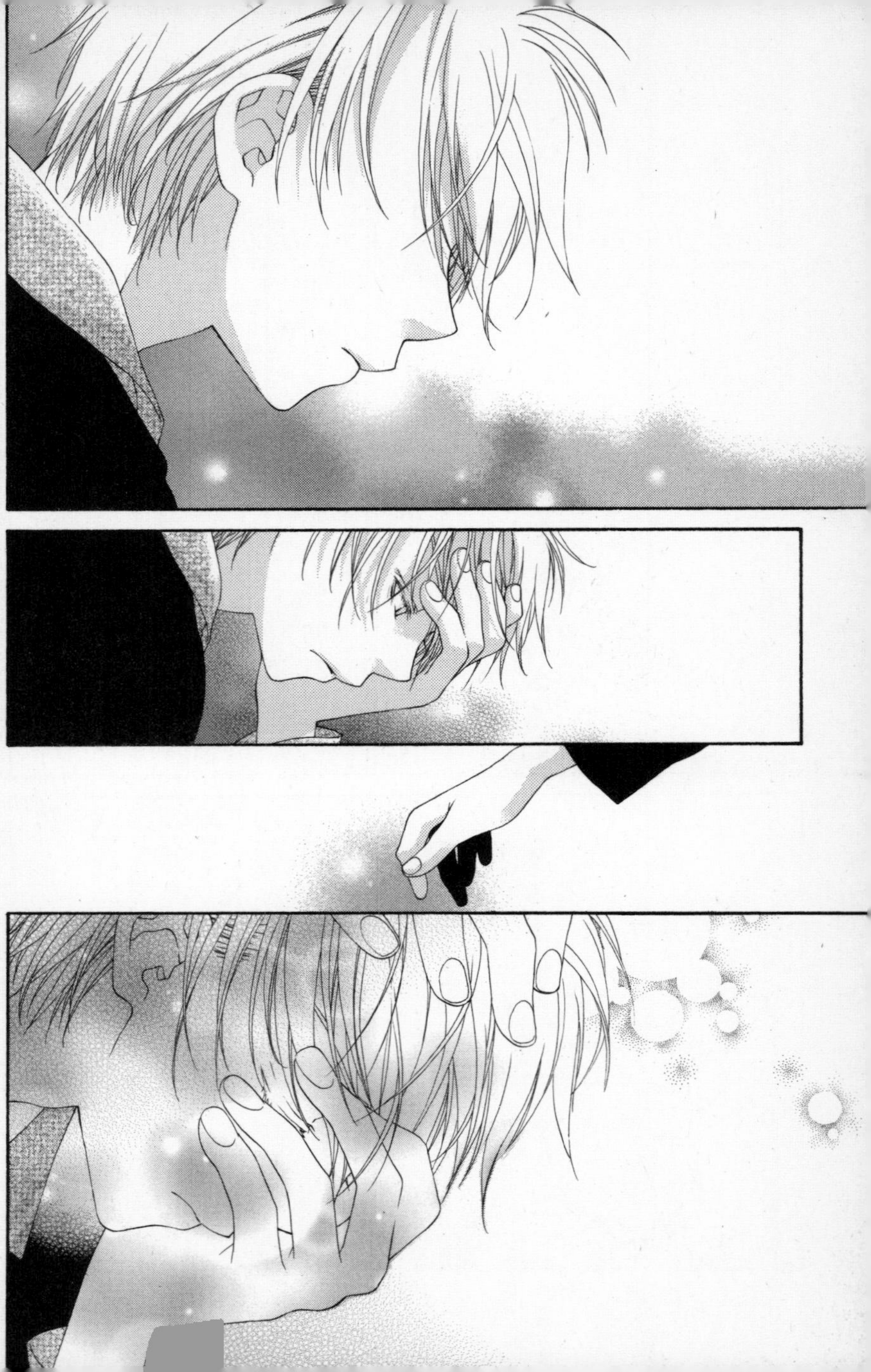

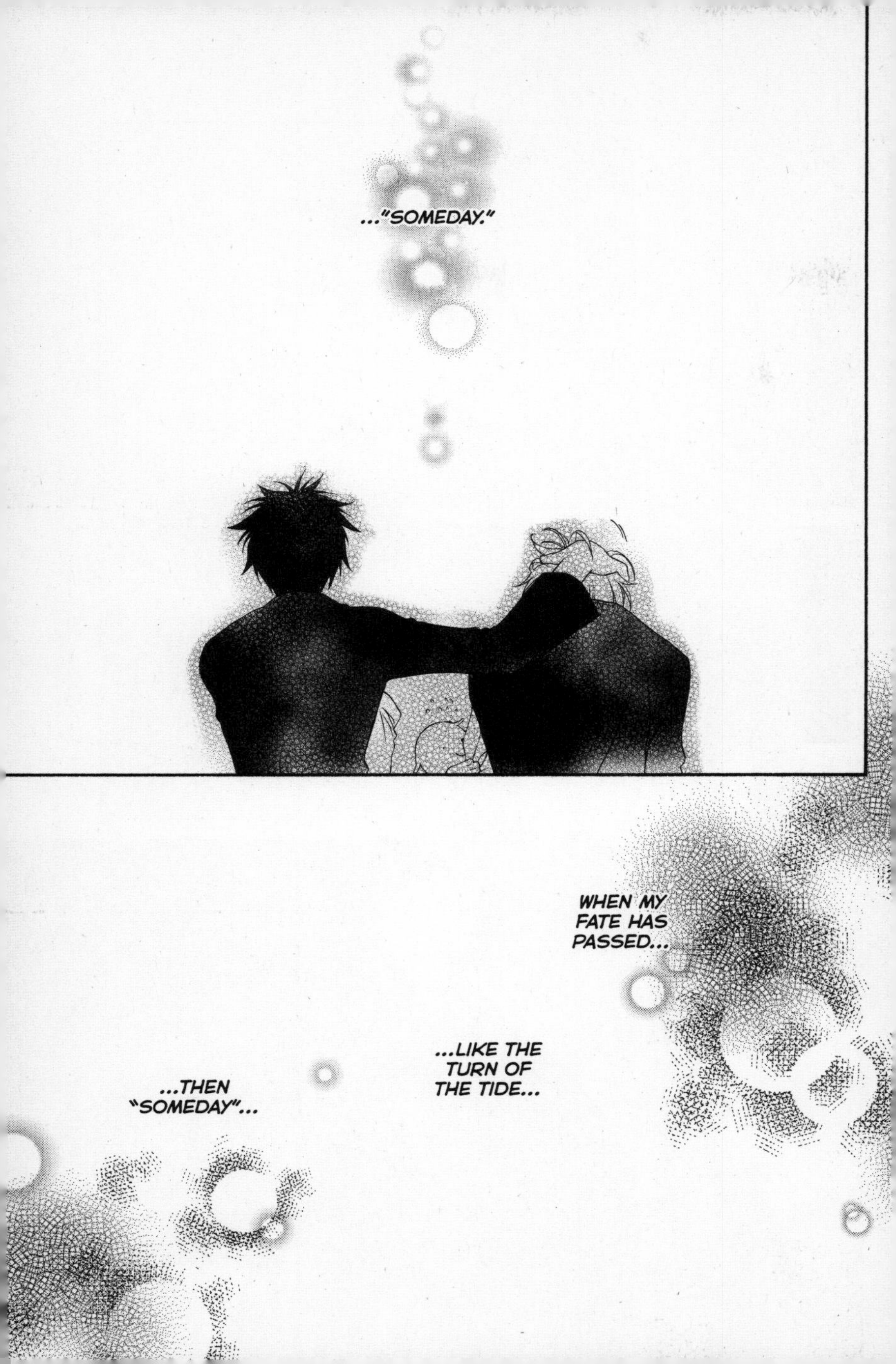
..."SOMEDAY."
WHEN MY FATE HAS PASSED...
...LIKE THE TURN OF THE TIDE...
...THEN "SOMEDAY"...

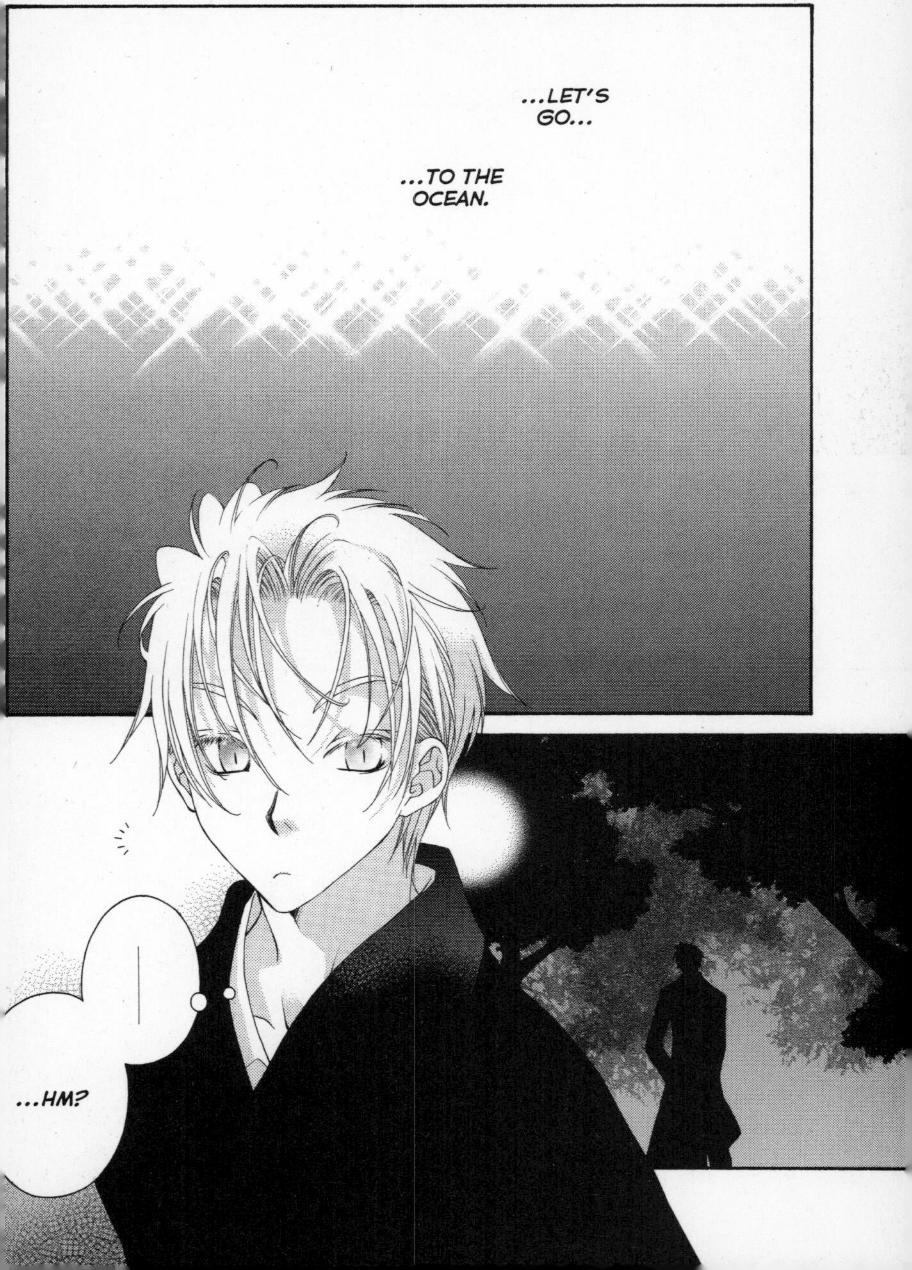

...LET'S GO...
...TO THE OCEAN.
...HM?

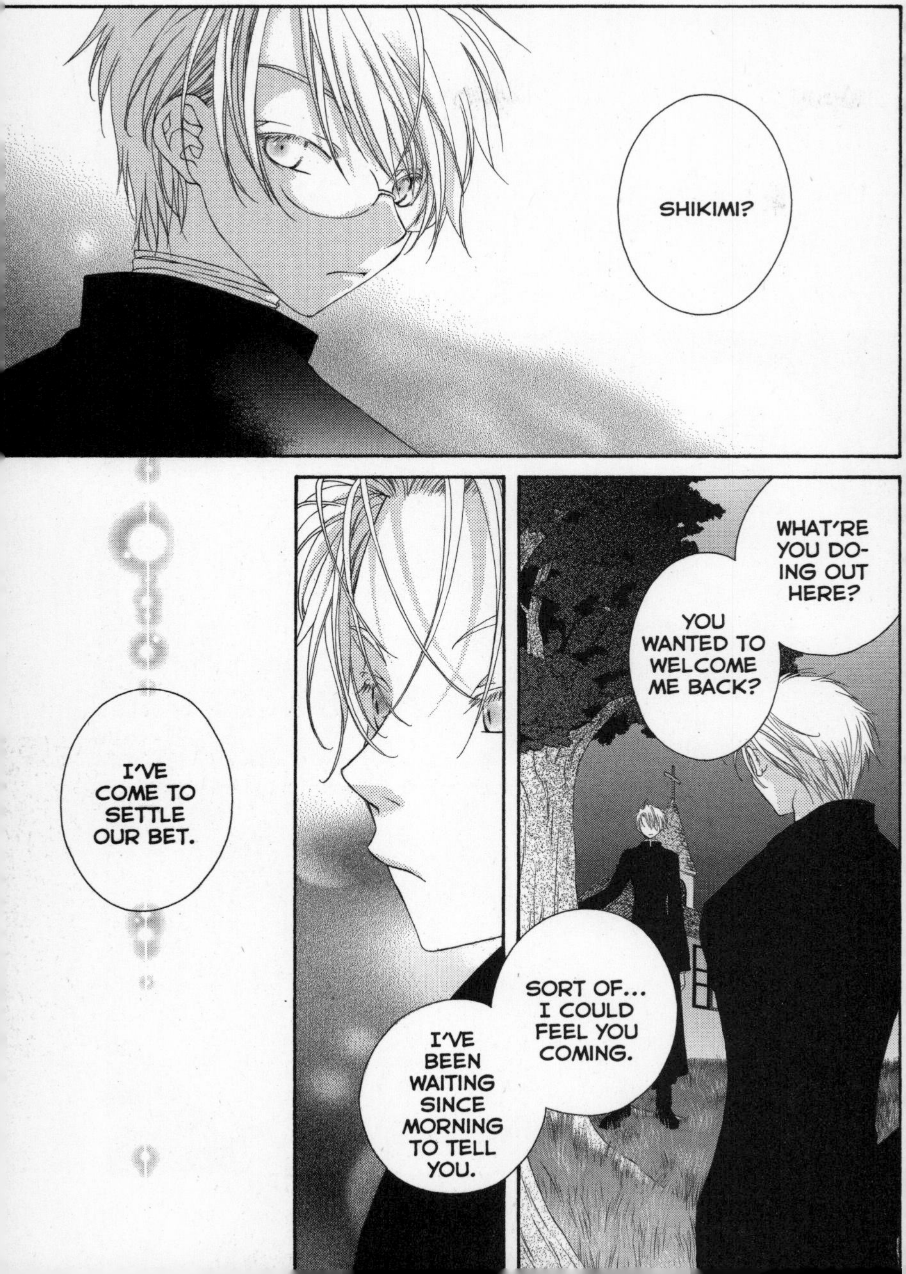
SHIKIMI?
WHAT'RE YOU DOING OUT HERE?
YOU WANTED TO WELCOME ME BACK?
SORT OF... I COULD FEEL YOU COMING.
I'VE BEEN WAITING SINCE MORNING TO TELL YOU.
I'VE COME TO SETTLE OUR BET.

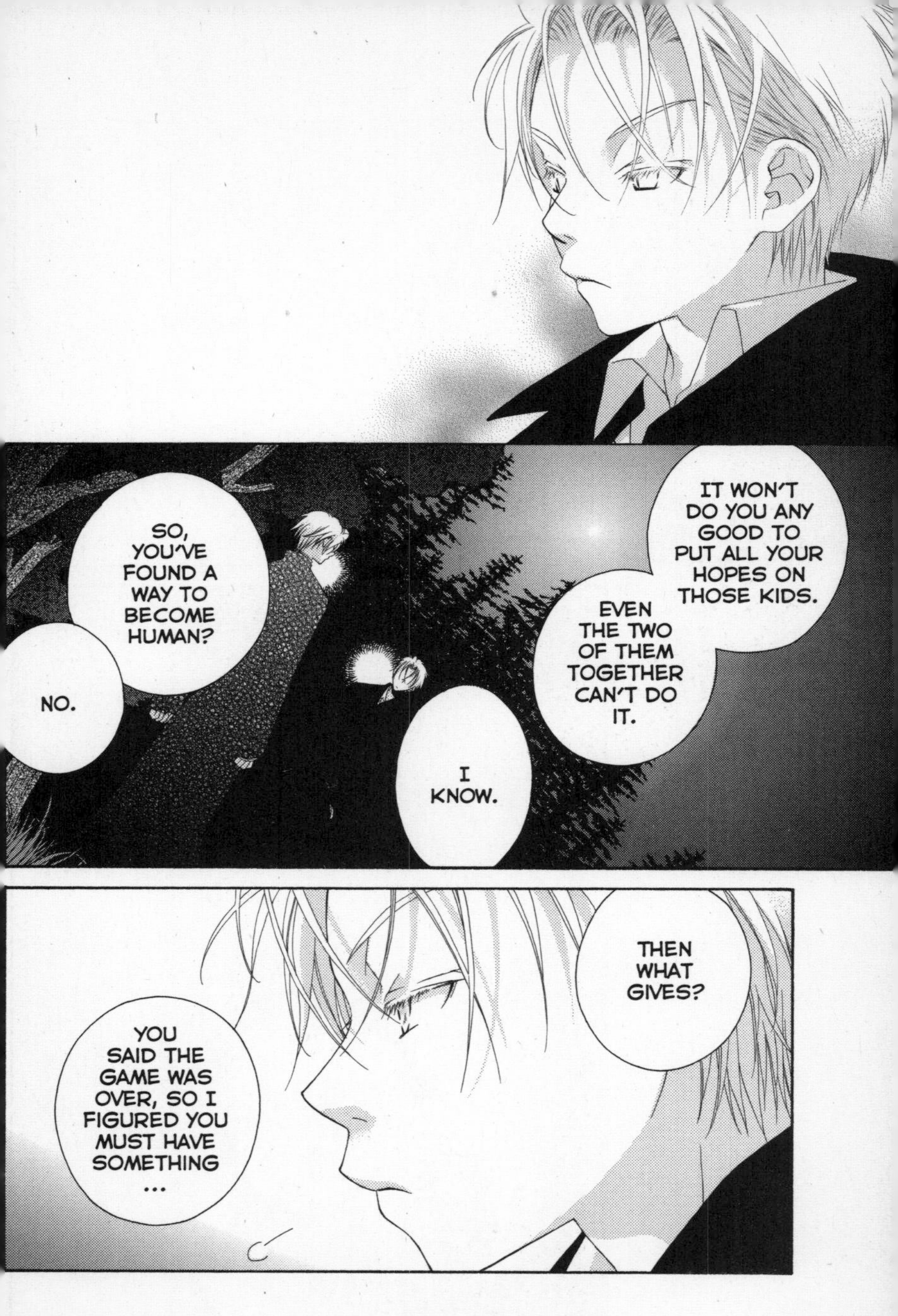
IT WON'T DO YOU ANY GOOD TO PUT ALL YOUR HOPES ON THOSE KIDS.
EVEN THE TWO OF THEM TOGETHER CAN'T DO IT.
I KNOW.
SO, YOU'VE FOUND A WAY TO BECOME HUMAN?
NO.
THEN WHAT GIVES?
YOU SAID THE GAME WAS OVER, SO I FIGURED YOU MUST HAVE SOMETHING ...

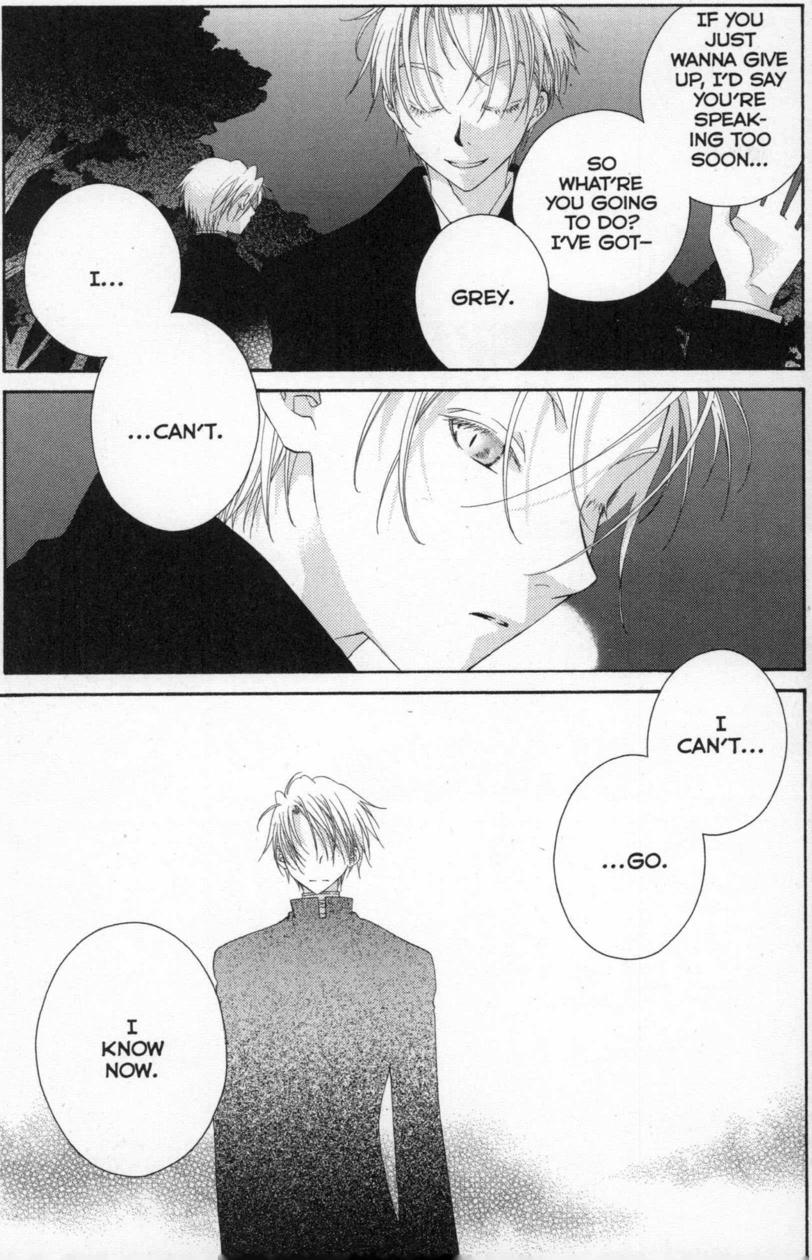
IF YOU JUST WANNA GIVE UP, I'D SAY YOU'RE SPEAK-ING TOO SOON...
SO WHAT'RE YOU GOING TO DO? I'VE GOT–
GREY.
I...
...CAN'T.
I CAN'T...
...GO.
I KNOW NOW.

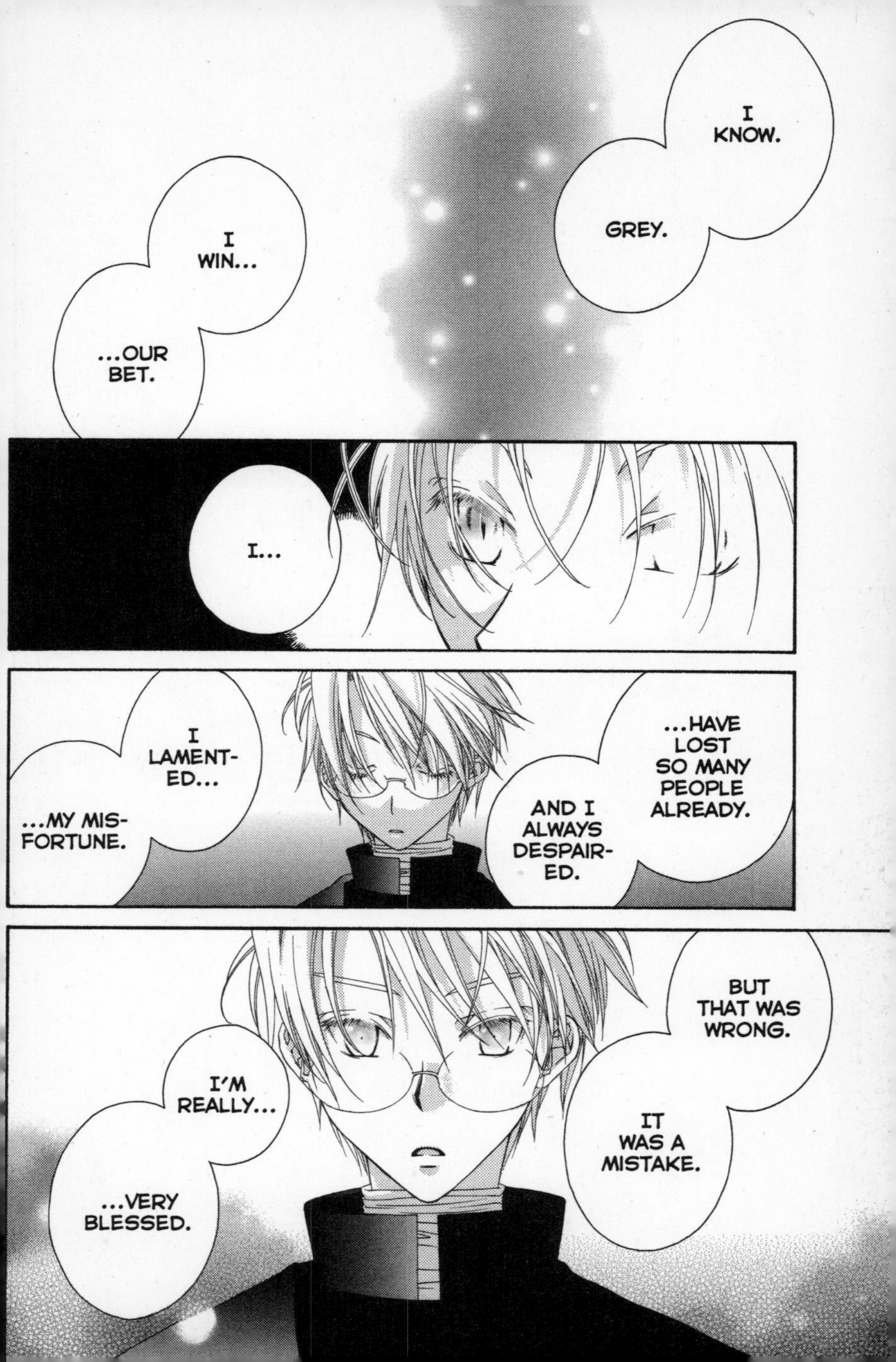
I KNOW.
GREY.
I WIN...
...OUR BET.
I...
...HAVE LOST SO MANY PEOPLE ALREADY.
AND I ALWAYS DESPAIR-ED.
I LAMENT-ED...
...MY MIS-FORTUNE.
BUT THAT WAS WRONG.
IT WAS A MISTAKE.
I'M REALLY...
...VERY BLESSED.

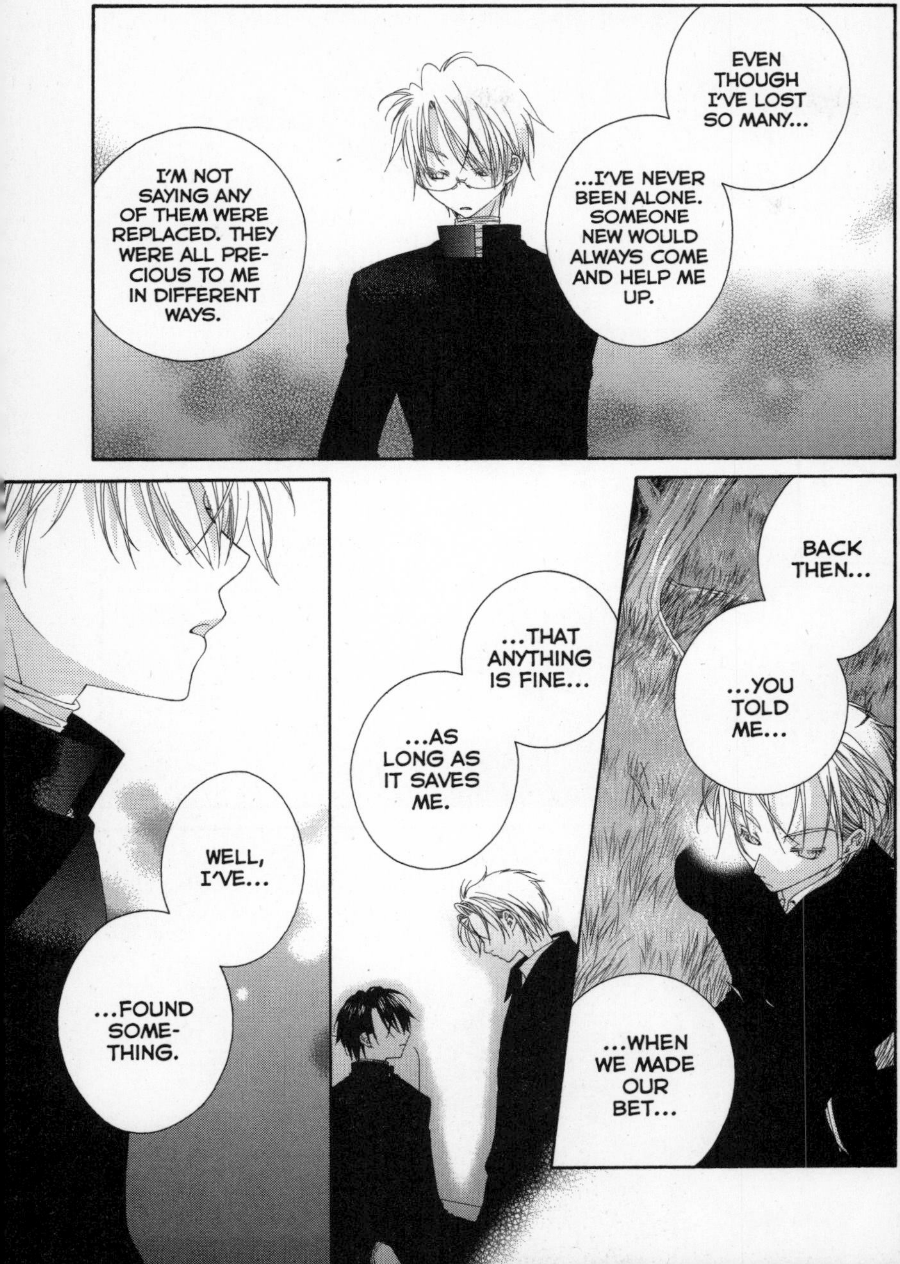
EVEN THOUGH I'VE LOST SO MANY...
...I'VE NEVER BEEN ALONE. SOMEONE NEW WOULD ALWAYS COME AND HELP ME UP.
I'M NOT SAYING ANY OF THEM WERE REPLACED. THEY WERE ALL PRE-CIOUS TO ME IN DIFFERENT WAYS.
BACK THEN...
...YOU TOLD ME...
...WHEN WE MADE OUR BET...
...THAT ANYTHING IS FINE...
...AS LONG AS IT SAVES ME.
WELL, I'VE...
...FOUND SOME-THING.

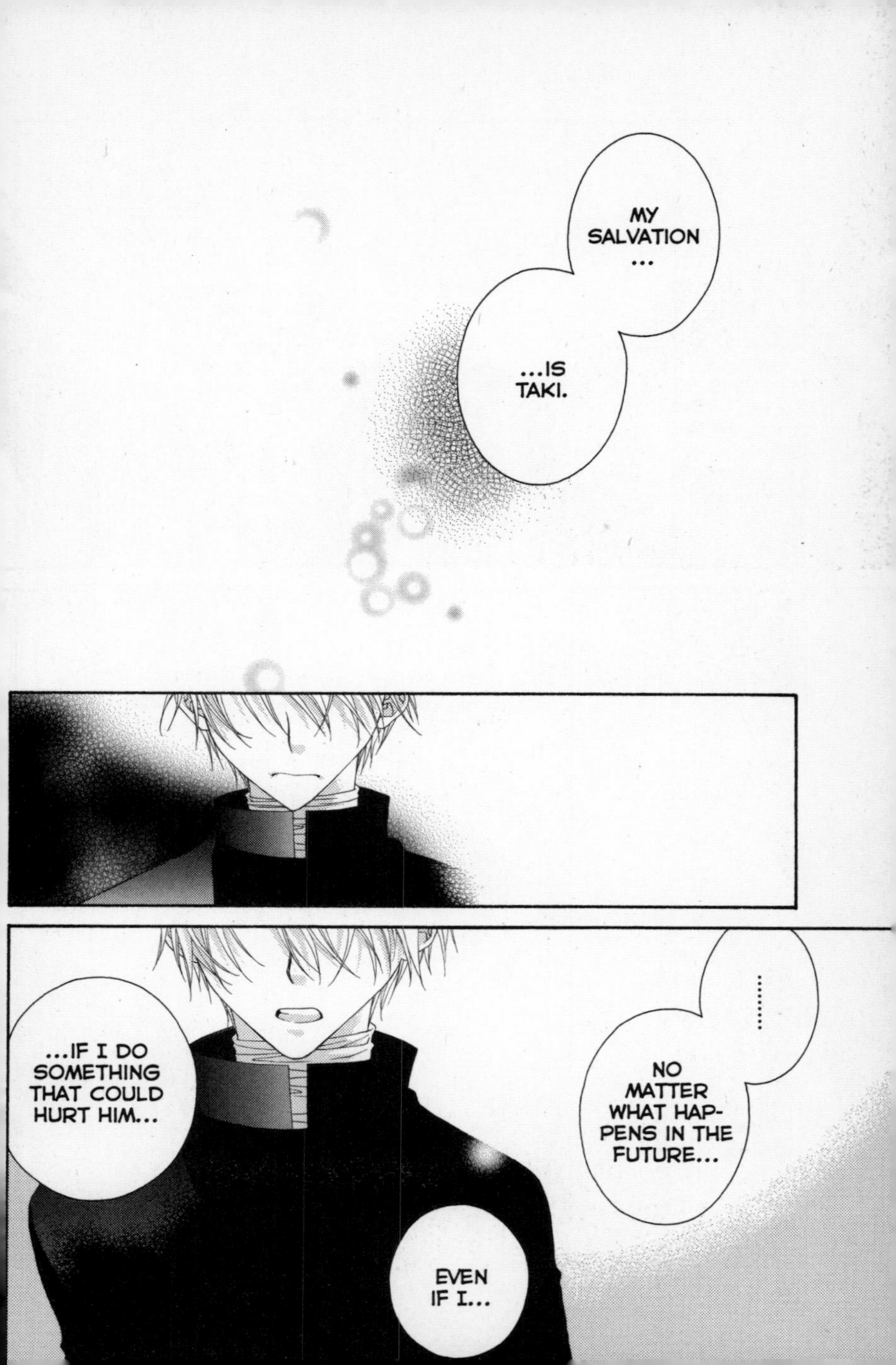
MY SALVATION ...
...IS TAKI.
......
NO MATTER WHAT HAP-PENS IN THE FUTURE...
EVEN IF I...
...IF I DO SOMETHING THAT COULD HURT HIM...

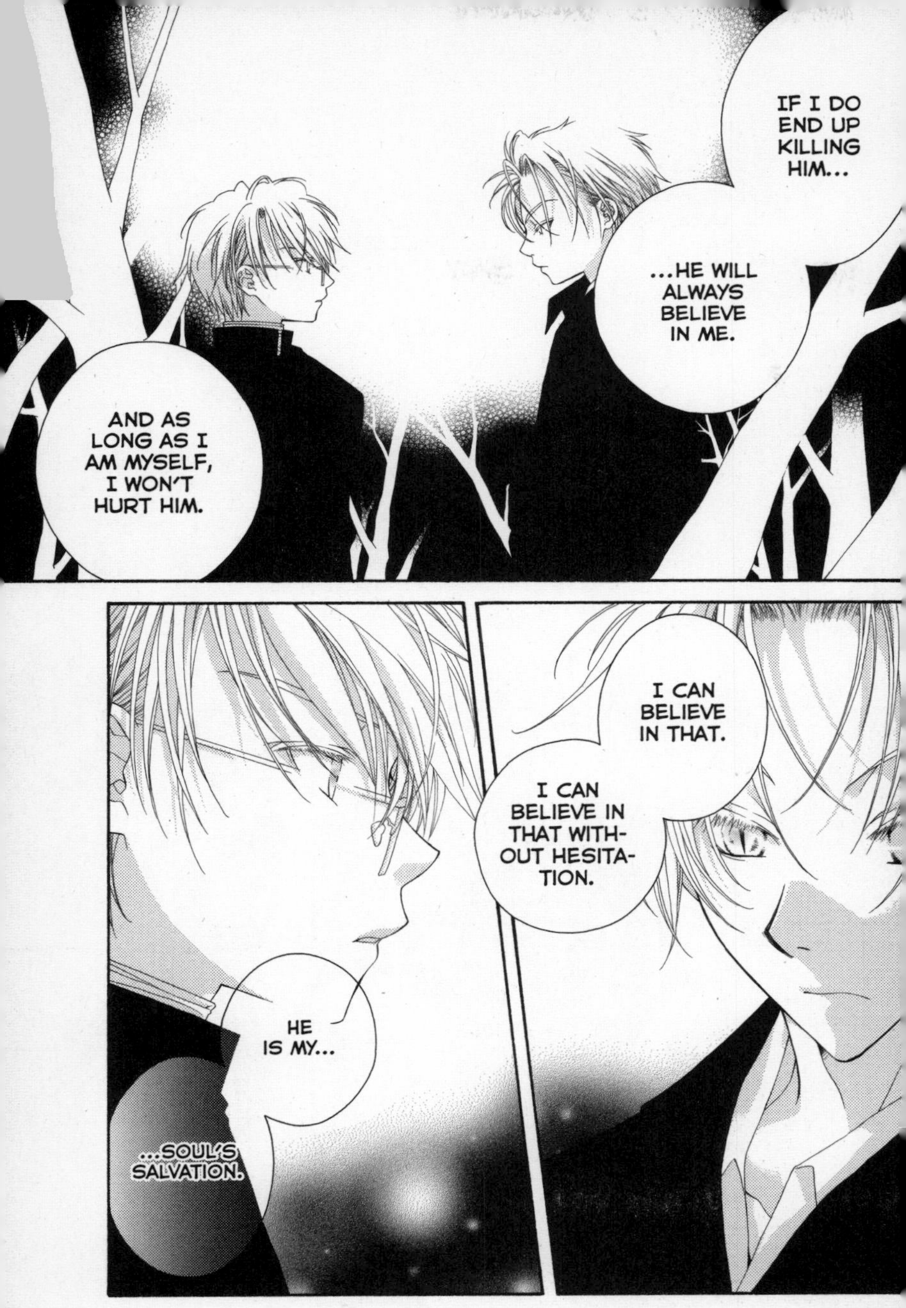
IF I DO END UP KILLING HIM...
...HE WILL ALWAYS BELIEVE IN ME.
AND AS LONG AS I AM MYSELF, I WON'T HURT HIM.
I CAN BELIEVE IN THAT.
I CAN BELIEVE IN THAT WITH-OUT HESITA-TION.
HE IS MY...
...SOUL'S SALVATION.

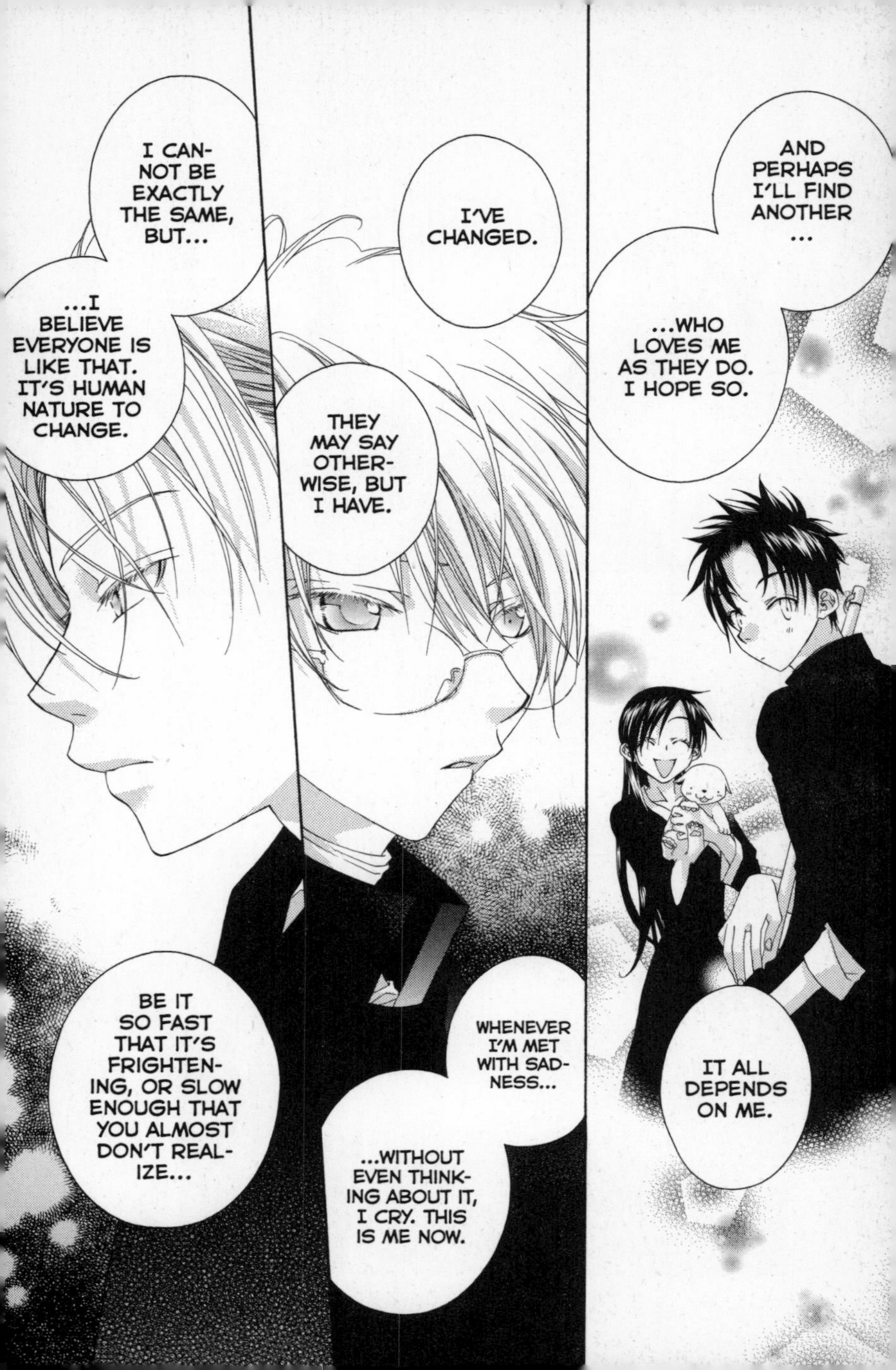
AND PERHAPS I'LL FIND ANOTHER ...
...WHO LOVES ME AS THEY DO. I HOPE SO.
IT ALL DEPENDS ON ME.
I'VE CHANGED.
THEY MAY SAY OTHERWISE, BUT I HAVE.
WHENEVER I'M MET WITH SADNESS...
...WITHOUT EVEN THINKING ABOUT IT, I CRY. THIS IS ME NOW.
I CANNOT BE EXACTLY THE SAME, BUT...
...I BELIEVE EVERYONE IS LIKE THAT. IT'S HUMAN NATURE TO CHANGE.
BE IT SO FAST THAT IT'S FRIGHTENING, OR SLOW ENOUGH THAT YOU ALMOST DON'T REALIZE...

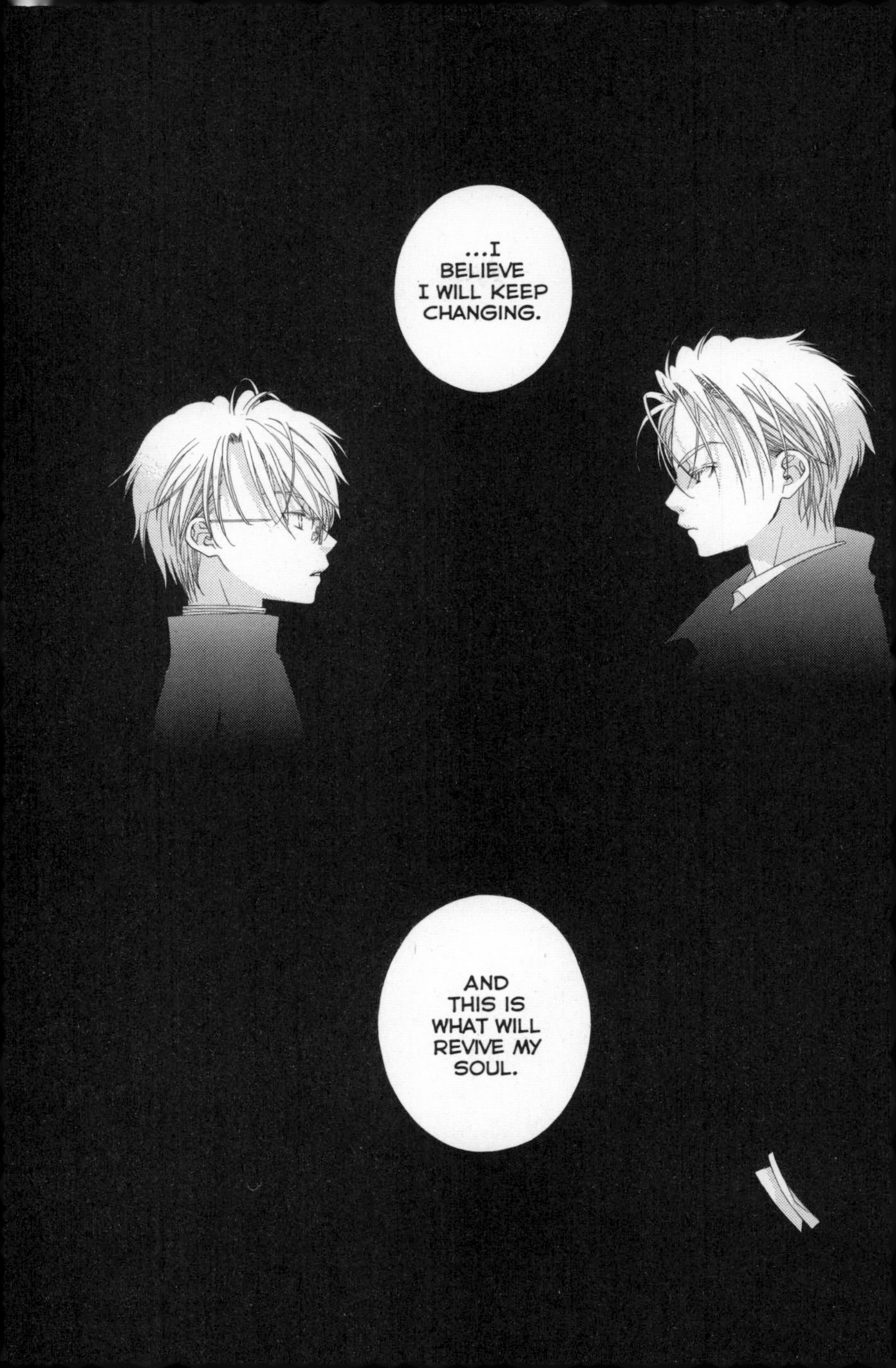
...I BELIEVE I WILL KEEP CHANGING.
AND THIS IS WHAT WILL REVIVE MY SOUL.

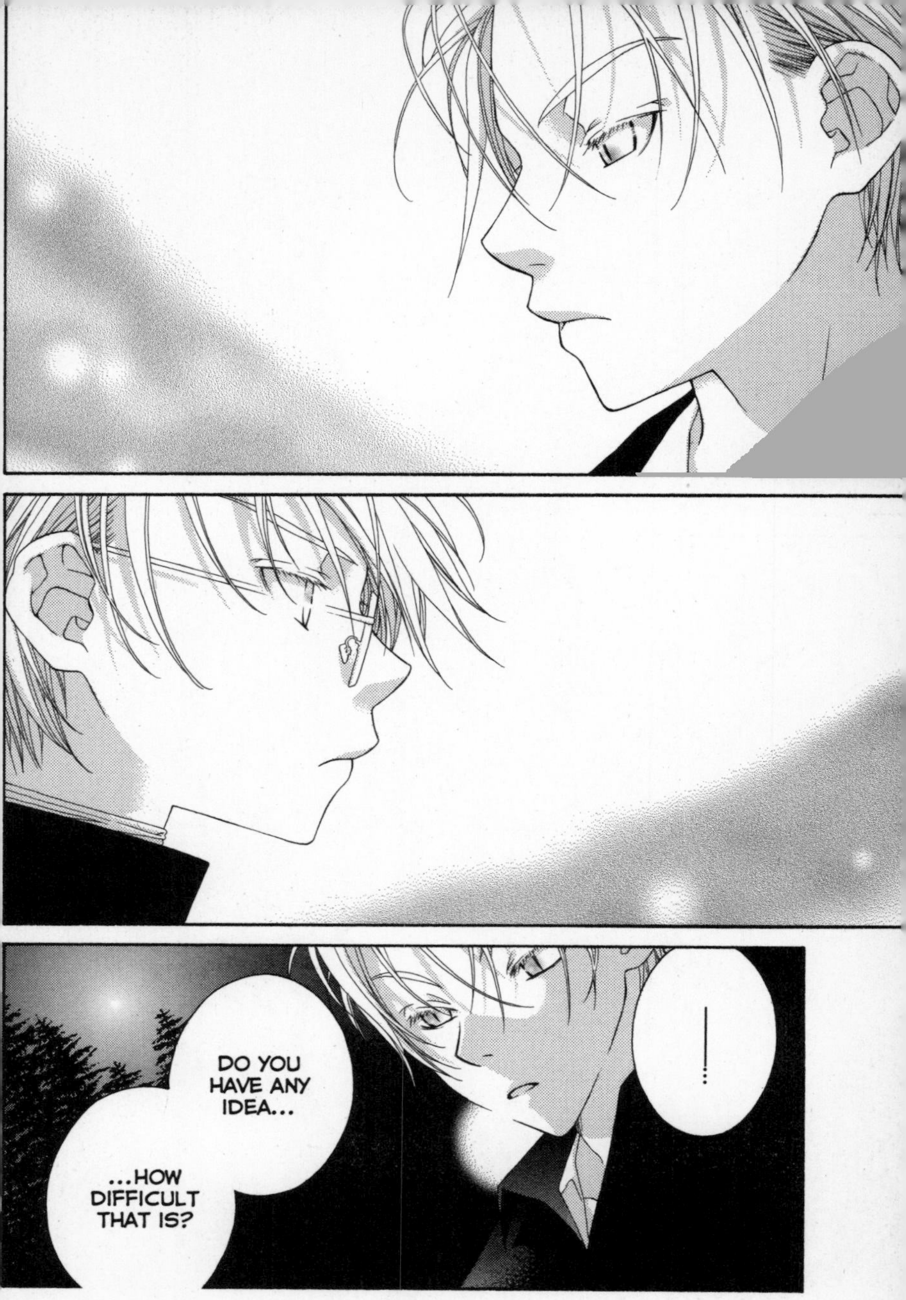
—!
DO YOU HAVE ANY IDEA...
...HOW DIFFICULT THAT IS?

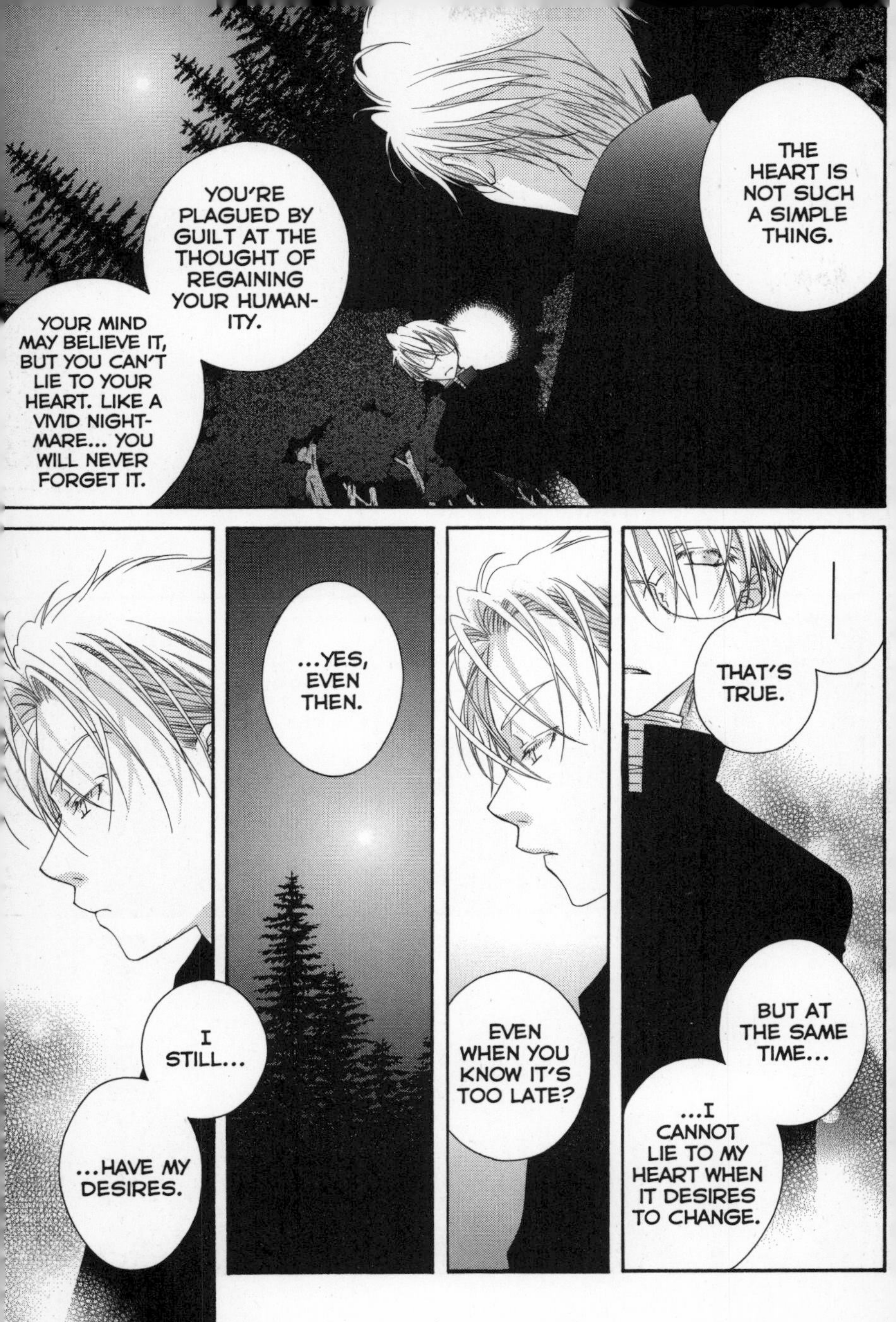
THE HEART IS NOT SUCH A SIMPLE THING.
YOU'RE PLAGUED BY GUILT AT THE THOUGHT OF REGAINING YOUR HUMAN-ITY.
YOUR MIND MAY BELIEVE IT, BUT YOU CAN'T LIE TO YOUR HEART. LIKE A VIVID NIGHT-MARE... YOU WILL NEVER FORGET IT.
THAT'S TRUE.
BUT AT THE SAME TIME...
...I CANNOT LIE TO MY HEART WHEN IT DESIRES TO CHANGE.
EVEN WHEN YOU KNOW IT'S TOO LATE?
...YES, EVEN THEN.
I STILL...
...HAVE MY DESIRES.

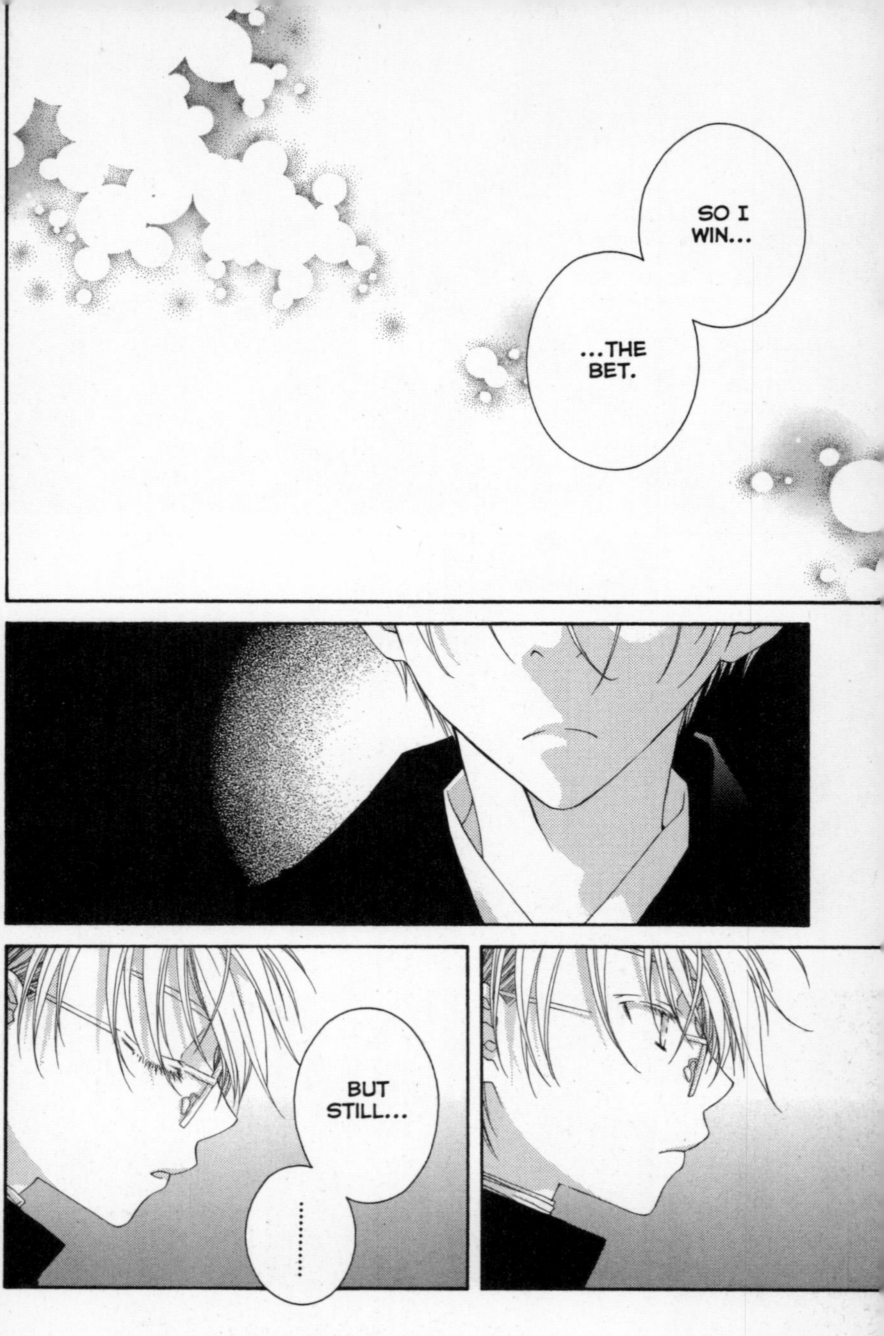
SO I WIN...
...THE BET.
BUT STILL...
....

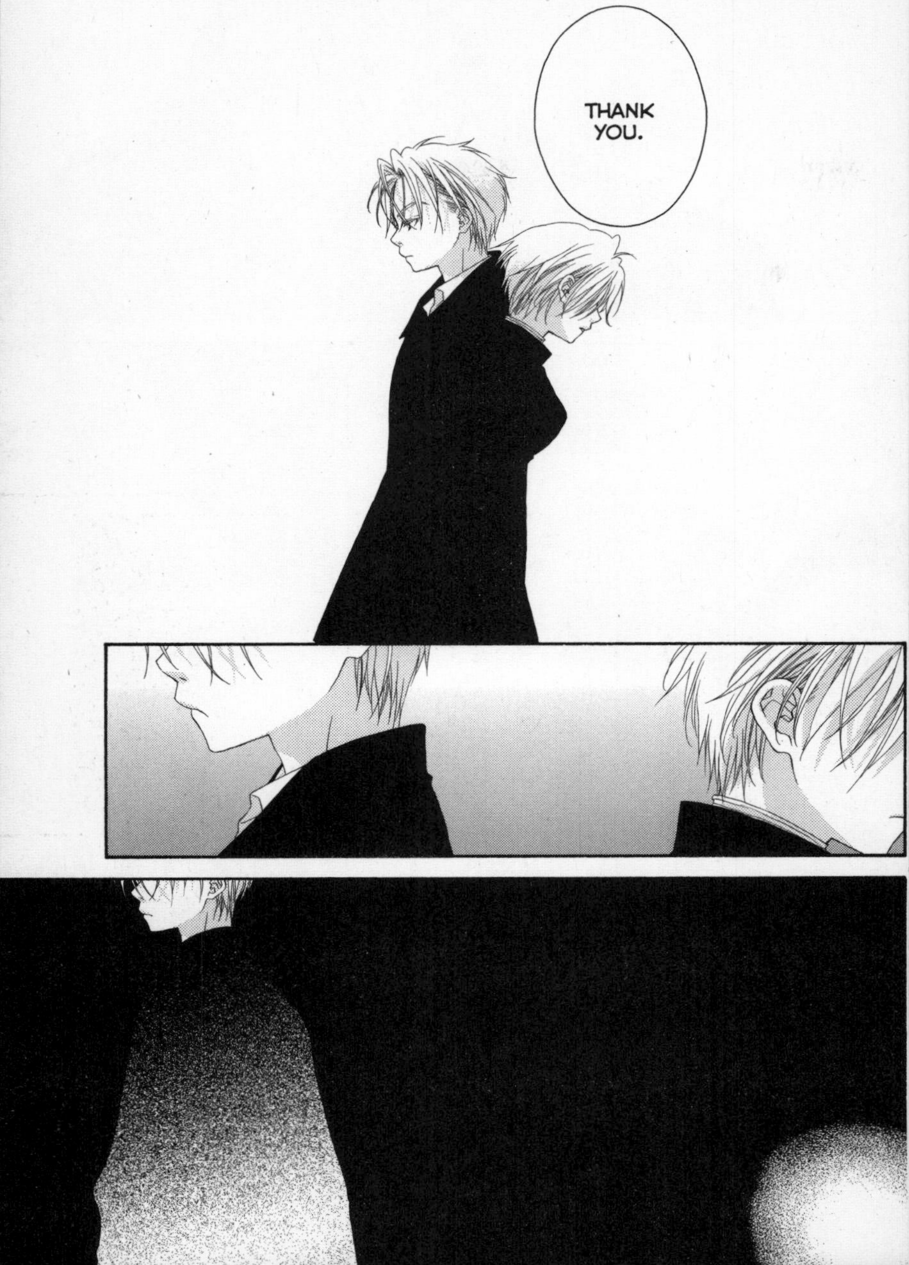
THANK YOU.

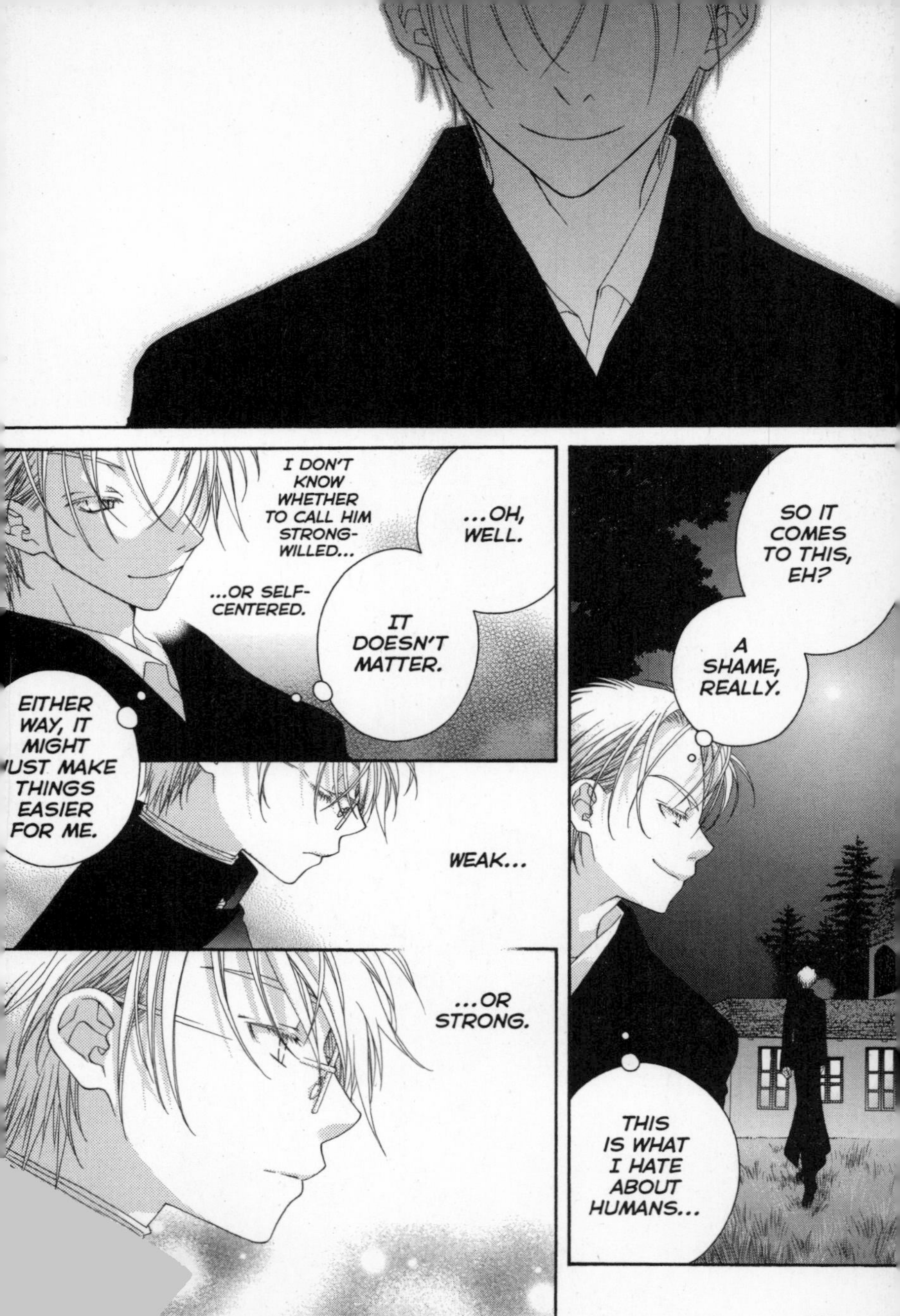
SO IT COMES TO THIS, EH?
A SHAME, REALLY.
THIS IS WHAT I HATE ABOUT HUMANS...
I DON'T KNOW WHETHER TO CALL HIM STRONG-WILLED...
...OR SELF-CENTERED.
...OH, WELL.
IT DOESN'T MATTER.
EITHER WAY, IT MIGHT JUST MAKE THINGS EASIER FOR ME.
WEAK...
...OR STRONG.

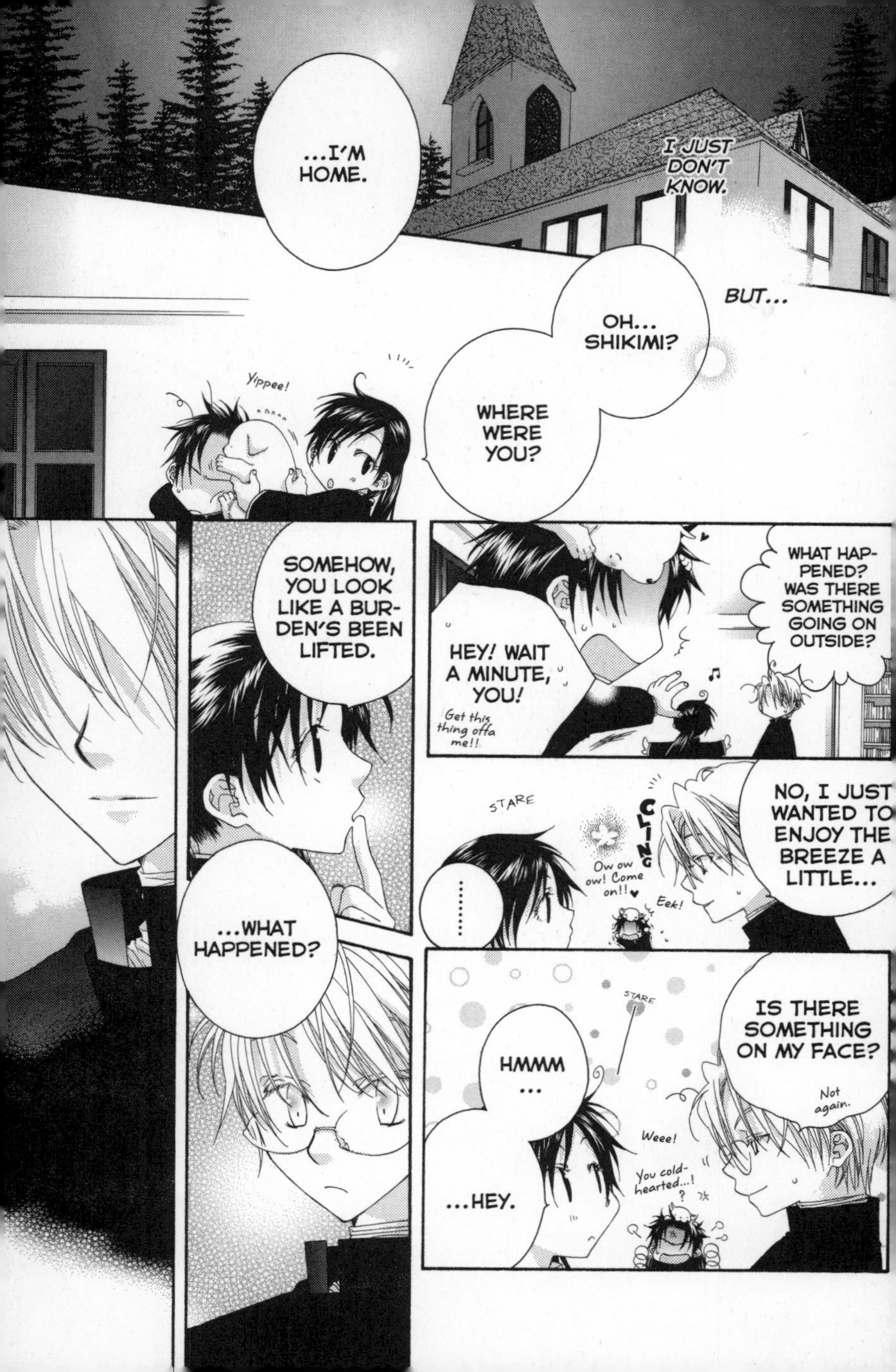
I JUST DON'T KNOW.
BUT...
...I'M HOME.
OH... SHIKIMI?
WHERE WERE YOU?
Yippee!
WHAT HAPPENED? WAS THERE SOMETHING GOING ON OUTSIDE?
HEY! WAIT A MINUTE, YOU!
Get this thing offa me!!
NO, I JUST WANTED TO ENJOY THE BREEZE A LITTLE...
CLING
Eek!
Ow ow ow! Come on!!
STARE
......
IS THERE SOMETHING ON MY FACE?
Not again.
STARE
HMMM ...
Weee!
You cold-hearted...!
...HEY.
SOMEHOW, YOU LOOK LIKE A BURDEN'S BEEN LIFTED.
...WHAT HAPPENED?

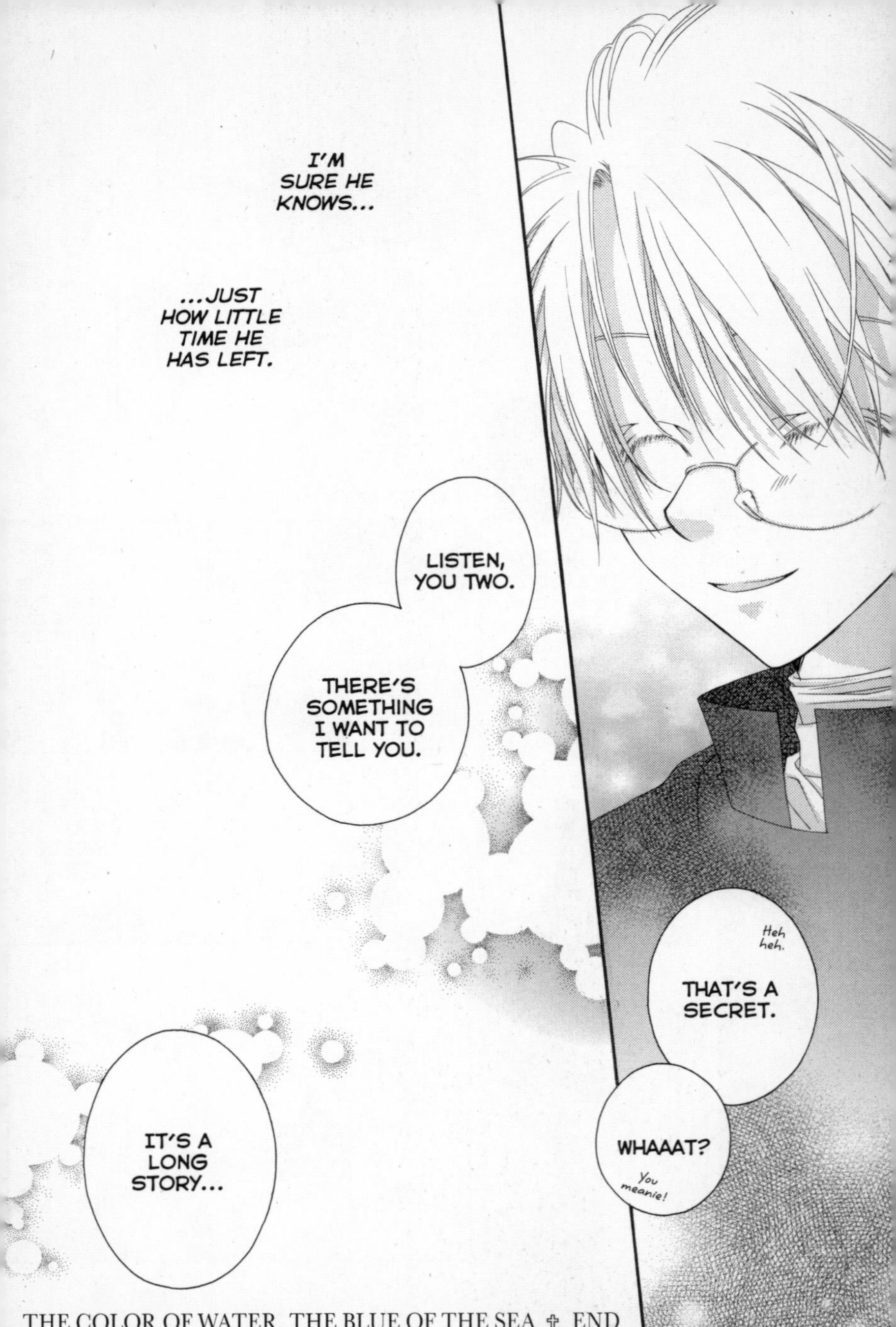
Heh heh.
THAT'S A SECRET.
WHAAAT?
You meanie!
I'M SURE HE KNOWS...
...JUST HOW LITTLE TIME HE HAS LEFT.
LISTEN, YOU TWO.
THERE'S SOMETHING I WANT TO TELL YOU.
IT'S A LONG STORY...

THE COLOR OF WATER, THE BLUE OF THE SEA ✞ END

The Forest at Night is Beautiful

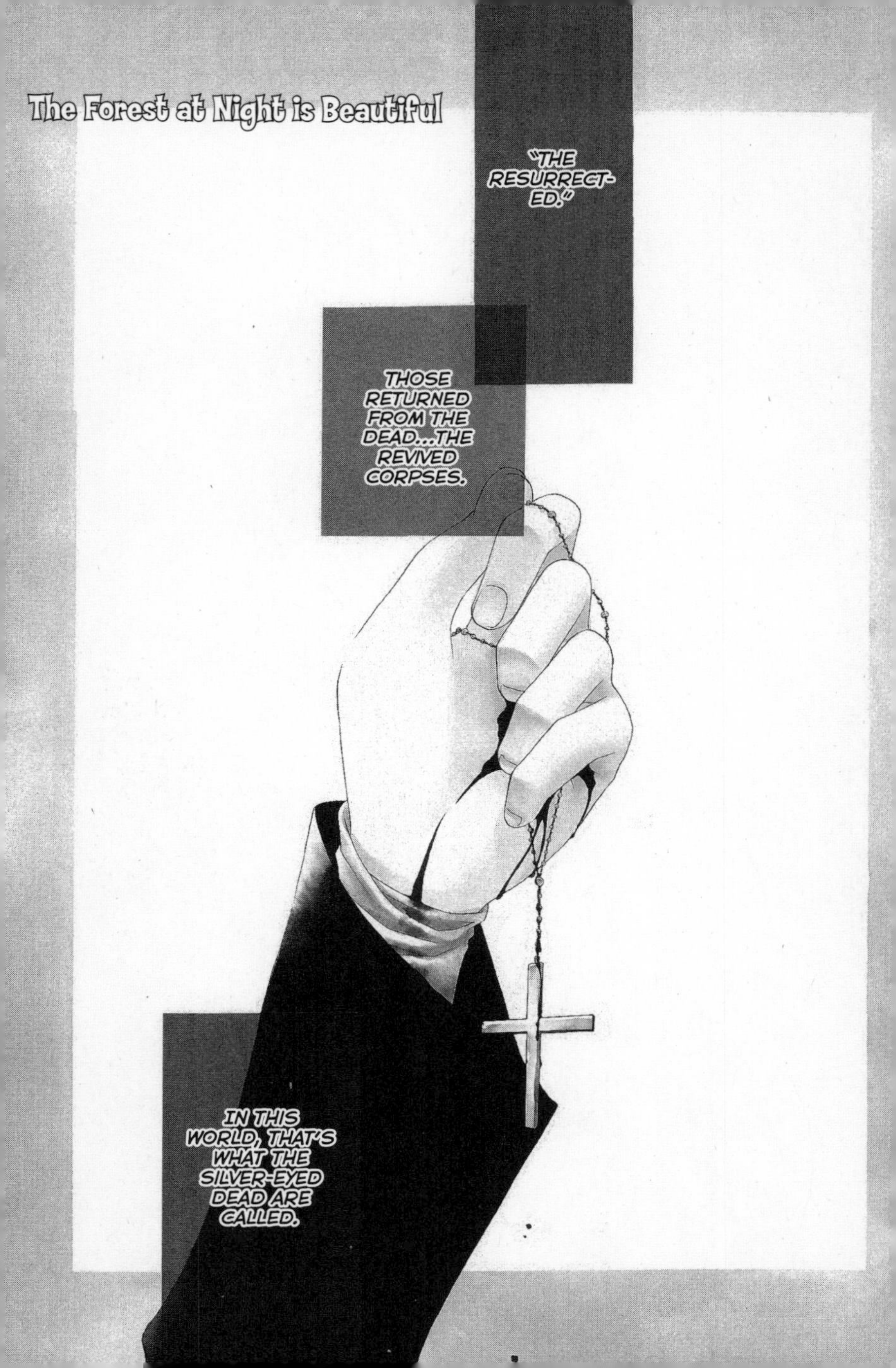
"THE RESURRECT-ED."
THOSE RETURNED FROM THE DEAD...THE REVIVED CORPSES.
IN THIS WORLD, THAT'S WHAT THE SILVER-EYED DEAD ARE CALLED.

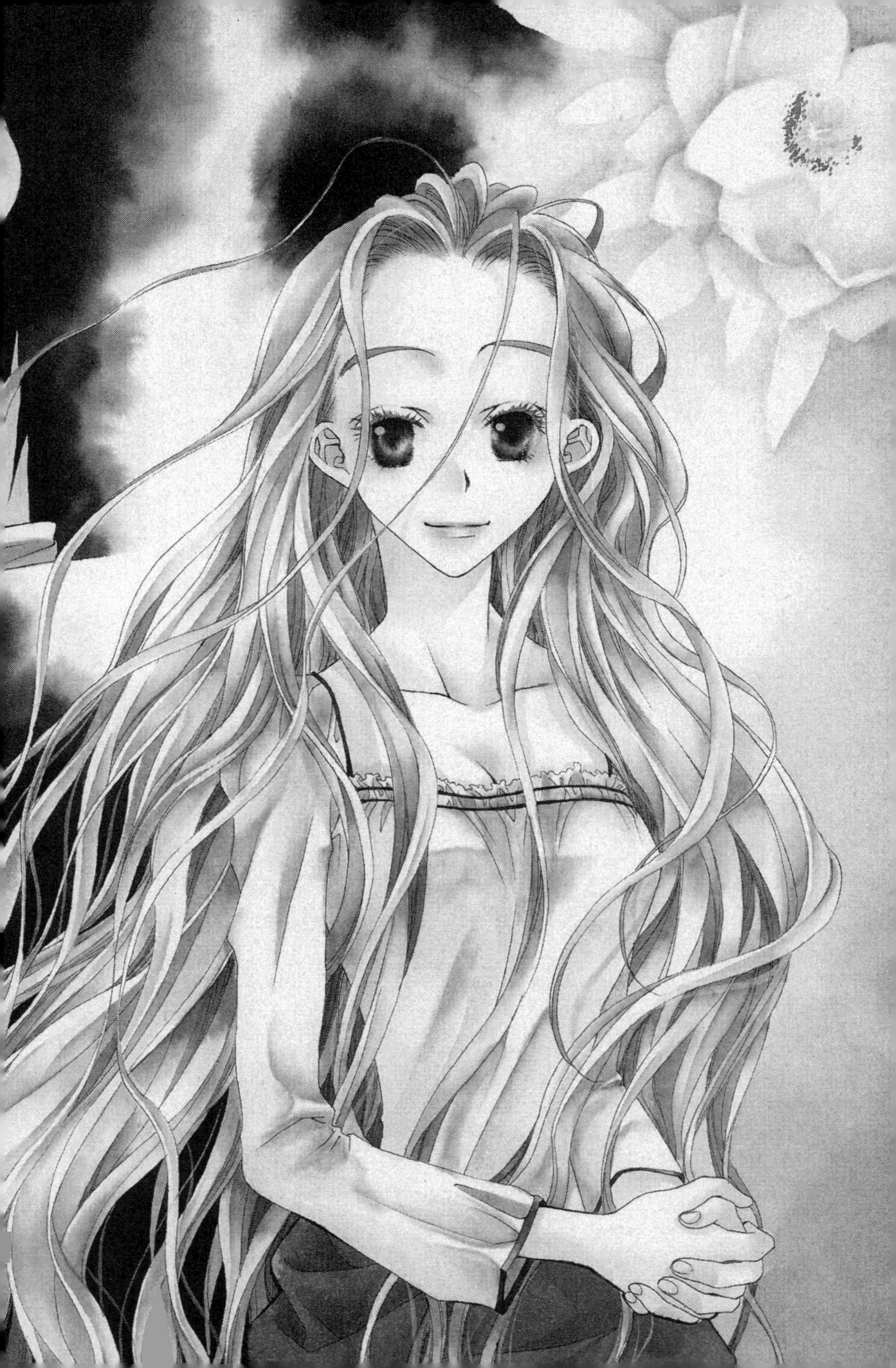

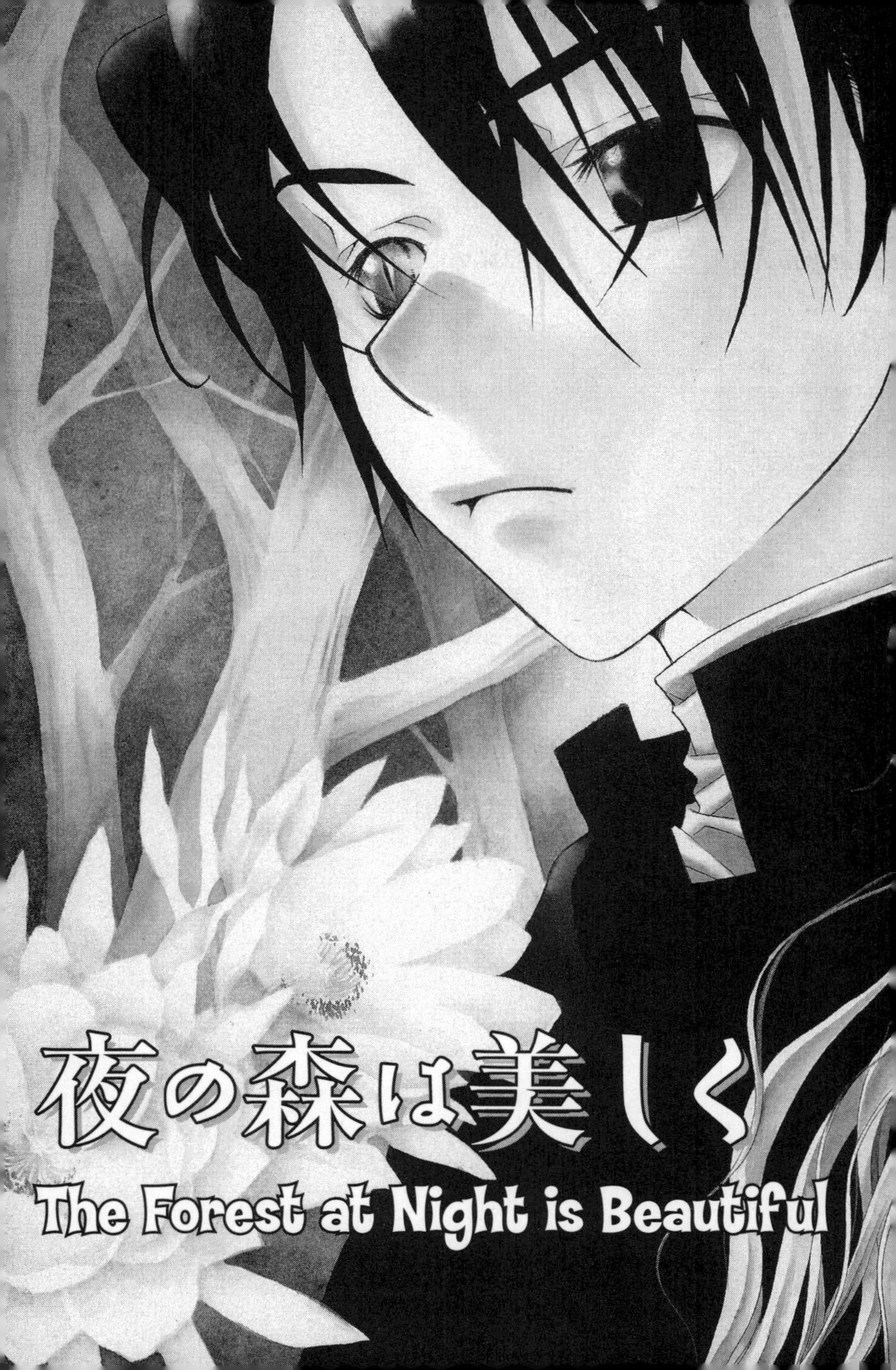
夜の森は美しく
The Forest at Night is Beautiful

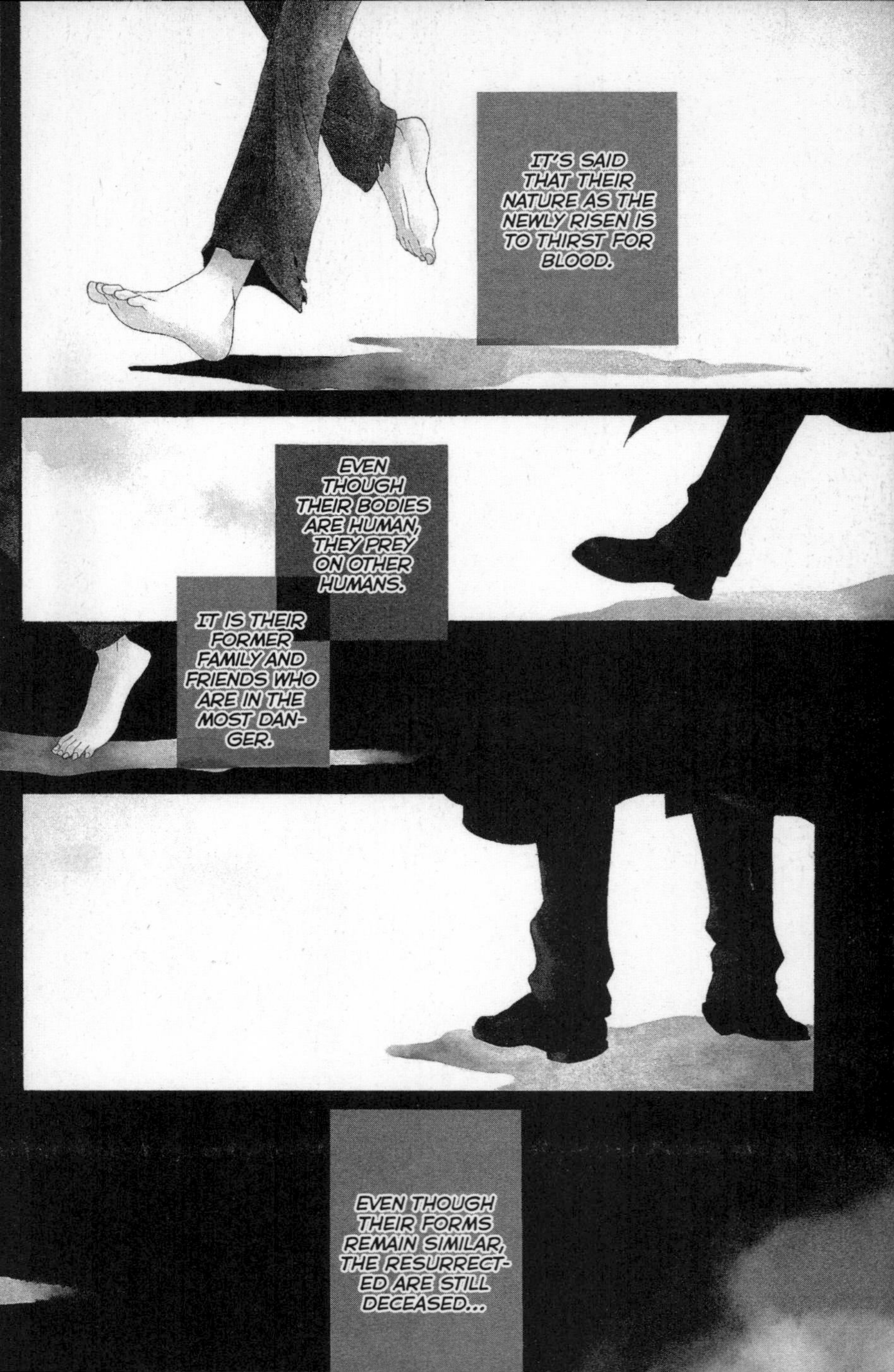
IT'S SAID THAT THEIR NATURE AS THE NEWLY RISEN IS TO THIRST FOR BLOOD.
EVEN THOUGH THEIR BODIES ARE HUMAN, THEY PREY ON OTHER HUMANS.
IT IS THEIR FORMER FAMILY AND FRIENDS WHO ARE IN THE MOST DAN-GER.
EVEN THOUGH THEIR FORMS REMAIN SIMILAR, THE RESURRECT-ED ARE STILL DECEASED...

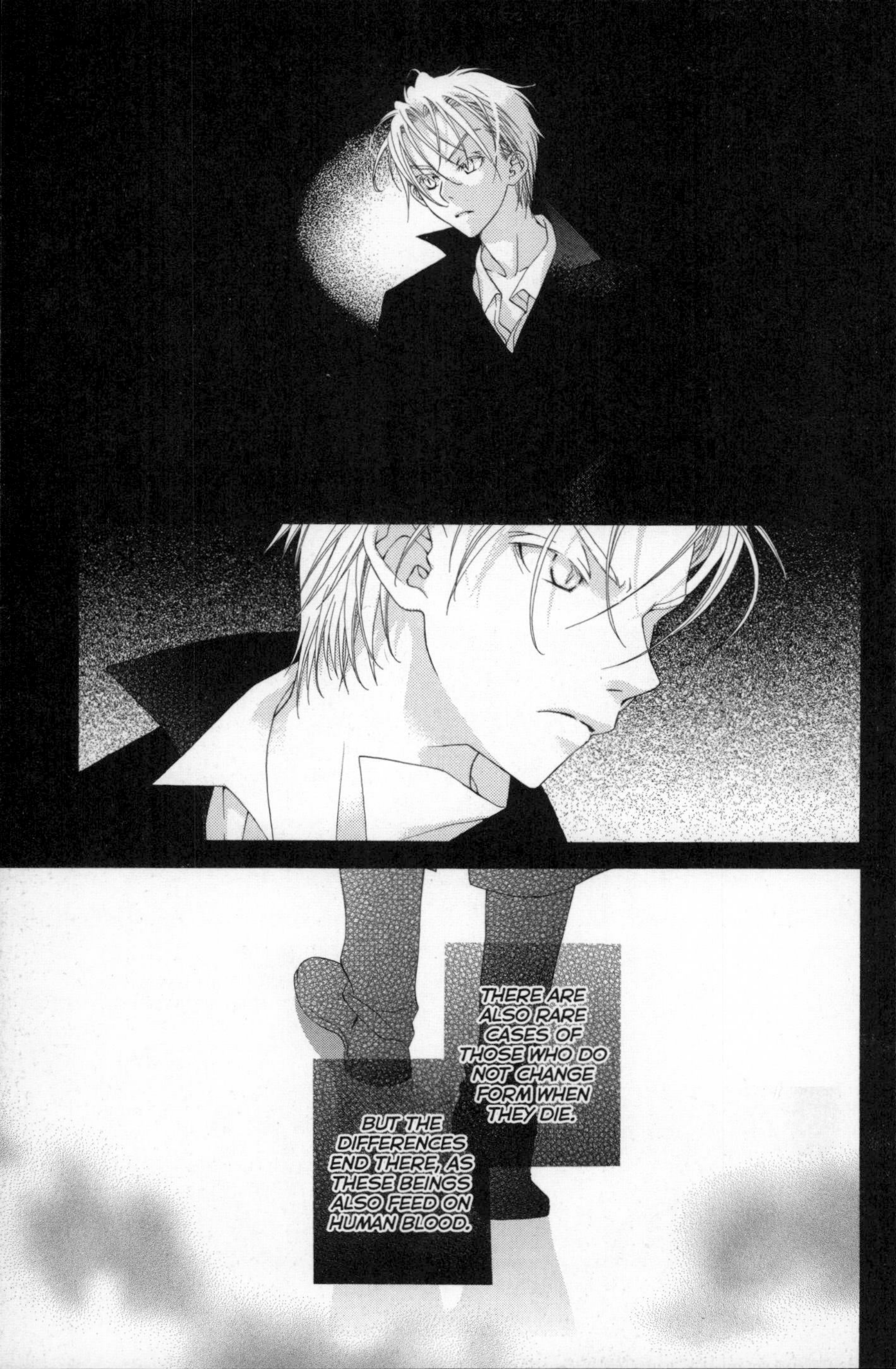
THERE ARE ALSO RARE CASES OF THOSE WHO DO NOT CHANGE FORM WHEN THEY DIE.
BUT THE DIFFERENCES END THERE, AS THESE BEINGS ALSO FEED ON HUMAN BLOOD.

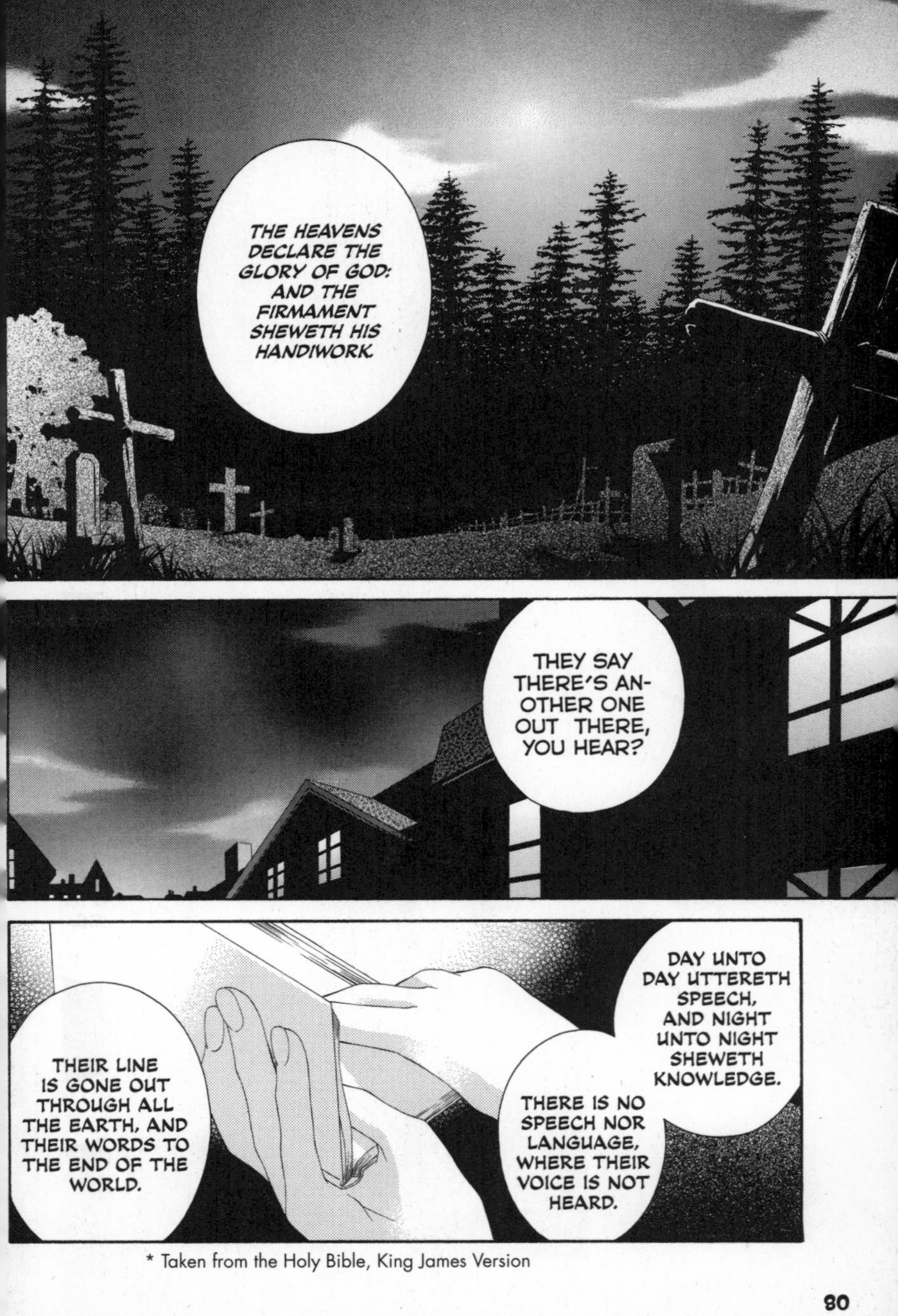
THE HEAVENS DECLARE THE GLORY OF GOD: AND THE FIRMAMENT SHEWETH HIS HANDIWORK.
THEY SAY THERE'S AN-OTHER ONE OUT THERE, YOU HEAR?
DAY UNTO DAY UTTERETH SPEECH, AND NIGHT UNTO NIGHT SHEWETH KNOWLEDGE.
THERE IS NO SPEECH NOR LANGUAGE, WHERE THEIR VOICE IS NOT HEARD.
THEIR LINE IS GONE OUT THROUGH ALL THE EARTH, AND THEIR WORDS TO THE END OF THE WORLD.

* Taken from the Holy Bible, King James Version

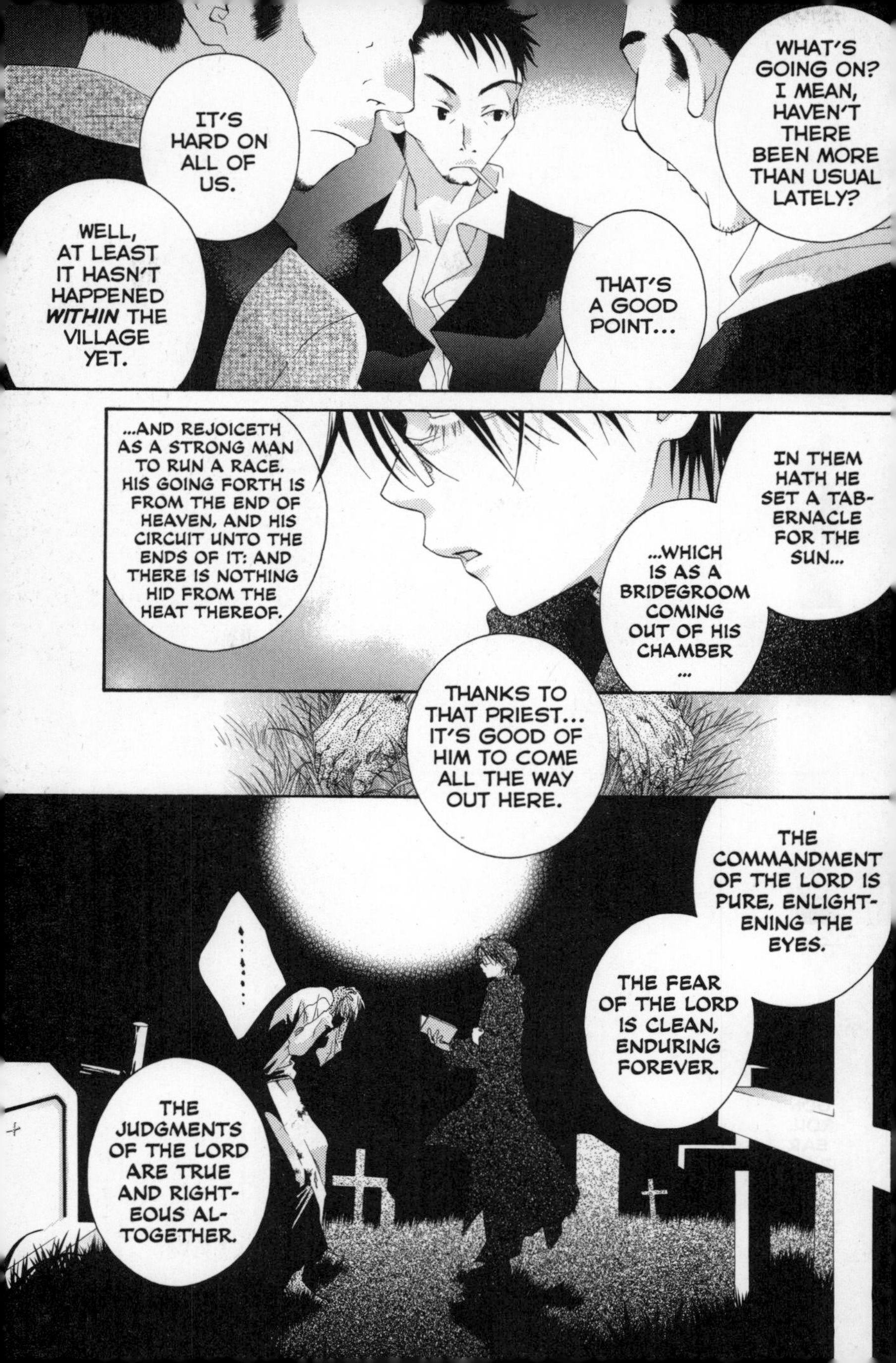

WHAT'S GOING ON? I MEAN, HAVEN'T THERE BEEN MORE THAN USUAL LATELY?
IT'S HARD ON ALL OF US.
WELL, AT LEAST IT HASN'T HAPPENED *WITHIN* THE VILLAGE YET.
THAT'S A GOOD POINT...
IN THEM HATH HE SET A TABERNACLE FOR THE SUN...
...WHICH IS AS A BRIDEGROOM COMING OUT OF HIS CHAMBER ...
...AND REJOICETH AS A STRONG MAN TO RUN A RACE. HIS GOING FORTH IS FROM THE END OF HEAVEN, AND HIS CIRCUIT UNTO THE ENDS OF IT: AND THERE IS NOTHING HID FROM THE HEAT THEREOF.
THANKS TO THAT PRIEST... IT'S GOOD OF HIM TO COME ALL THE WAY OUT HERE.
THE COMMANDMENT OF THE LORD IS PURE, ENLIGHTENING THE EYES.
THE FEAR OF THE LORD IS CLEAN, ENDURING FOREVER.
......
THE JUDGMENTS OF THE LORD ARE TRUE AND RIGHTEOUS ALTOGETHER.

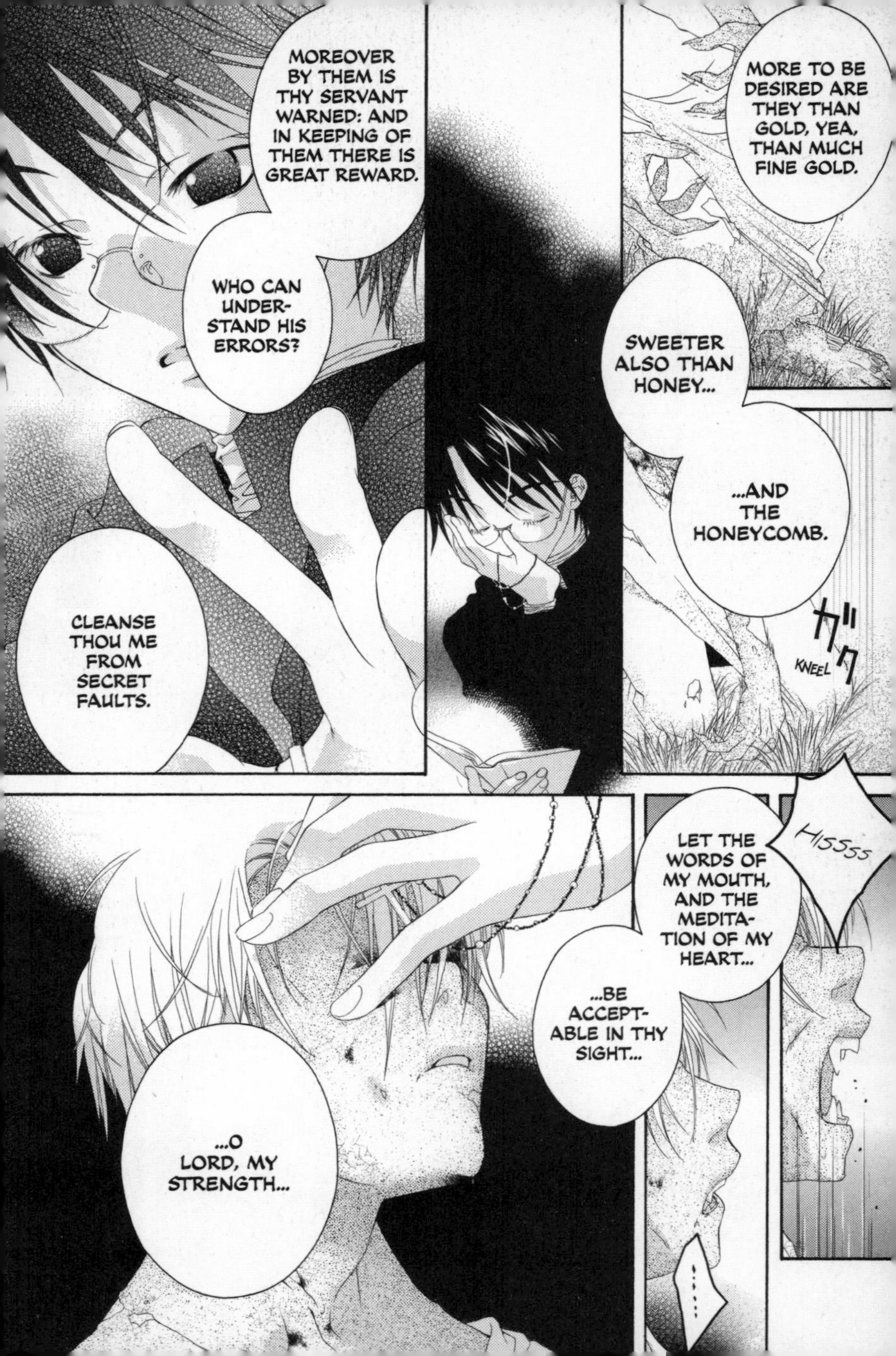
MORE TO BE DESIRED ARE THEY THAN GOLD, YEA, THAN MUCH FINE GOLD.
SWEETER ALSO THAN HONEY...
...AND THE HONEYCOMB.
ガク
KNEEL
MOREOVER BY THEM IS THY SERVANT WARNED: AND IN KEEPING OF THEM THERE IS GREAT REWARD.
WHO CAN UNDER-STAND HIS ERRORS?
CLEANSE THOU ME FROM SECRET FAULTS.
HISSSS
......
LET THE WORDS OF MY MOUTH, AND THE MEDITA-TION OF MY HEART...
...BE ACCEPT-ABLE IN THY SIGHT...
...O LORD, MY STRENGTH...

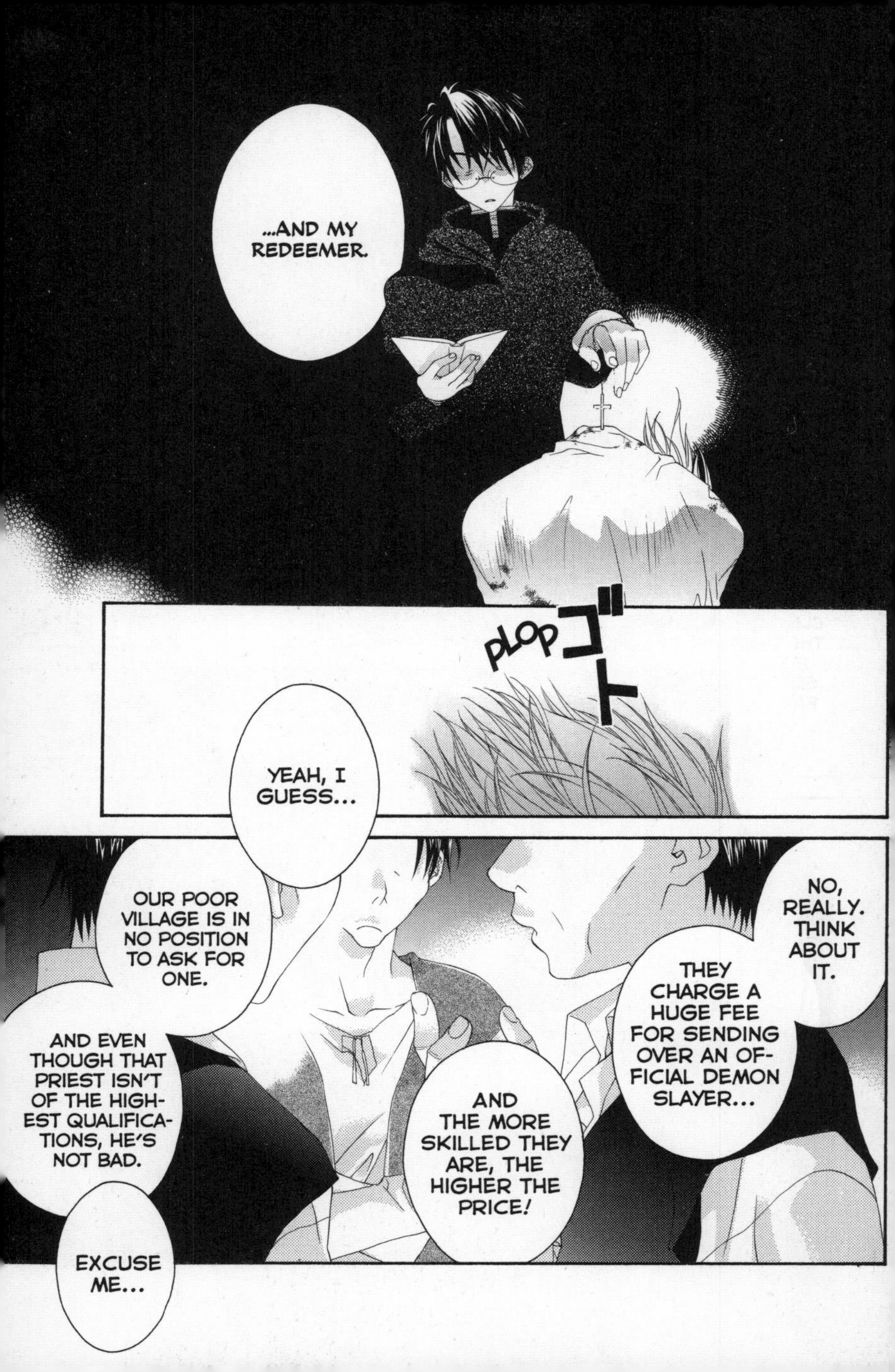
...AND MY REDEEMER.
PLOP
ゴト
YEAH, I GUESS...
NO, REALLY. THINK ABOUT IT.
THEY CHARGE A HUGE FEE FOR SENDING OVER AN OFFICIAL DEMON SLAYER...
AND THE MORE SKILLED THEY ARE, THE HIGHER THE PRICE!
OUR POOR VILLAGE IS IN NO POSITION TO ASK FOR ONE.
AND EVEN THOUGH THAT PRIEST ISN'T OF THE HIGHEST QUALIFICATIONS, HE'S NOT BAD.
EXCUSE ME...

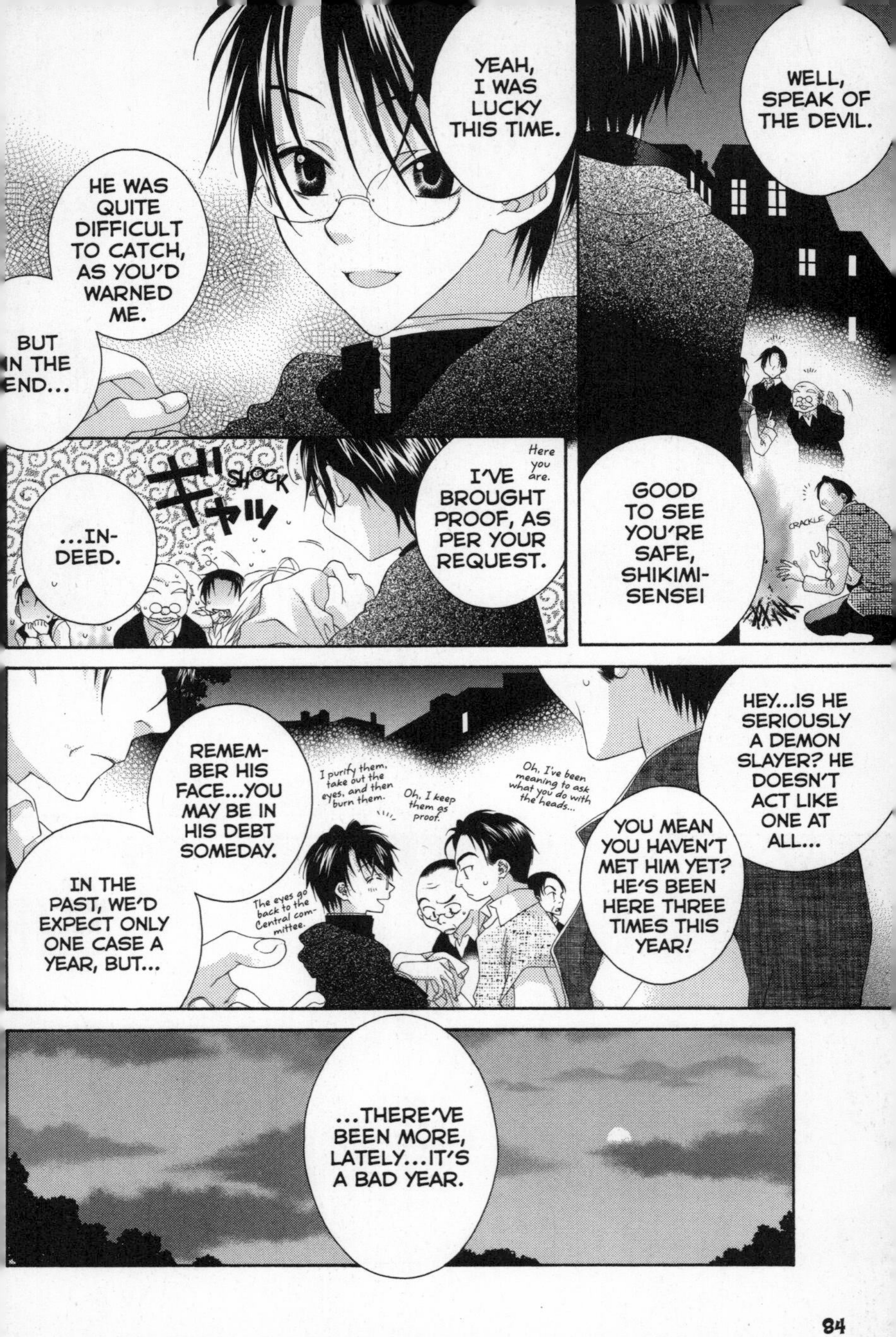
WELL, SPEAK OF THE DEVIL.
GOOD TO SEE YOU'RE SAFE, SHIKIMI-SENSEI
CRACKLE
YEAH, I WAS LUCKY THIS TIME.
HE WAS QUITE DIFFICULT TO CATCH, AS YOU'D WARNED ME.
BUT IN THE END...
Here you are.
I'VE BROUGHT PROOF, AS PER YOUR REQUEST.
SHOCK
...IN-DEED.
HEY...IS HE SERIOUSLY A DEMON SLAYER? HE DOESN'T ACT LIKE ONE AT ALL...
YOU MEAN YOU HAVEN'T MET HIM YET? HE'S BEEN HERE THREE TIMES THIS YEAR!
Oh, I've been meaning to ask what you do with the heads...
Oh, I keep them as proof.
I purify them, take out the eyes, and then burn them.
The eyes go back to the Central committee.
REMEMBER HIS FACE...YOU MAY BE IN HIS DEBT SOMEDAY.
IN THE PAST, WE'D EXPECT ONLY ONE CASE A YEAR, BUT...
...THERE'VE BEEN MORE, LATELY...IT'S A BAD YEAR.

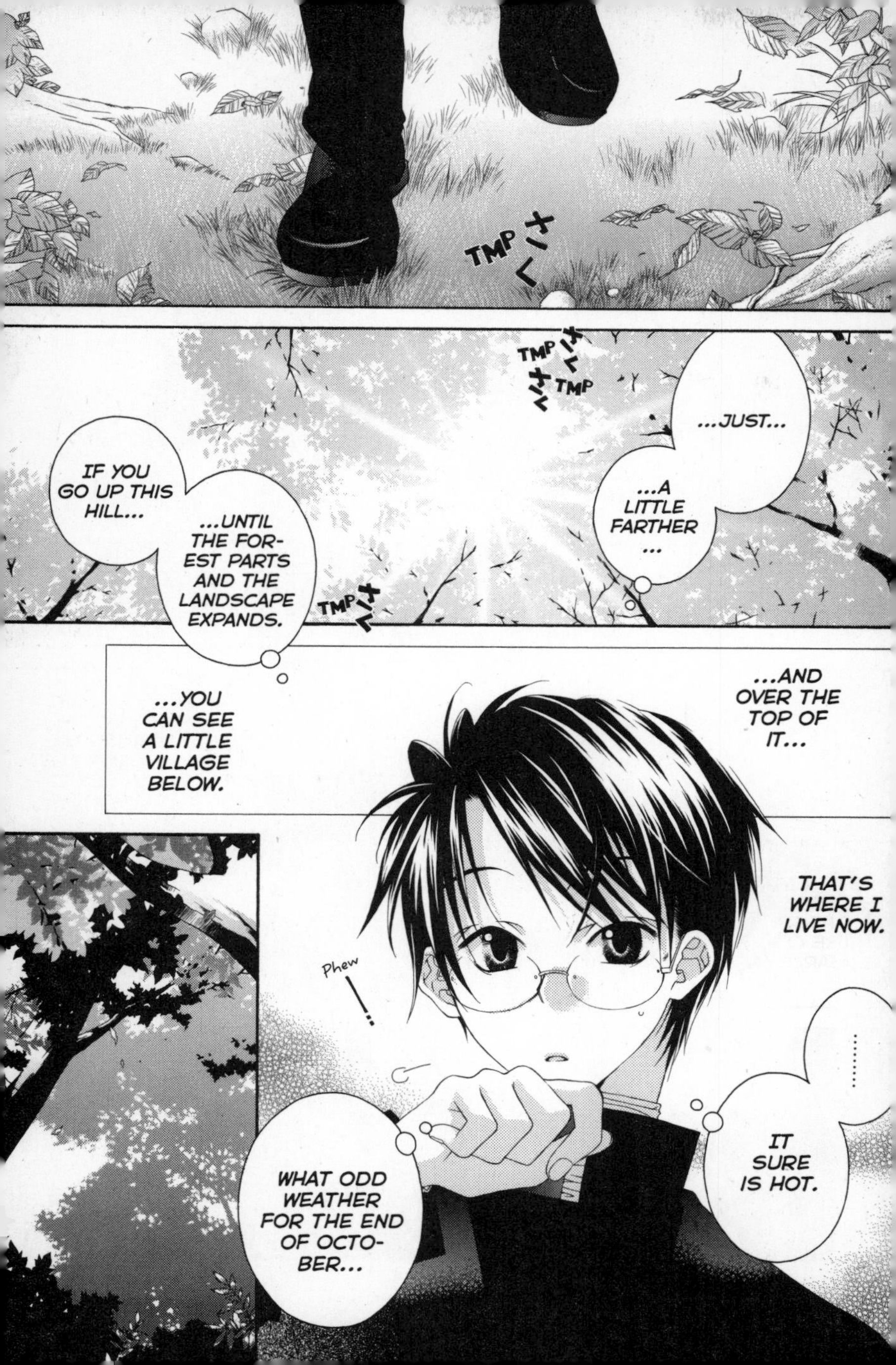
TMP
...JUST...
...A LITTLE FARTHER ...
TMP TMP
IF YOU GO UP THIS HILL...
...UNTIL THE FOR-EST PARTS AND THE LANDSCAPE EXPANDS.
TMP
...AND OVER THE TOP OF IT...
...YOU CAN SEE A LITTLE VILLAGE BELOW.
THAT'S WHERE I LIVE NOW.
......
IT SURE IS HOT.
Phew
WHAT ODD WEATHER FOR THE END OF OCTO-BER...

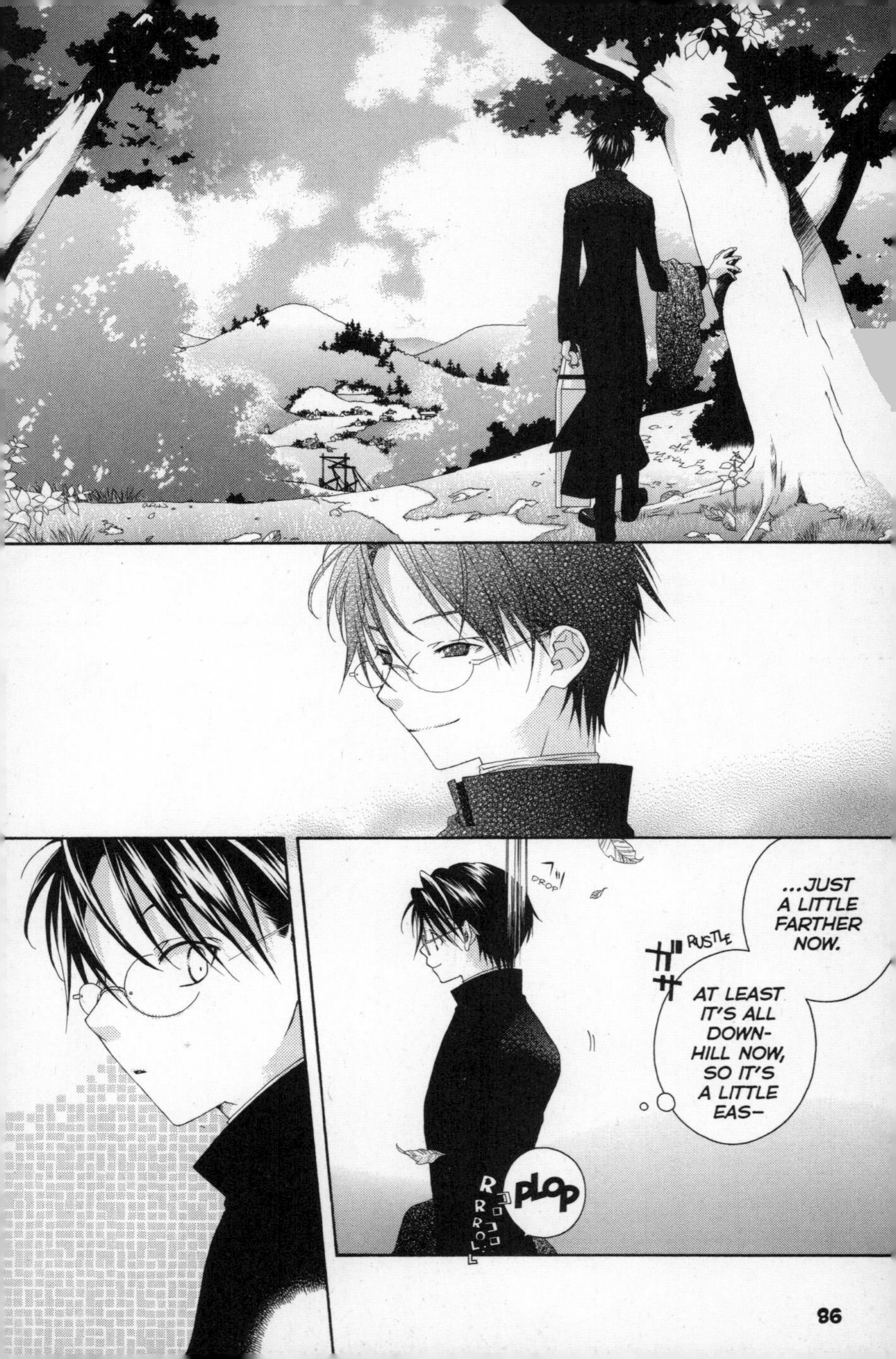
...JUST A LITTLE FARTHER NOW.
DROP
ガサ RUSTLE
AT LEAST IT'S ALL DOWN-HILL NOW, SO IT'S A LITTLE EAS—
PLOP
RRROL

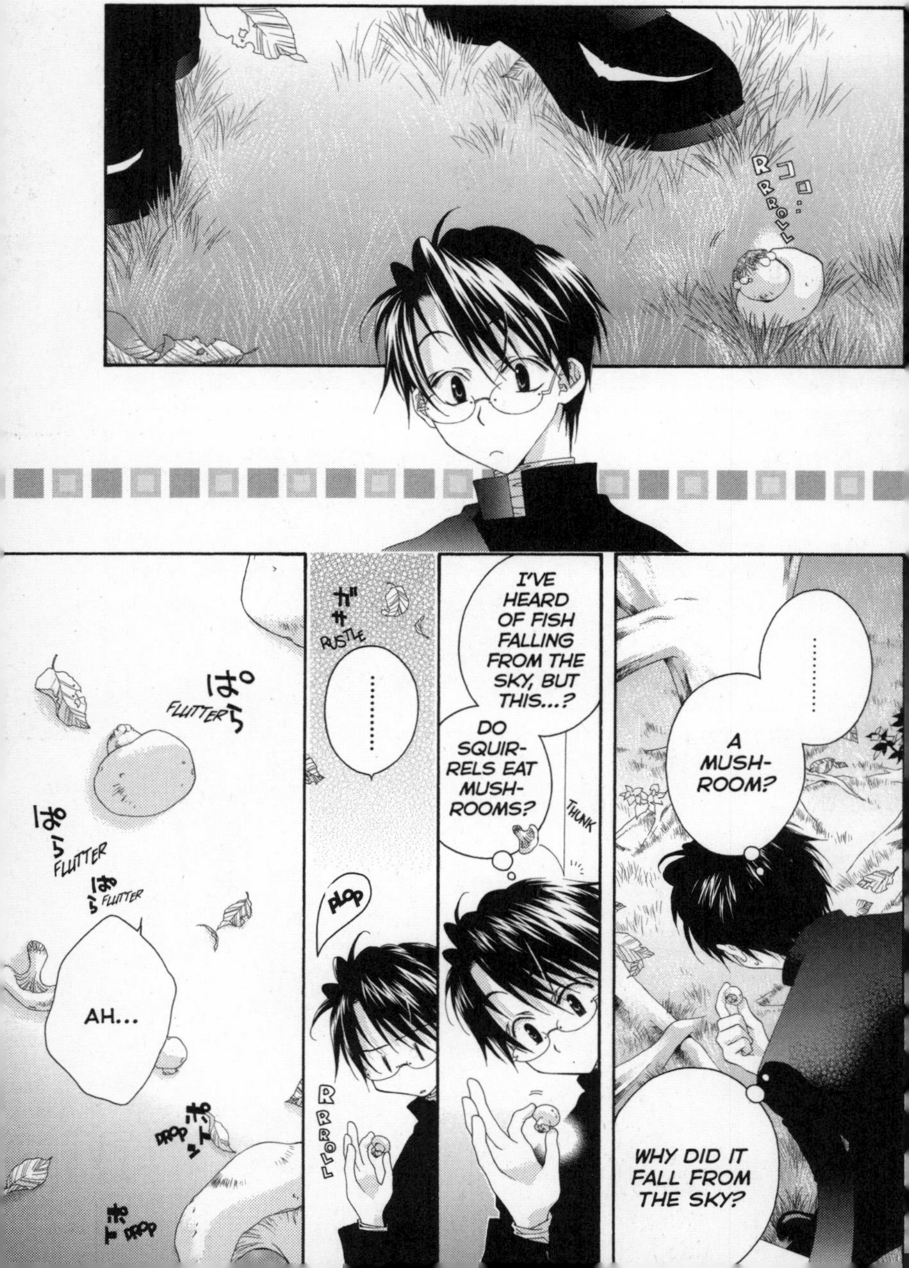
コロ…
RRROLL
……
A MUSHROOM?
WHY DID IT FALL FROM THE SKY?
I'VE HEARD OF FISH FALLING FROM THE SKY, BUT THIS...?
DO SQUIRRELS EAT MUSHROOMS?
THUNK
ガサ
RUSTLE
……
PLOP
RRROLL
ぱら
FLUTTER
ぱら
FLUTTER
ぱら
FLUTTER
AH...
ポト
DROP
ポト
DROP

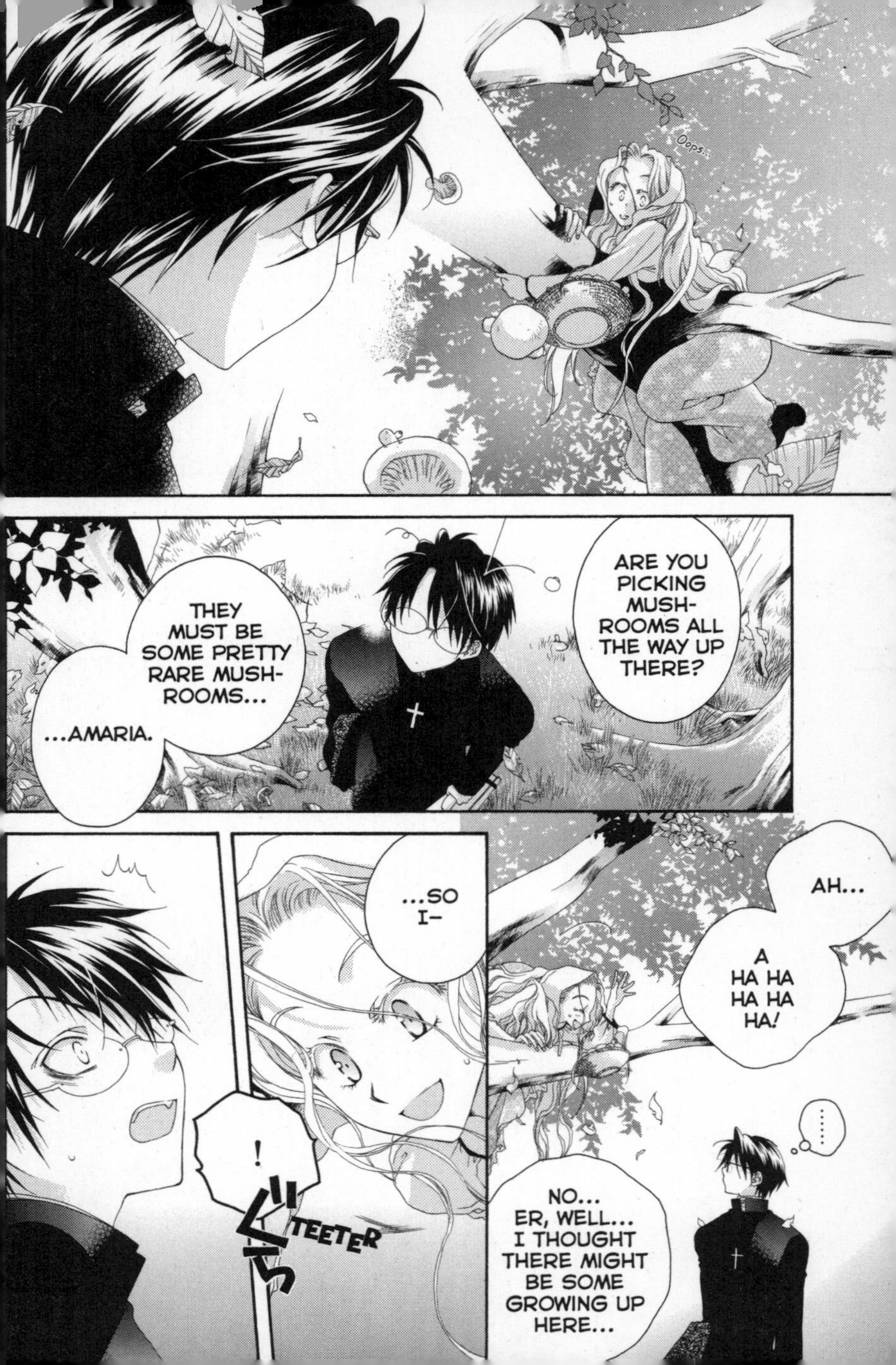
Oops...
ARE YOU PICKING MUSH-ROOMS ALL THE WAY UP THERE?
THEY MUST BE SOME PRETTY RARE MUSH-ROOMS...
...AMARIA.
AH...
A HA HA HA HA HA!
......
NO... ER, WELL... I THOUGHT THERE MIGHT BE SOME GROWING UP HERE...
...SO I-
TEETER
!

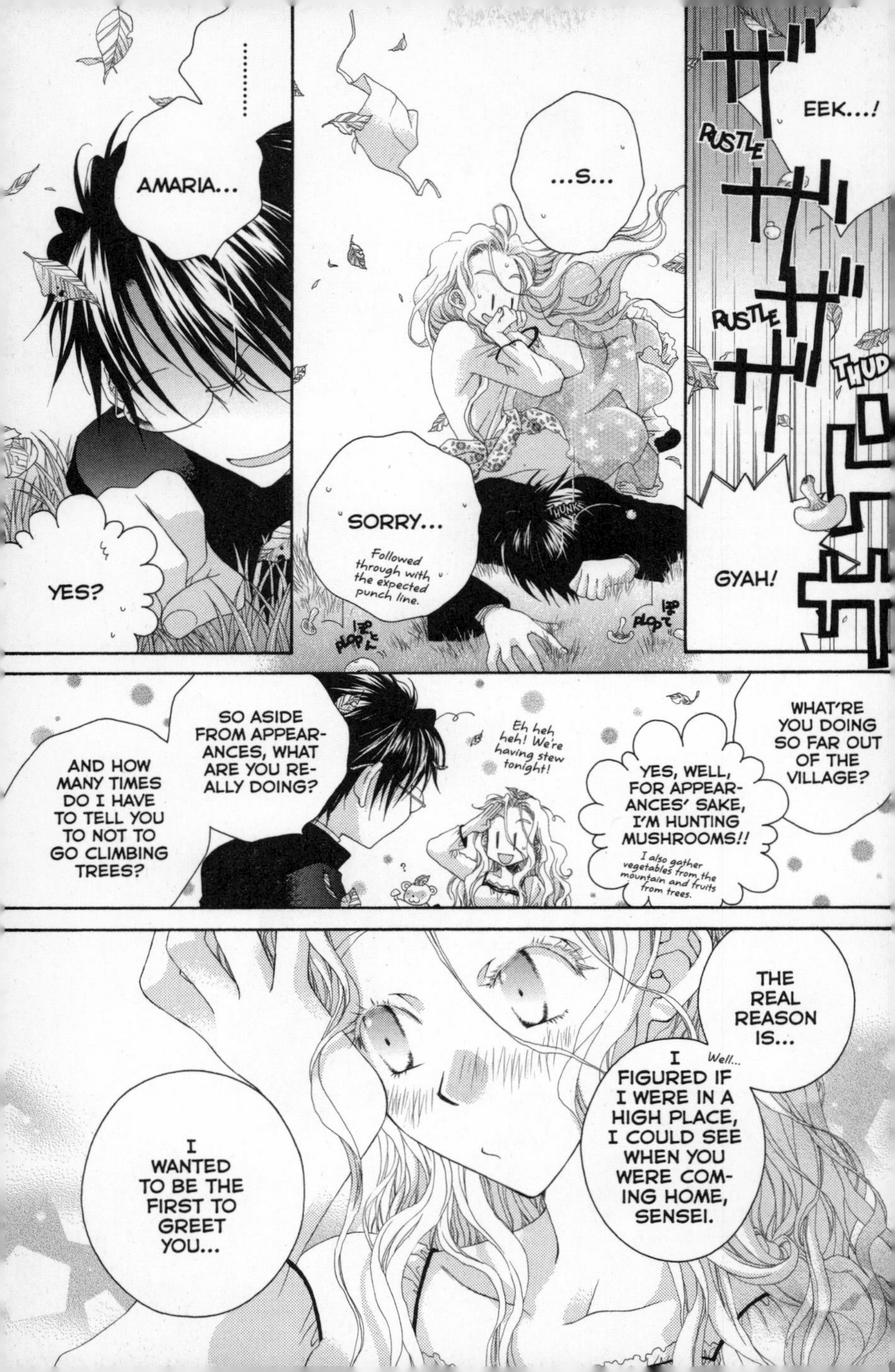
EEK...!
RUSTLE
RUSTLE
THUD
GYAH!
...S...
SORRY...
Followed through with the expected punch line.
PLOP
PLOP
......
AMARIA...
YES?
WHAT'RE YOU DOING SO FAR OUT OF THE VILLAGE?
YES, WELL, FOR APPEAR-ANCES' SAKE, I'M HUNTING MUSHROOMS!!
I also gather vegetables from the mountain and fruits from trees.
Eh heh heh! We're having stew tonight!
SO ASIDE FROM APPEAR-ANCES, WHAT ARE YOU RE-ALLY DOING?
AND HOW MANY TIMES DO I HAVE TO TELL YOU TO NOT TO GO CLIMBING TREES?
THE REAL REASON IS...
Well...
I FIGURED IF I WERE IN A HIGH PLACE, I COULD SEE WHEN YOU WERE COM-ING HOME, SENSEI.
I WANTED TO BE THE FIRST TO GREET YOU...

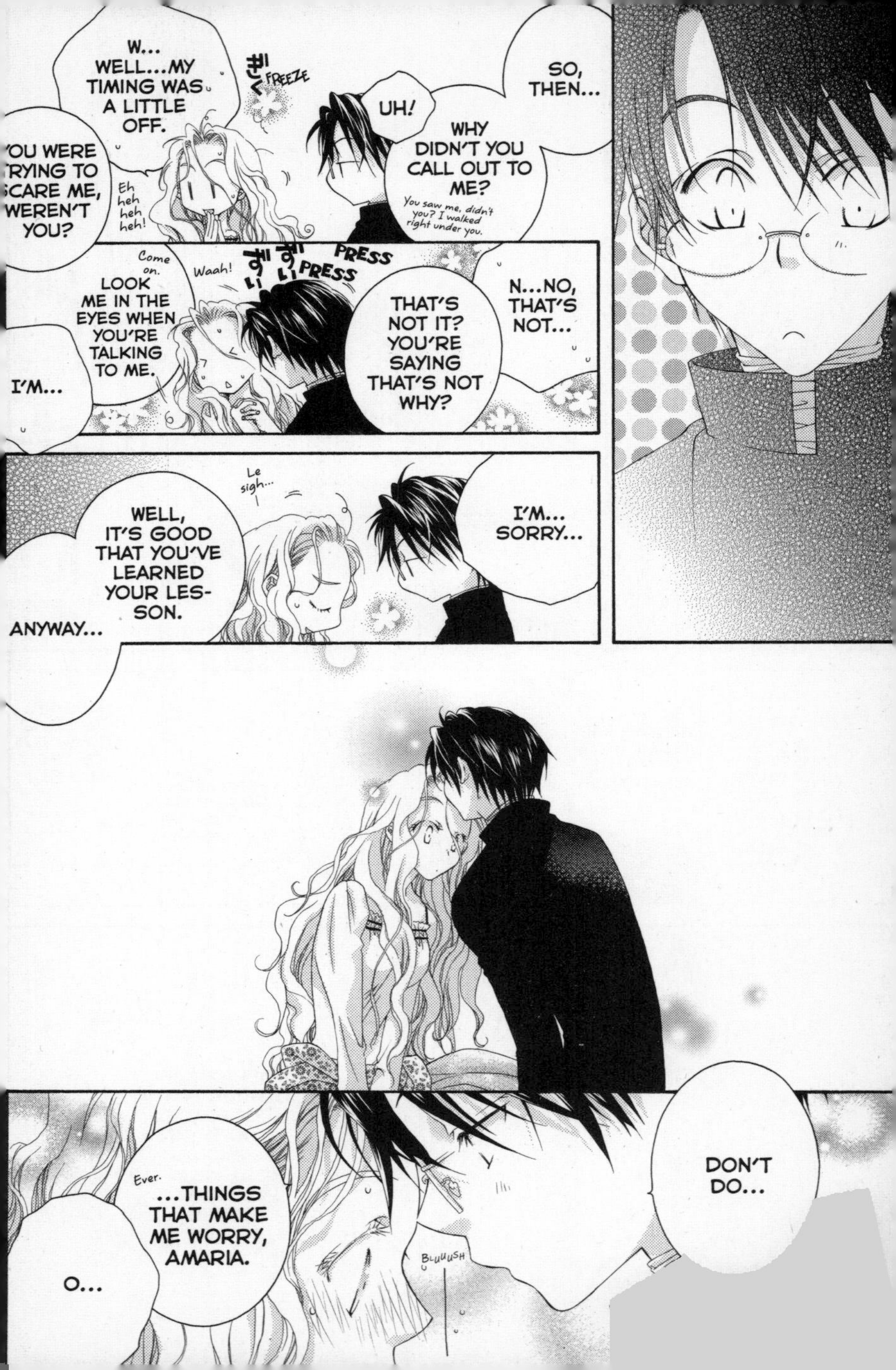

SO, THEN...
UH!
WHY DIDN'T YOU CALL OUT TO ME?
You saw me, didn't you? I walked right under you.
FREEZE
W... WELL...MY TIMING WAS A LITTLE OFF.
Eh heh heh heh!
OU WERE RYING TO CARE ME, WEREN'T YOU?
N...NO, THAT'S NOT...
THAT'S NOT IT? YOU'RE SAYING THAT'S NOT WHY?
PRESS
PRESS
Waah!
Come on.
LOOK ME IN THE EYES WHEN YOU'RE TALKING TO ME.
I'M...
I'M... SORRY...
Le sigh...
WELL, IT'S GOOD THAT YOU'VE LEARNED YOUR LES-SON.
ANYWAY...
DON'T DO...
Ever.
...THINGS THAT MAKE ME WORRY, AMARIA.
BLUUUSH
O...

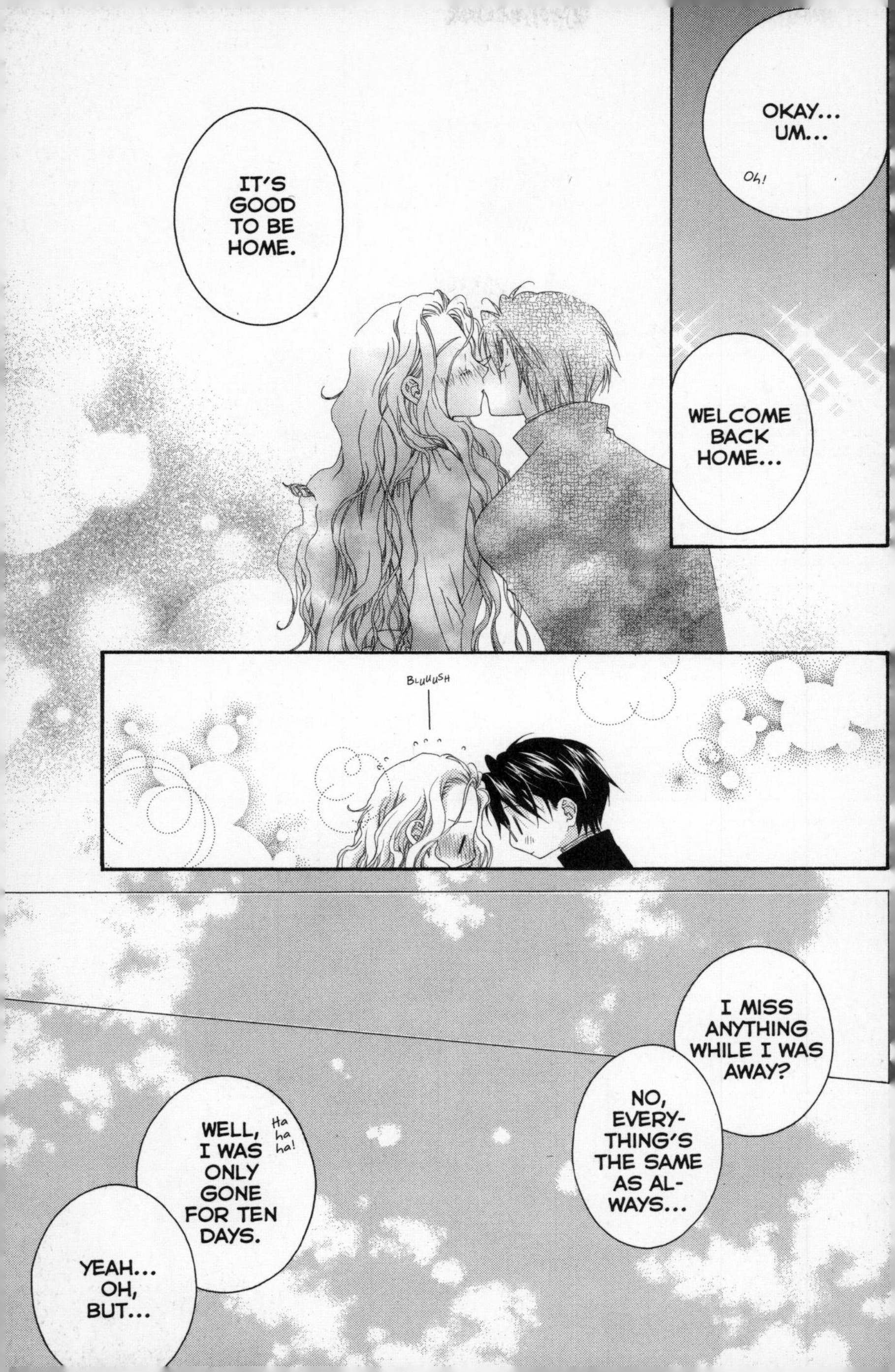
OKAY... UM...
Oh!
WELCOME BACK HOME...
IT'S GOOD TO BE HOME.
BLUUUSH
I MISS ANYTHING WHILE I WAS AWAY?
NO, EVERY-THING'S THE SAME AS AL-WAYS...
WELL, I WAS ONLY GONE FOR TEN DAYS.
Ha ha ha!
YEAH... OH, BUT...

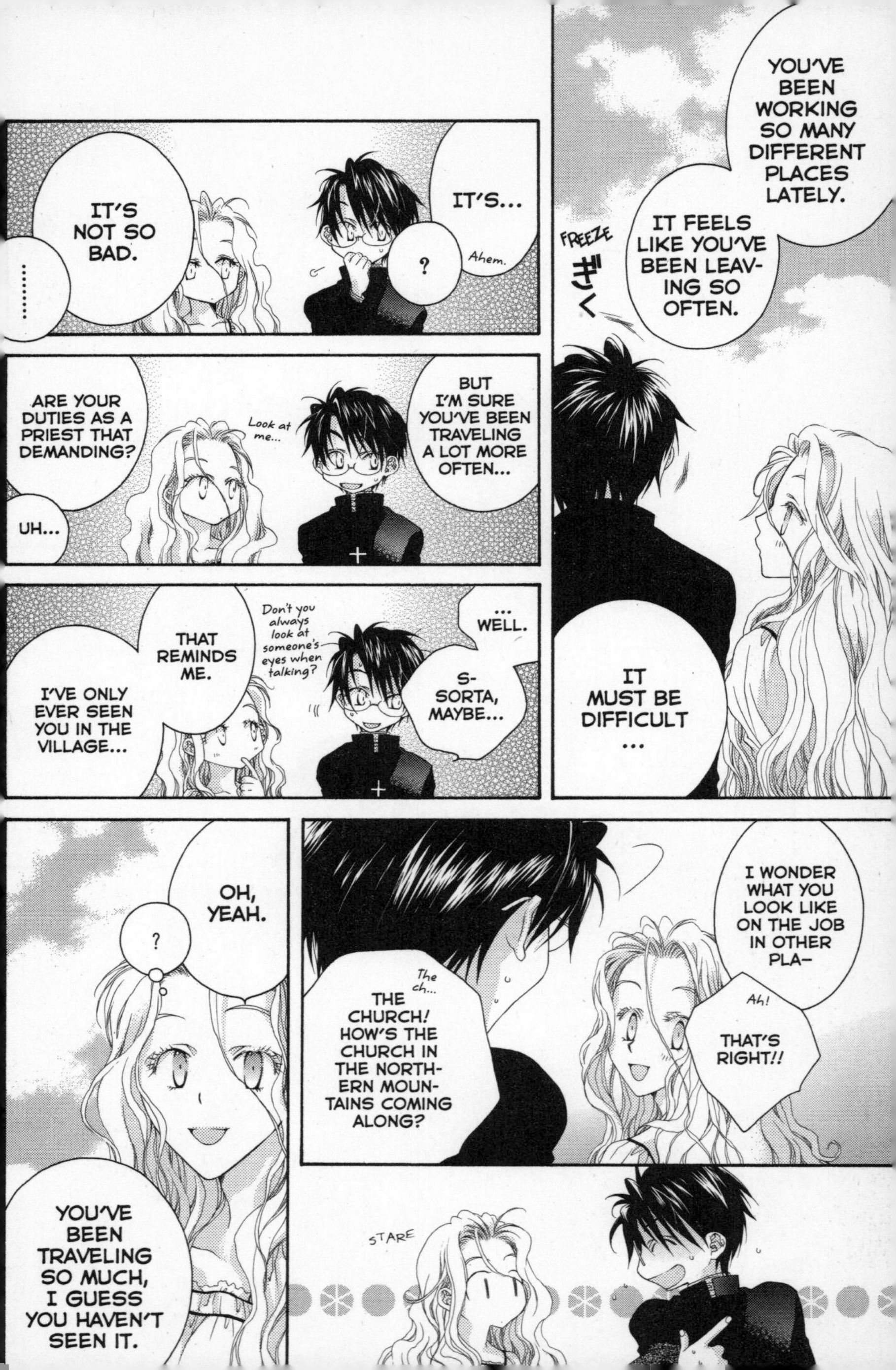
YOU'VE BEEN WORKING SO MANY DIFFERENT PLACES LATELY.
IT FEELS LIKE YOU'VE BEEN LEAVING SO OFTEN.
FREEZE
ぎく
IT MUST BE DIFFICULT ...
IT'S...
Ahem.
?
IT'S NOT SO BAD.
......
BUT I'M SURE YOU'VE BEEN TRAVELING A LOT MORE OFTEN...
Look at me...
ARE YOUR DUTIES AS A PRIEST THAT DEMANDING?
UH...
... WELL.
S-SORTA, MAYBE...
Don't you always look at someone's eyes when talking?
THAT REMINDS ME.
I'VE ONLY EVER SEEN YOU IN THE VILLAGE...
I WONDER WHAT YOU LOOK LIKE ON THE JOB IN OTHER PLA–
The ch...
THE CHURCH! HOW'S THE CHURCH IN THE NORTHERN MOUNTAINS COMING ALONG?
Ah!
THAT'S RIGHT!!
STARE
OH, YEAH.
?
YOU'VE BEEN TRAVELING SO MUCH, I GUESS YOU HAVEN'T SEEN IT.

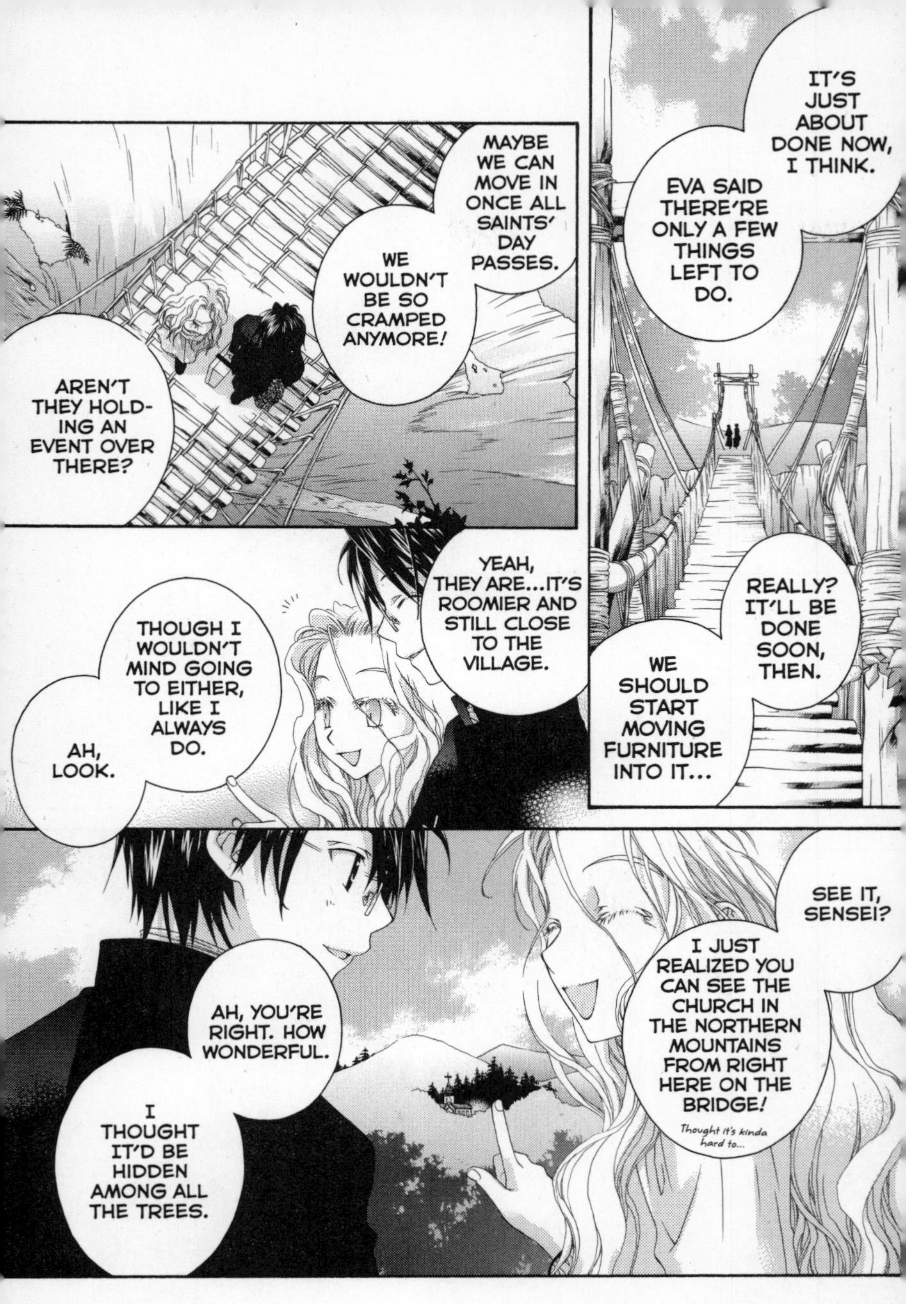
IT'S JUST ABOUT DONE NOW, I THINK.
EVA SAID THERE'RE ONLY A FEW THINGS LEFT TO DO.
REALLY? IT'LL BE DONE SOON, THEN.
WE SHOULD START MOVING FURNITURE INTO IT...
MAYBE WE CAN MOVE IN ONCE ALL SAINTS' DAY PASSES.
WE WOULDN'T BE SO CRAMPED ANYMORE!
AREN'T THEY HOLDING AN EVENT OVER THERE?
YEAH, THEY ARE...IT'S ROOMIER AND STILL CLOSE TO THE VILLAGE.
THOUGH I WOULDN'T MIND GOING TO EITHER, LIKE I ALWAYS DO.
AH, LOOK.
SEE IT, SENSEI?
I JUST REALIZED YOU CAN SEE THE CHURCH IN THE NORTHERN MOUNTAINS FROM RIGHT HERE ON THE BRIDGE!
Thought it's kinda hard to...
AH, YOU'RE RIGHT. HOW WONDERFUL.
I THOUGHT IT'D BE HIDDEN AMONG ALL THE TREES.

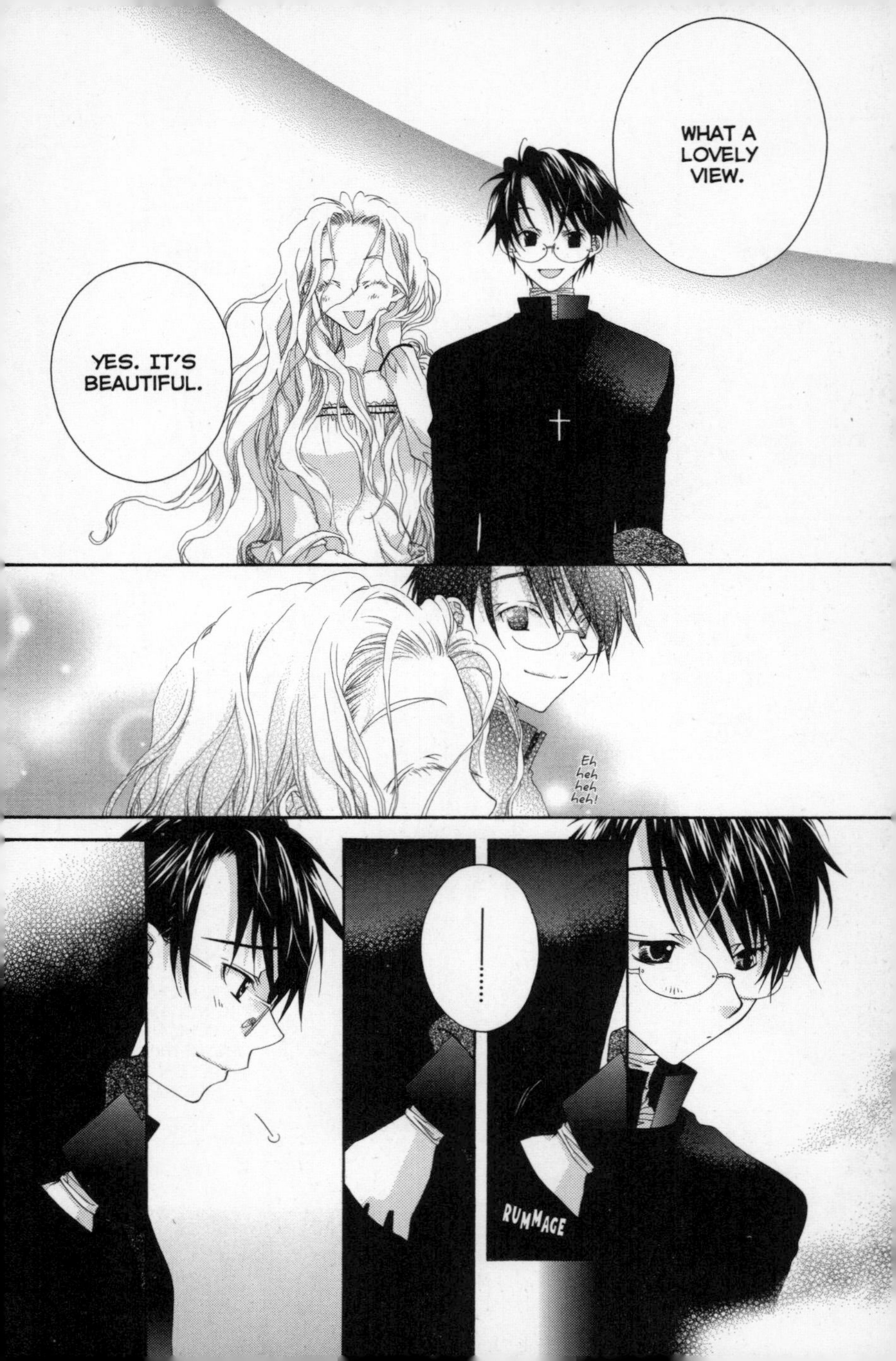
WHAT A LOVELY VIEW.
YES. IT'S BEAUTIFUL.
Eh heh heh heh!
RUMMAGE
—......

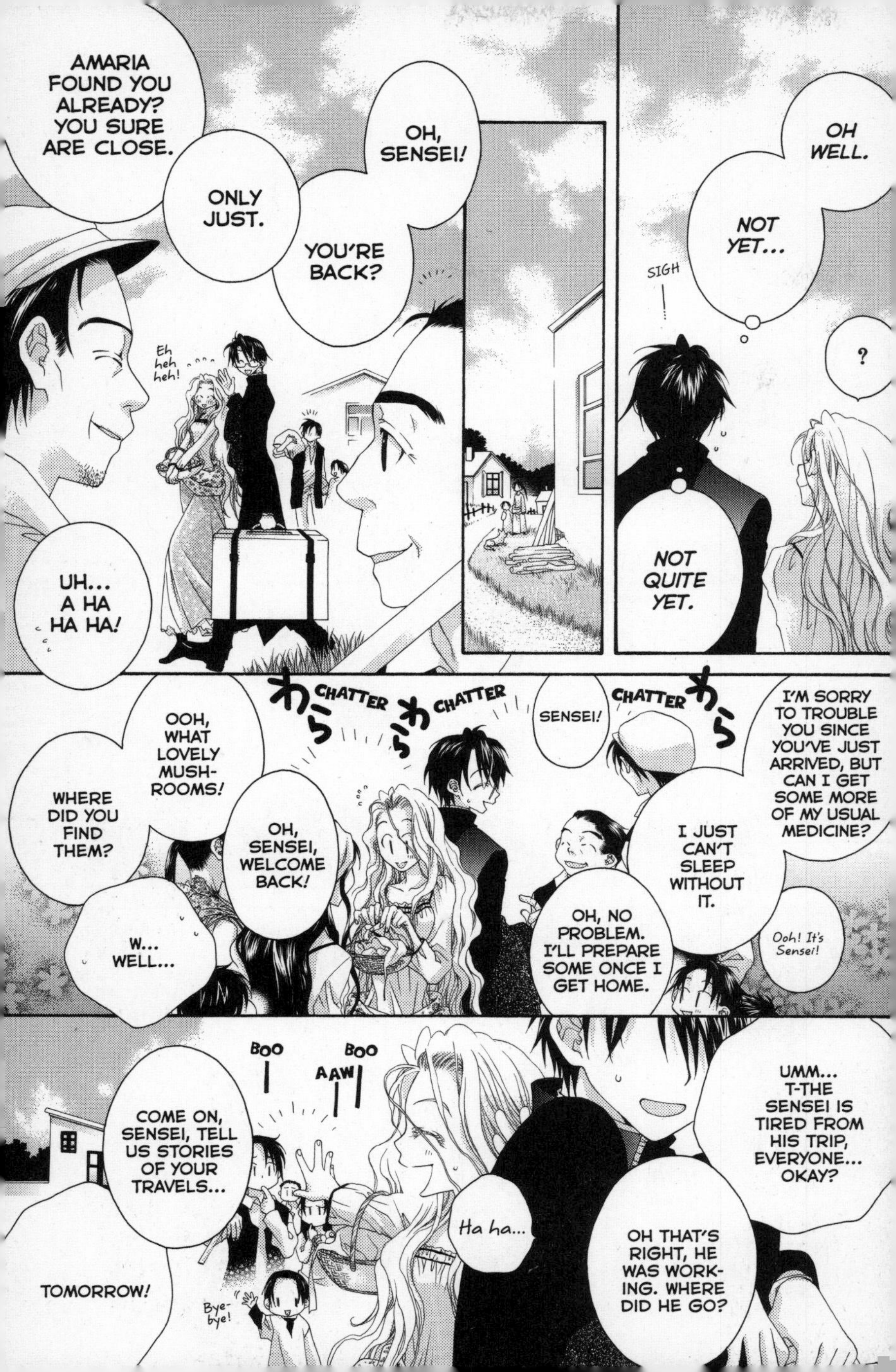
OH WELL.
NOT YET...
SIGH
?
NOT QUITE YET.
OH, SENSEI!
YOU'RE BACK?
ONLY JUST.
AMARIA FOUND YOU ALREADY? YOU SURE ARE CLOSE.
Eh heh heh!
UH... A HA HA HA!
I'M SORRY TO TROUBLE YOU SINCE YOU'VE JUST ARRIVED, BUT CAN I GET SOME MORE OF MY USUAL MEDICINE?
I JUST CAN'T SLEEP WITHOUT IT.
Ooh! It's Sensei!
わら CHATTER
SENSEI!
OH, NO PROBLEM. I'LL PREPARE SOME ONCE I GET HOME.
わら CHATTER
わら CHATTER
OH, SENSEI, WELCOME BACK!
OOH, WHAT LOVELY MUSH-ROOMS!
WHERE DID YOU FIND THEM?
W... WELL...
UMM... T-THE SENSEI IS TIRED FROM HIS TRIP, EVERYONE... OKAY?
OH THAT'S RIGHT, HE WAS WORK-ING. WHERE DID HE GO?
Ha ha...
BOO
AAW
BOO
COME ON, SENSEI, TELL US STORIES OF YOUR TRAVELS...
TOMORROW!
Bye-bye!

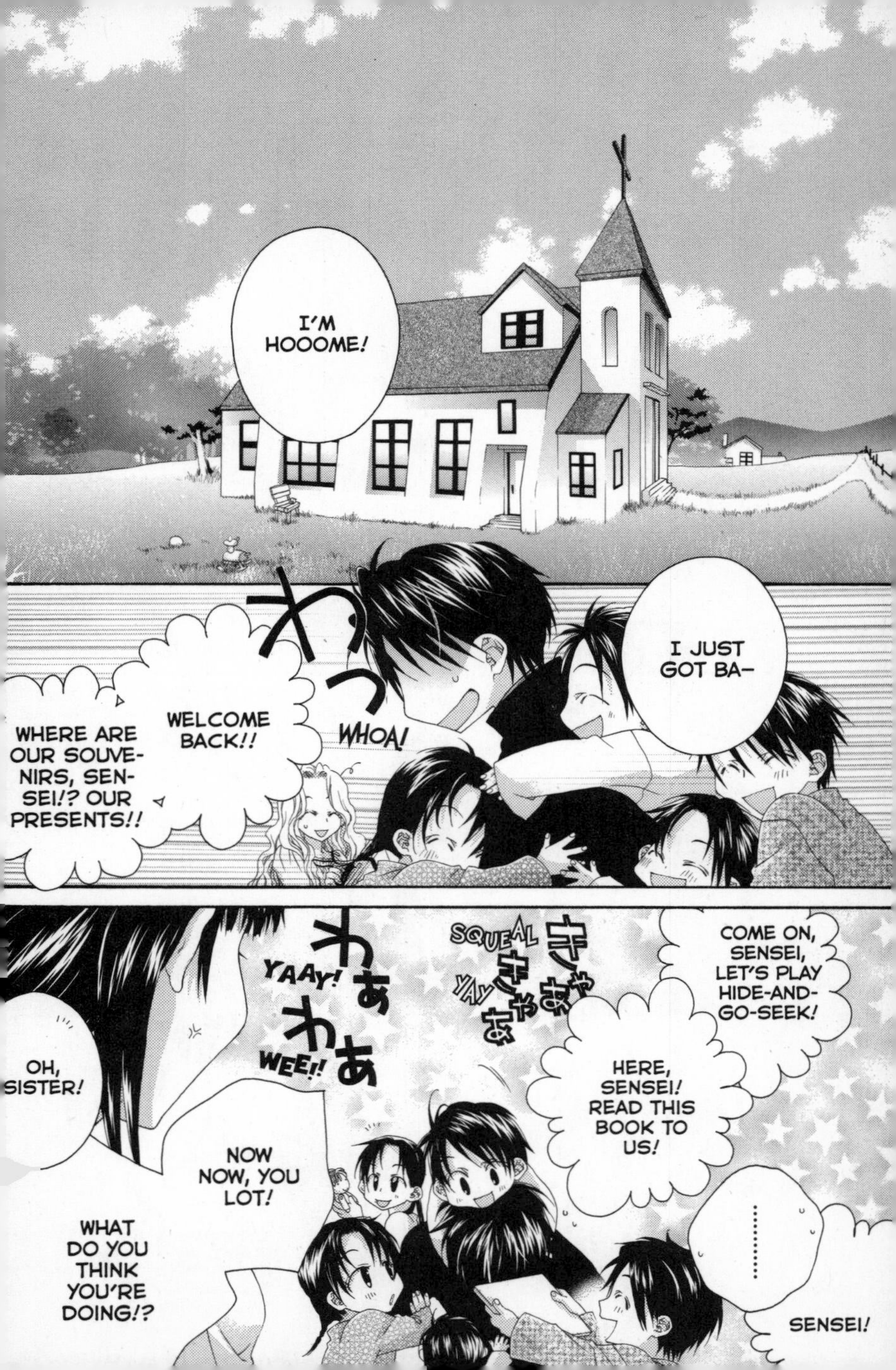

I'M HOOOME!
I JUST GOT BA–
わっ
WHOA!
WELCOME BACK!!
WHERE ARE OUR SOUVENIRS, SENSEI!? OUR PRESENTS!!
COME ON, SENSEI, LET'S PLAY HIDE-AND-GO-SEEK!
きゃあきゃあ
SQUEAL
YAY
HERE, SENSEI! READ THIS BOOK TO US!
わぁわぁ
YAAY!
WEE!!
......
SENSEI!
NOW NOW, YOU LOT!
OH, SISTER!
WHAT DO YOU THINK YOU'RE DOING!?

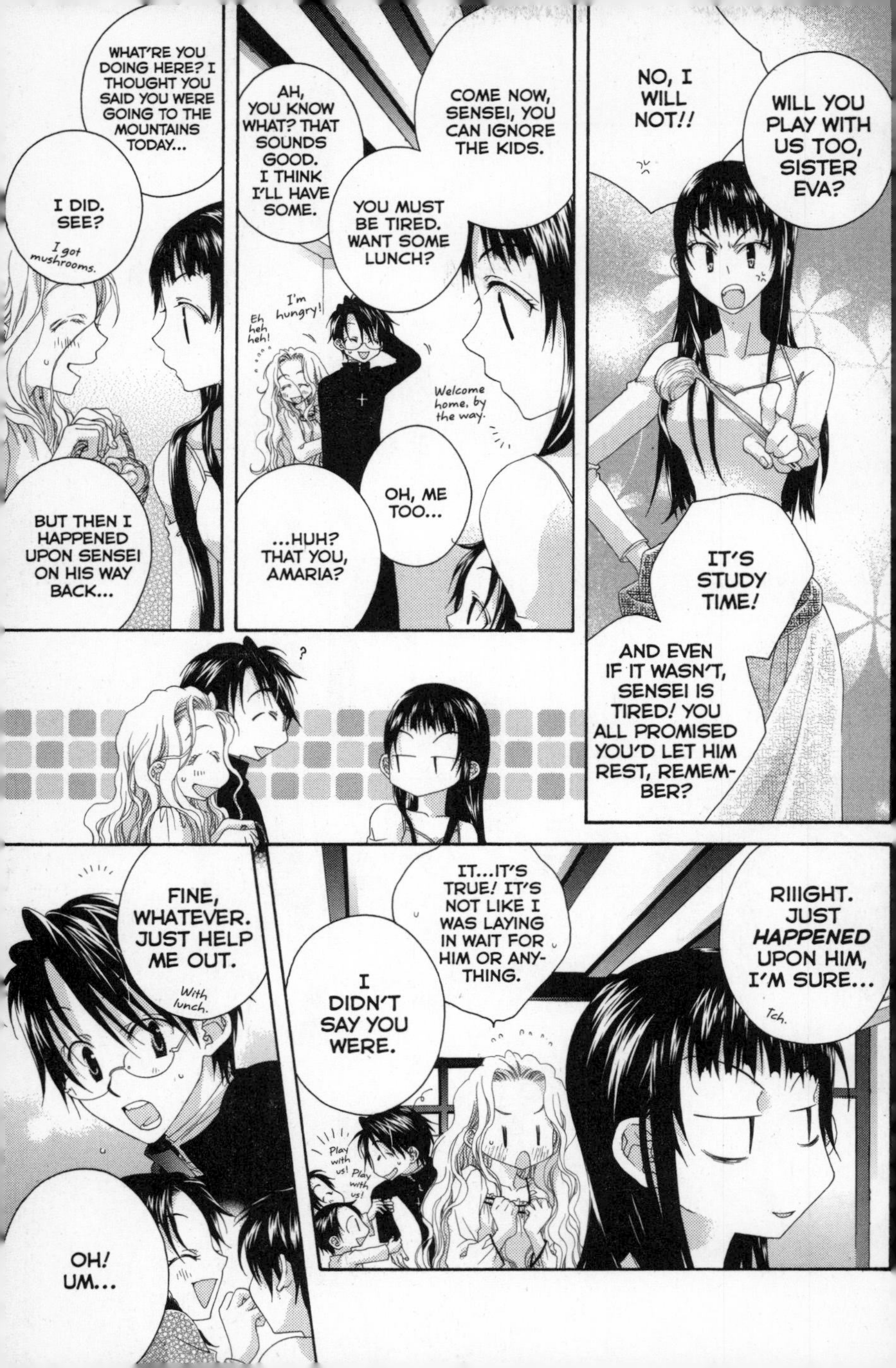
WILL YOU PLAY WITH US TOO, SISTER EVA?
NO, I WILL NOT!!
IT'S STUDY TIME!
AND EVEN IF IT WASN'T, SENSEI IS TIRED! YOU ALL PROMISED YOU'D LET HIM REST, REMEMBER?
COME NOW, SENSEI, YOU CAN IGNORE THE KIDS.
YOU MUST BE TIRED. WANT SOME LUNCH?
AH, YOU KNOW WHAT? THAT SOUNDS GOOD. I THINK I'LL HAVE SOME.
I'm hungry!
Eh heh heh!
Welcome home, by the way.
OH, ME TOO...
...HUH? THAT YOU, AMARIA?
WHAT'RE YOU DOING HERE? I THOUGHT YOU SAID YOU WERE GOING TO THE MOUNTAINS TODAY...
I DID. SEE?
I got mushrooms.
BUT THEN I HAPPENED UPON SENSEI ON HIS WAY BACK...
?
RIIIGHT. JUST HAPPENED UPON HIM, I'M SURE...
Tch.
IT...IT'S TRUE! IT'S NOT LIKE I WAS LAYING IN WAIT FOR HIM OR ANYTHING.
I DIDN'T SAY YOU WERE.
Play with us!
Play with us!
FINE, WHATEVER. JUST HELP ME OUT.
With lunch.
OH! UM...

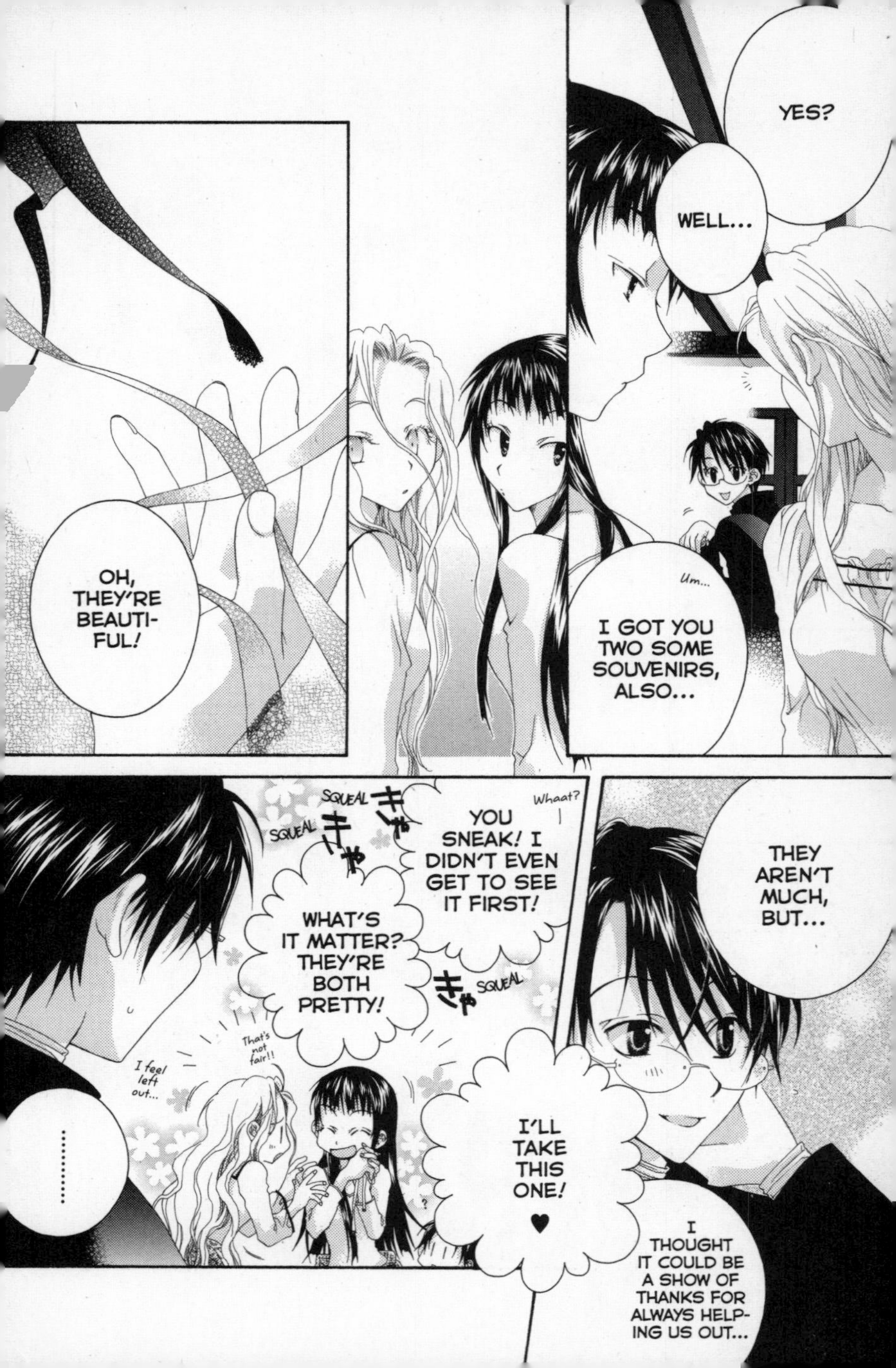
YES?
WELL...
Um...
I GOT YOU TWO SOME SOUVENIRS, ALSO...
OH, THEY'RE BEAUTI-FUL!
THEY AREN'T MUCH, BUT...
I THOUGHT IT COULD BE A SHOW OF THANKS FOR ALWAYS HELP-ING US OUT...
Whaat?
YOU SNEAK! I DIDN'T EVEN GET TO SEE IT FIRST!
きゃ SQUEAL
きゃ SQUEAL
WHAT'S IT MATTER? THEY'RE BOTH PRETTY!
きゃ SQUEAL
I'LL TAKE THIS ONE! ♥
That's not fair!!
I feel left out...
....

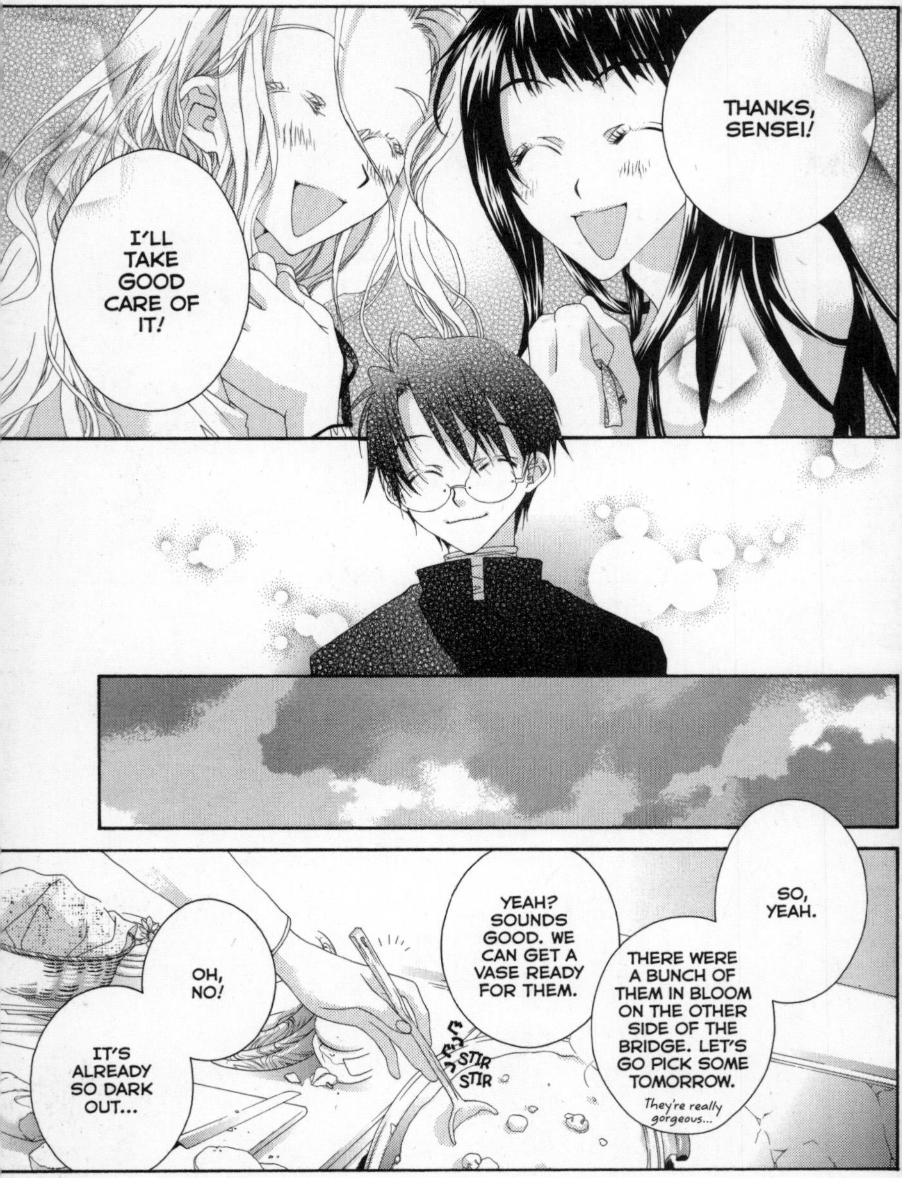
THANKS, SENSEI!
I'LL TAKE GOOD CARE OF IT!
SO, YEAH.
THERE WERE A BUNCH OF THEM IN BLOOM ON THE OTHER SIDE OF THE BRIDGE. LET'S GO PICK SOME TOMORROW.
They're really gorgeous...
YEAH? SOUNDS GOOD. WE CAN GET A VASE READY FOR THEM.
STIR STIR
OH, NO!
IT'S ALREADY SO DARK OUT...

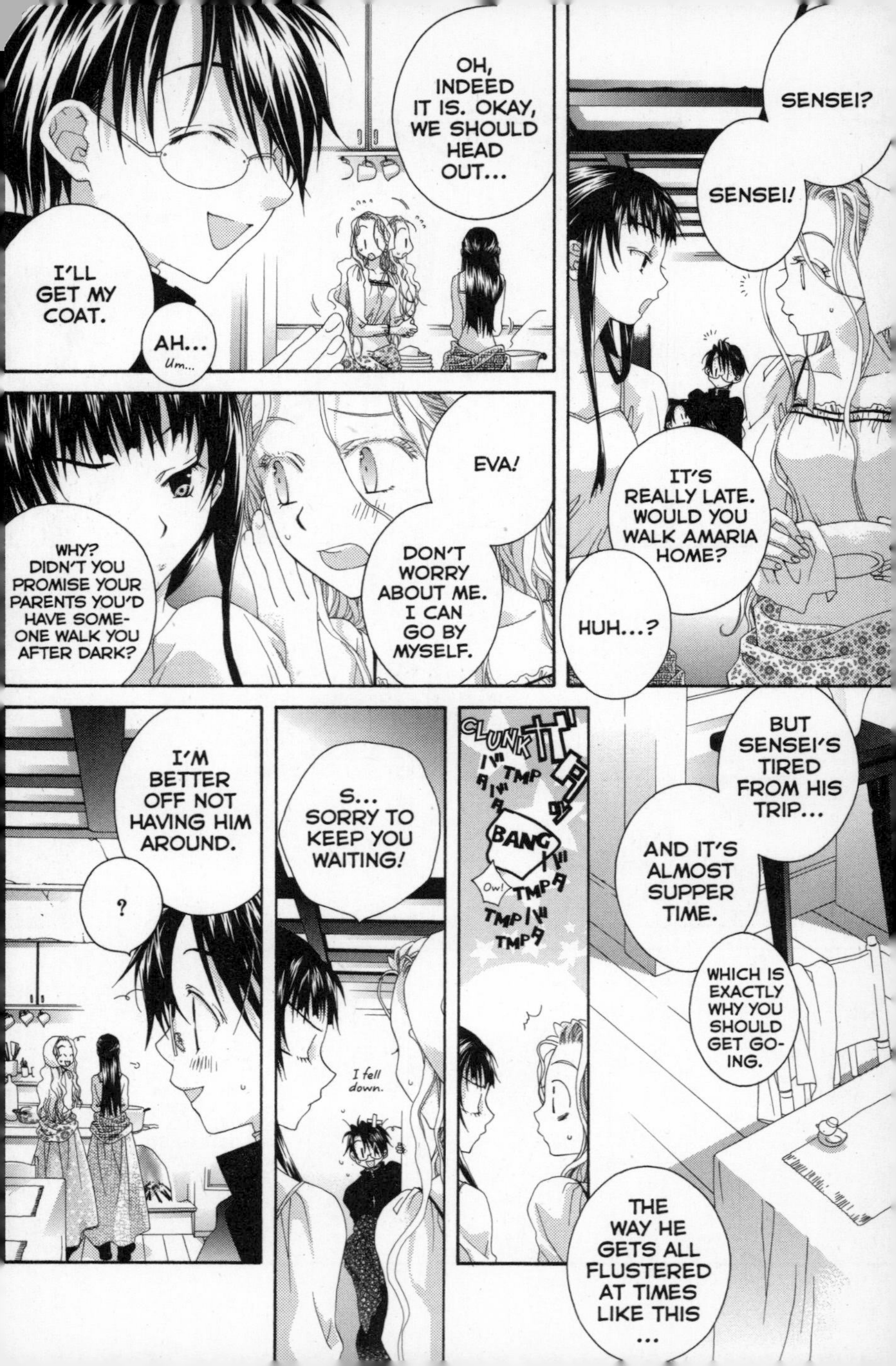
SENSEI?
SENSEI!
IT'S REALLY LATE. WOULD YOU WALK AMARIA HOME?
HUH...?
OH, INDEED IT IS. OKAY, WE SHOULD HEAD OUT...
I'LL GET MY COAT.
AH...
Um...
EVA!
DON'T WORRY ABOUT ME. I CAN GO BY MYSELF.
WHY? DIDN'T YOU PROMISE YOUR PARENTS YOU'D HAVE SOME-ONE WALK YOU AFTER DARK?
BUT SENSEI'S TIRED FROM HIS TRIP...
AND IT'S ALMOST SUPPER TIME.
WHICH IS EXACTLY WHY YOU SHOULD GET GO-ING.
THE WAY HE GETS ALL FLUSTERED AT TIMES LIKE THIS ...
CLUNK
TMP
BANG
Ow!
TMP
TMP
TMP
S... SORRY TO KEEP YOU WAITING!
I fell down.
I'M BETTER OFF NOT HAVING HIM AROUND.
?

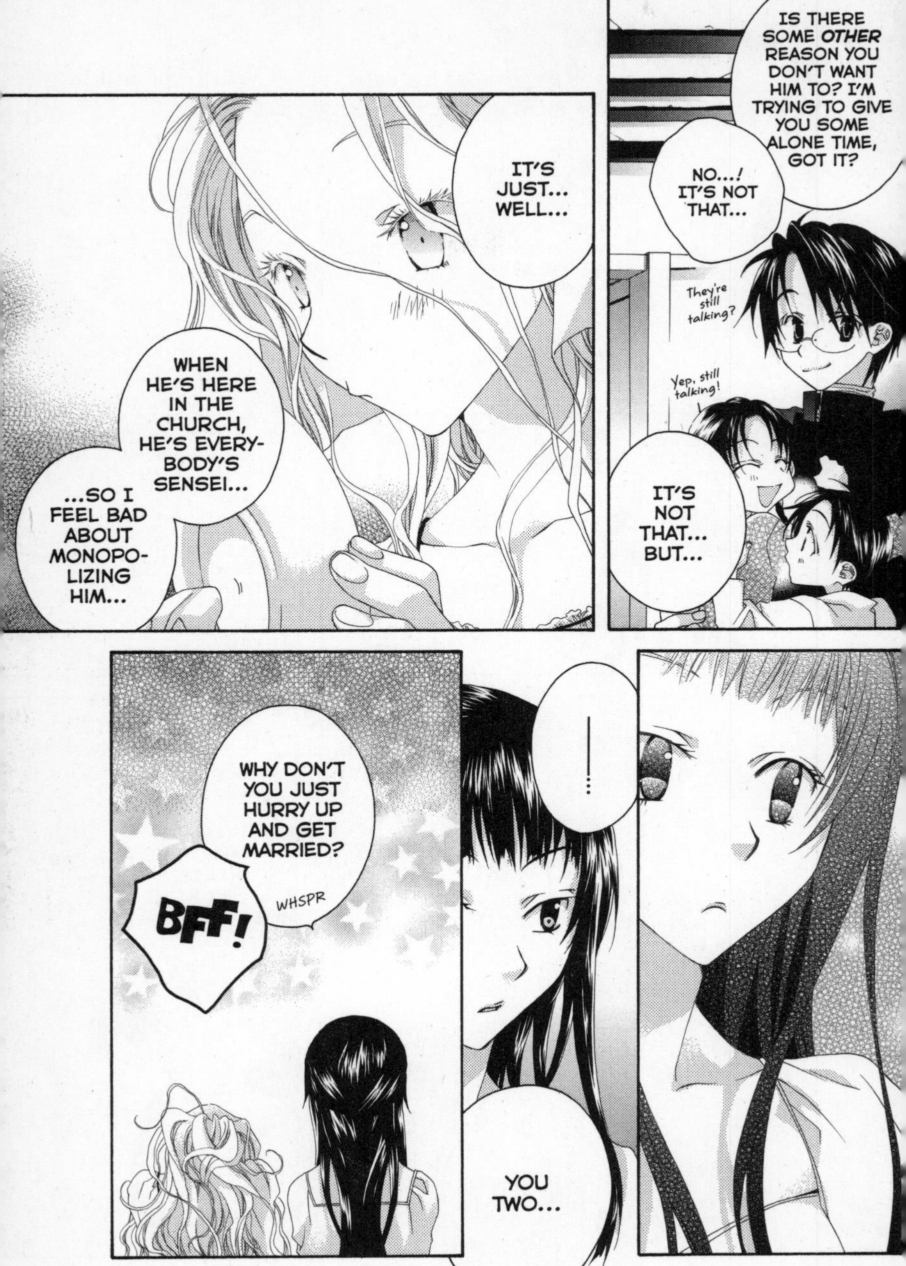
IS THERE SOME *OTHER* REASON YOU DON'T WANT HIM TO? I'M TRYING TO GIVE YOU SOME ALONE TIME, GOT IT?
NO...! IT'S NOT THAT...
They're still talking?
Yep, still talking!
IT'S NOT THAT... BUT...
IT'S JUST... WELL...
WHEN HE'S HERE IN THE CHURCH, HE'S EVERY-BODY'S SENSEI...
...SO I FEEL BAD ABOUT MONOPO-LIZING HIM...
......
YOU TWO...
WHY DON'T YOU JUST HURRY UP AND GET MARRIED?
WHSPR
BFF!

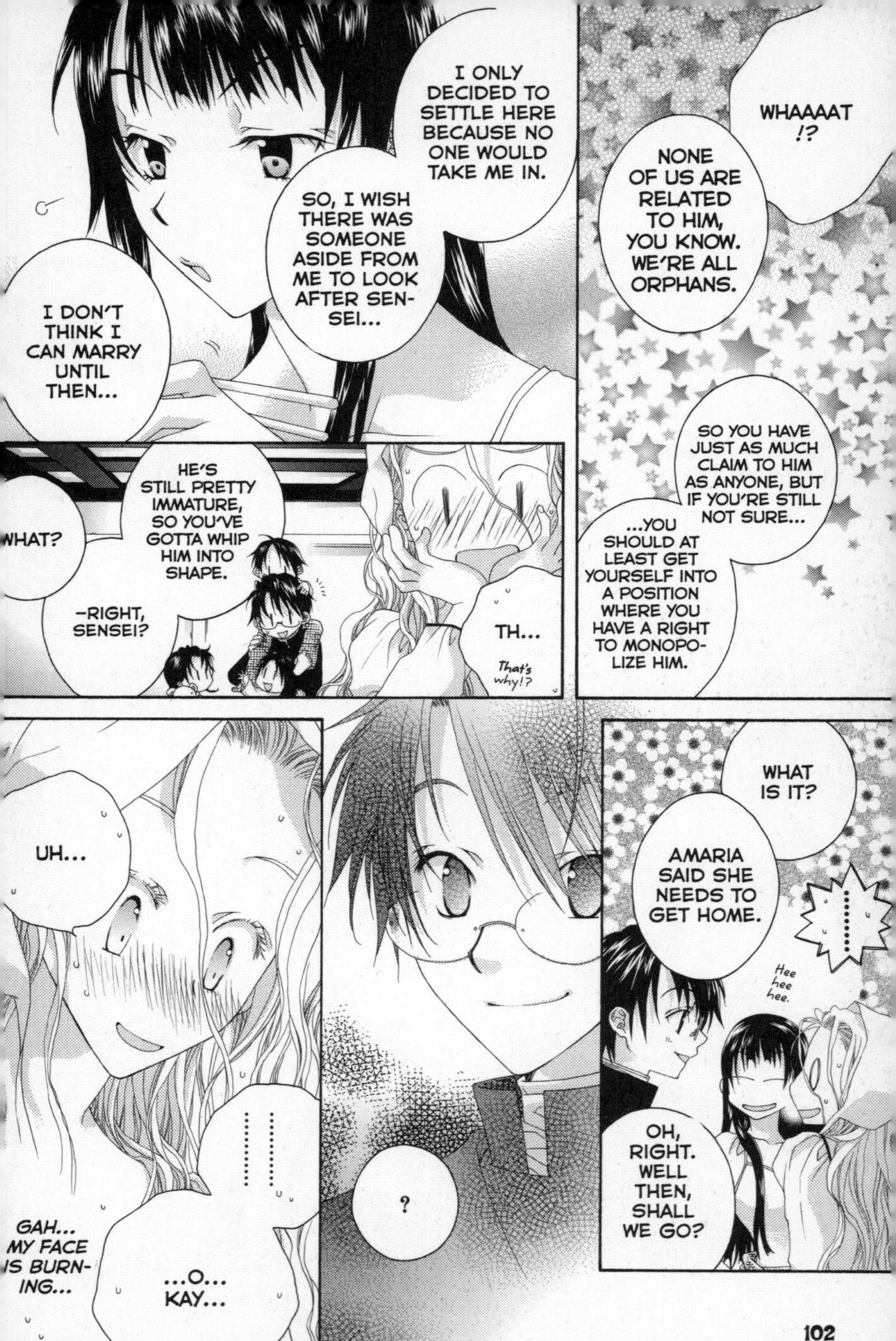

WHAAAAT !?
NONE OF US ARE RELATED TO HIM, YOU KNOW. WE'RE ALL ORPHANS.
SO YOU HAVE JUST AS MUCH CLAIM TO HIM AS ANYONE, BUT IF YOU'RE STILL NOT SURE...
...YOU SHOULD AT LEAST GET YOURSELF INTO A POSITION WHERE YOU HAVE A RIGHT TO MONOPO-LIZE HIM.
I ONLY DECIDED TO SETTLE HERE BECAUSE NO ONE WOULD TAKE ME IN.
SO, I WISH THERE WAS SOMEONE ASIDE FROM ME TO LOOK AFTER SEN-SEI...
I DON'T THINK I CAN MARRY UNTIL THEN...
TH...
That's why!?
WHAT?
HE'S STILL PRETTY IMMATURE, SO YOU'VE GOTTA WHIP HIM INTO SHAPE.
-RIGHT, SENSEI?
WHAT IS IT?
AMARIA SAID SHE NEEDS TO GET HOME.
......
Hee hee hee.
OH, RIGHT. WELL THEN, SHALL WE GO?
?
UH...
......
GAH... MY FACE IS BURNING...
...O... KAY...

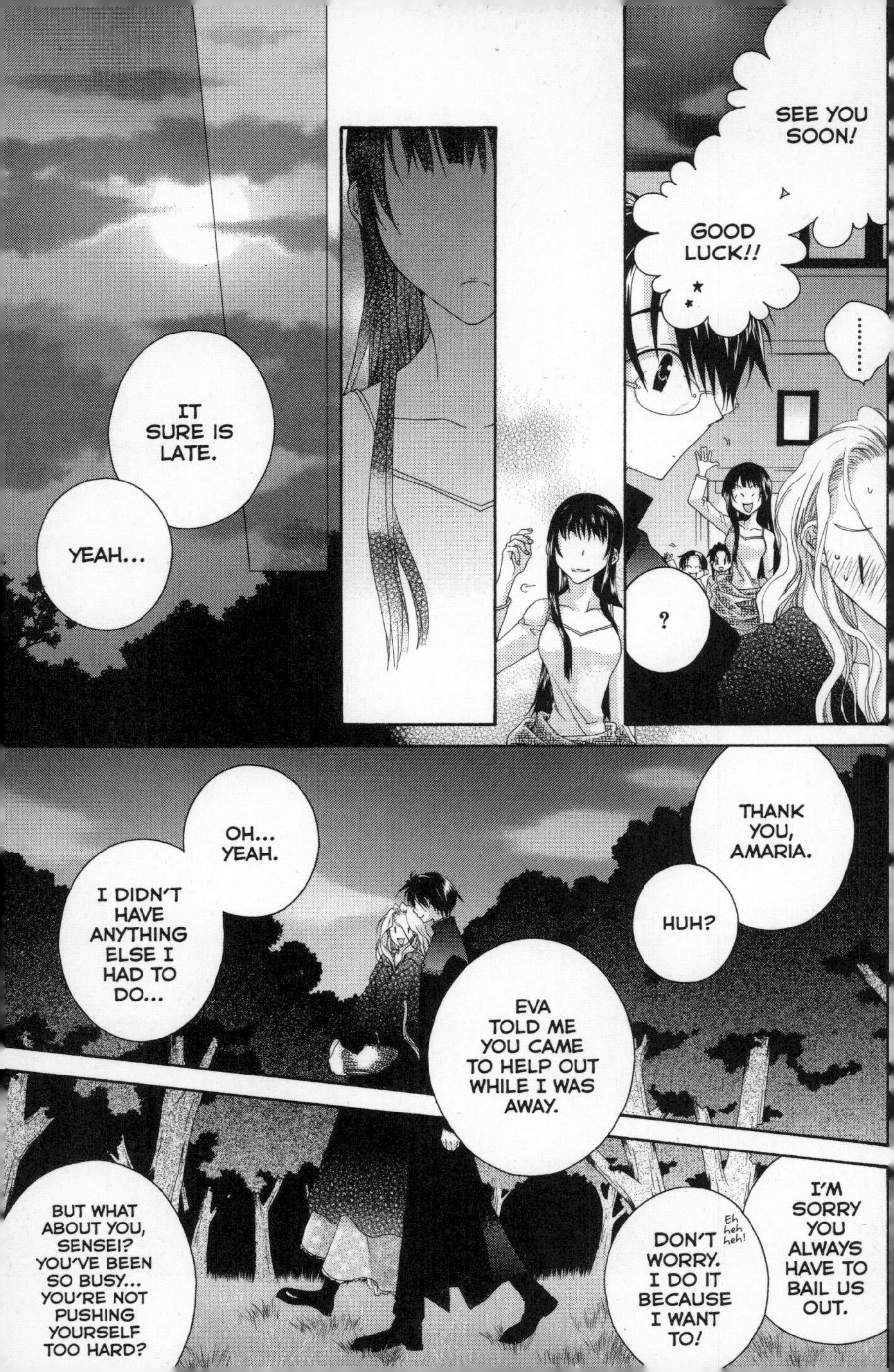
SEE YOU SOON!
GOOD LUCK!!
......
?
IT SURE IS LATE.
YEAH...
THANK YOU, AMARIA.
HUH?
OH... YEAH.
I DIDN'T HAVE ANYTHING ELSE I HAD TO DO...
EVA TOLD ME YOU CAME TO HELP OUT WHILE I WAS AWAY.
I'M SORRY YOU ALWAYS HAVE TO BAIL US OUT.
Eh heh heh!
DON'T WORRY. I DO IT BECAUSE I WANT TO!
BUT WHAT ABOUT YOU, SENSEI? YOU'VE BEEN SO BUSY... YOU'RE NOT PUSHING YOURSELF TOO HARD?

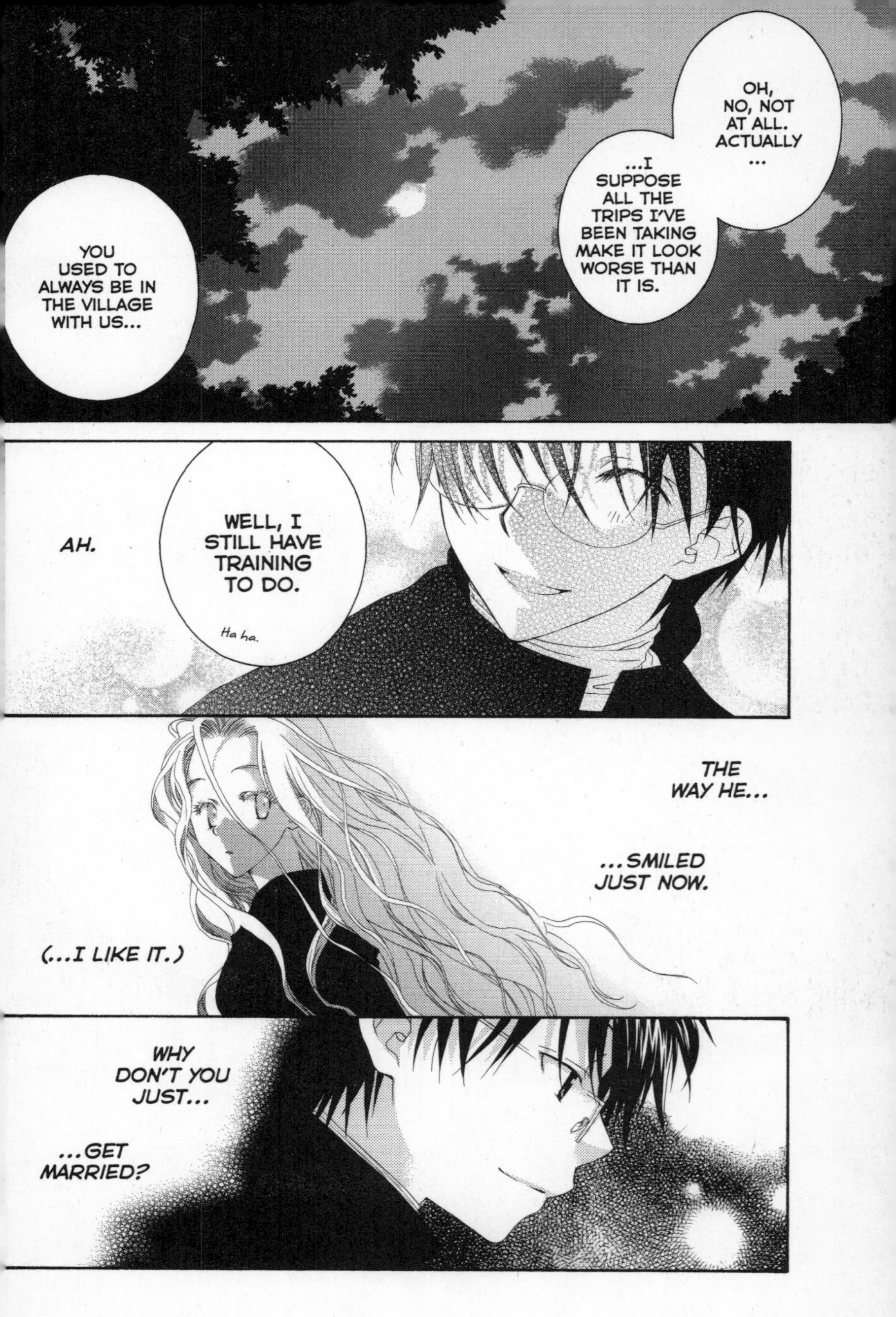
OH, NO, NOT AT ALL. ACTUALLY ...
...I SUPPOSE ALL THE TRIPS I'VE BEEN TAKING MAKE IT LOOK WORSE THAN IT IS.
YOU USED TO ALWAYS BE IN THE VILLAGE WITH US...
WELL, I STILL HAVE TRAINING TO DO.
Ha ha.
AH.
THE WAY HE...
...SMILED JUST NOW.
(...I LIKE IT.)
WHY DON'T YOU JUST...
...GET MARRIED?

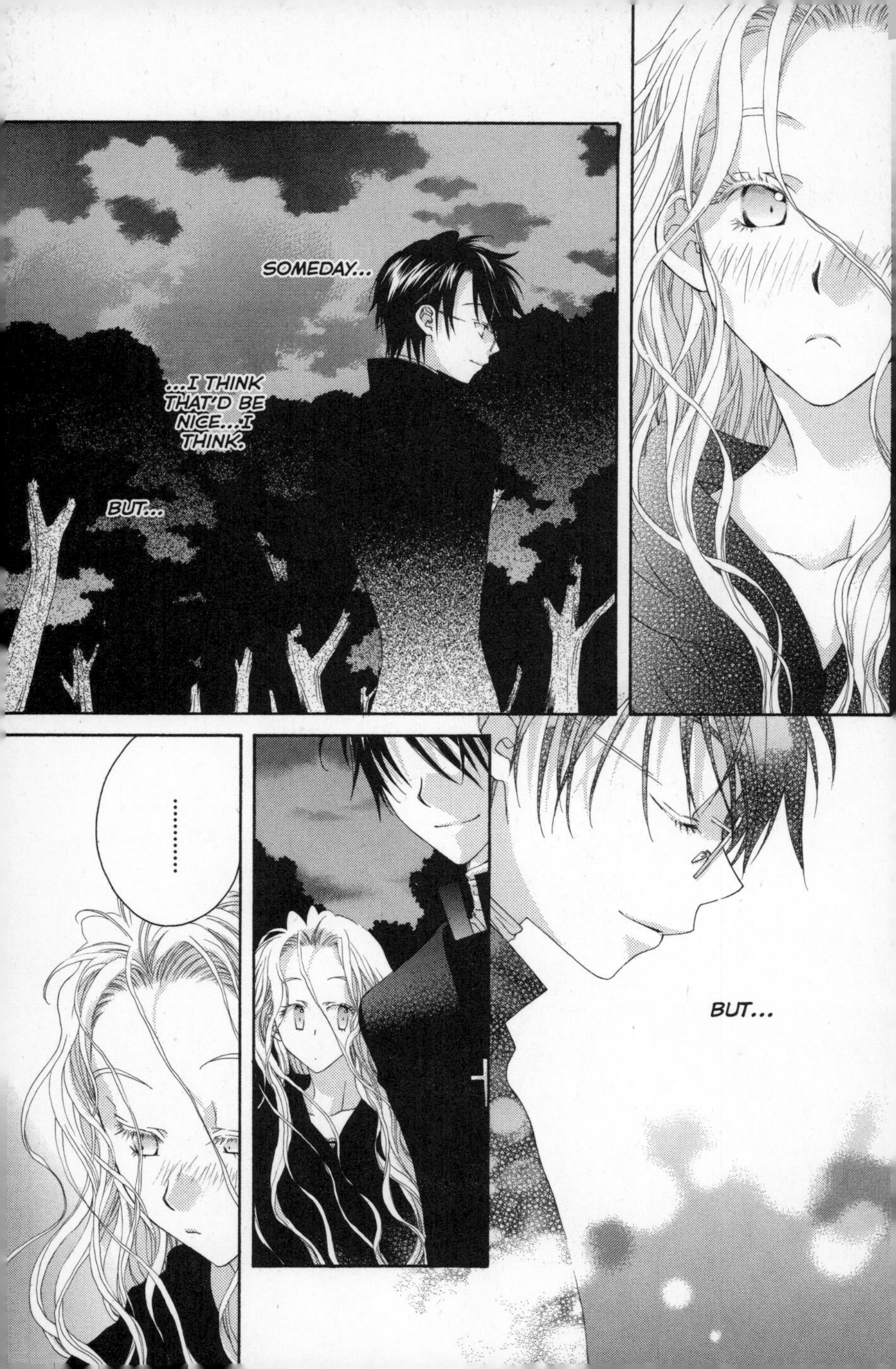
SOMEDAY...
...I THINK THAT'D BE NICE...I THINK.
BUT...
BUT...
....

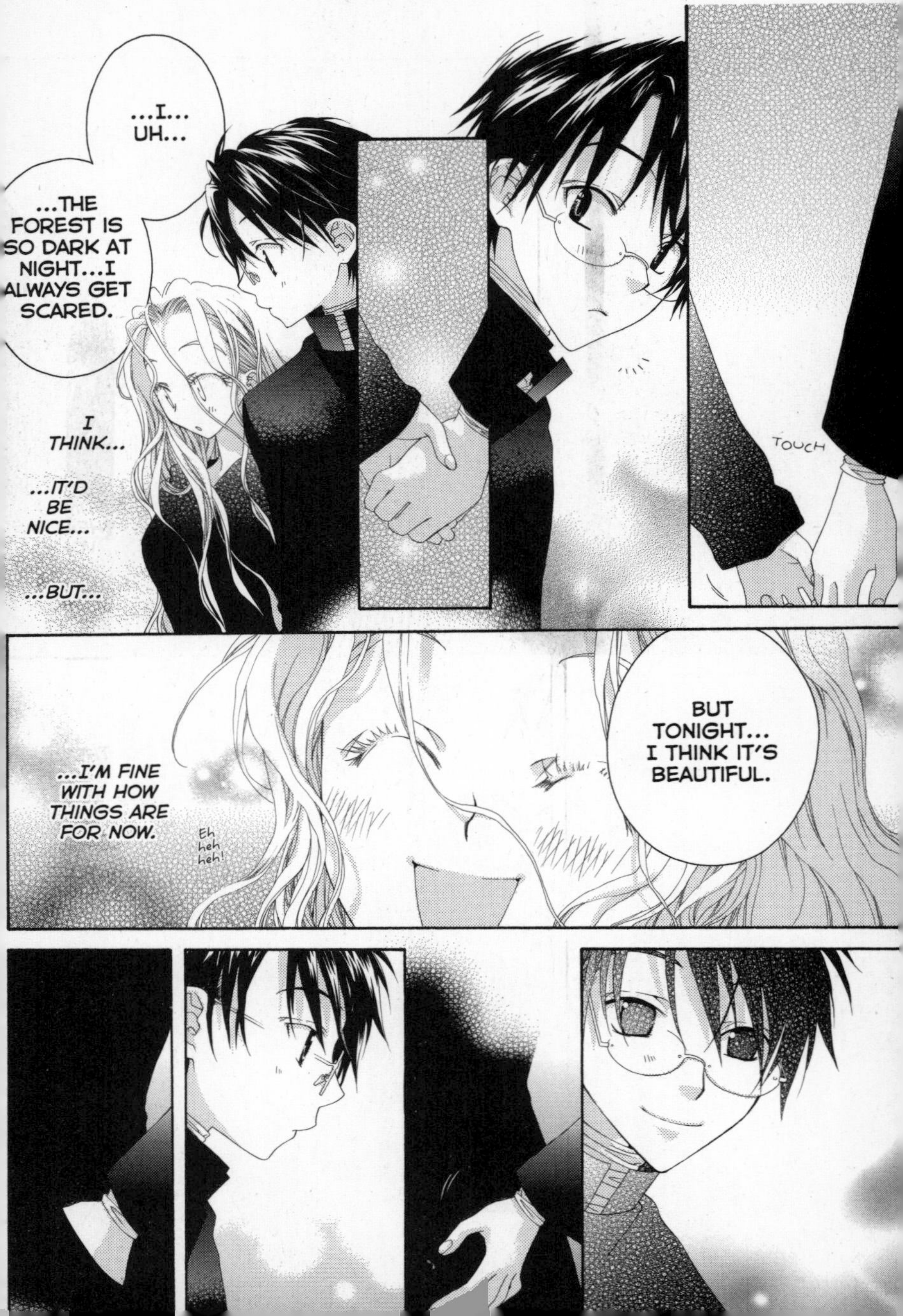
TOUCH
...I... UH...
...THE FOREST IS SO DARK AT NIGHT...I ALWAYS GET SCARED.
I THINK...
...IT'D BE NICE...
...BUT...
BUT TONIGHT... I THINK IT'S BEAUTIFUL.
Eh heh heh!
...I'M FINE WITH HOW THINGS ARE FOR NOW.

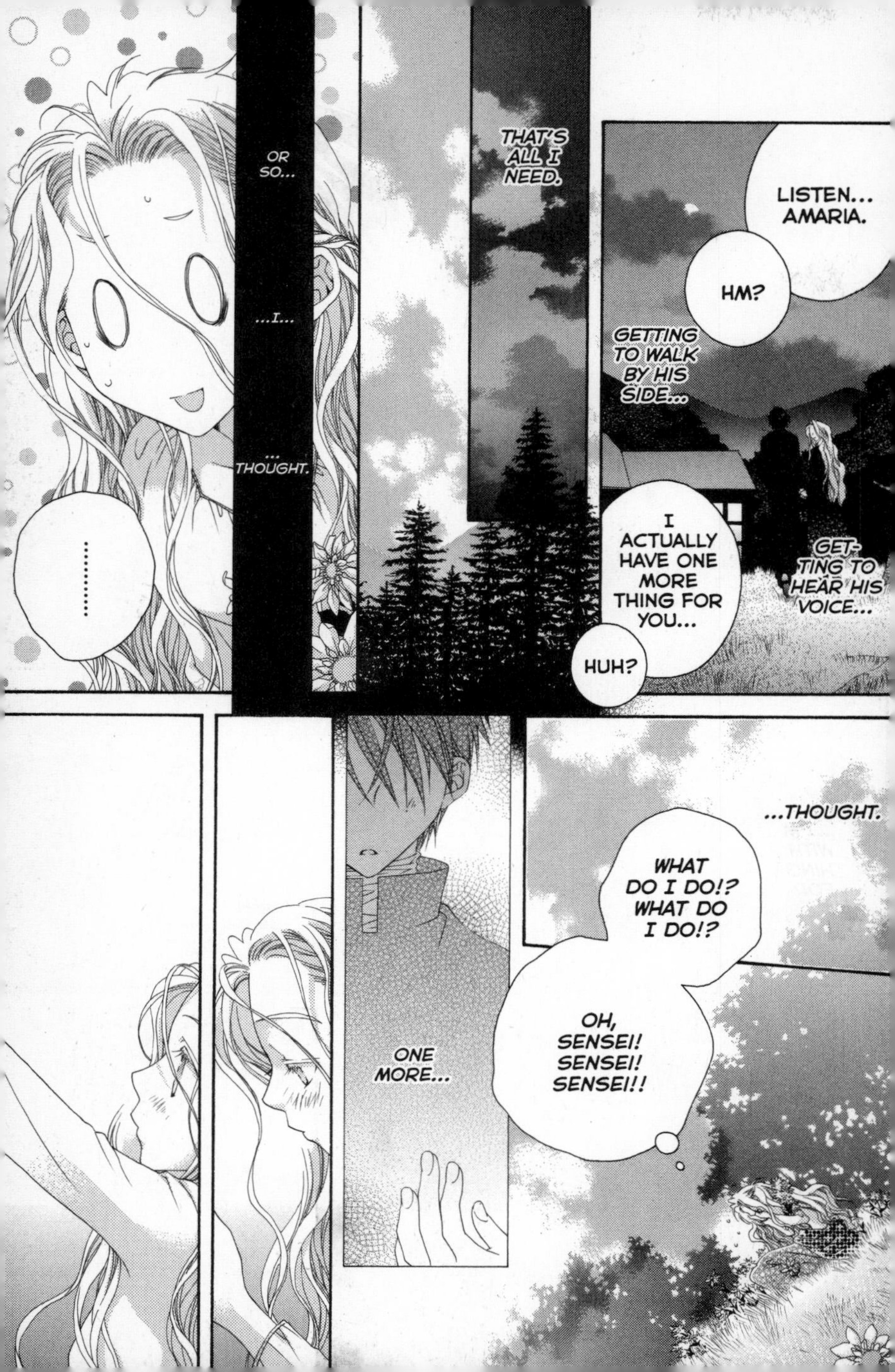
LISTEN... AMARIA.
HM?
GETTING TO WALK BY HIS SIDE...
GET-TING TO HEAR HIS VOICE...
I ACTUALLY HAVE ONE MORE THING FOR YOU...
HUH?
THAT'S ALL I NEED.
OR SO...
...I...
...THOUGHT.
......
...THOUGHT.
WHAT DO I DO!? WHAT DO I DO!?
OH, SENSEI! SENSEI! SENSEI!!
ONE MORE...

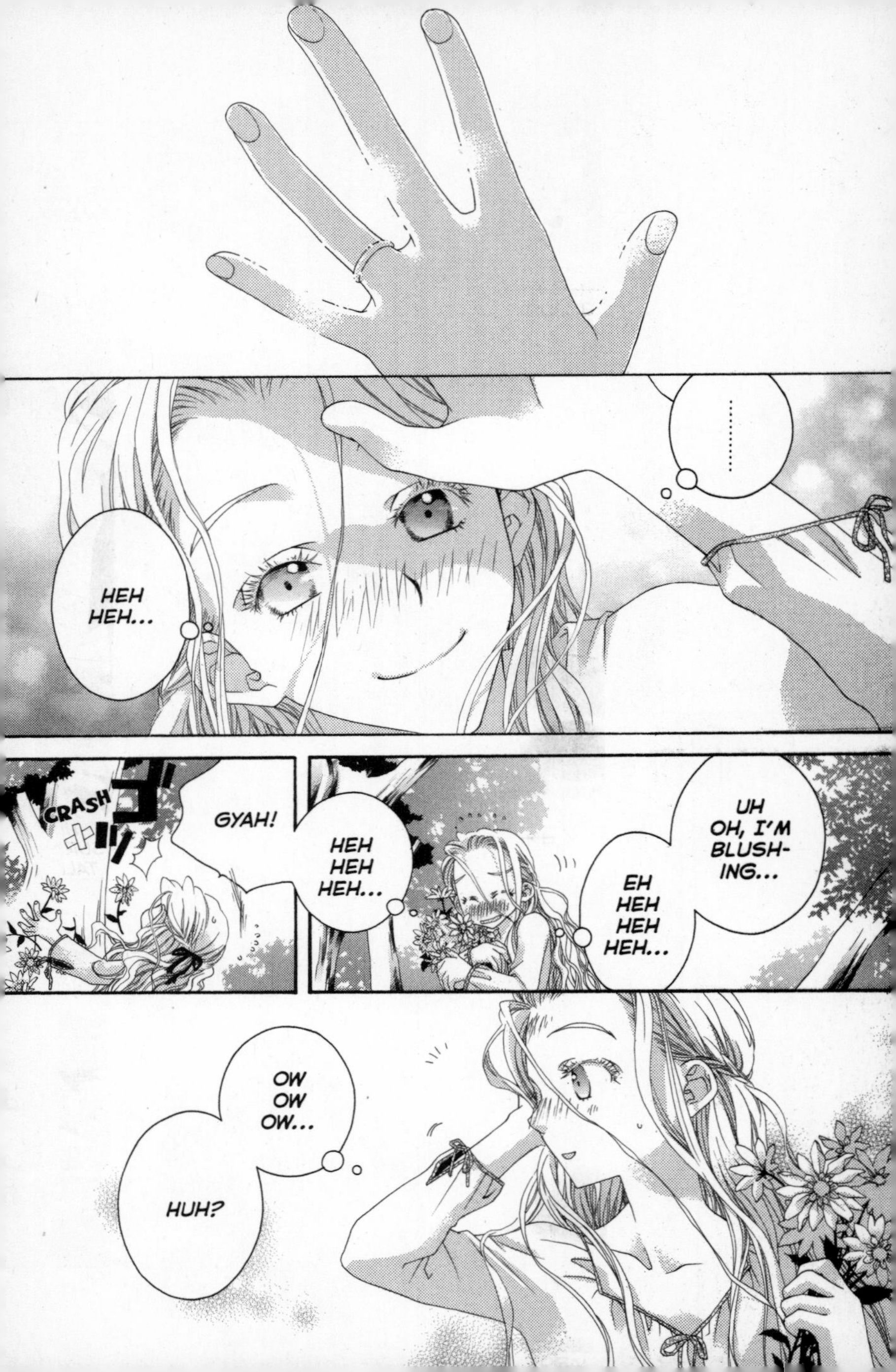
......
HEH HEH...
UH OH, I'M BLUSHING...
EH HEH HEH HEH...
HEH HEH HEH...
GYAH!
CRASH
OW OW OW...
HUH?

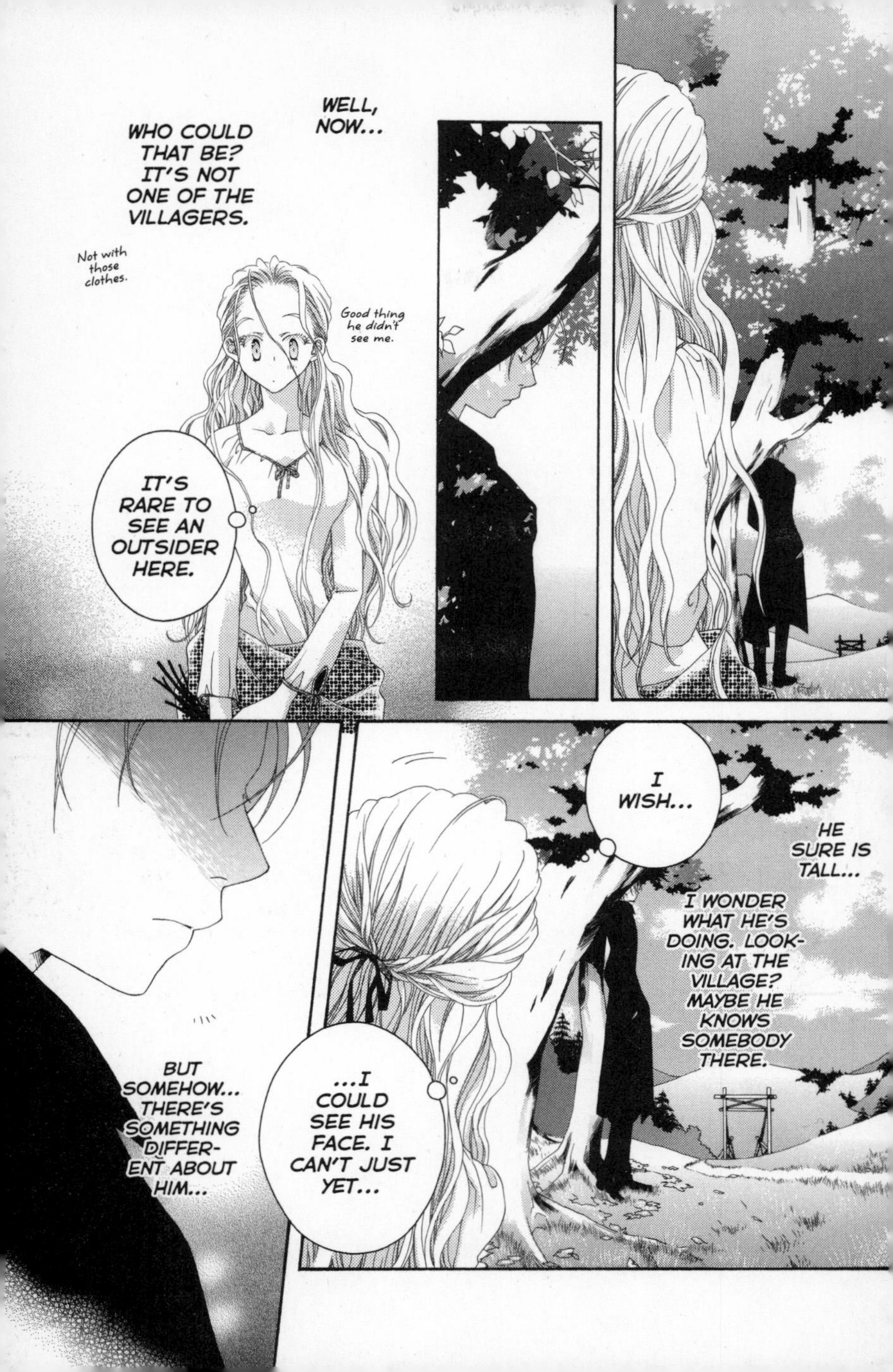
WELL, NOW...
WHO COULD THAT BE? IT'S NOT ONE OF THE VILLAGERS.
Not with those clothes.
Good thing he didn't see me.
IT'S RARE TO SEE AN OUTSIDER HERE.
HE SURE IS TALL...
I WONDER WHAT HE'S DOING. LOOK-ING AT THE VILLAGE? MAYBE HE KNOWS SOMEBODY THERE.
I WISH...
...I COULD SEE HIS FACE. I CAN'T JUST YET...
BUT SOMEHOW... THERE'S SOMETHING DIFFER-ENT ABOUT HIM...

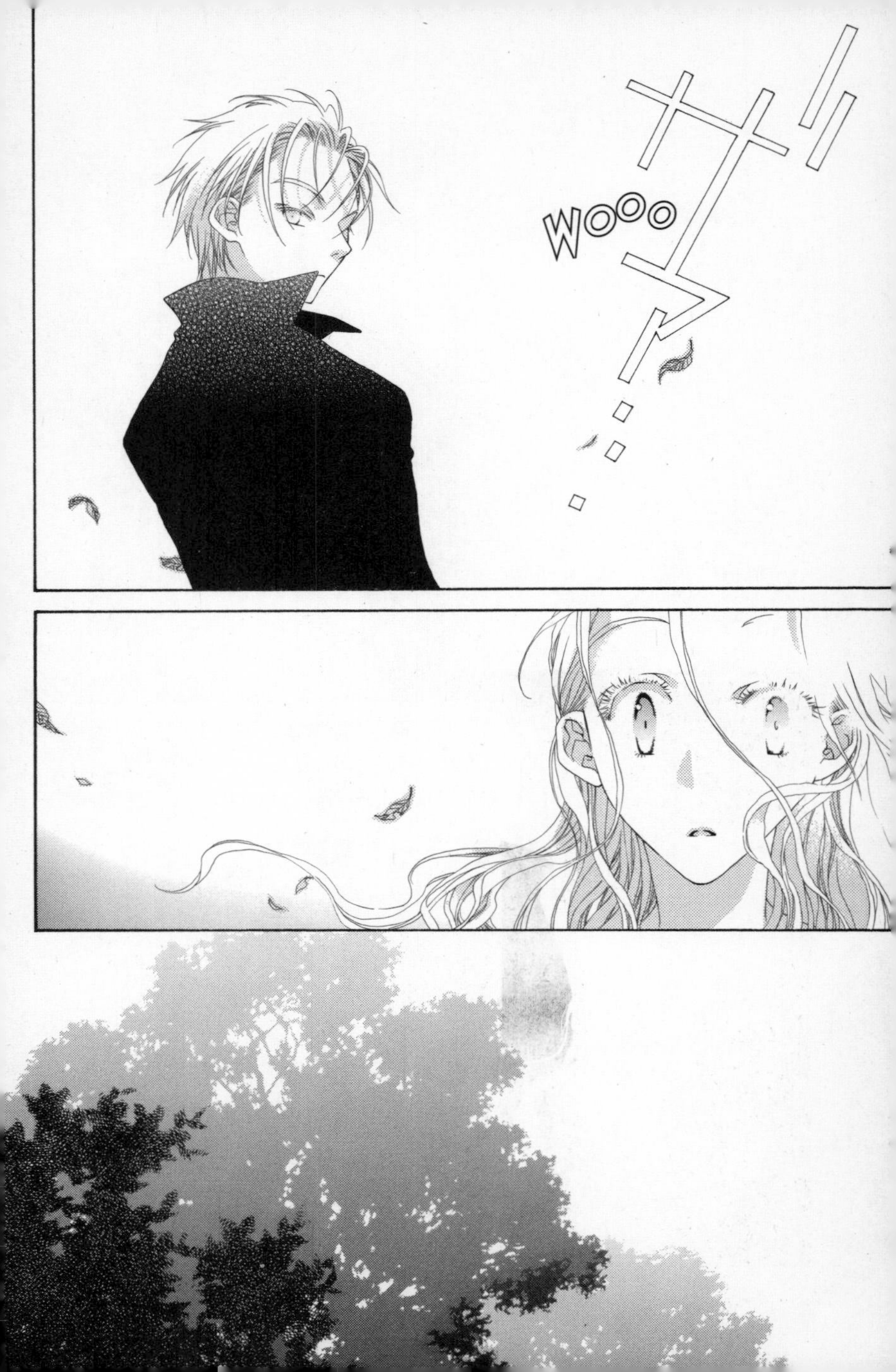
WOOO

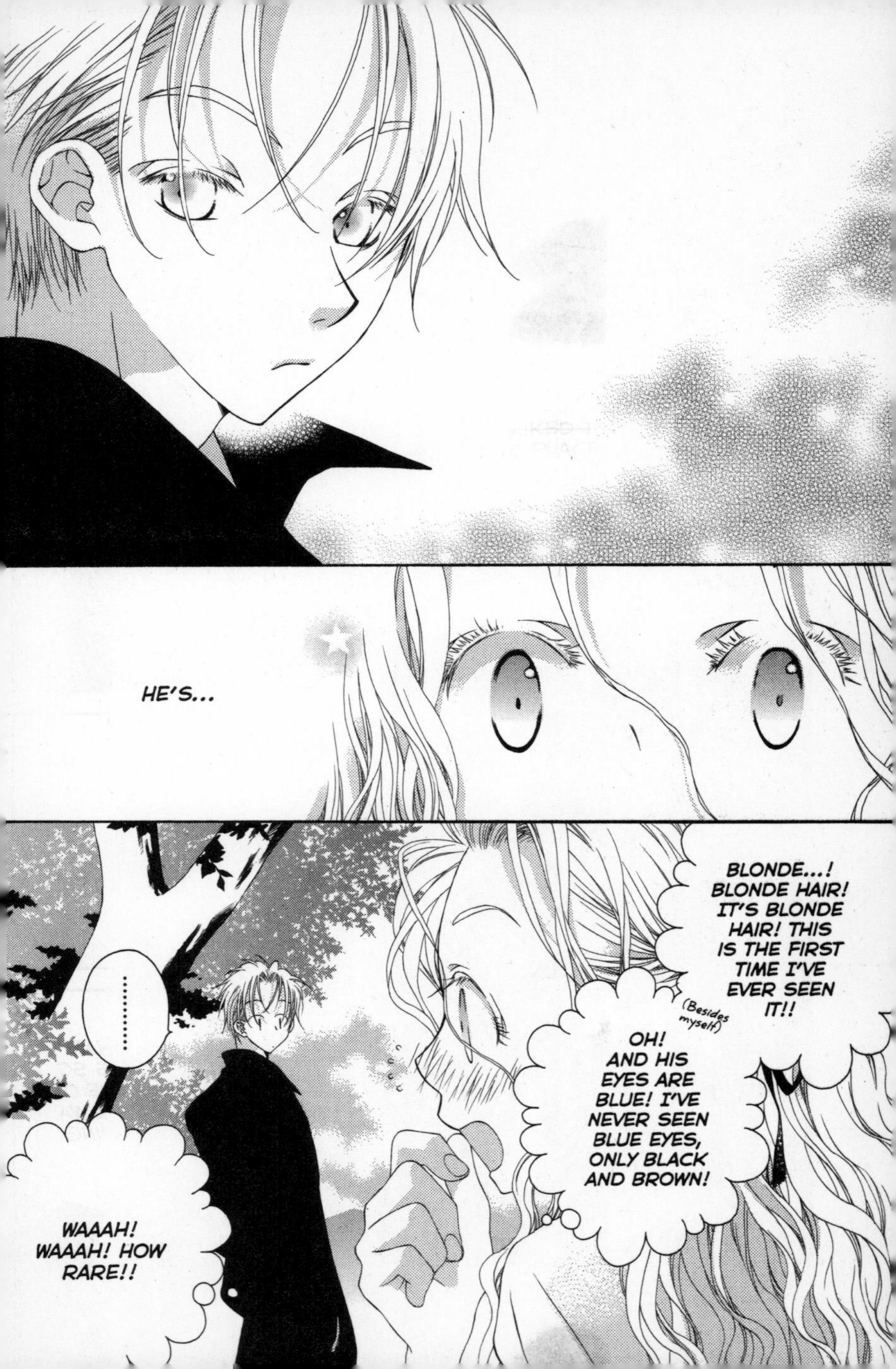
HE'S...
BLONDE...! BLONDE HAIR! IT'S BLONDE HAIR! THIS IS THE FIRST TIME I'VE EVER SEEN IT!!
(Besides myself)
OH! AND HIS EYES ARE BLUE! I'VE NEVER SEEN BLUE EYES, ONLY BLACK AND BROWN!
......
WAAAH! WAAAH! HOW RARE!!

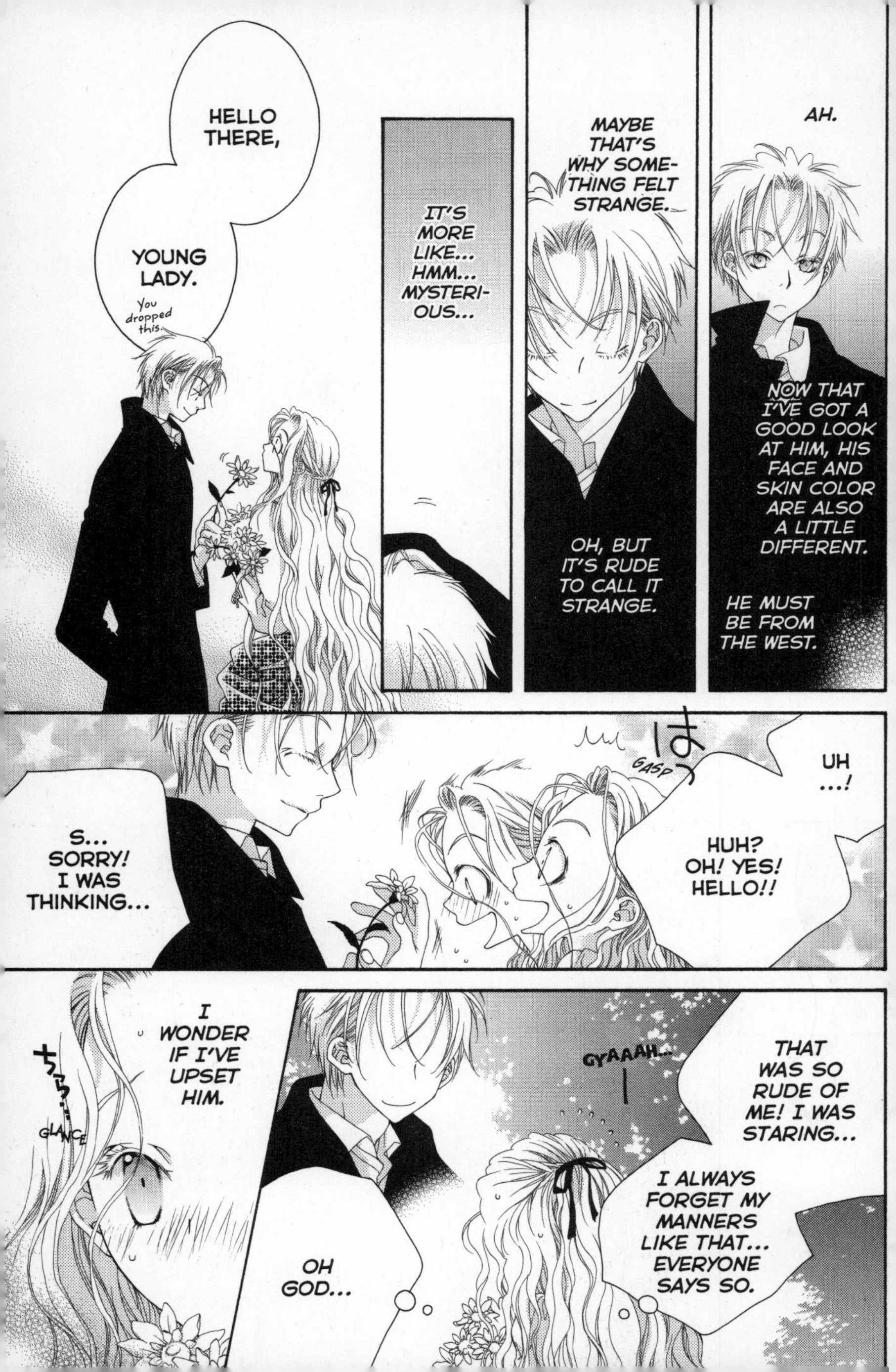
AH.
NOW THAT I'VE GOT A GOOD LOOK AT HIM, HIS FACE AND SKIN COLOR ARE ALSO A LITTLE DIFFERENT.
HE MUST BE FROM THE WEST.
MAYBE THAT'S WHY SOMETHING FELT STRANGE.
OH, BUT IT'S RUDE TO CALL IT STRANGE.
IT'S MORE LIKE... HMM... MYSTERIOUS...
HELLO THERE,
YOUNG LADY.
You dropped this.
UH ...!
GASP
HUH? OH! YES! HELLO!!
S... SORRY! I WAS THINKING...
THAT WAS SO RUDE OF ME! I WAS STARING...
GYAAAH...
I ALWAYS FORGET MY MANNERS LIKE THAT... EVERYONE SAYS SO.
OH GOD...
I WONDER IF I'VE UPSET HIM.
GLANCE

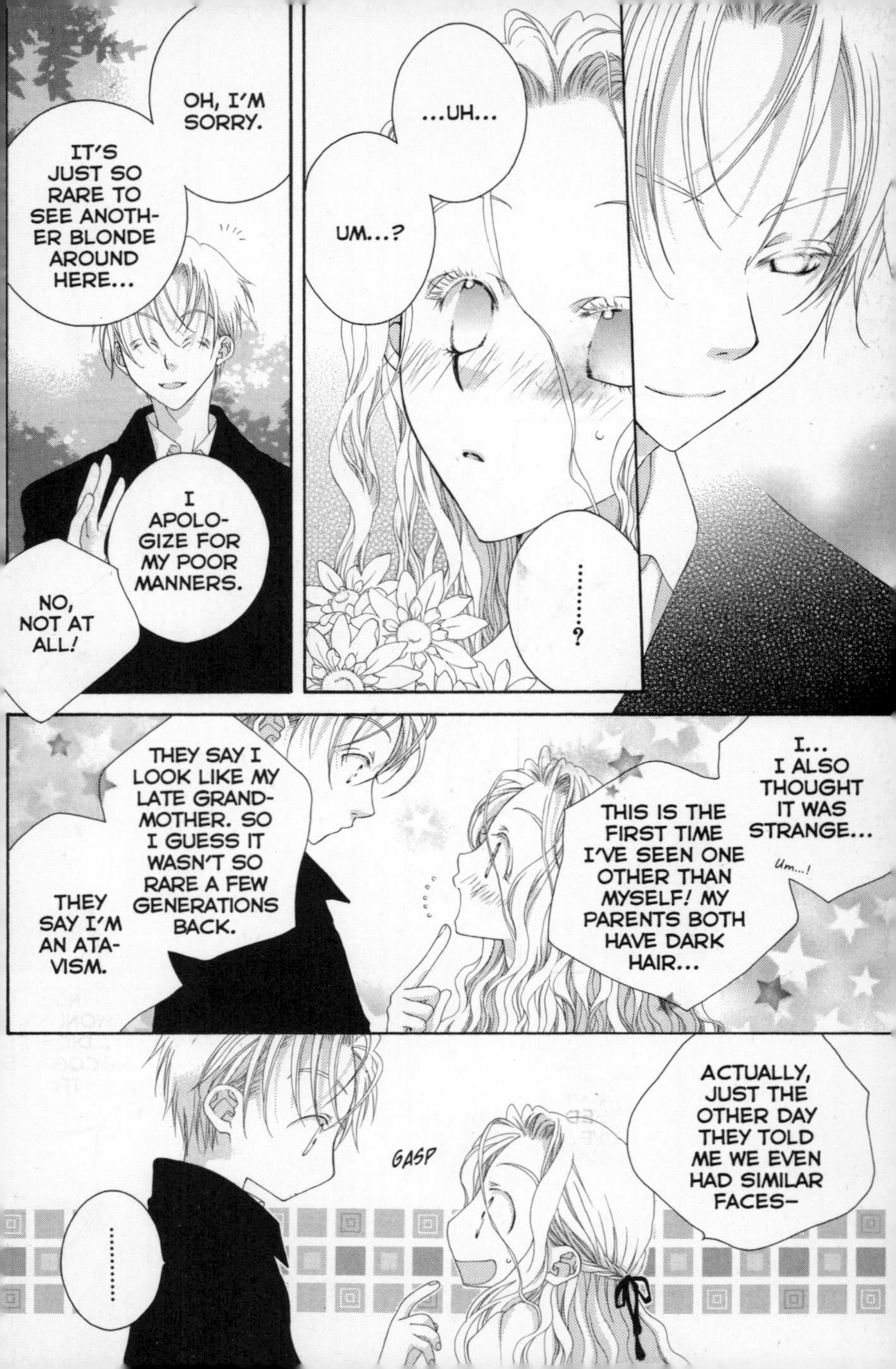

...UH...
UM...?
......?
OH, I'M SORRY.
IT'S JUST SO RARE TO SEE ANOTHER BLONDE AROUND HERE...
I APOLOGIZE FOR MY POOR MANNERS.
NO, NOT AT ALL!
I... I ALSO THOUGHT IT WAS STRANGE...
Um...!
THIS IS THE FIRST TIME I'VE SEEN ONE OTHER THAN MYSELF! MY PARENTS BOTH HAVE DARK HAIR...
THEY SAY I LOOK LIKE MY LATE GRANDMOTHER. SO I GUESS IT WASN'T SO RARE A FEW GENERATIONS BACK.
THEY SAY I'M AN ATAVISM.
ACTUALLY, JUST THE OTHER DAY THEY TOLD ME WE EVEN HAD SIMILAR FACES—
GASP
......

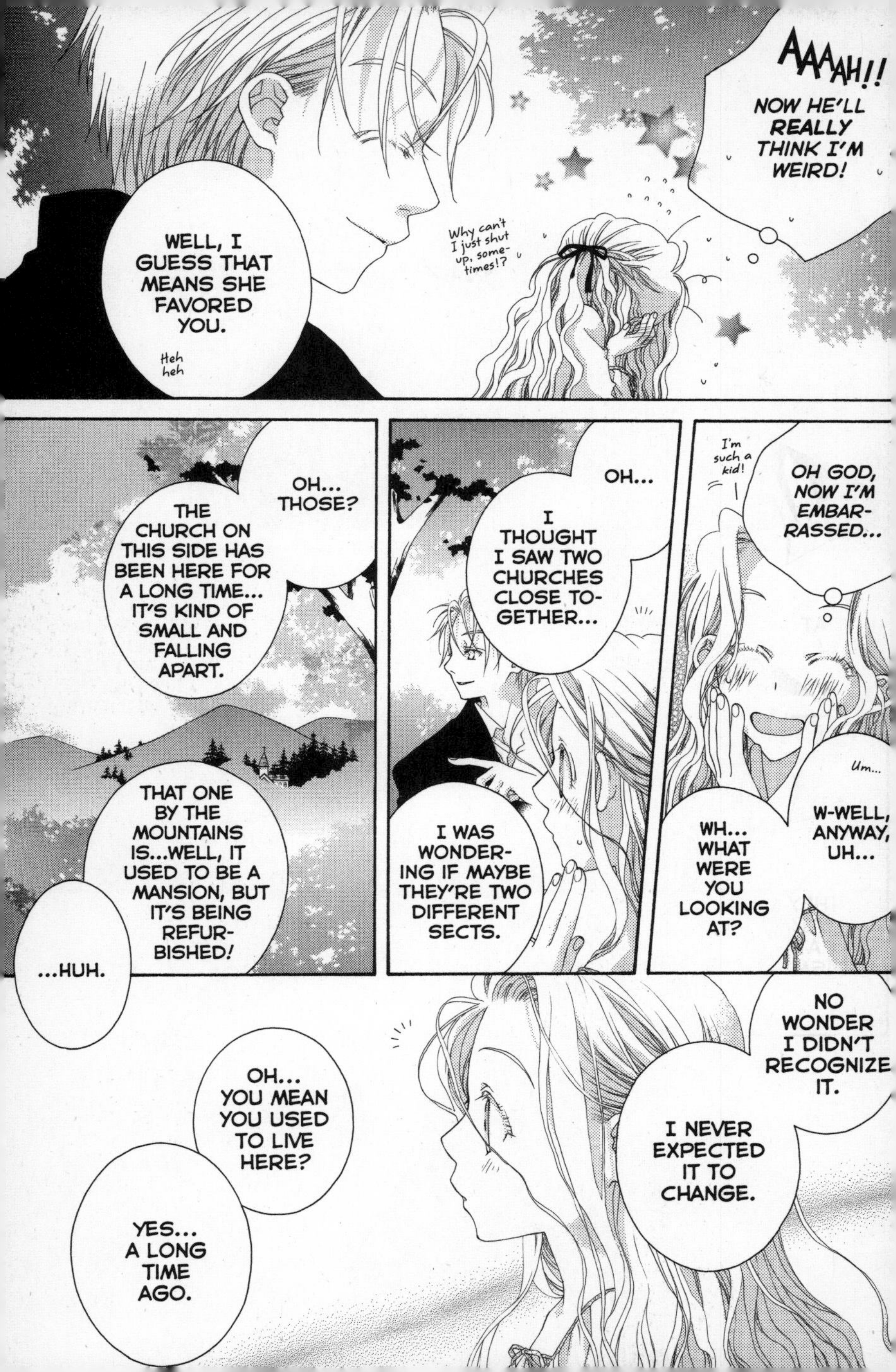
AAAAH!!
NOW HE'LL REALLY THINK I'M WEIRD!
Why can't I just shut up, some-times!?
WELL, I GUESS THAT MEANS SHE FAVORED YOU.
Heh heh
I'm such a kid!
OH GOD, NOW I'M EMBAR-RASSED...
Um...
W-WELL, ANYWAY, UH...
WH... WHAT WERE YOU LOOKING AT?
OH...
I THOUGHT I SAW TWO CHURCHES CLOSE TO-GETHER...
I WAS WONDER-ING IF MAYBE THEY'RE TWO DIFFERENT SECTS.
OH... THOSE?
THE CHURCH ON THIS SIDE HAS BEEN HERE FOR A LONG TIME... IT'S KIND OF SMALL AND FALLING APART.
THAT ONE BY THE MOUNTAINS IS...WELL, IT USED TO BE A MANSION, BUT IT'S BEING REFUR-BISHED!
...HUH.
NO WONDER I DIDN'T RECOGNIZE IT.
I NEVER EXPECTED IT TO CHANGE.
OH... YOU MEAN YOU USED TO LIVE HERE?
YES... A LONG TIME AGO.

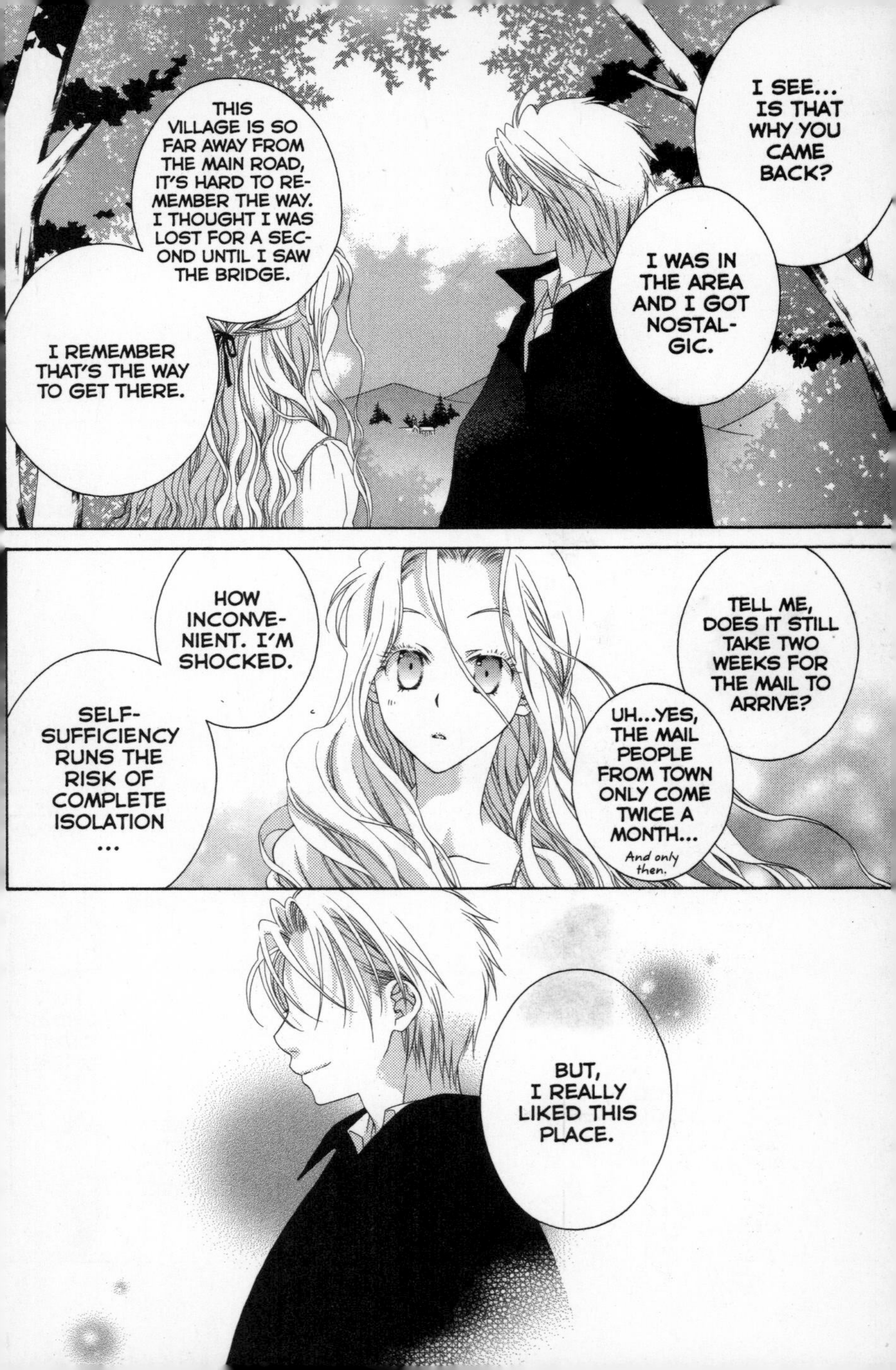
I SEE... IS THAT WHY YOU CAME BACK?
I WAS IN THE AREA AND I GOT NOSTALGIC.
THIS VILLAGE IS SO FAR AWAY FROM THE MAIN ROAD, IT'S HARD TO REMEMBER THE WAY. I THOUGHT I WAS LOST FOR A SECOND UNTIL I SAW THE BRIDGE.
I REMEMBER THAT'S THE WAY TO GET THERE.
TELL ME, DOES IT STILL TAKE TWO WEEKS FOR THE MAIL TO ARRIVE?
UH...YES, THE MAIL PEOPLE FROM TOWN ONLY COME TWICE A MONTH...
And only then.
HOW INCONVENIENT. I'M SHOCKED.
SELF-SUFFICIENCY RUNS THE RISK OF COMPLETE ISOLATION ...
BUT, I REALLY LIKED THIS PLACE.

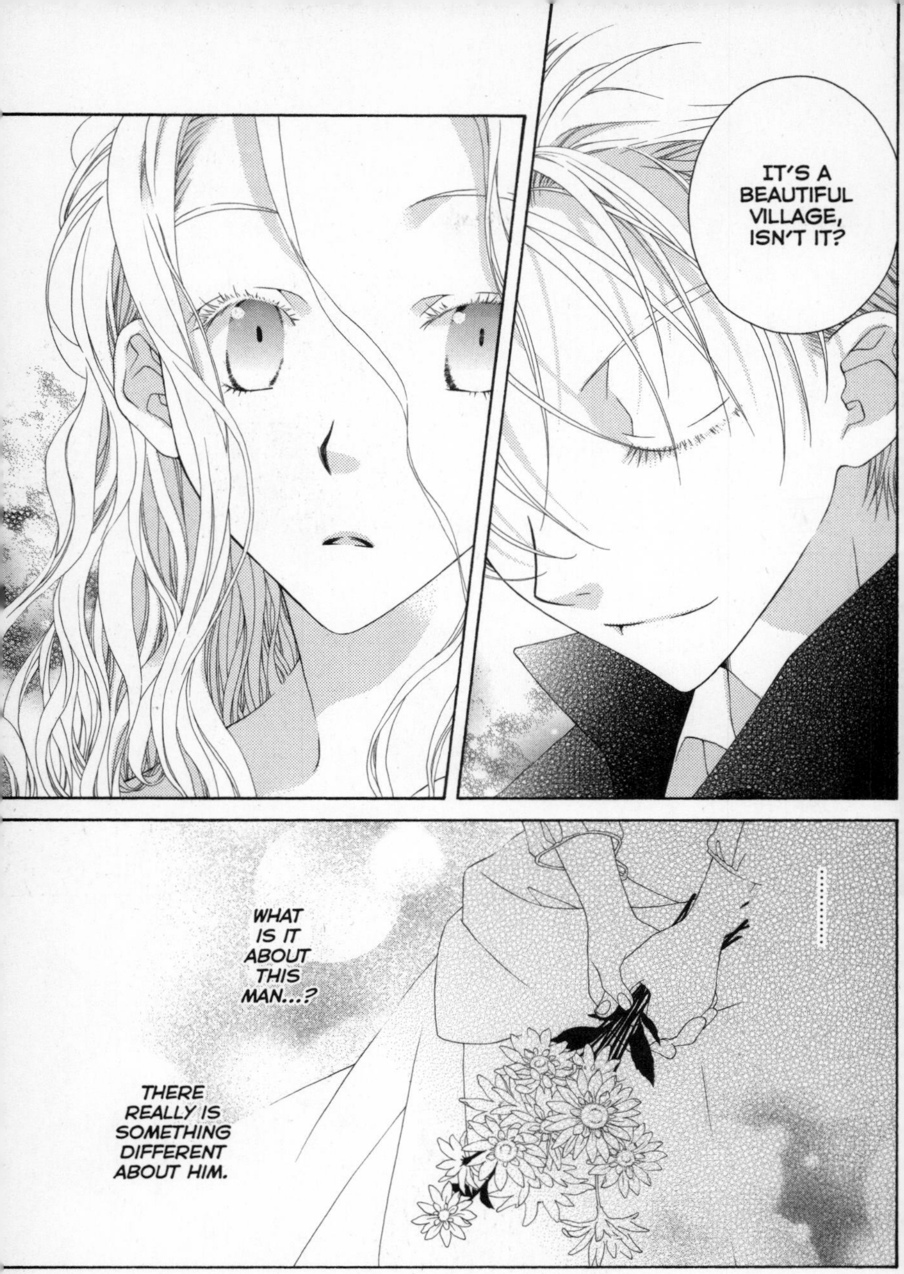
IT'S A BEAUTIFUL VILLAGE, ISN'T IT?
......
WHAT IS IT ABOUT THIS MAN...?
THERE REALLY IS SOMETHING DIFFERENT ABOUT HIM.

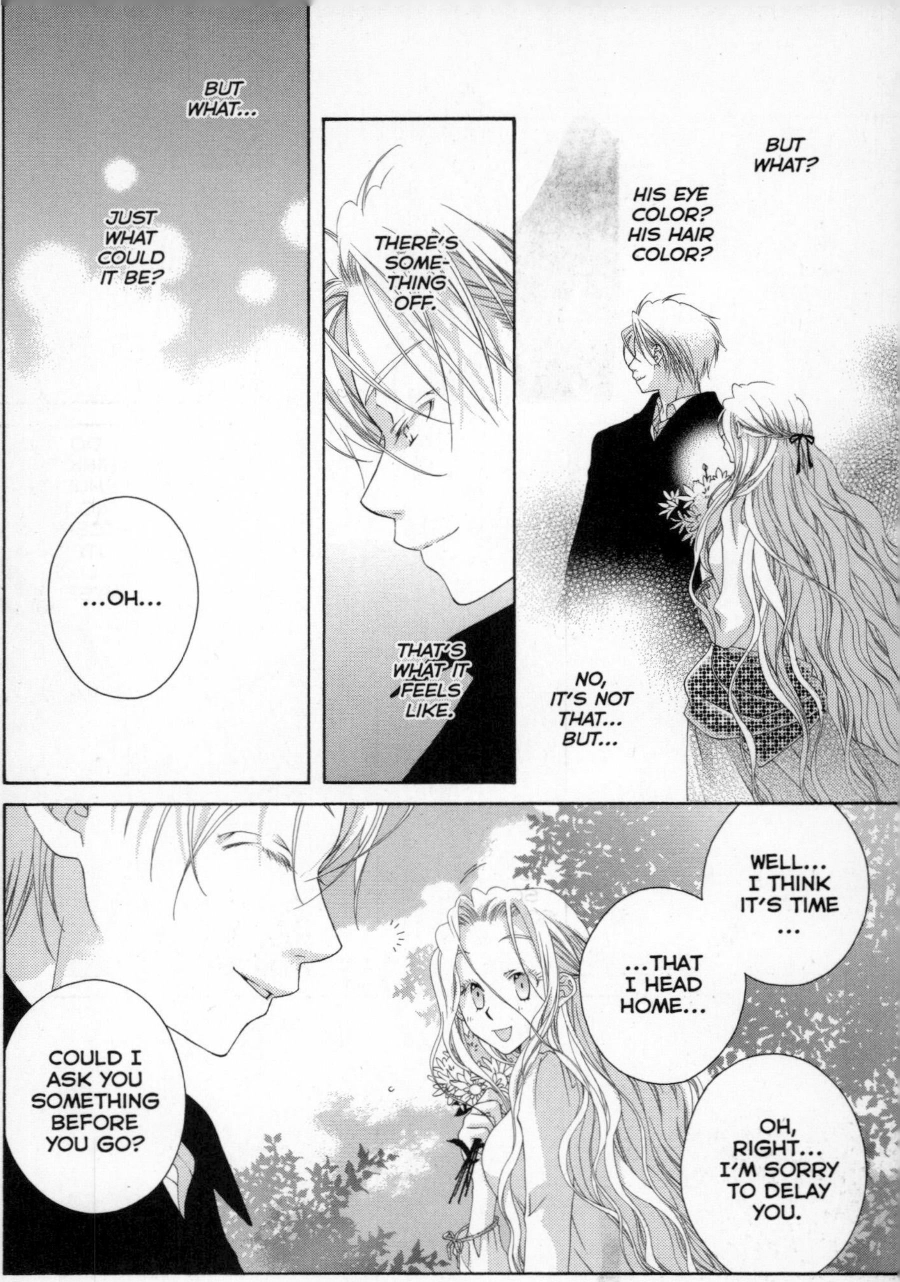
BUT WHAT?
HIS EYE COLOR? HIS HAIR COLOR?
NO, IT'S NOT THAT... BUT...
THERE'S SOME-THING OFF.
THAT'S WHAT IT FEELS LIKE.
BUT WHAT...
JUST WHAT COULD IT BE?
...OH...
WELL... I THINK IT'S TIME ...
...THAT I HEAD HOME...
OH, RIGHT... I'M SORRY TO DELAY YOU.
COULD I ASK YOU SOMETHING BEFORE YOU GO?

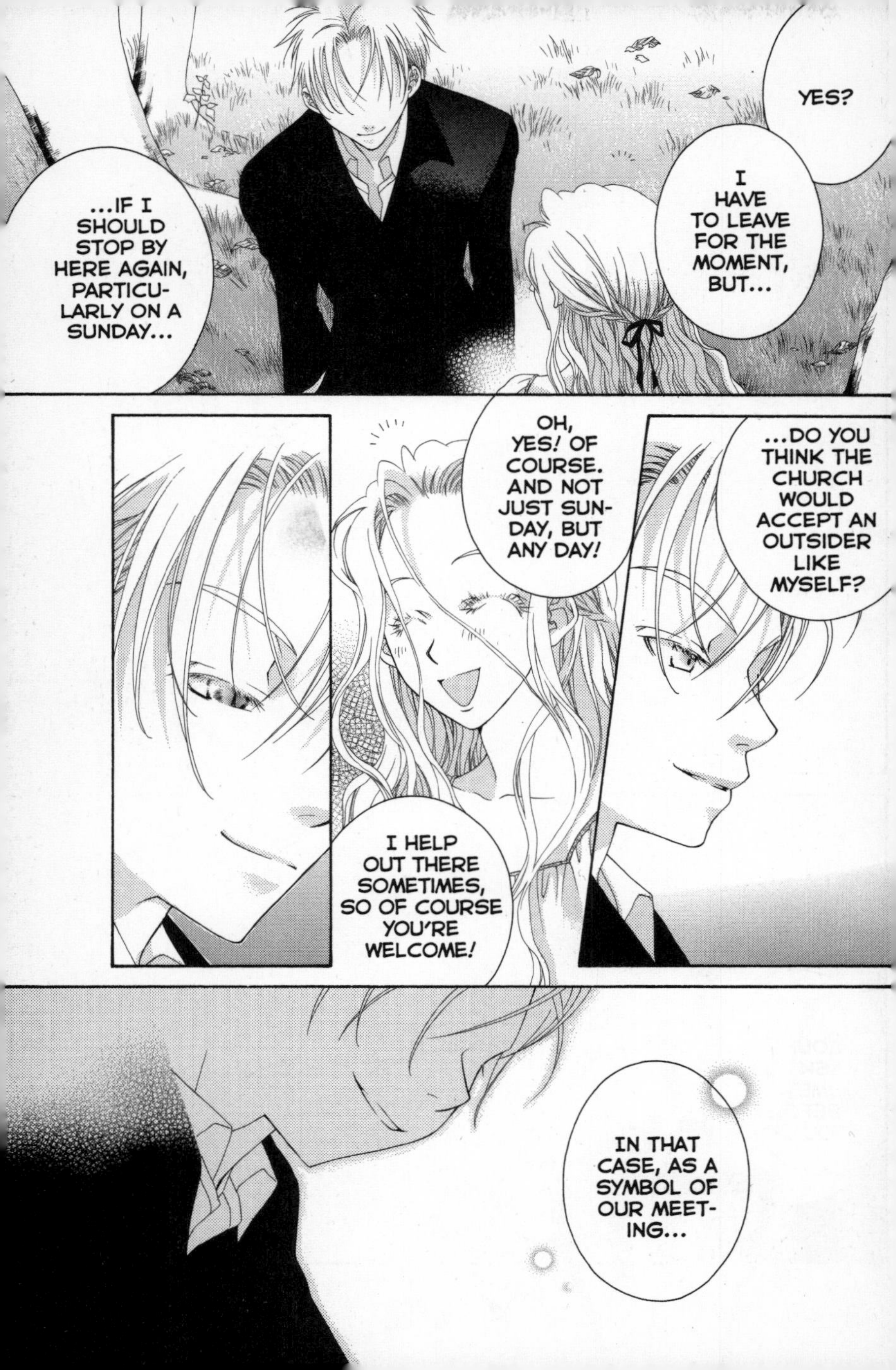
YES?
I HAVE TO LEAVE FOR THE MOMENT, BUT...
...IF I SHOULD STOP BY HERE AGAIN, PARTICULARLY ON A SUNDAY...
...DO YOU THINK THE CHURCH WOULD ACCEPT AN OUTSIDER LIKE MYSELF?
OH, YES! OF COURSE. AND NOT JUST SUNDAY, BUT ANY DAY!
I HELP OUT THERE SOMETIMES, SO OF COURSE YOU'RE WELCOME!
IN THAT CASE, AS A SYMBOL OF OUR MEETING...

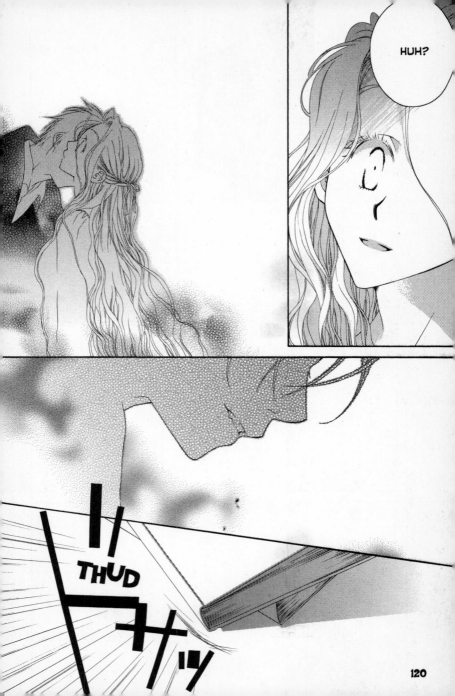

HUH?

THUD

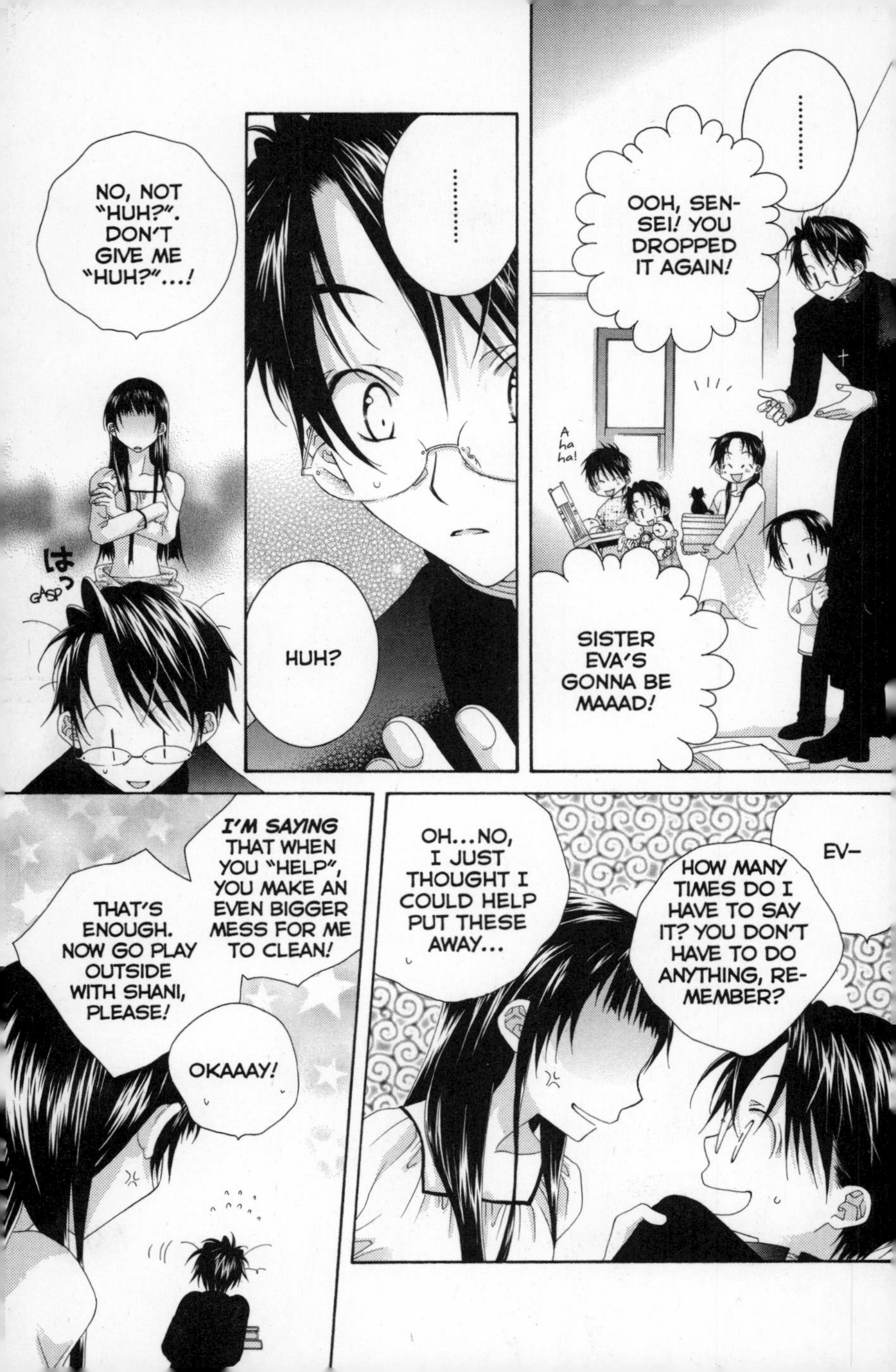
......
OOH, SEN-SEI! YOU DROPPED IT AGAIN!
A ha ha!
SISTER EVA'S GONNA BE MAAAD!
......
HUH?
NO, NOT "HUH?". DON'T GIVE ME "HUH?"...!
はっ
GASP
EV–
HOW MANY TIMES DO I HAVE TO SAY IT? YOU DON'T HAVE TO DO ANYTHING, RE-MEMBER?
OH...NO, I JUST THOUGHT I COULD HELP PUT THESE AWAY...
I'M SAYING THAT WHEN YOU "HELP", YOU MAKE AN EVEN BIGGER MESS FOR ME TO CLEAN!
THAT'S ENOUGH. NOW GO PLAY OUTSIDE WITH SHANI, PLEASE!
OKAAAY!

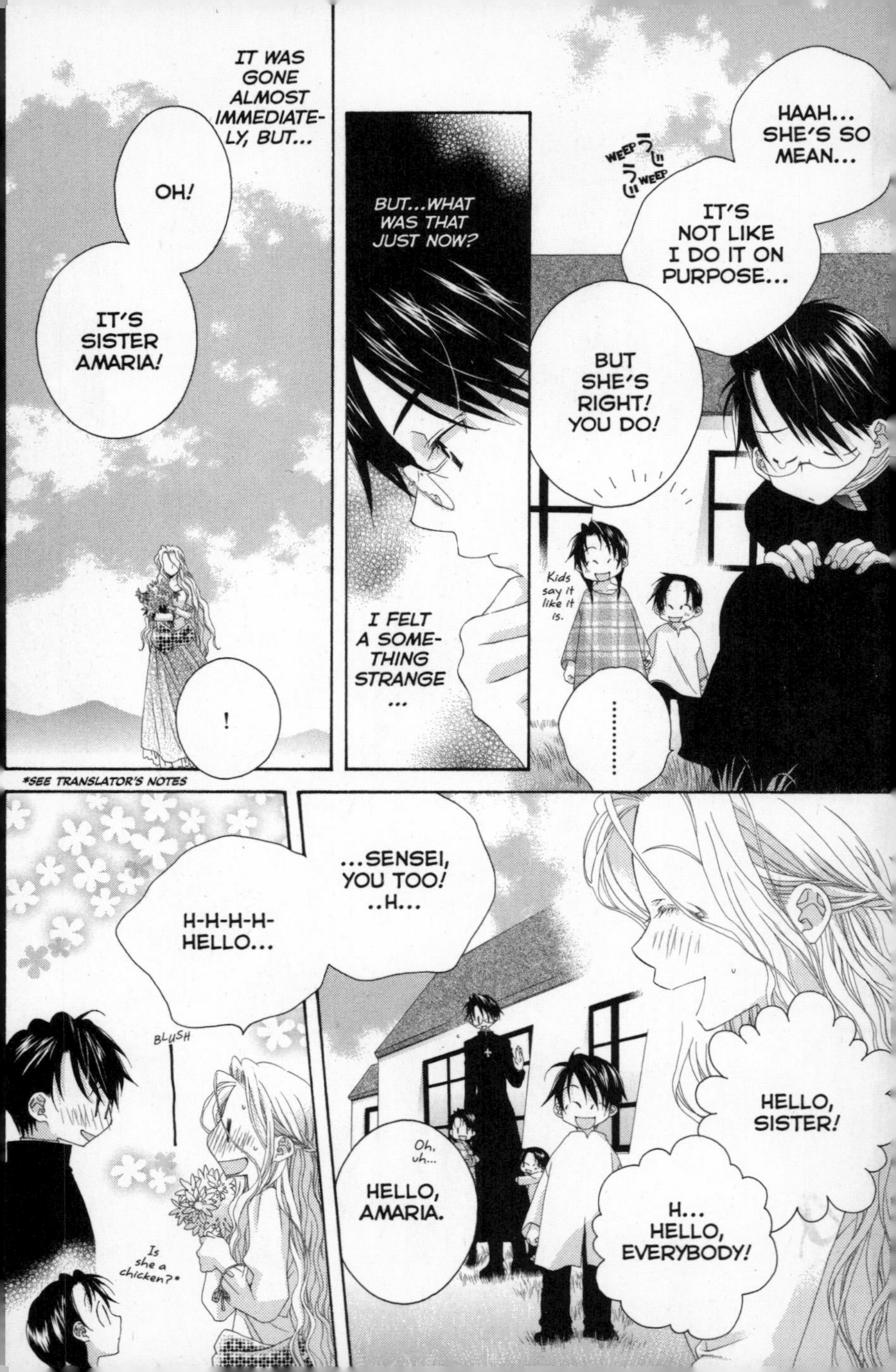
HAAH... SHE'S SO MEAN...
WEEP WEEP
IT'S NOT LIKE I DO IT ON PURPOSE...
BUT SHE'S RIGHT! YOU DO!
Kids say it like it is.
....
BUT...WHAT WAS THAT JUST NOW?
I FELT A SOMETHING STRANGE ...
IT WAS GONE ALMOST IMMEDIATELY, BUT...
OH!
IT'S SISTER AMARIA!
!
HELLO, SISTER!
H... HELLO, EVERYBODY!
Oh, uh...
HELLO, AMARIA.
...SENSEI, YOU TOO! ..H...
H-H-H-H-HELLO...
BLUSH
Is she a chicken?*

*SEE TRANSLATOR'S NOTES

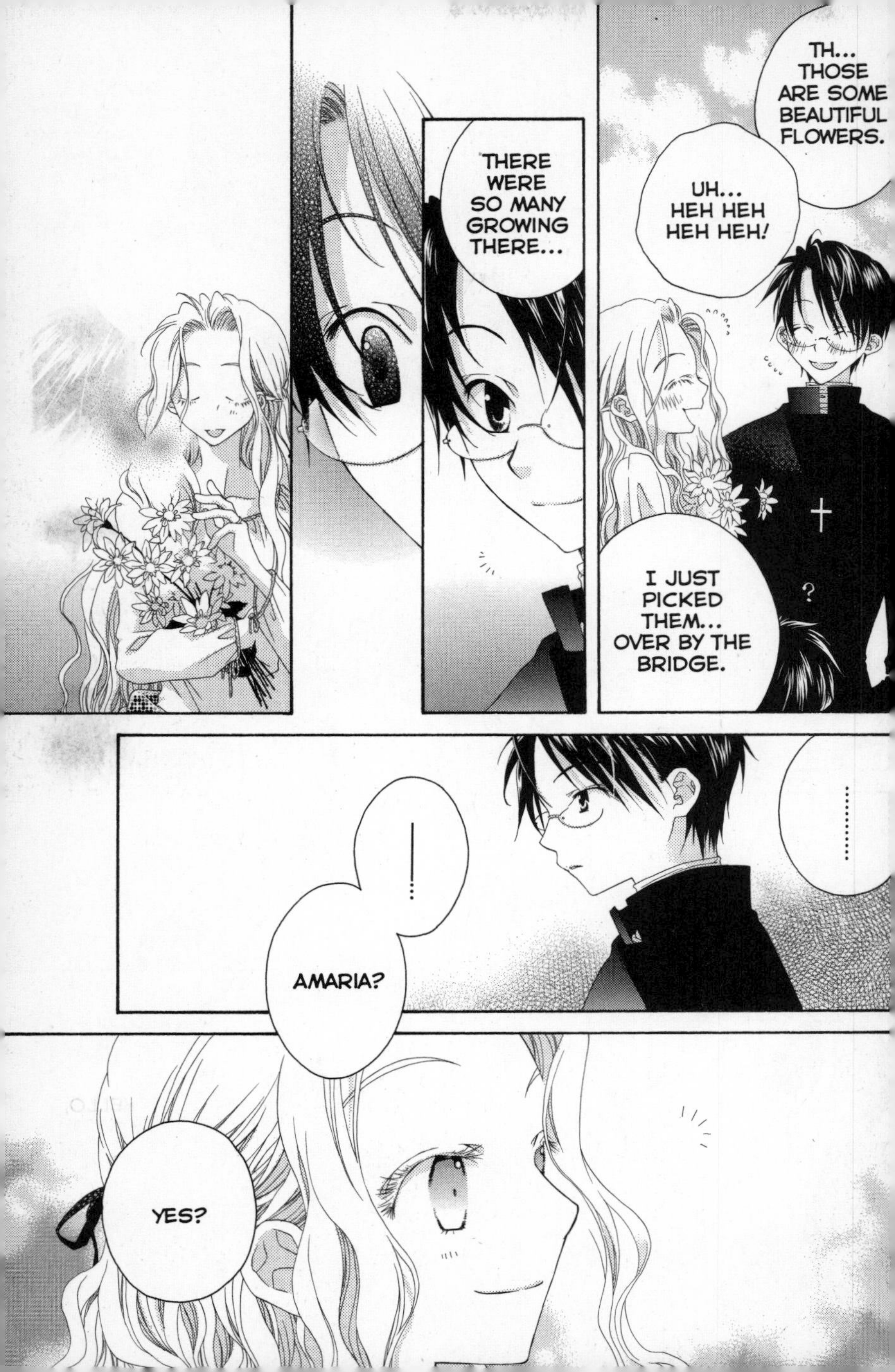
TH... THOSE ARE SOME BEAUTIFUL FLOWERS.
UH... HEH HEH HEH HEH!
I JUST PICKED THEM... OVER BY THE BRIDGE.
THERE WERE SO MANY GROWING THERE...
......
—...
AMARIA?
YES?

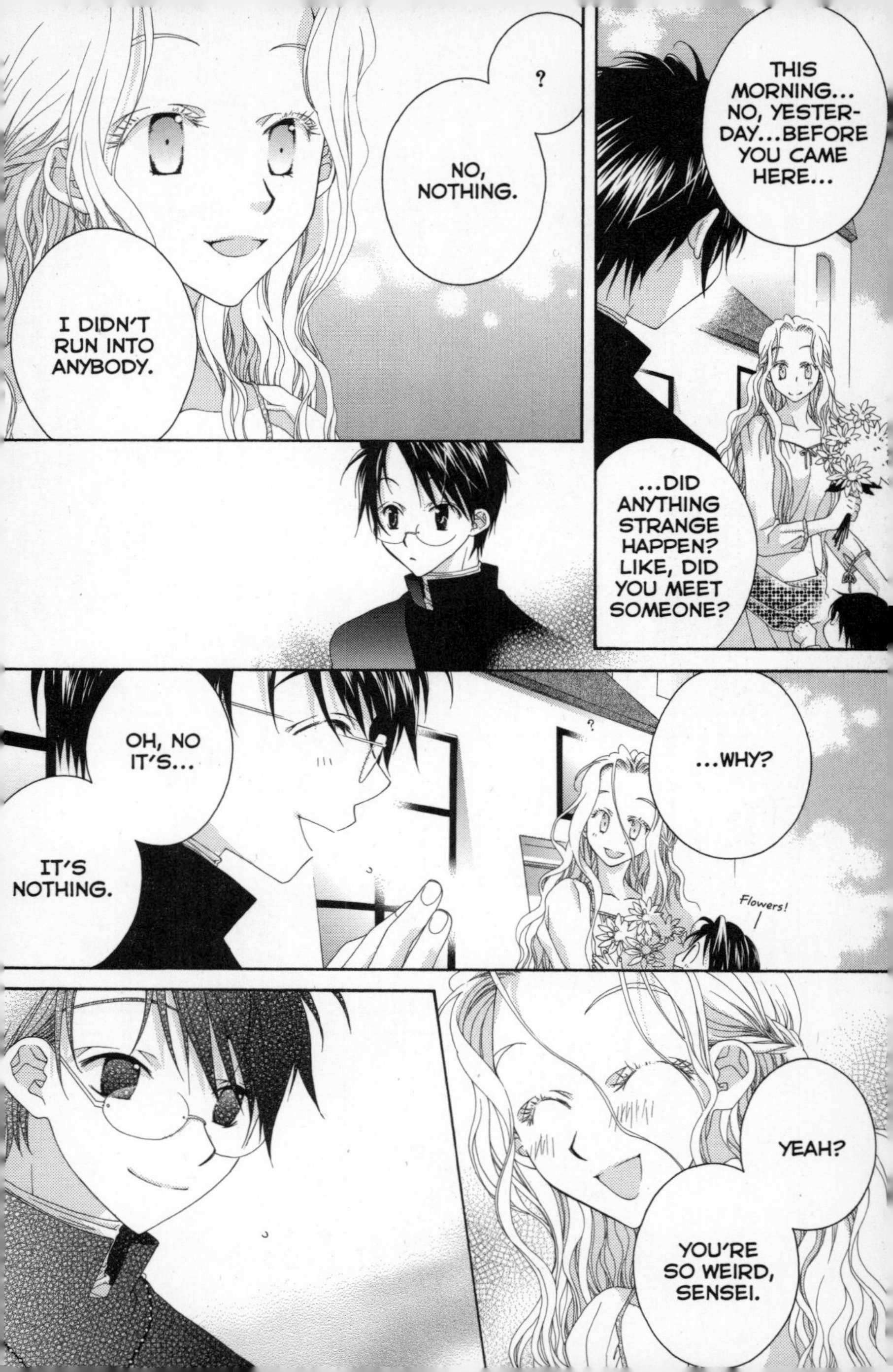
THIS MORNING... NO, YESTER-DAY...BEFORE YOU CAME HERE...
...DID ANYTHING STRANGE HAPPEN? LIKE, DID YOU MEET SOMEONE?
?
NO, NOTHING.
I DIDN'T RUN INTO ANYBODY.
?
...WHY?
Flowers!
OH, NO IT'S...
IT'S NOTHING.
YEAH?
YOU'RE SO WEIRD, SENSEI.

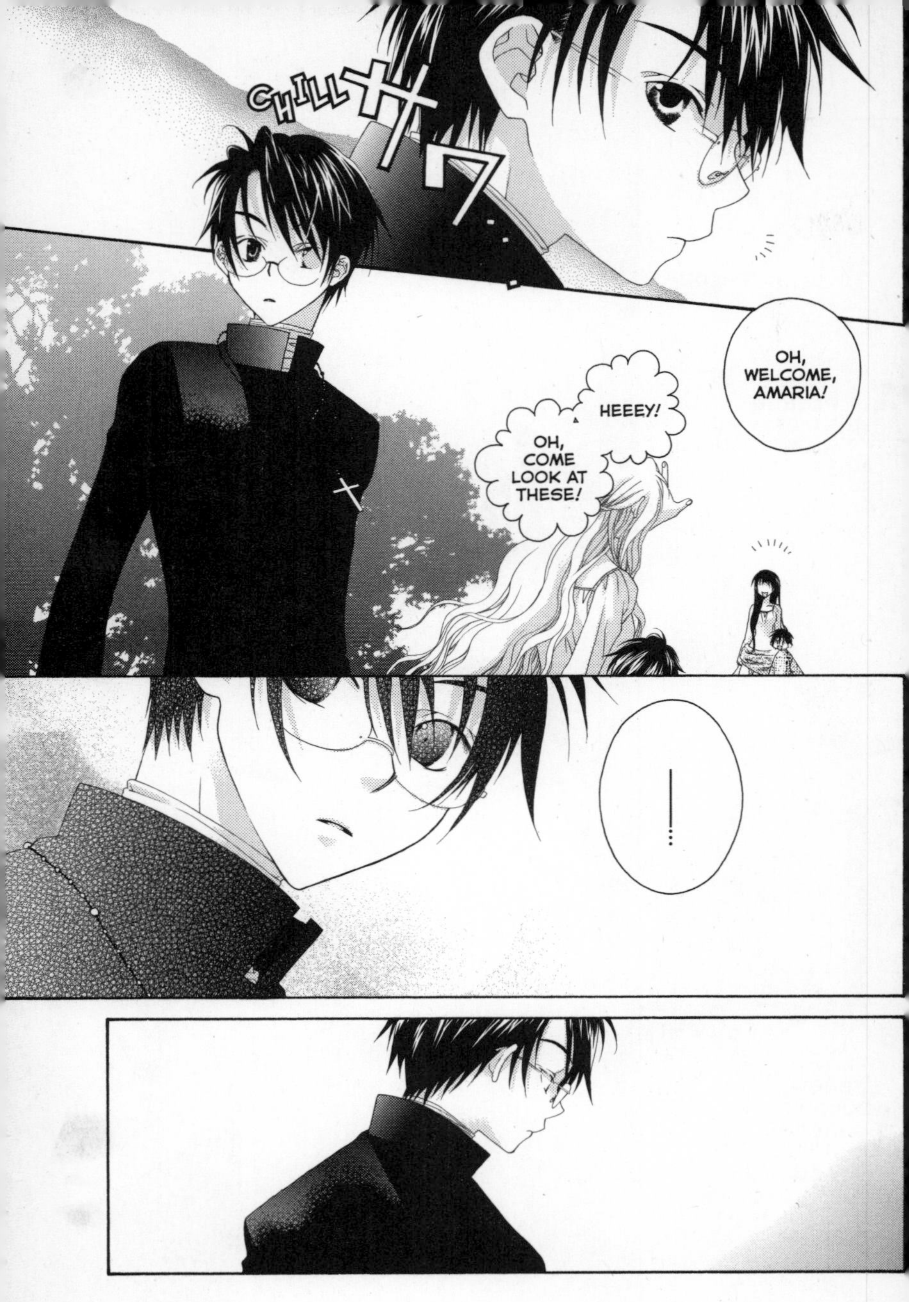
CHILL
OH, WELCOME, AMARIA!
HEEEY!
OH, COME LOOK AT THESE!
—...

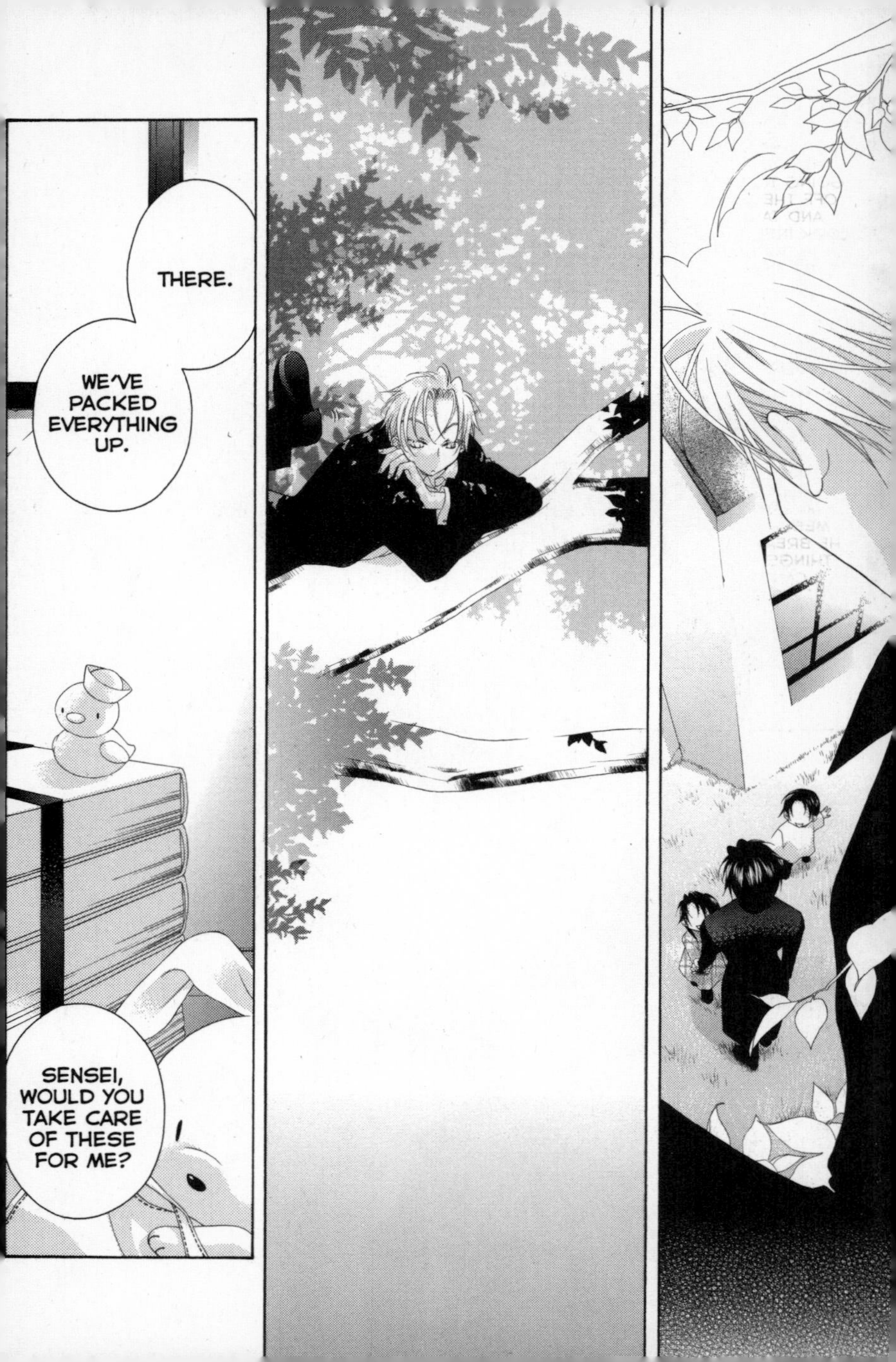
THERE.
WE'VE PACKED EVERYTHING UP.
SENSEI, WOULD YOU TAKE CARE OF THESE FOR ME?

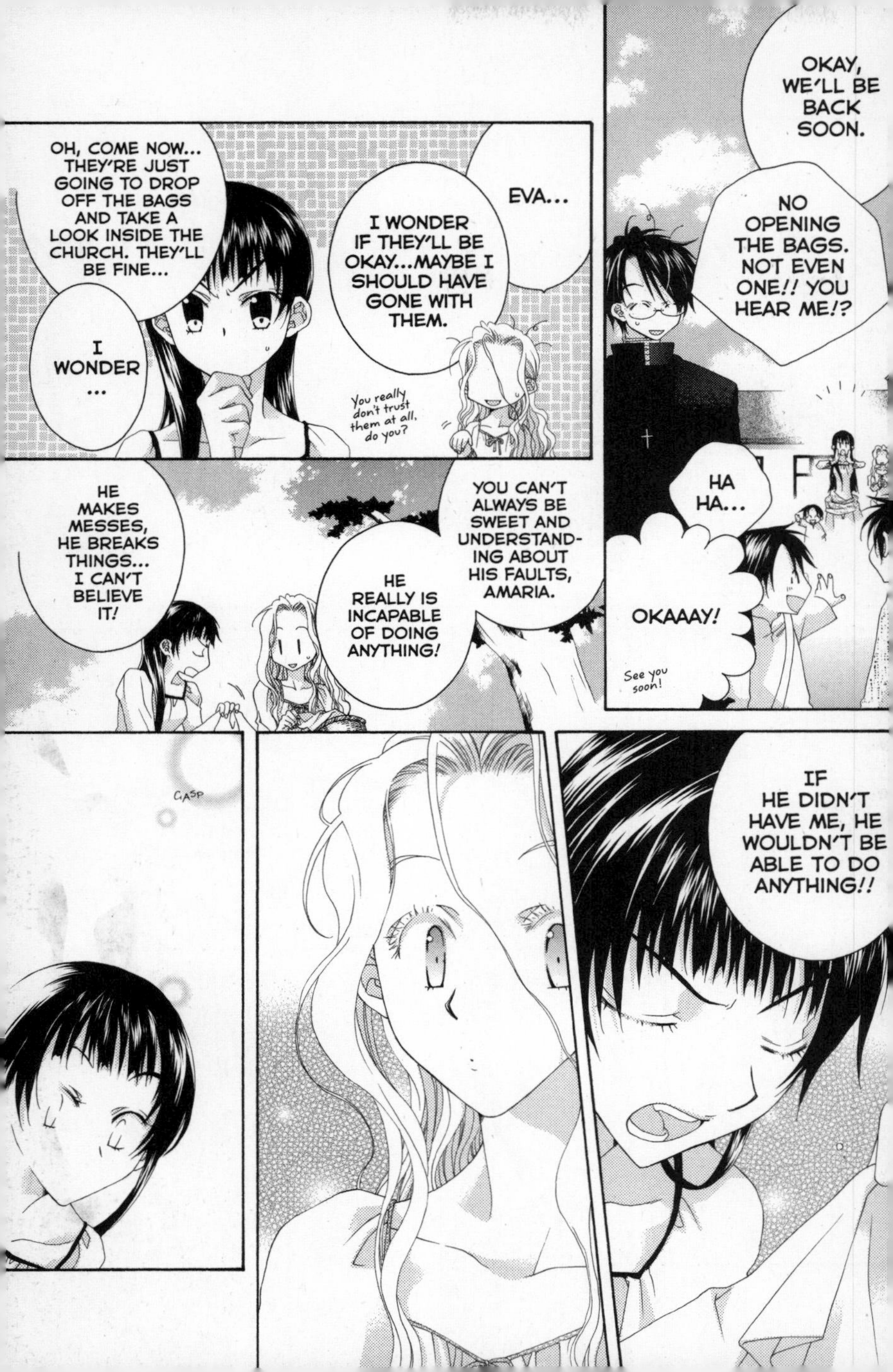
OKAY, WE'LL BE BACK SOON.
NO OPENING THE BAGS. NOT EVEN ONE!! YOU HEAR ME!?
HA HA...
OKAAAY!
See you soon!
EVA...
I WONDER IF THEY'LL BE OKAY...MAYBE I SHOULD HAVE GONE WITH THEM.
OH, COME NOW... THEY'RE JUST GOING TO DROP OFF THE BAGS AND TAKE A LOOK INSIDE THE CHURCH. THEY'LL BE FINE...
I WONDER...
You really don't trust them at all, do you?
YOU CAN'T ALWAYS BE SWEET AND UNDERSTANDING ABOUT HIS FAULTS, AMARIA.
HE MAKES MESSES, HE BREAKS THINGS... I CAN'T BELIEVE IT!
HE REALLY IS INCAPABLE OF DOING ANYTHING!
IF HE DIDN'T HAVE ME, HE WOULDN'T BE ABLE TO DO ANYTHING!!
GASP

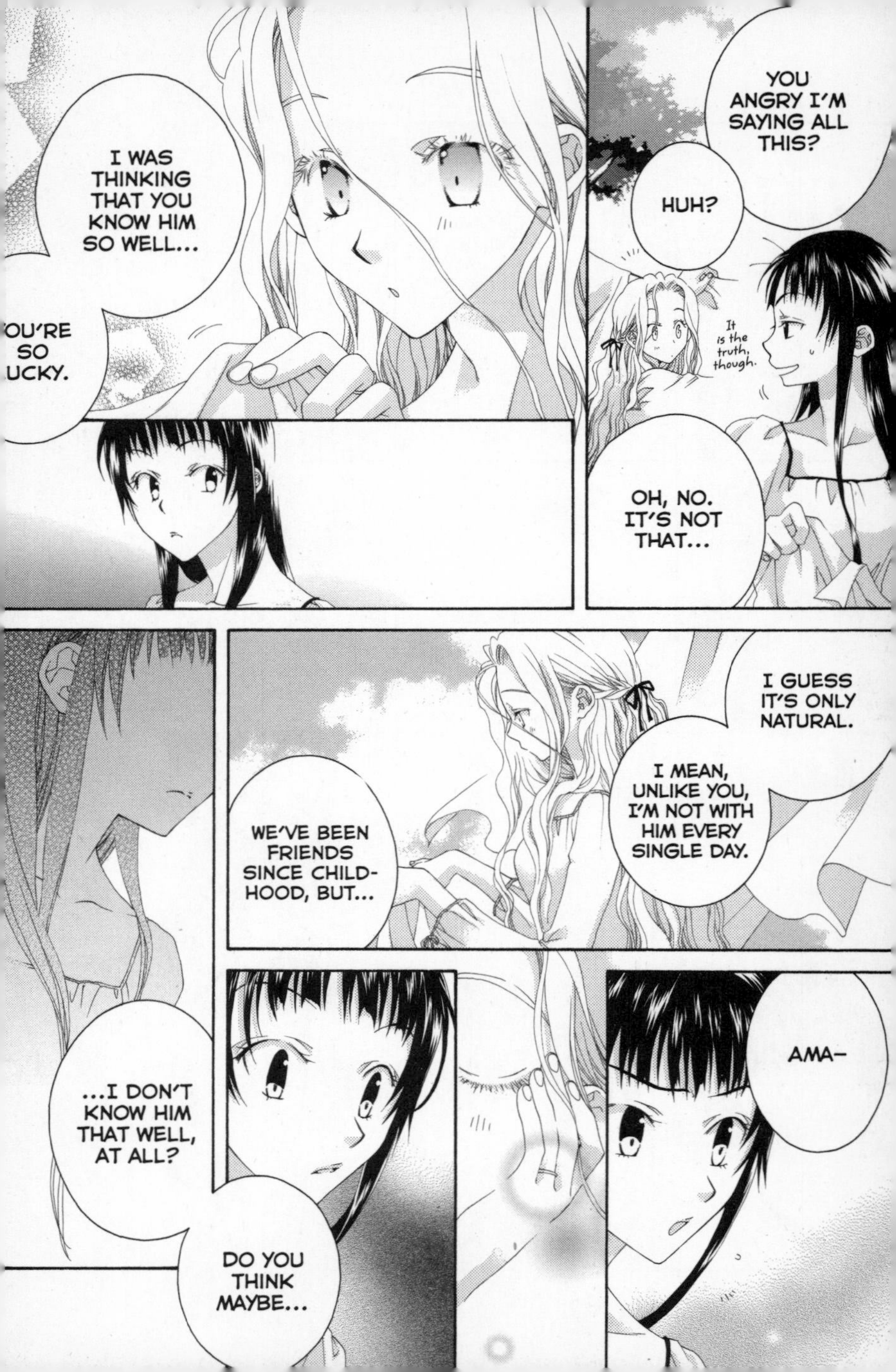
YOU ANGRY I'M SAYING ALL THIS?
HUH?
It is the truth, though.
OH, NO. IT'S NOT THAT...
I WAS THINKING THAT YOU KNOW HIM SO WELL...
OU'RE SO UCKY.
I GUESS IT'S ONLY NATURAL.
I MEAN, UNLIKE YOU, I'M NOT WITH HIM EVERY SINGLE DAY.
WE'VE BEEN FRIENDS SINCE CHILD-HOOD, BUT...
AMA-
DO YOU THINK MAYBE...
...I DON'T KNOW HIM THAT WELL, AT ALL?

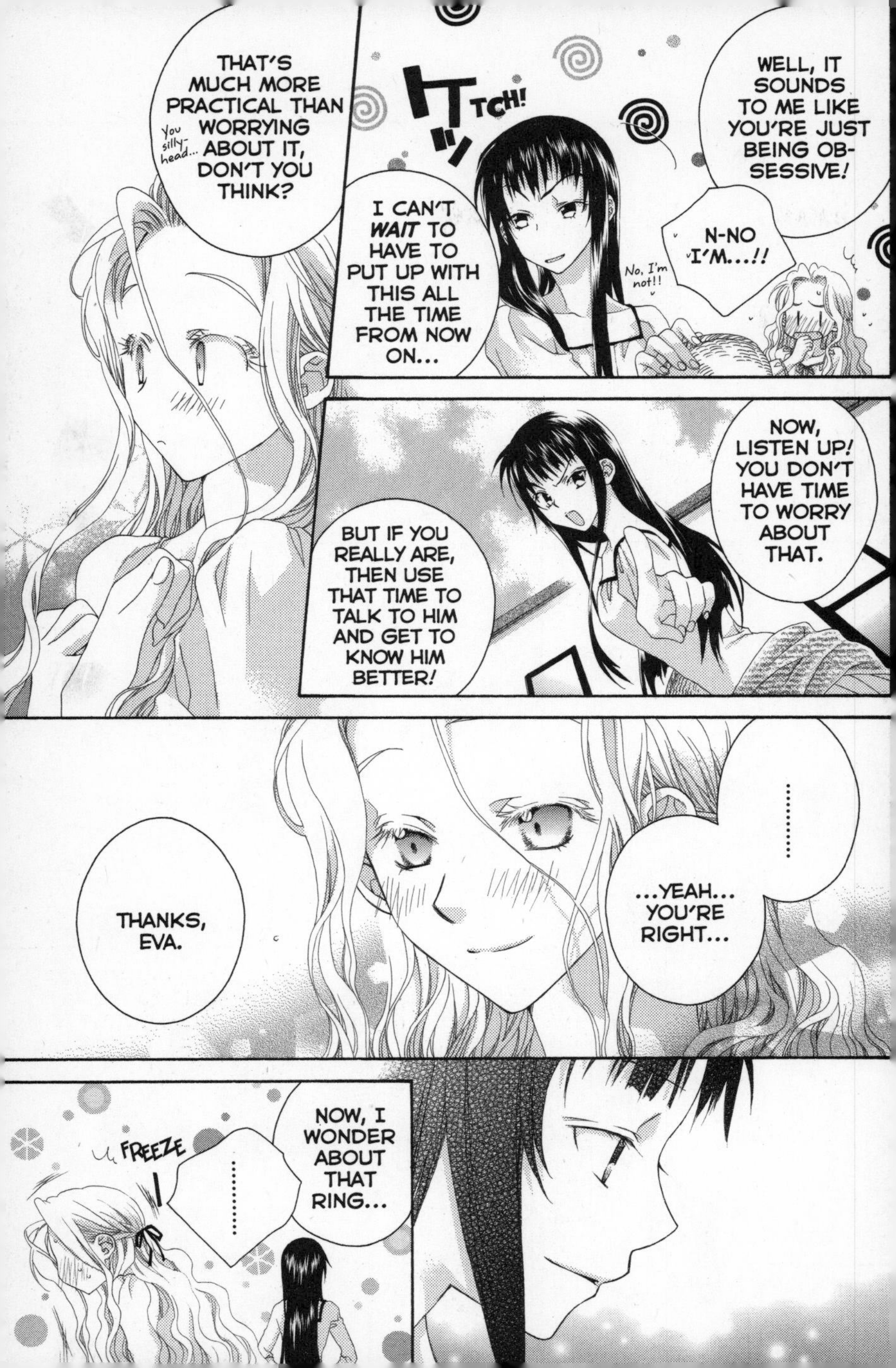
WELL, IT SOUNDS TO ME LIKE YOU'RE JUST BEING OB-SESSIVE!
N-NO I'M...!!
No, I'm not!!
TCH!
I CAN'T *WAIT* TO HAVE TO PUT UP WITH THIS ALL THE TIME FROM NOW ON...
NOW, LISTEN UP! YOU DON'T HAVE TIME TO WORRY ABOUT THAT.
BUT IF YOU REALLY ARE, THEN USE THAT TIME TO TALK TO HIM AND GET TO KNOW HIM BETTER!
THAT'S MUCH MORE PRACTICAL THAN WORRYING ABOUT IT, DON'T YOU THINK?
You silly-head...
......
...YEAH... YOU'RE RIGHT...
THANKS, EVA.
NOW, I WONDER ABOUT THAT RING...
FREEZE
......

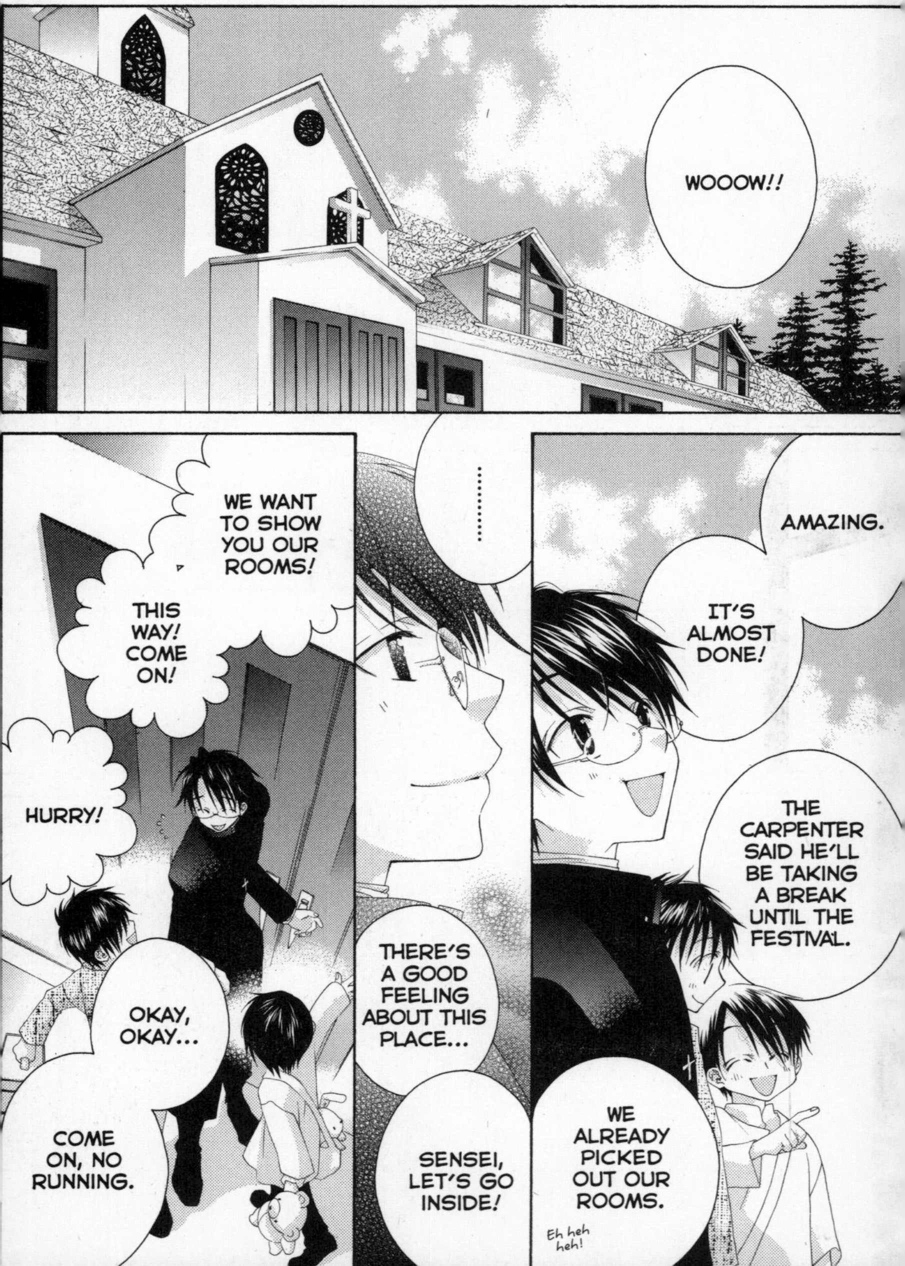
WOOOW!!
AMAZING.
IT'S ALMOST DONE!
THE CARPENTER SAID HE'LL BE TAKING A BREAK UNTIL THE FESTIVAL.
WE ALREADY PICKED OUT OUR ROOMS.
Eh heh heh!
....
THERE'S A GOOD FEELING ABOUT THIS PLACE...
SENSEI, LET'S GO INSIDE!
WE WANT TO SHOW YOU OUR ROOMS!
THIS WAY! COME ON!
HURRY!
OKAY, OKAY...
COME ON, NO RUNNING.

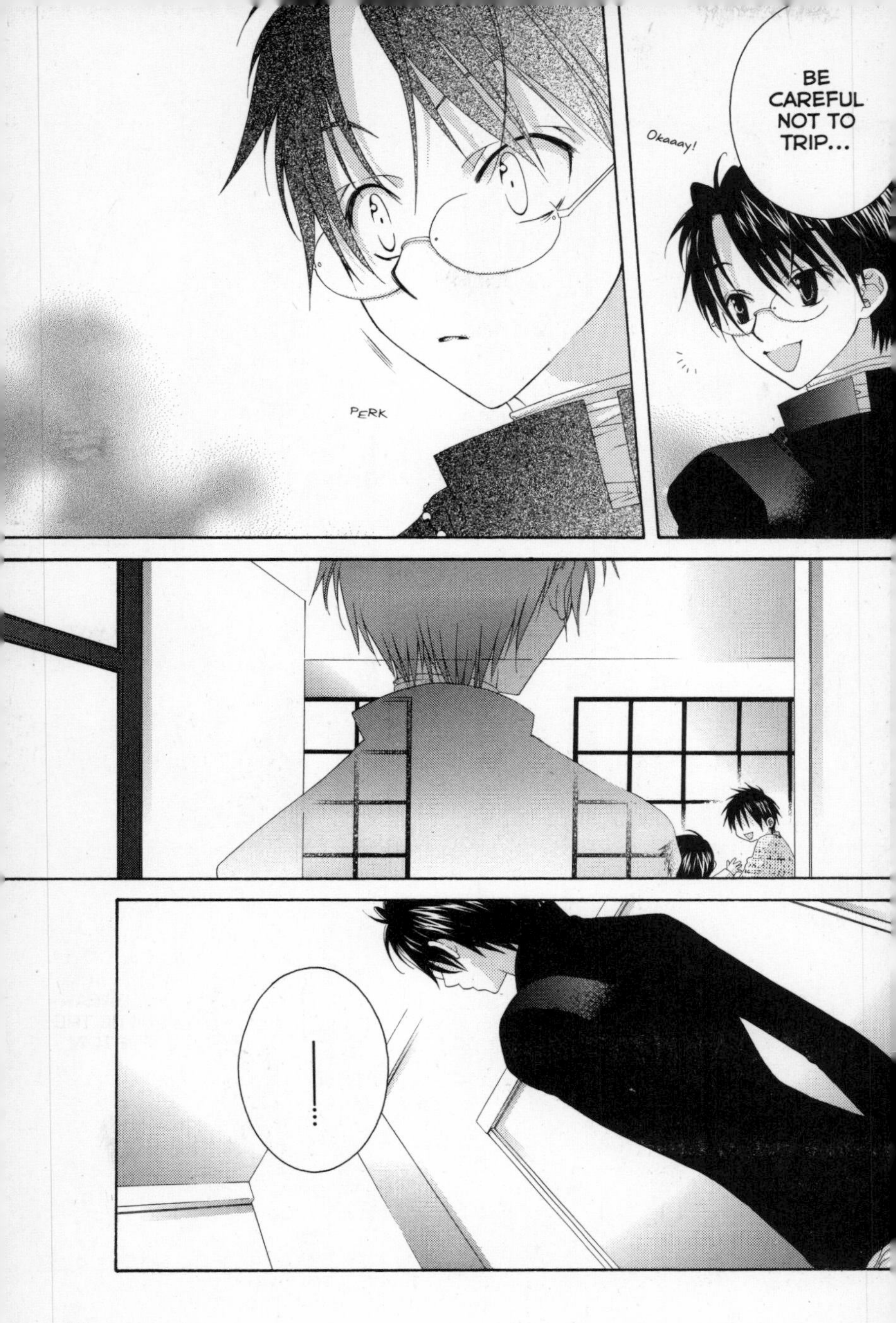
BE CAREFUL NOT TO TRIP...
Okaaay!
PERK
—...

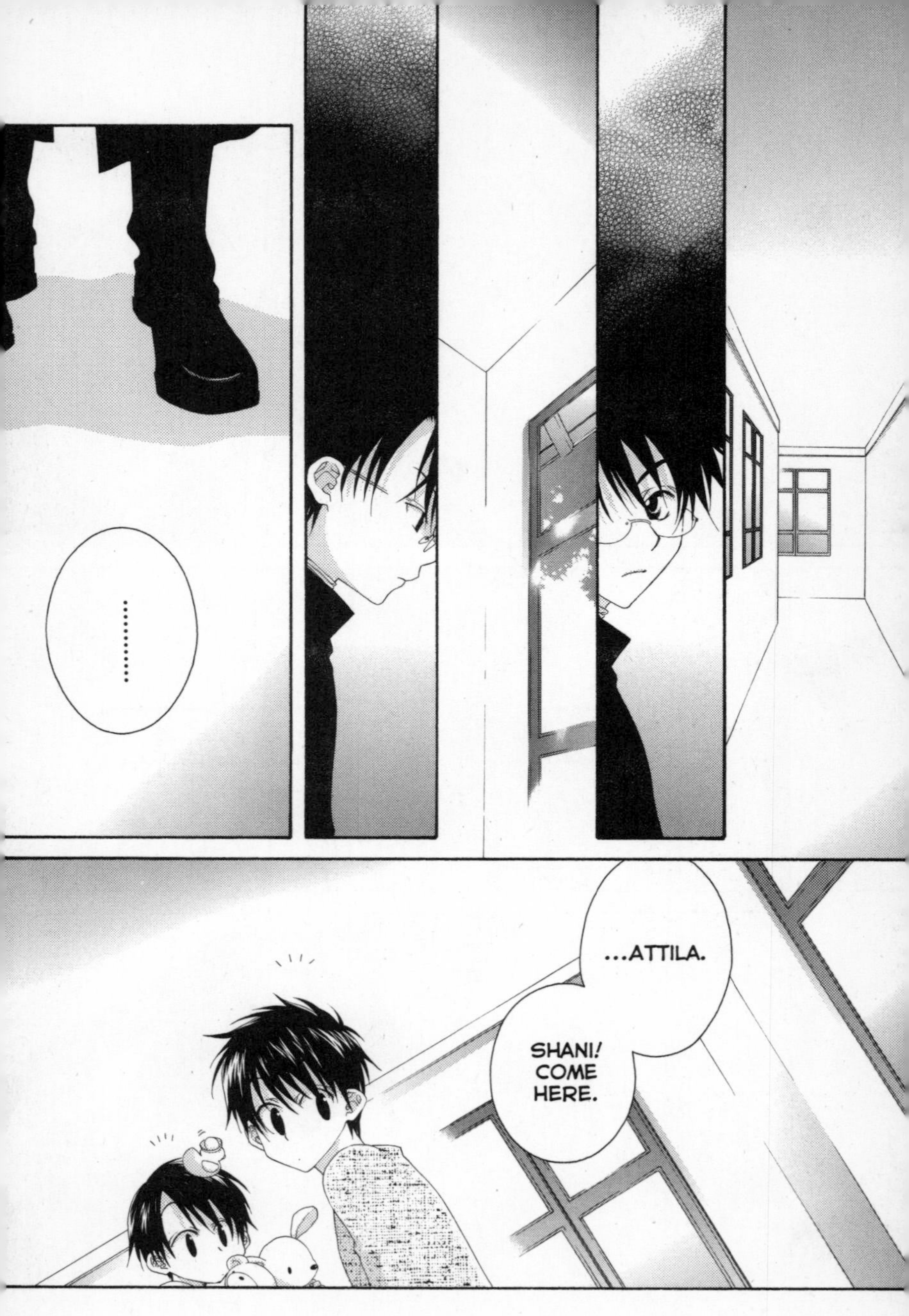

....
...ATTILA.
SHANI! COME HERE.

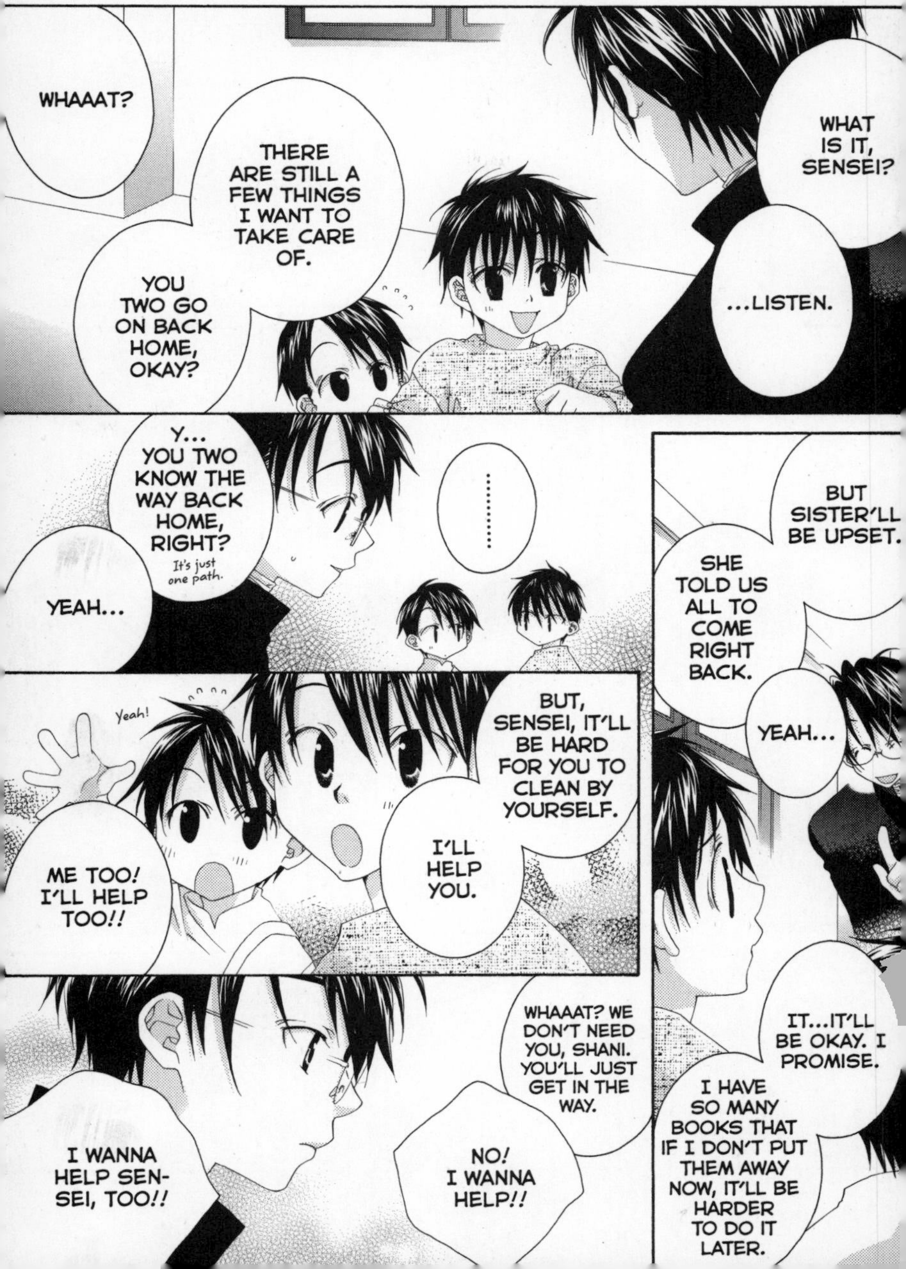
WHAT IS IT, SENSEI?
...LISTEN.
THERE ARE STILL A FEW THINGS I WANT TO TAKE CARE OF.
YOU TWO GO ON BACK HOME, OKAY?
WHAAAT?
BUT SISTER'LL BE UPSET.
SHE TOLD US ALL TO COME RIGHT BACK.
YEAH...
IT...IT'LL BE OKAY. I PROMISE.
I HAVE SO MANY BOOKS THAT IF I DON'T PUT THEM AWAY NOW, IT'LL BE HARDER TO DO IT LATER.
Y... YOU TWO KNOW THE WAY BACK HOME, RIGHT?
It's just one path.
......
YEAH...
BUT, SENSEI, IT'LL BE HARD FOR YOU TO CLEAN BY YOURSELF.
I'LL HELP YOU.
Yeah!
ME TOO! I'LL HELP TOO!!
WHAAAT? WE DON'T NEED YOU, SHANI. YOU'LL JUST GET IN THE WAY.
NO! I WANNA HELP!!
I WANNA HELP SEN-SEI, TOO!!

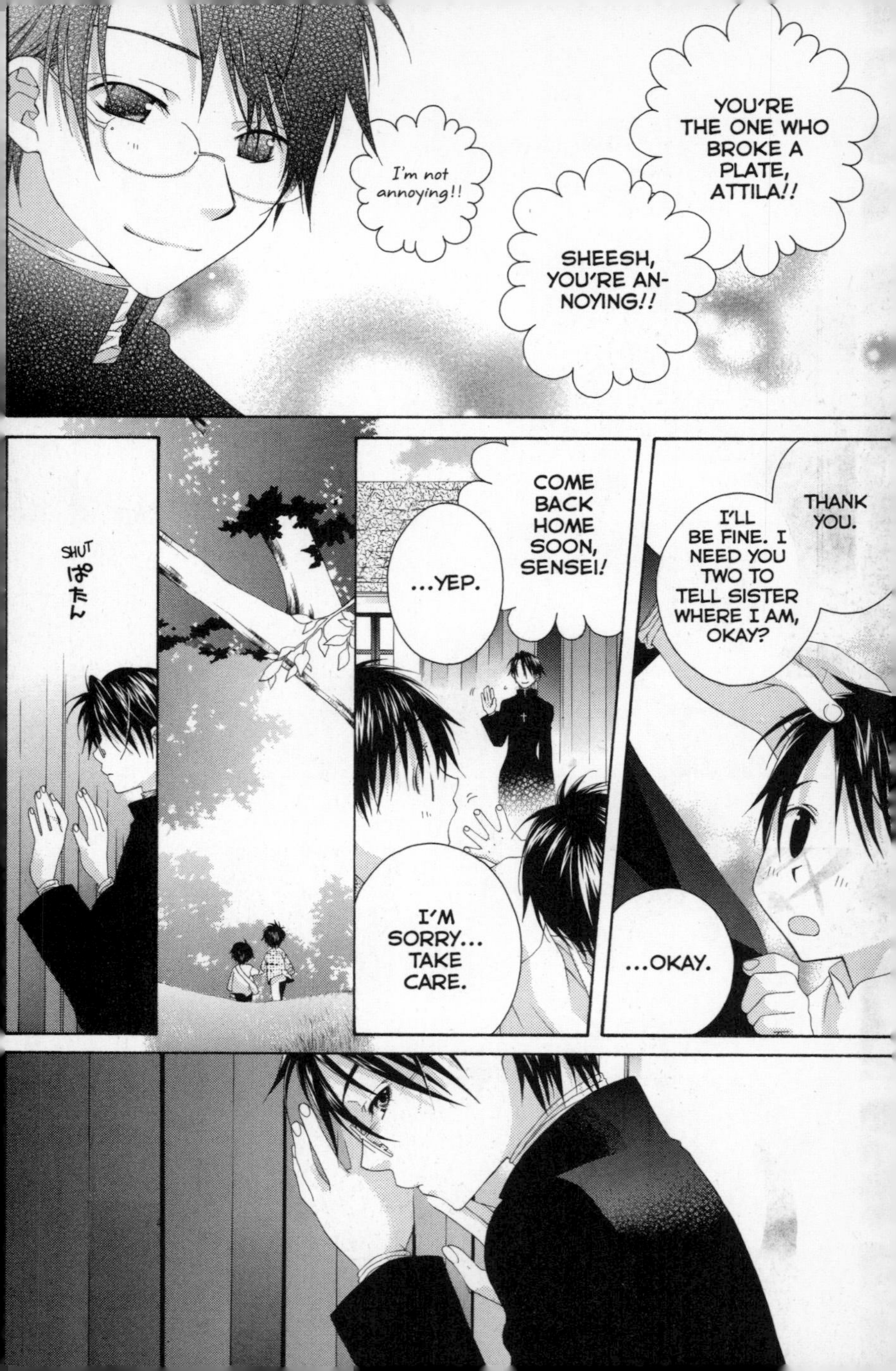
YOU'RE THE ONE WHO BROKE A PLATE, ATTILA!!
SHEESH, YOU'RE AN-NOYING!!
I'm not annoying!!
THANK YOU.
I'LL BE FINE. I NEED YOU TWO TO TELL SISTER WHERE I AM, OKAY?
...OKAY.
COME BACK HOME SOON, SENSEI!
...YEP.
I'M SORRY... TAKE CARE.
SHUT
ぱたん

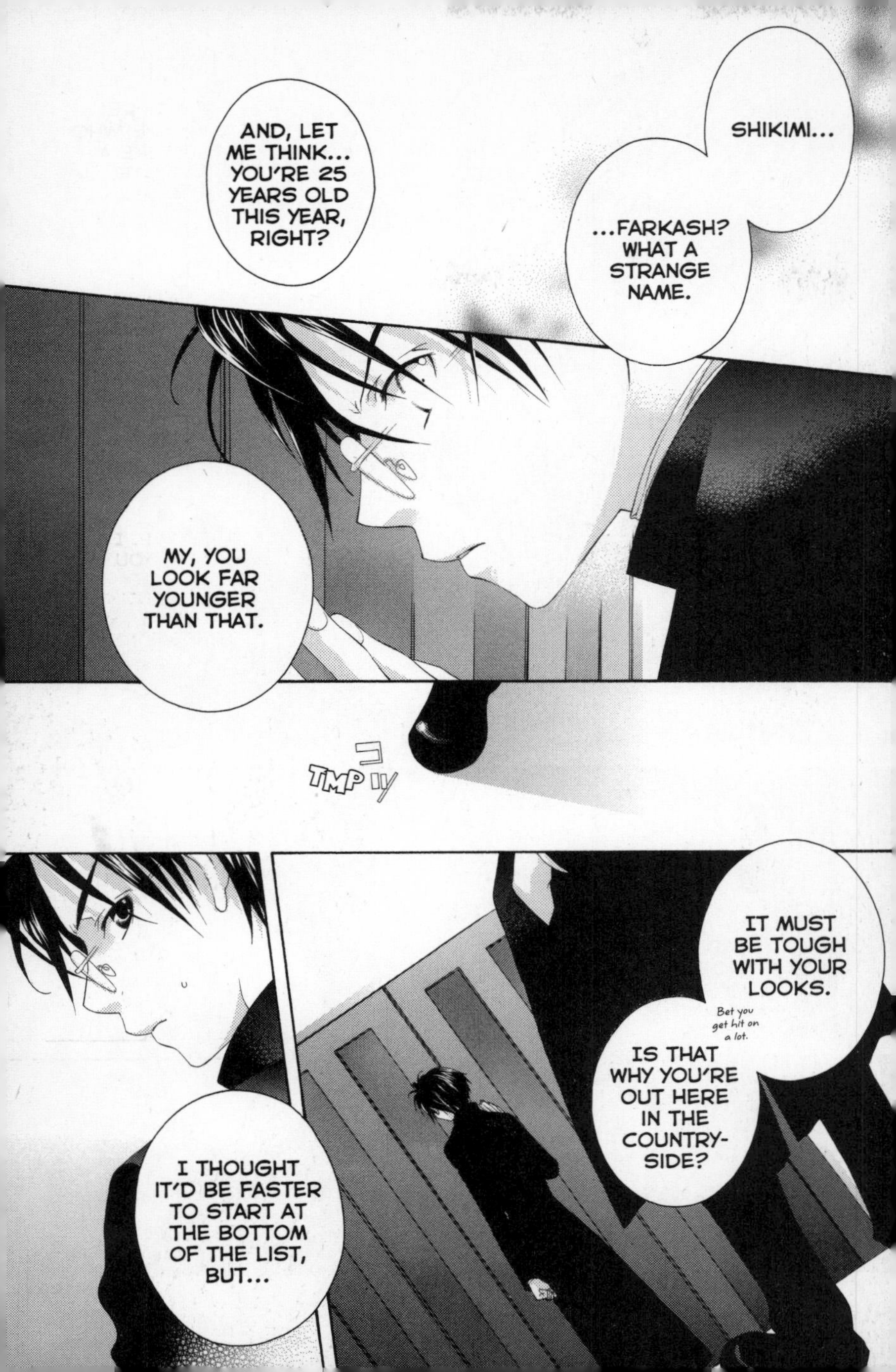
SHIKIMI...
...FARKASH? WHAT A STRANGE NAME.
AND, LET ME THINK... YOU'RE 25 YEARS OLD THIS YEAR, RIGHT?
MY, YOU LOOK FAR YOUNGER THAN THAT.
TMP
IT MUST BE TOUGH WITH YOUR LOOKS.
Bet you get hit on a lot.
IS THAT WHY YOU'RE OUT HERE IN THE COUNTRY-SIDE?
I THOUGHT IT'D BE FASTER TO START AT THE BOTTOM OF THE LIST, BUT...

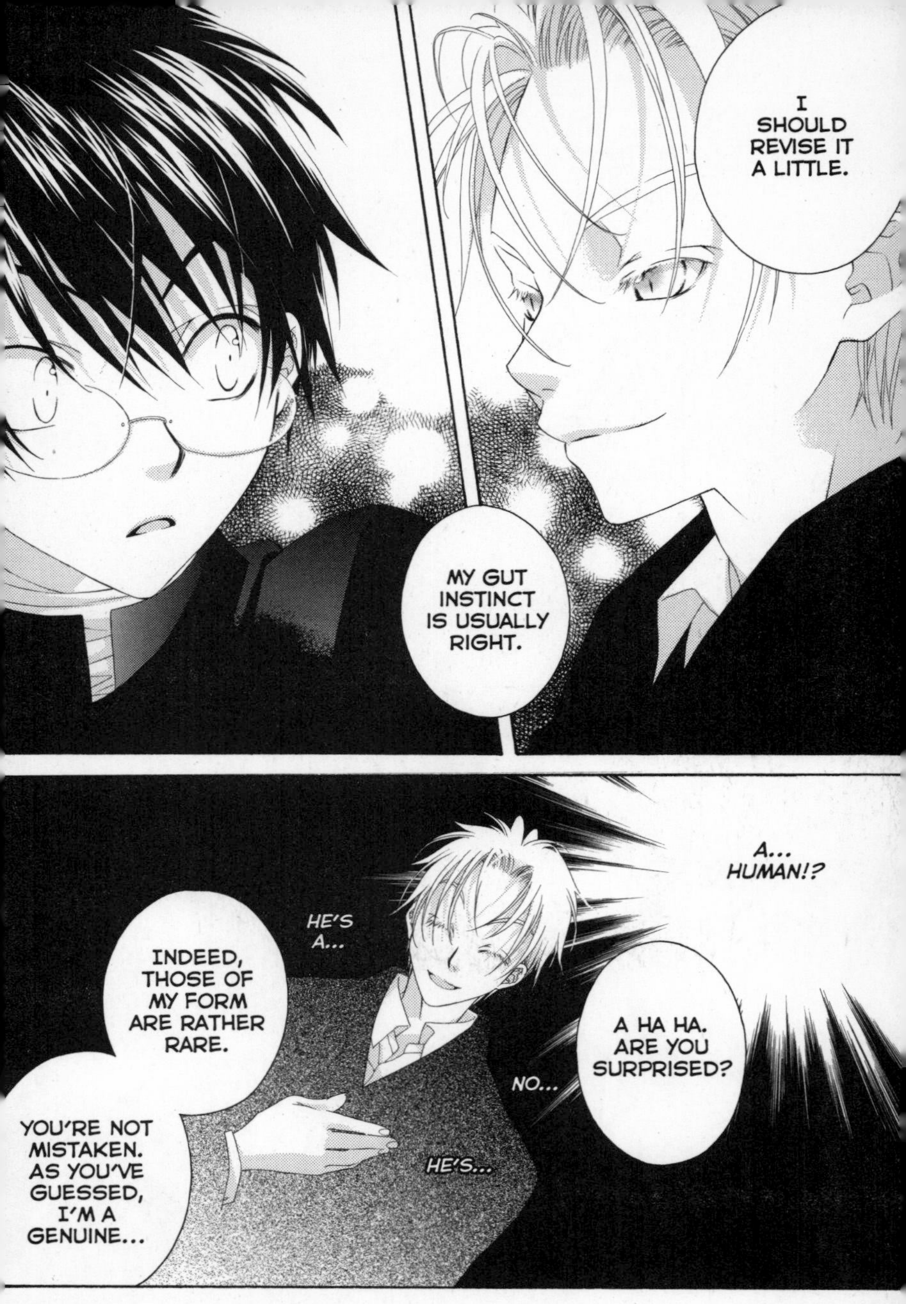
I SHOULD REVISE IT A LITTLE.
MY GUT INSTINCT IS USUALLY RIGHT.
A... HUMAN!?
A HA HA. ARE YOU SURPRISED?
NO...
HE'S...
HE'S A...
YOU'RE NOT MISTAKEN. AS YOU'VE GUESSED, I'M A GENUINE...
INDEED, THOSE OF MY FORM ARE RATHER RARE.

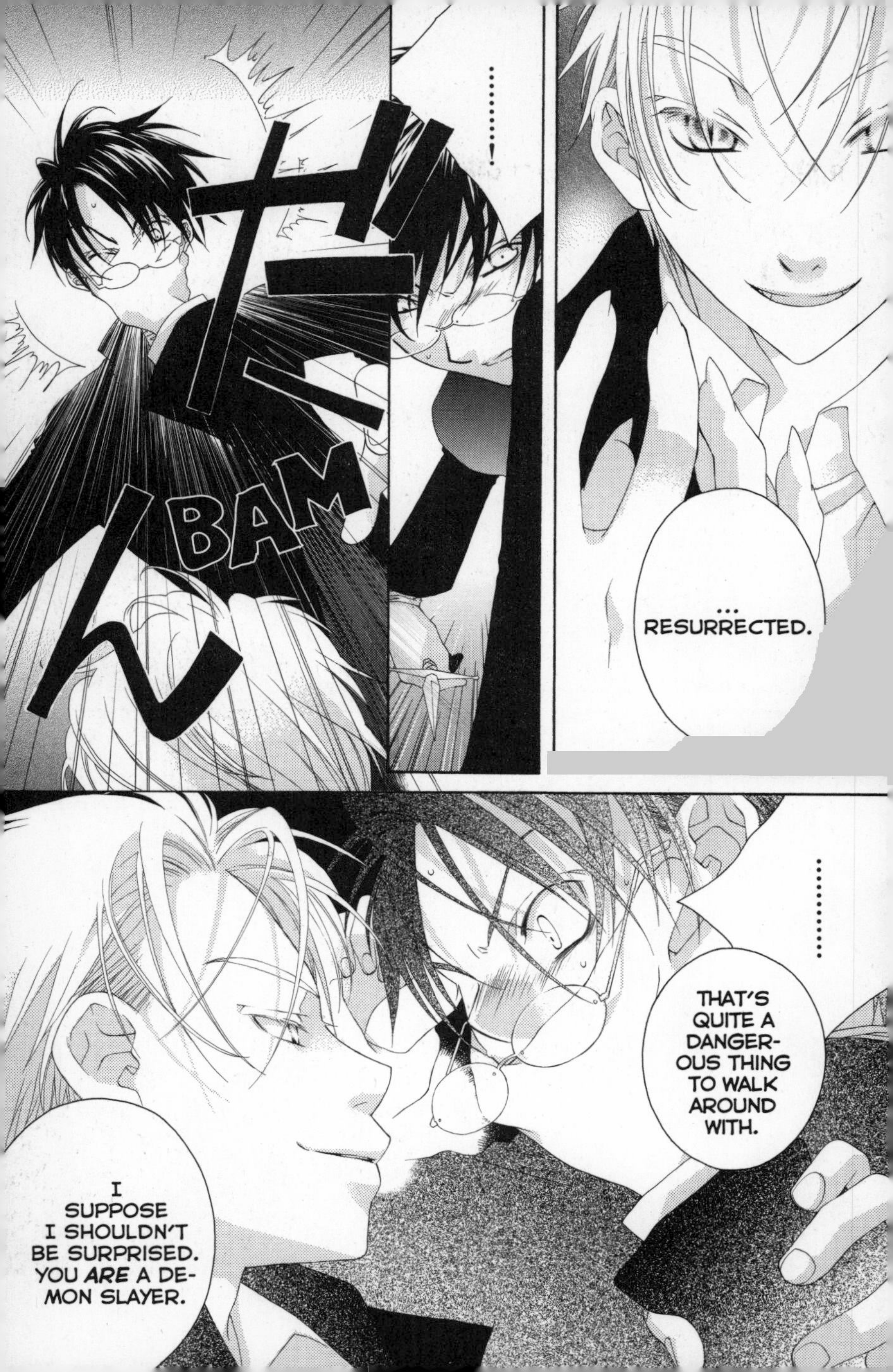
...RESURRECTED.
......!
BAM
....
THAT'S QUITE A DANGER-OUS THING TO WALK AROUND WITH.
I SUPPOSE I SHOULDN'T BE SURPRISED. YOU *ARE* A DE-MON SLAYER.

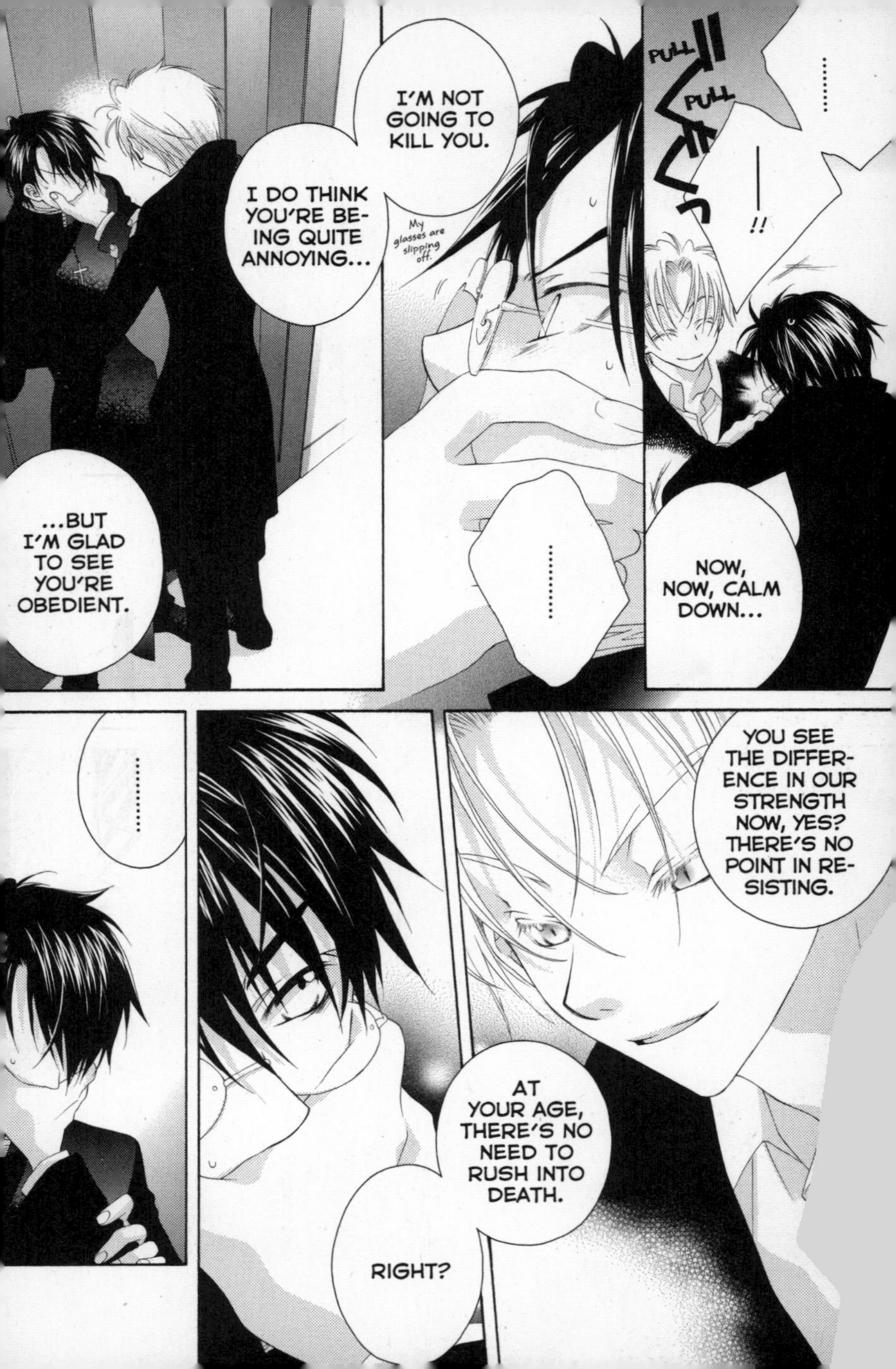

......
PULL
PULL
——!!
NOW, NOW, CALM DOWN...
I'M NOT GOING TO KILL YOU.
My glasses are slipping off.
I DO THINK YOU'RE BE-ING QUITE ANNOYING...
....
...BUT I'M GLAD TO SEE YOU'RE OBEDIENT.
YOU SEE THE DIFFER-ENCE IN OUR STRENGTH NOW, YES? THERE'S NO POINT IN RE-SISTING.
AT YOUR AGE, THERE'S NO NEED TO RUSH INTO DEATH.
RIGHT?
....

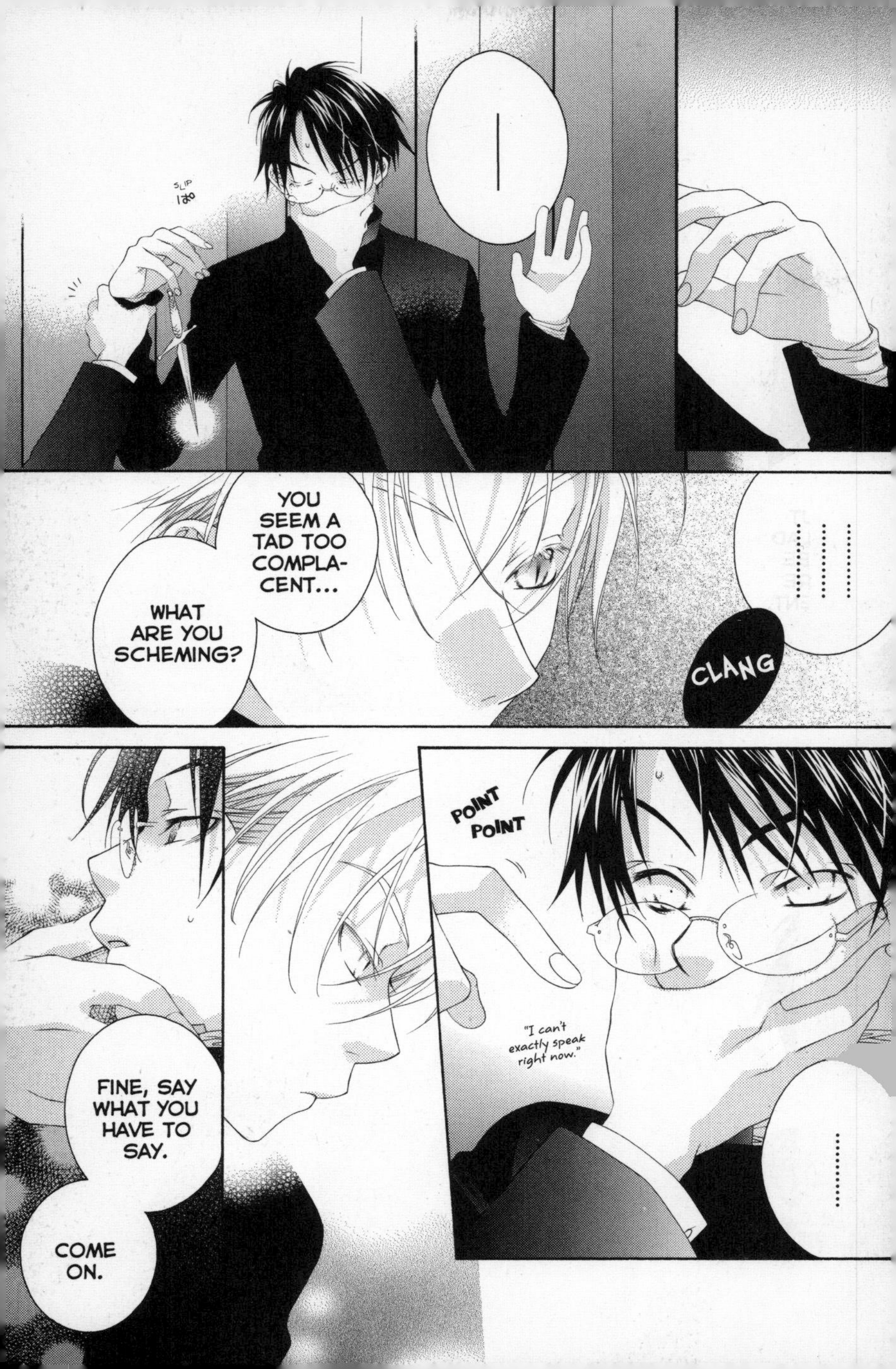
SLIP
......
CLANG
YOU SEEM A TAD TOO COMPLACENT...
WHAT ARE YOU SCHEMING?
POINT POINT
"I can't exactly speak right now."
......
FINE, SAY WHAT YOU HAVE TO SAY.
COME ON.

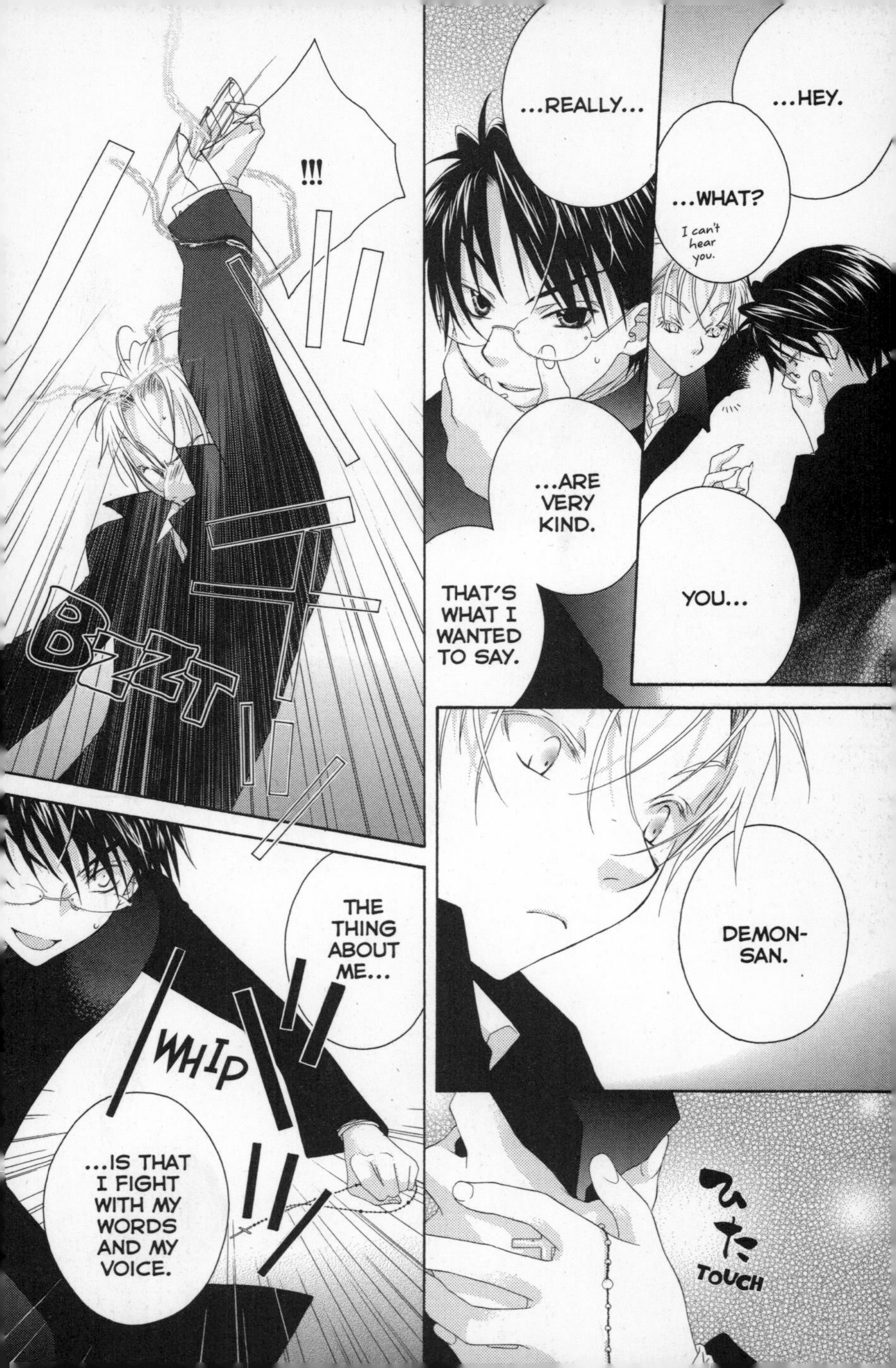
...HEY.
...WHAT?
I can't hear you.
YOU...
...REALLY...
...ARE VERY KIND.
THAT'S WHAT I WANTED TO SAY.
!!!
BZZT
DEMON-SAN.
TOUCH
THE THING ABOUT ME...
...IS THAT I FIGHT WITH MY WORDS AND MY VOICE.
WHIP

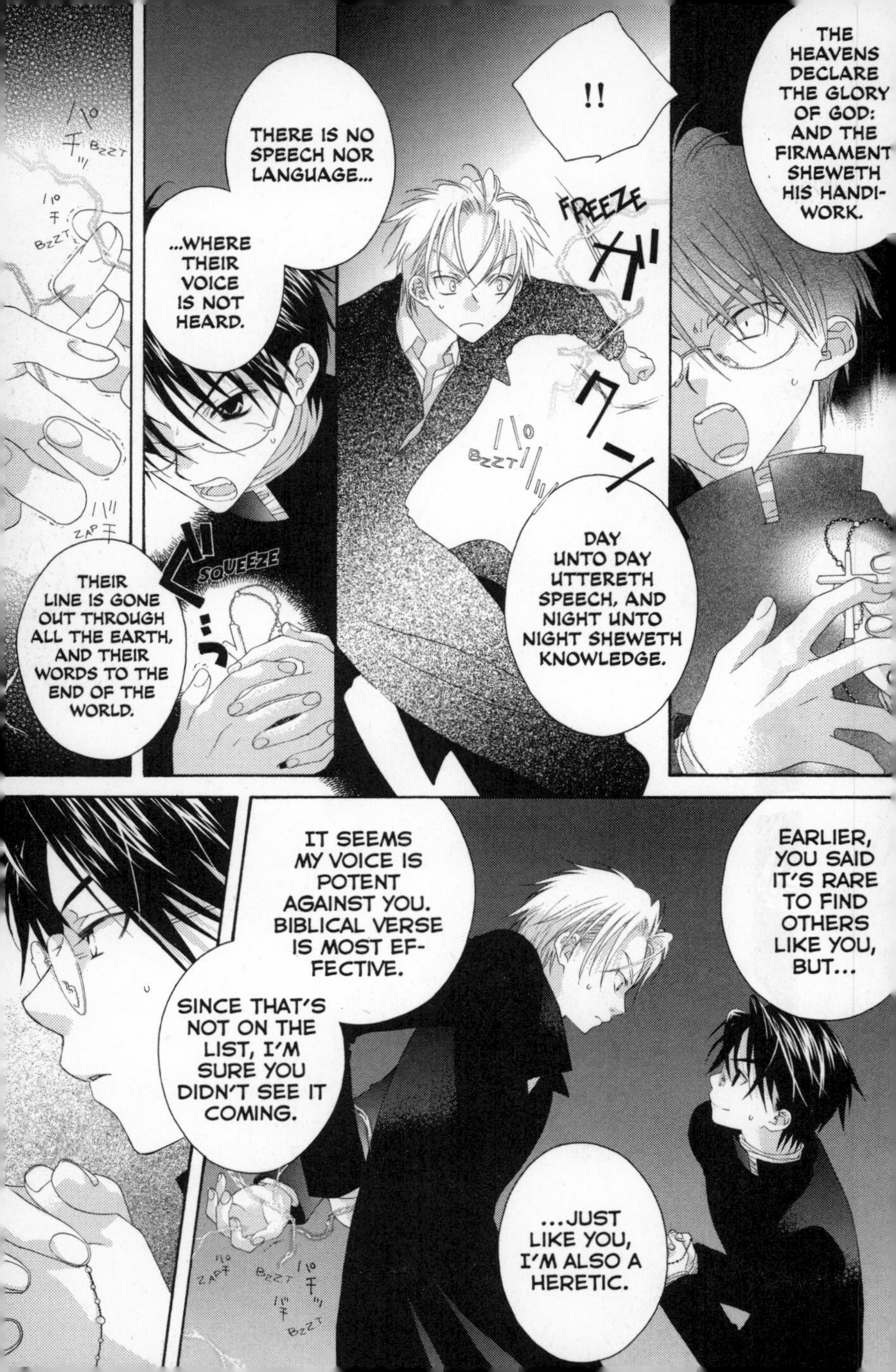

THE HEAVENS DECLARE THE GLORY OF GOD: AND THE FIRMAMENT SHEWETH HIS HANDI-WORK.
!!
FREEZE
BZZT
DAY UNTO DAY UTTERETH SPEECH, AND NIGHT UNTO NIGHT SHEWETH KNOWLEDGE.
THERE IS NO SPEECH NOR LANGUAGE...
...WHERE THEIR VOICE IS NOT HEARD.
SQUEEZE
THEIR LINE IS GONE OUT THROUGH ALL THE EARTH, AND THEIR WORDS TO THE END OF THE WORLD.
BZZT
BZZT
ZAP
EARLIER, YOU SAID IT'S RARE TO FIND OTHERS LIKE YOU, BUT...
IT SEEMS MY VOICE IS POTENT AGAINST YOU. BIBLICAL VERSE IS MOST EF-FECTIVE.
SINCE THAT'S NOT ON THE LIST, I'M SURE YOU DIDN'T SEE IT COMING.
...JUST LIKE YOU, I'M ALSO A HERETIC.
ZAP
BZZT
BZZT

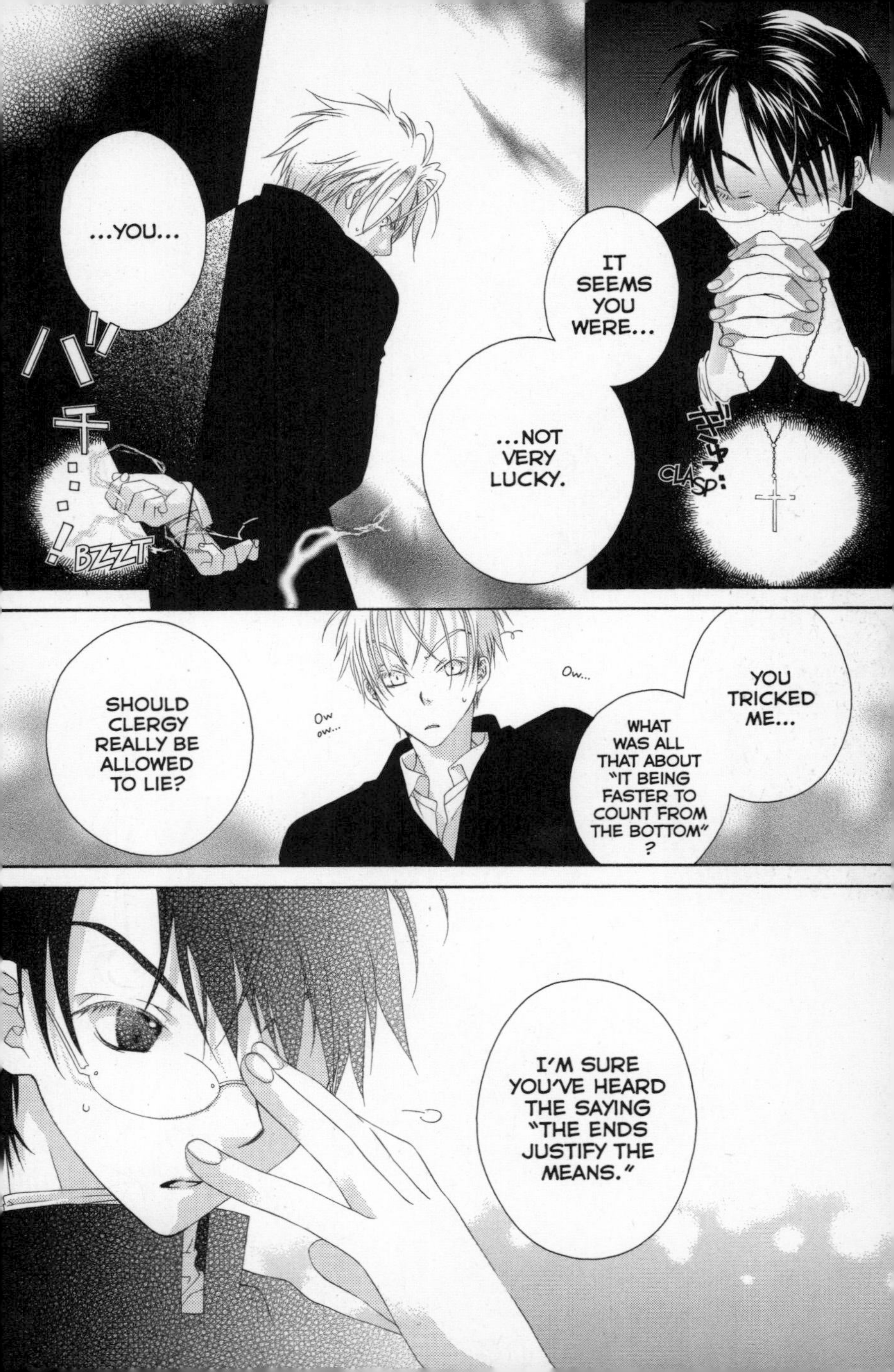

IT SEEMS YOU WERE...
...NOT VERY LUCKY.
CLASP
...YOU...
BZZZT
YOU TRICKED ME...
WHAT WAS ALL THAT ABOUT "IT BEING FASTER TO COUNT FROM THE BOTTOM"?
Ow...
Ow ow...
SHOULD CLERGY REALLY BE ALLOWED TO LIE?
I'M SURE YOU'VE HEARD THE SAYING "THE ENDS JUSTIFY THE MEANS."

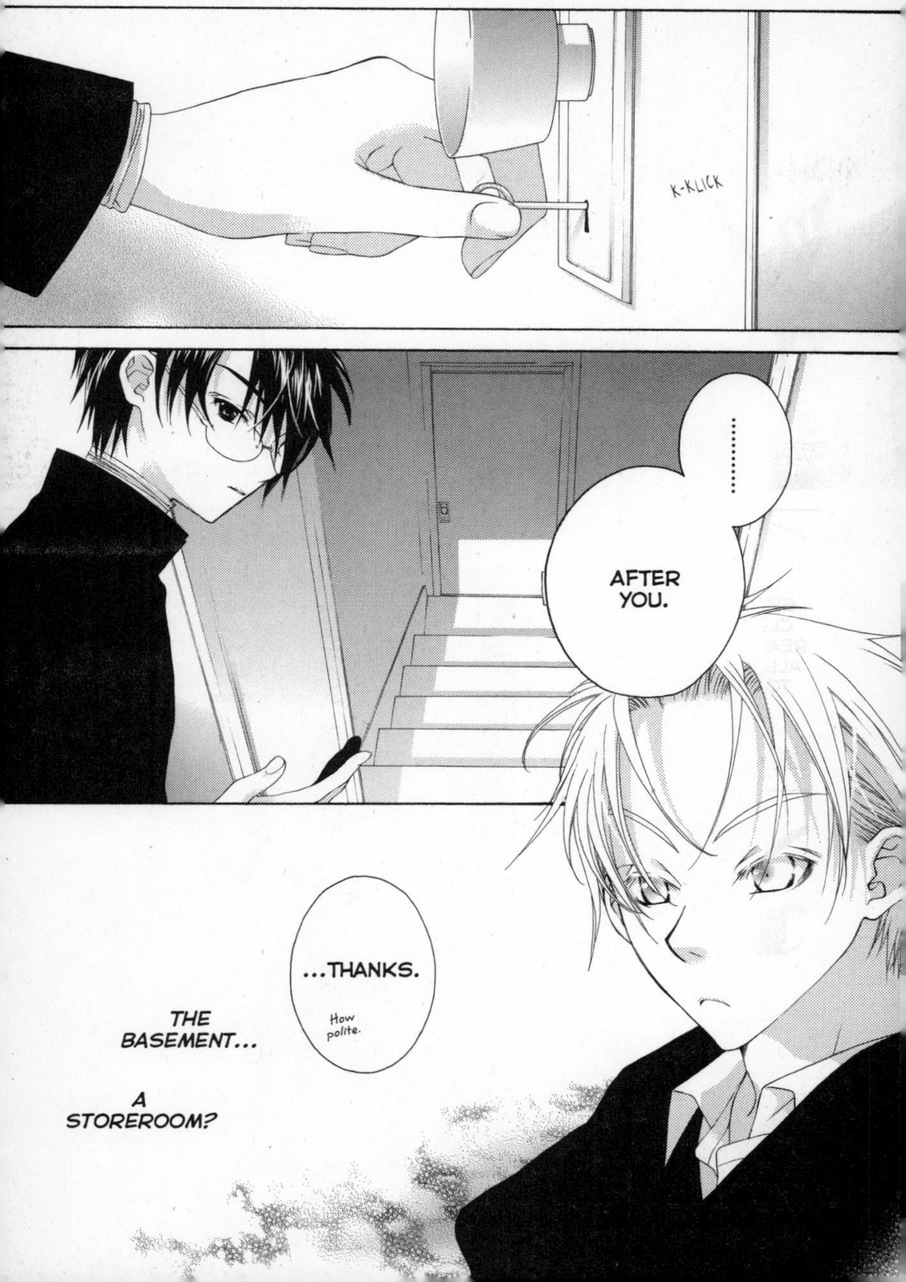
K-KLICK
......
AFTER YOU.
...THANKS.
How polite.
THE BASEMENT...
A STOREROOM?

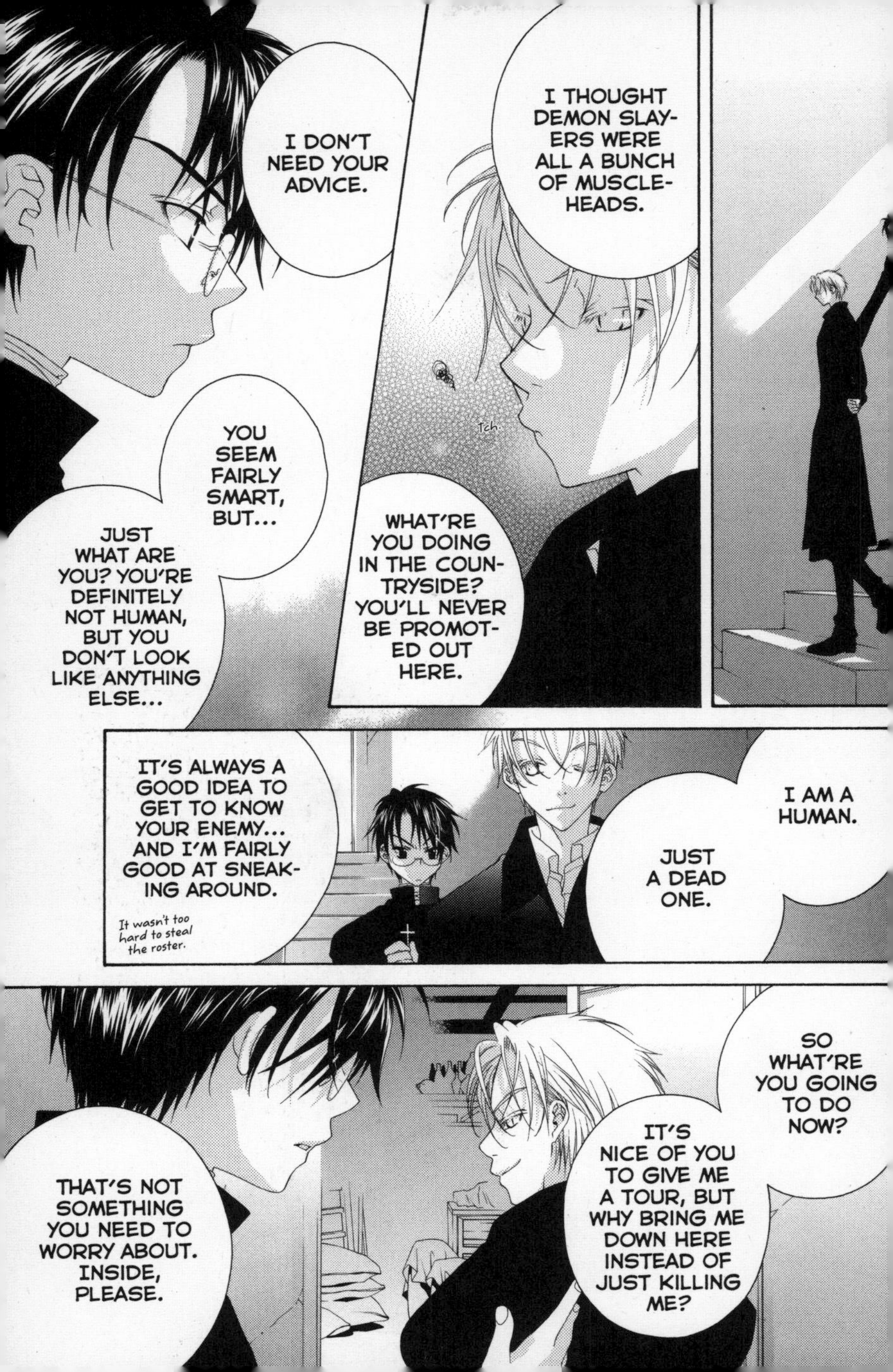
I THOUGHT DEMON SLAYERS WERE ALL A BUNCH OF MUSCLEHEADS.
Tch.
WHAT'RE YOU DOING IN THE COUNTRYSIDE? YOU'LL NEVER BE PROMOTED OUT HERE.
I DON'T NEED YOUR ADVICE.
YOU SEEM FAIRLY SMART, BUT...
JUST WHAT ARE YOU? YOU'RE DEFINITELY NOT HUMAN, BUT YOU DON'T LOOK LIKE ANYTHING ELSE...
I AM A HUMAN.
JUST A DEAD ONE.
IT'S ALWAYS A GOOD IDEA TO GET TO KNOW YOUR ENEMY... AND I'M FAIRLY GOOD AT SNEAKING AROUND.
It wasn't too hard to steal the roster.
SO WHAT'RE YOU GOING TO DO NOW?
IT'S NICE OF YOU TO GIVE ME A TOUR, BUT WHY BRING ME DOWN HERE INSTEAD OF JUST KILLING ME?
THAT'S NOT SOMETHING YOU NEED TO WORRY ABOUT. INSIDE, PLEASE.

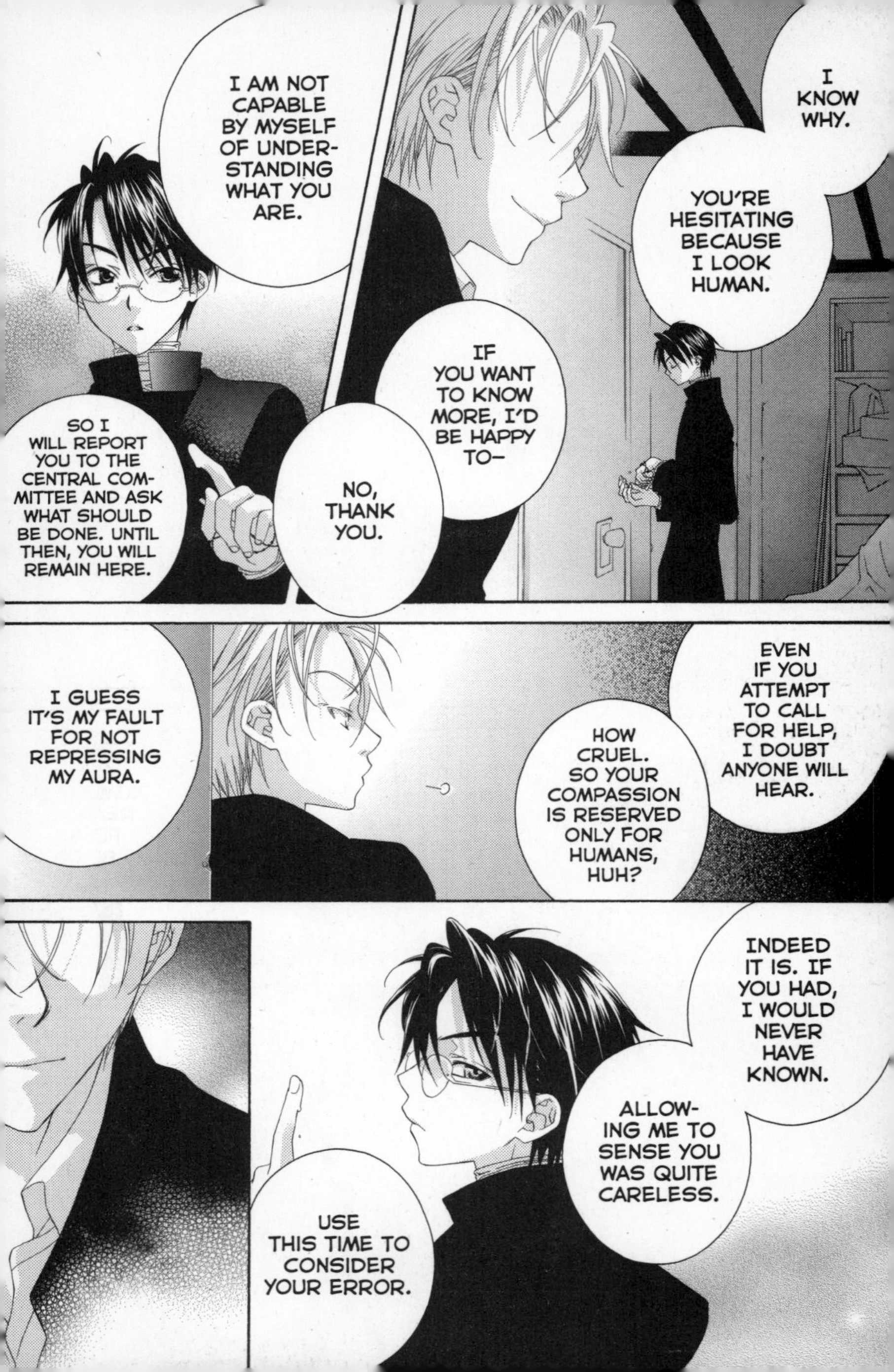
I KNOW WHY.
YOU'RE HESITATING BECAUSE I LOOK HUMAN.
IF YOU WANT TO KNOW MORE, I'D BE HAPPY TO–
NO, THANK YOU.
I AM NOT CAPABLE BY MYSELF OF UNDER-STANDING WHAT YOU ARE.
SO I WILL REPORT YOU TO THE CENTRAL COM-MITTEE AND ASK WHAT SHOULD BE DONE. UNTIL THEN, YOU WILL REMAIN HERE.
EVEN IF YOU ATTEMPT TO CALL FOR HELP, I DOUBT ANYONE WILL HEAR.
HOW CRUEL. SO YOUR COMPASSION IS RESERVED ONLY FOR HUMANS, HUH?
I GUESS IT'S MY FAULT FOR NOT REPRESSING MY AURA.
INDEED IT IS. IF YOU HAD, I WOULD NEVER HAVE KNOWN.
ALLOW-ING ME TO SENSE YOU WAS QUITE CARELESS.
USE THIS TIME TO CONSIDER YOUR ERROR.

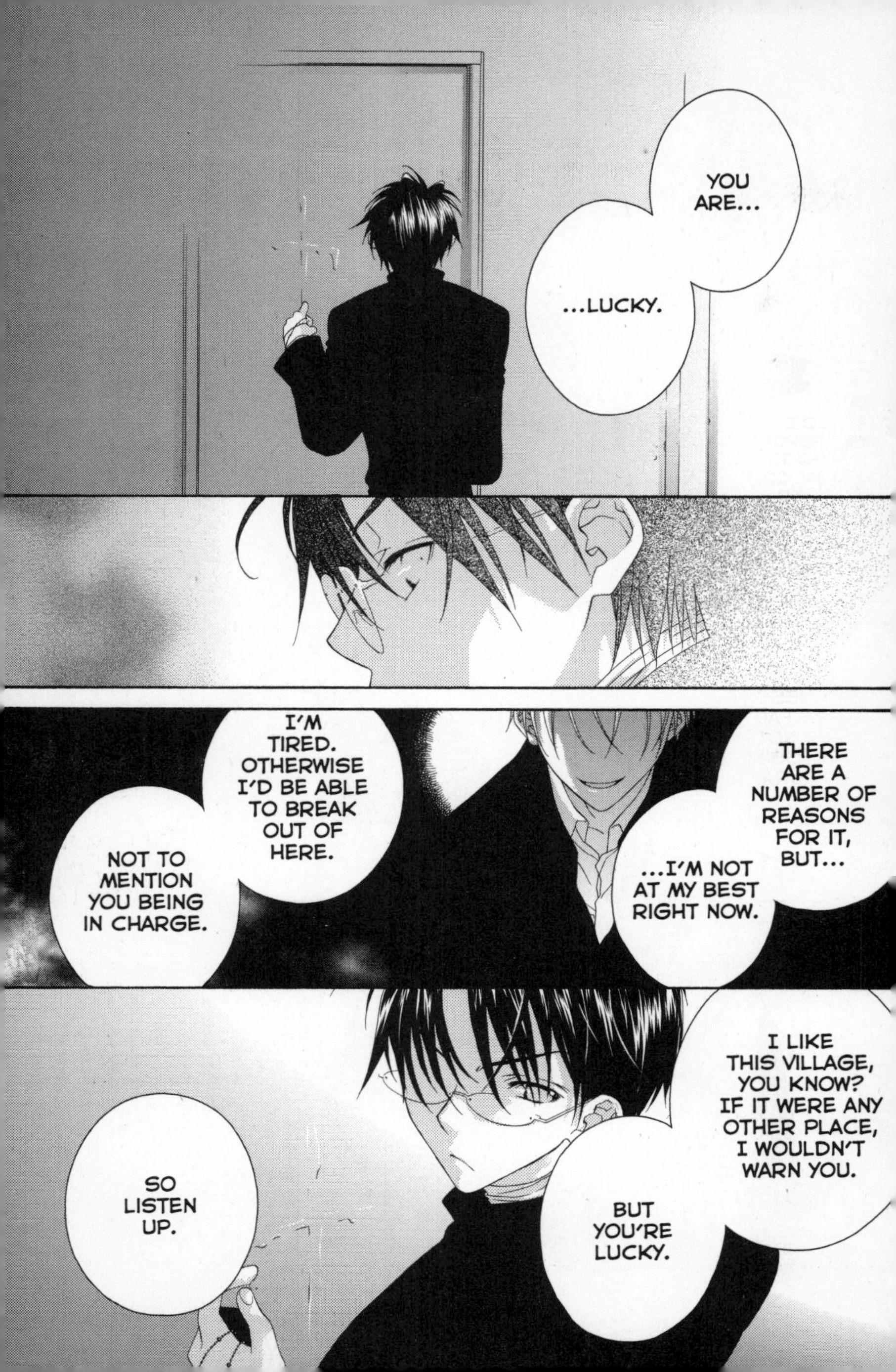
YOU ARE...
...LUCKY.
THERE ARE A NUMBER OF REASONS FOR IT, BUT...
...I'M NOT AT MY BEST RIGHT NOW.
I'M TIRED. OTHERWISE I'D BE ABLE TO BREAK OUT OF HERE.
NOT TO MENTION YOU BEING IN CHARGE.
I LIKE THIS VILLAGE, YOU KNOW? IF IT WERE ANY OTHER PLACE, I WOULDN'T WARN YOU.
BUT YOU'RE LUCKY.
SO LISTEN UP.

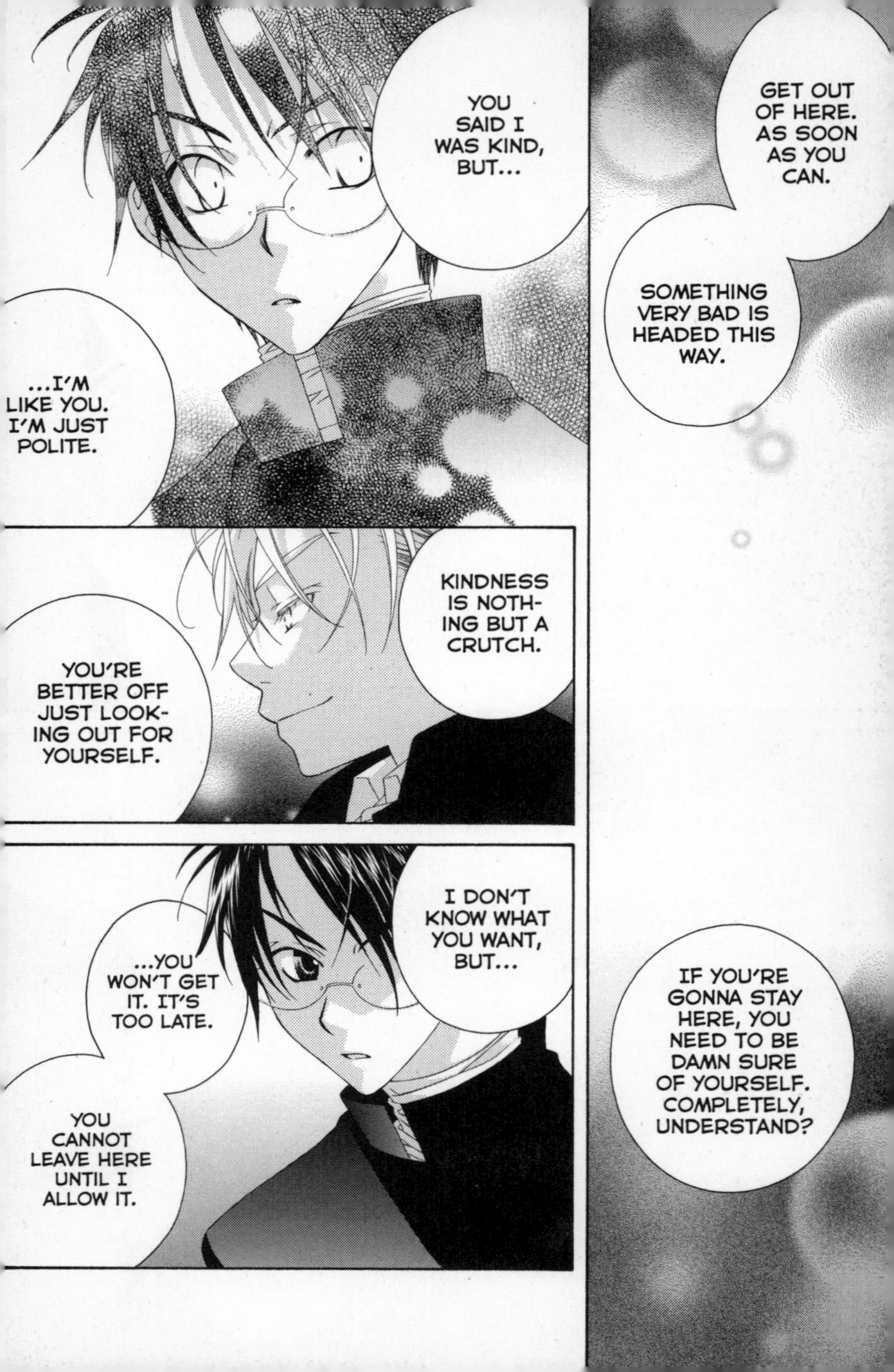
GET OUT OF HERE. AS SOON AS YOU CAN.
SOMETHING VERY BAD IS HEADED THIS WAY.
IF YOU'RE GONNA STAY HERE, YOU NEED TO BE DAMN SURE OF YOURSELF. COMPLETELY, UNDERSTAND?
YOU SAID I WAS KIND, BUT...
...I'M LIKE YOU. I'M JUST POLITE.
KINDNESS IS NOTHING BUT A CRUTCH.
YOU'RE BETTER OFF JUST LOOKING OUT FOR YOURSELF.
I DON'T KNOW WHAT YOU WANT, BUT...
...YOU WON'T GET IT. IT'S TOO LATE.
YOU CANNOT LEAVE HERE UNTIL I ALLOW IT.

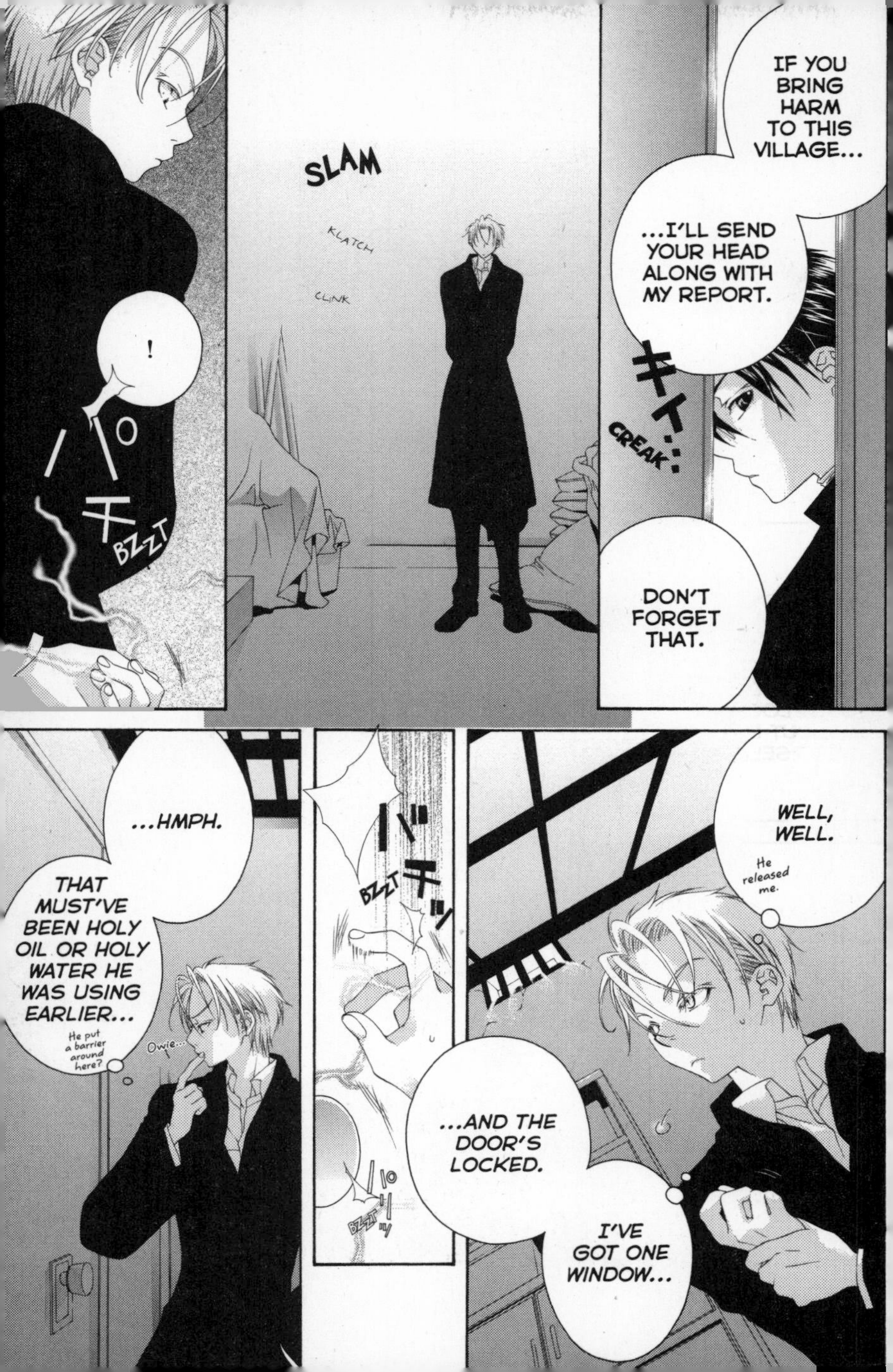
IF YOU BRING HARM TO THIS VILLAGE...
...I'LL SEND YOUR HEAD ALONG WITH MY REPORT.
CREAK
DON'T FORGET THAT.
SLAM
KLATCH
CLINK
!
BZZT
WELL, WELL.
He released me.
...AND THE DOOR'S LOCKED.
I'VE GOT ONE WINDOW...
BZZT
BZZT
...HMPH.
THAT MUST'VE BEEN HOLY OIL OR HOLY WATER HE WAS USING EARLIER...
He put a barrier around here?
Owie...

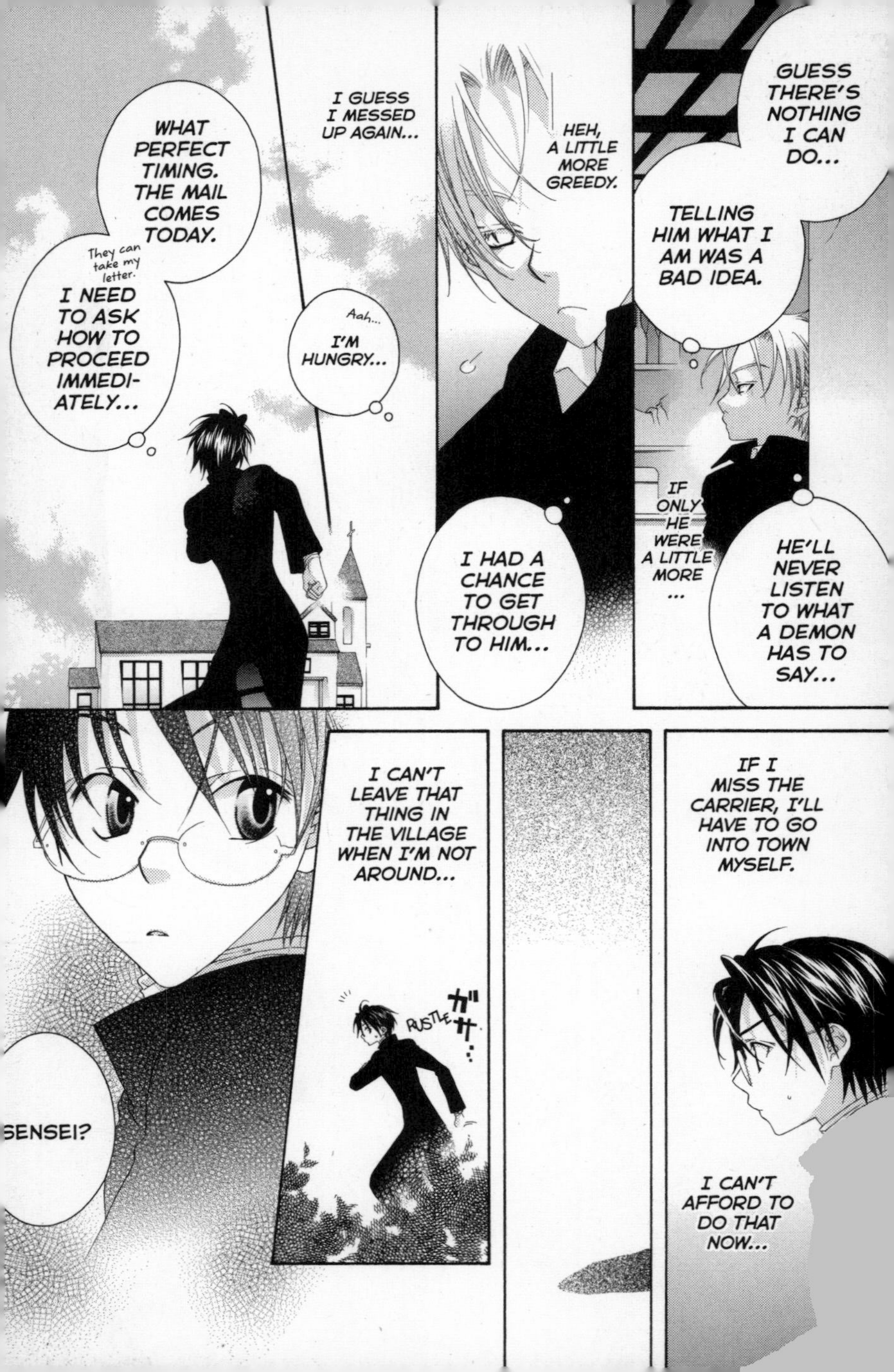
GUESS THERE'S NOTHING I CAN DO...
TELLING HIM WHAT I AM WAS A BAD IDEA.
HE'LL NEVER LISTEN TO WHAT A DEMON HAS TO SAY...
IF ONLY HE WERE A LITTLE MORE ...
HEH, A LITTLE MORE GREEDY.
I HAD A CHANCE TO GET THROUGH TO HIM...
I GUESS I MESSED UP AGAIN...
Aah...
I'M HUNGRY...
WHAT PERFECT TIMING. THE MAIL COMES TODAY.
They can take my letter.
I NEED TO ASK HOW TO PROCEED IMMEDIATELY...
IF I MISS THE CARRIER, I'LL HAVE TO GO INTO TOWN MYSELF.
I CAN'T AFFORD TO DO THAT NOW...
I CAN'T LEAVE THAT THING IN THE VILLAGE WHEN I'M NOT AROUND...
RUSTLE
ガサ
SENSEI?

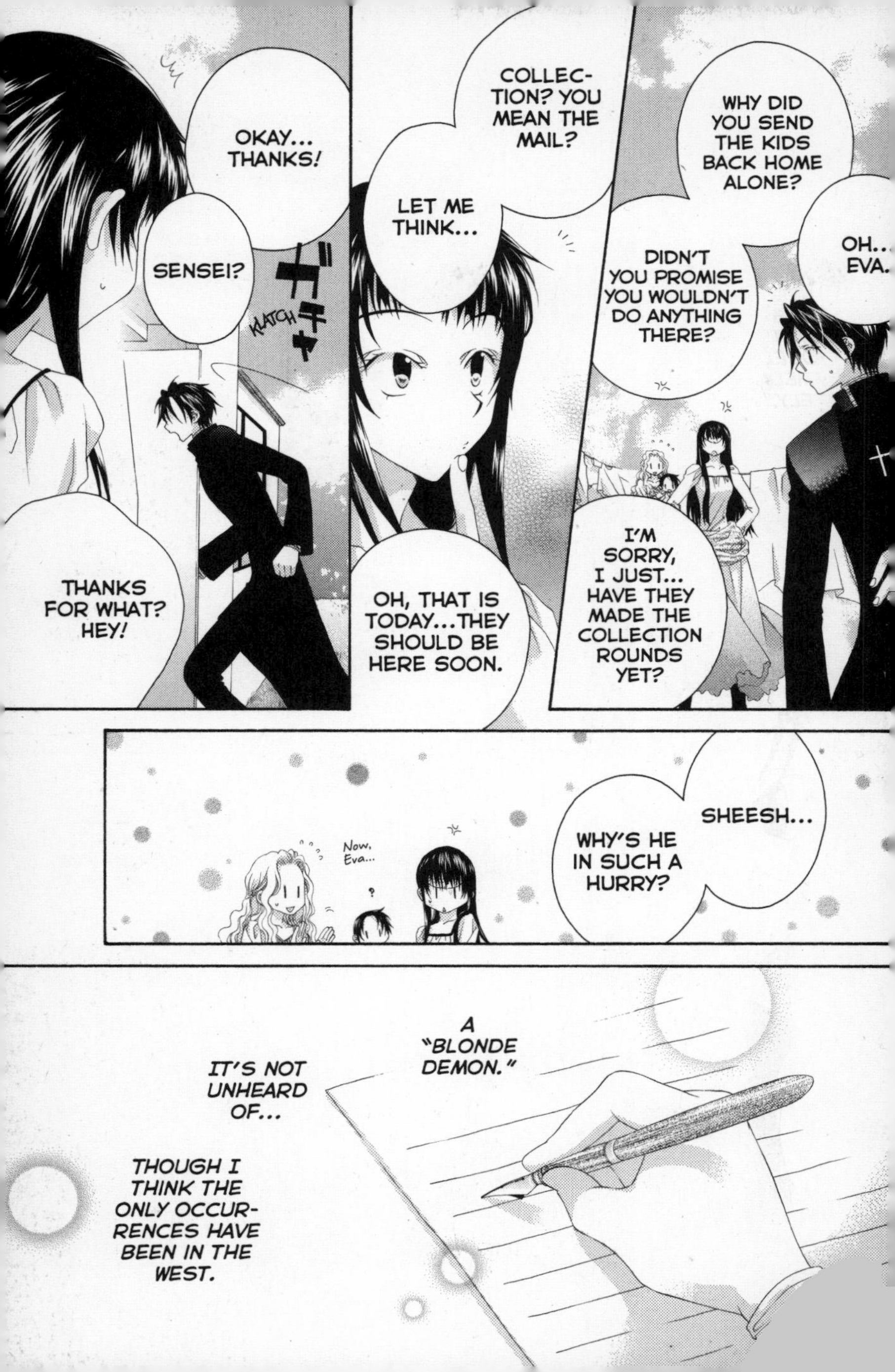

WHY DID YOU SEND THE KIDS BACK HOME ALONE?
OH... EVA.
DIDN'T YOU PROMISE YOU WOULDN'T DO ANYTHING THERE?
I'M SORRY, I JUST... HAVE THEY MADE THE COLLECTION ROUNDS YET?
COLLEC-TION? YOU MEAN THE MAIL?
LET ME THINK...
OH, THAT IS TODAY...THEY SHOULD BE HERE SOON.
OKAY... THANKS!
ガチャ
KLATCH
SENSEI?
THANKS FOR WHAT? HEY!
SHEESH...
WHY'S HE IN SUCH A HURRY?
Now, Eva...
A "BLONDE DEMON."
IT'S NOT UNHEARD OF...
THOUGH I THINK THE ONLY OCCUR-RENCES HAVE BEEN IN THE WEST.

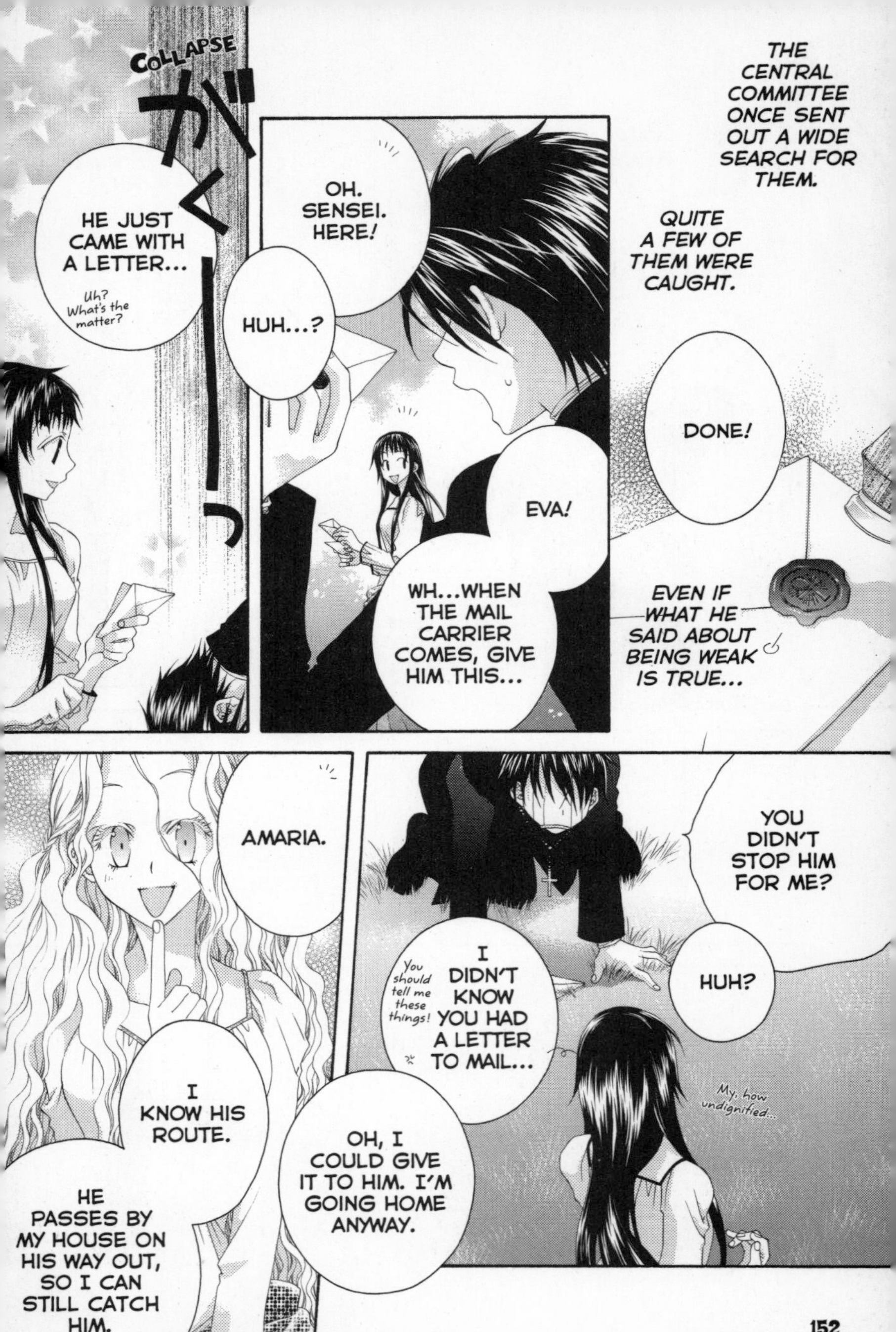
THE CENTRAL COMMITTEE ONCE SENT OUT A WIDE SEARCH FOR THEM.
QUITE A FEW OF THEM WERE CAUGHT.
DONE!
EVEN IF WHAT HE SAID ABOUT BEING WEAK IS TRUE...
OH. SENSEI. HERE!
HUH...?
EVA!
WH...WHEN THE MAIL CARRIER COMES, GIVE HIM THIS...
COLLAPSE
HE JUST CAME WITH A LETTER...
Uh? What's the matter?
YOU DIDN'T STOP HIM FOR ME?
HUH?
I DIDN'T KNOW YOU HAD A LETTER TO MAIL...
You should tell me these things!
My, how undignified...
AMARIA.
OH, I COULD GIVE IT TO HIM. I'M GOING HOME ANYWAY.
I KNOW HIS ROUTE.
HE PASSES BY MY HOUSE ON HIS WAY OUT, SO I CAN STILL CATCH HIM.

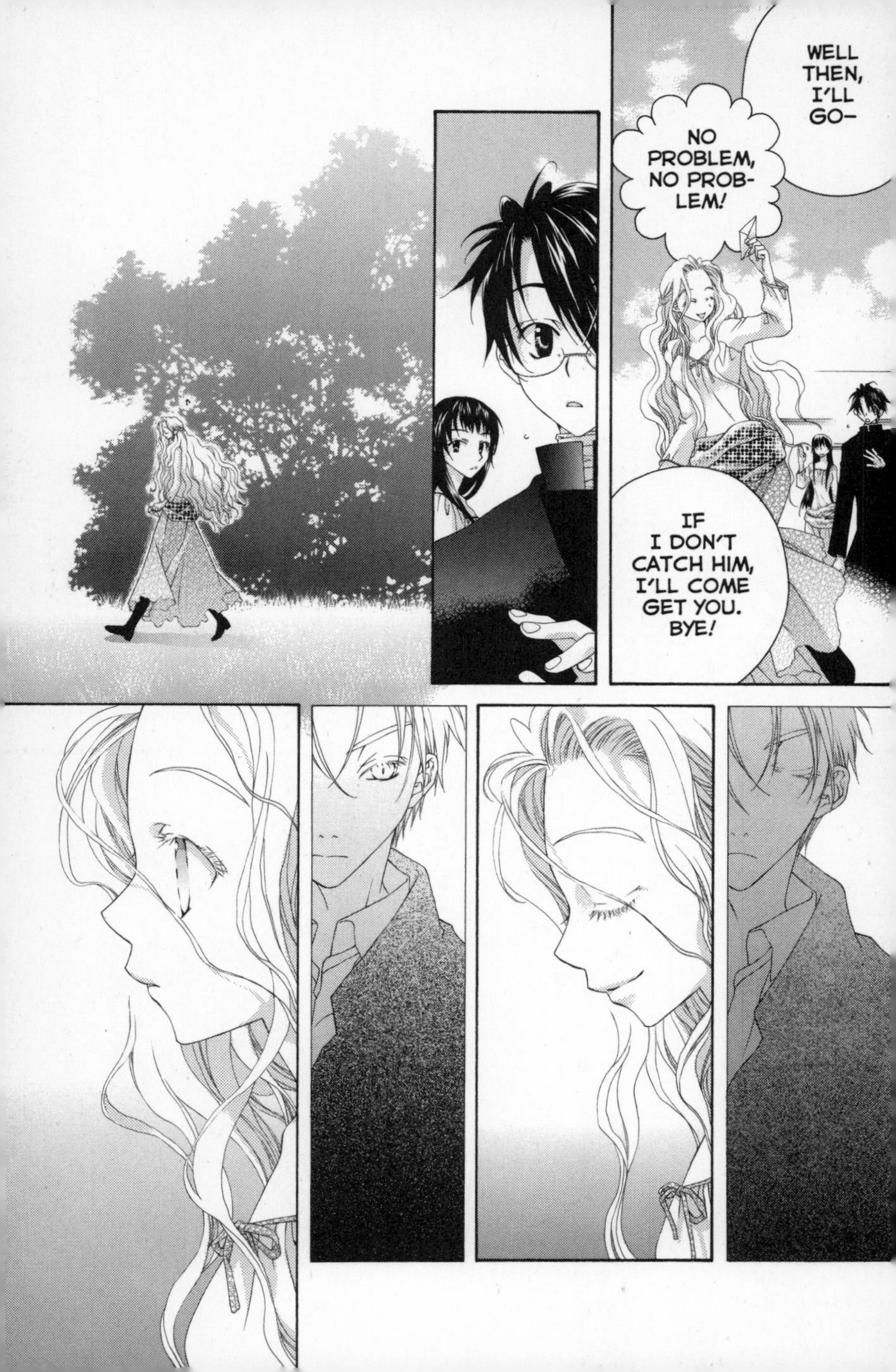
WELL THEN, I'LL GO—
NO PROBLEM, NO PROB-LEM!
IF I DON'T CATCH HIM, I'LL COME GET YOU. BYE!

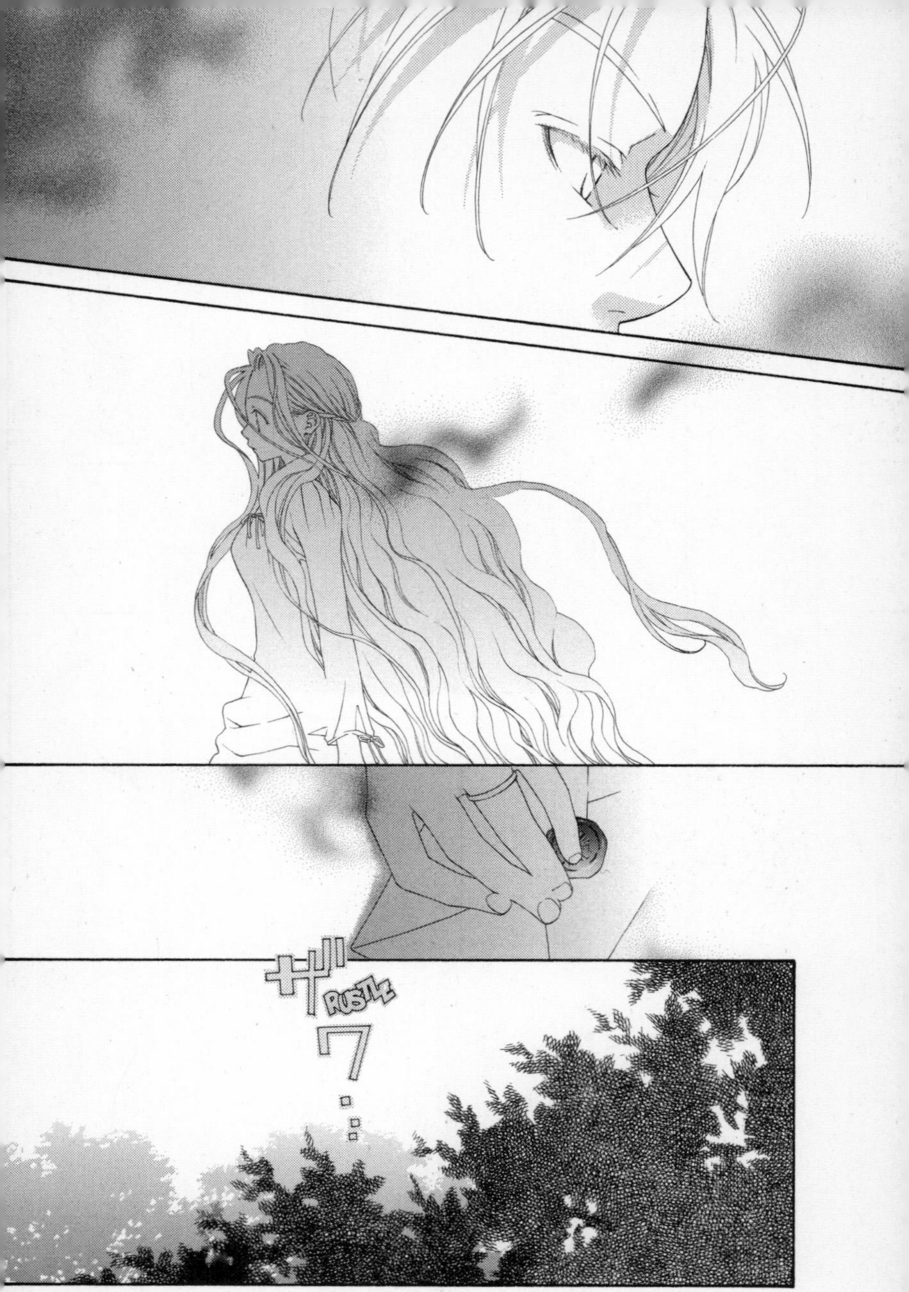
ザワ…
RUSTLE

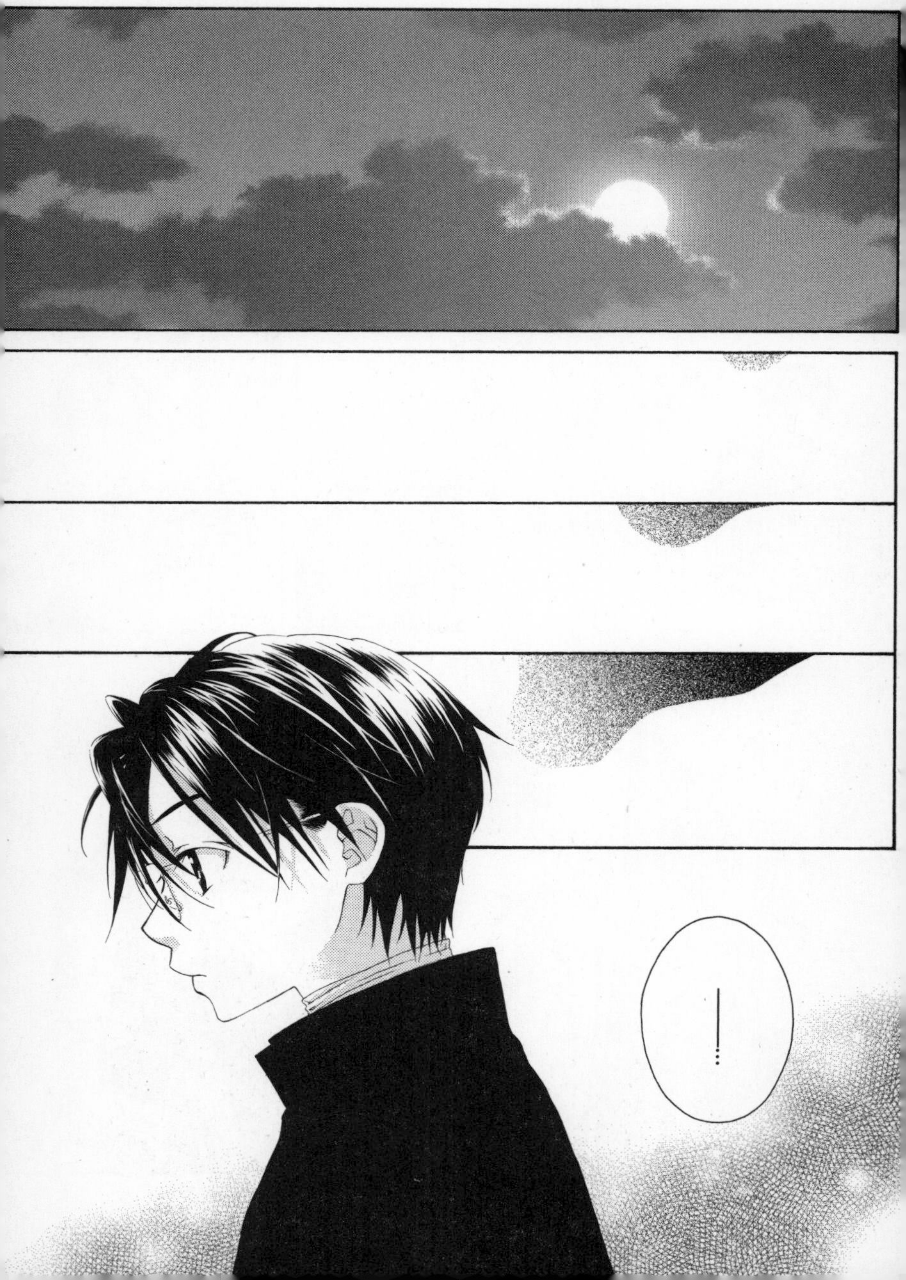
―…

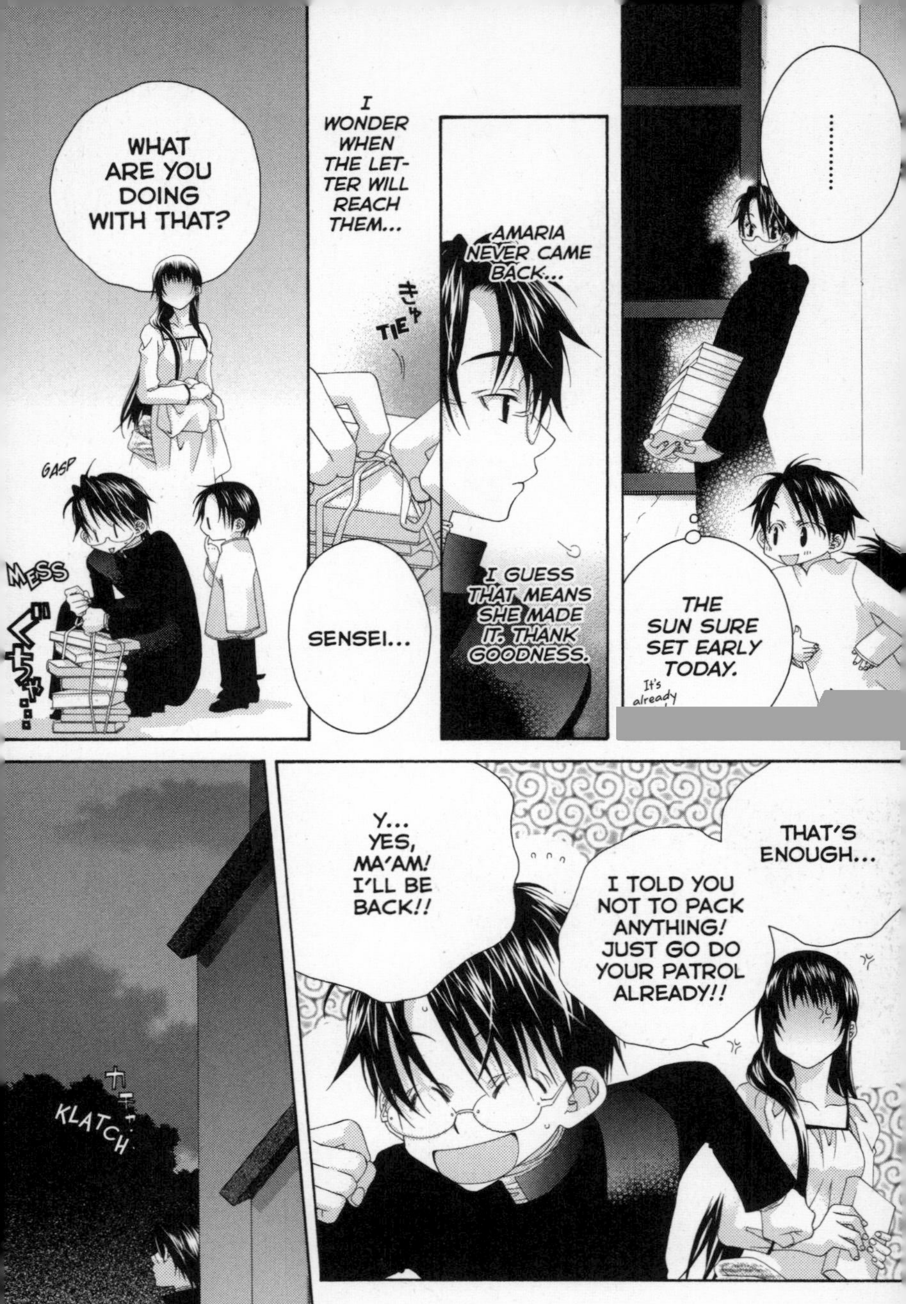

......
THE SUN SURE SET EARLY TODAY.
It's already
AMARIA NEVER CAME BACK...
I GUESS THAT MEANS SHE MADE IT. THANK GOODNESS.
I WONDER WHEN THE LETTER WILL REACH THEM...
TIE
SENSEI...
WHAT ARE YOU DOING WITH THAT?
GASP
MESS
THAT'S ENOUGH...
I TOLD YOU NOT TO PACK ANYTHING! JUST GO DO YOUR PATROL ALREADY!!
Y... YES, MA'AM! I'LL BE BACK!!
KLATCH

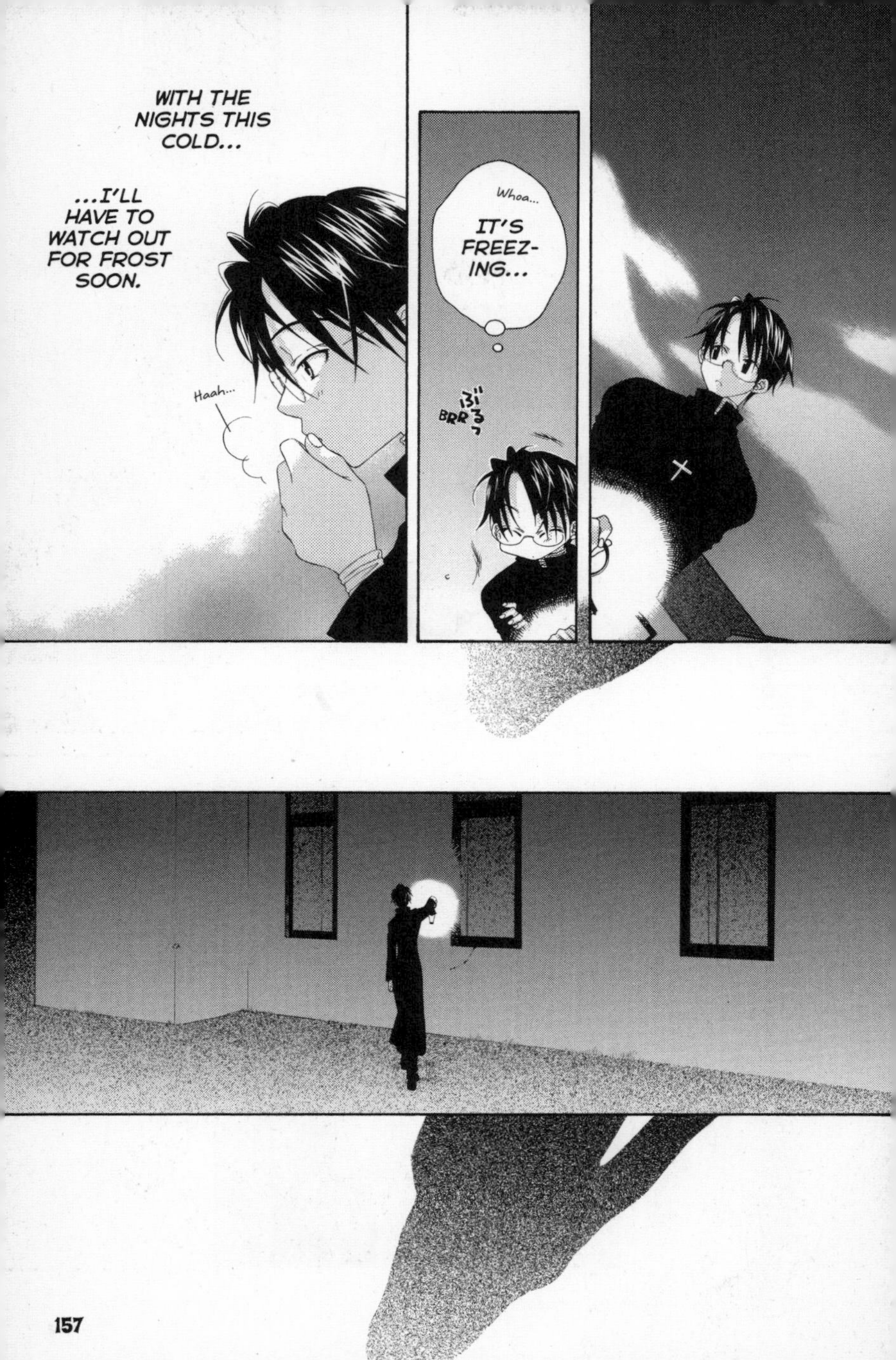
Whoa...
IT'S FREEZ-ING...
BRR ぶるっ
WITH THE NIGHTS THIS COLD...
...I'LL HAVE TO WATCH OUT FOR FROST SOON.
Haah...

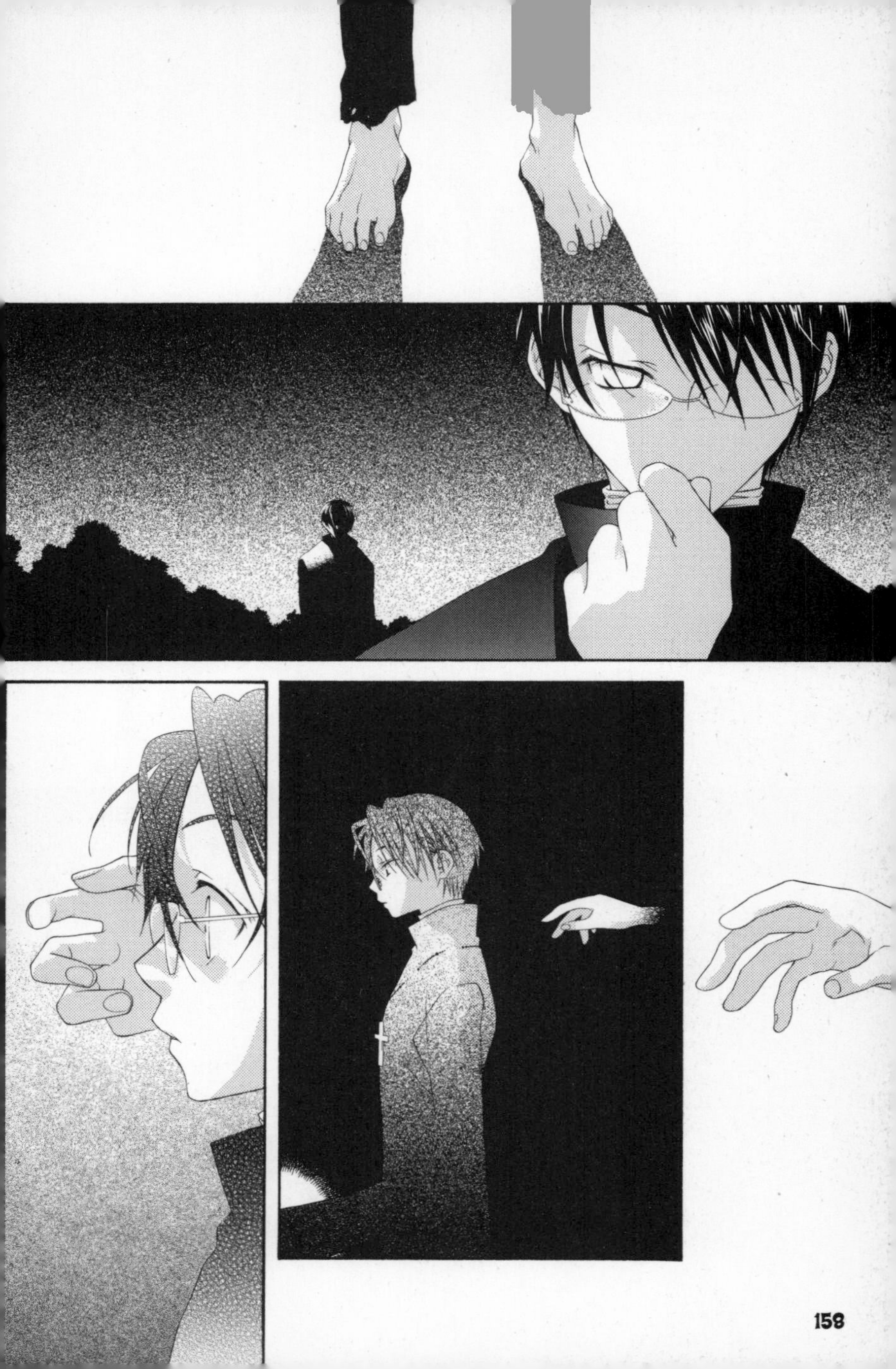

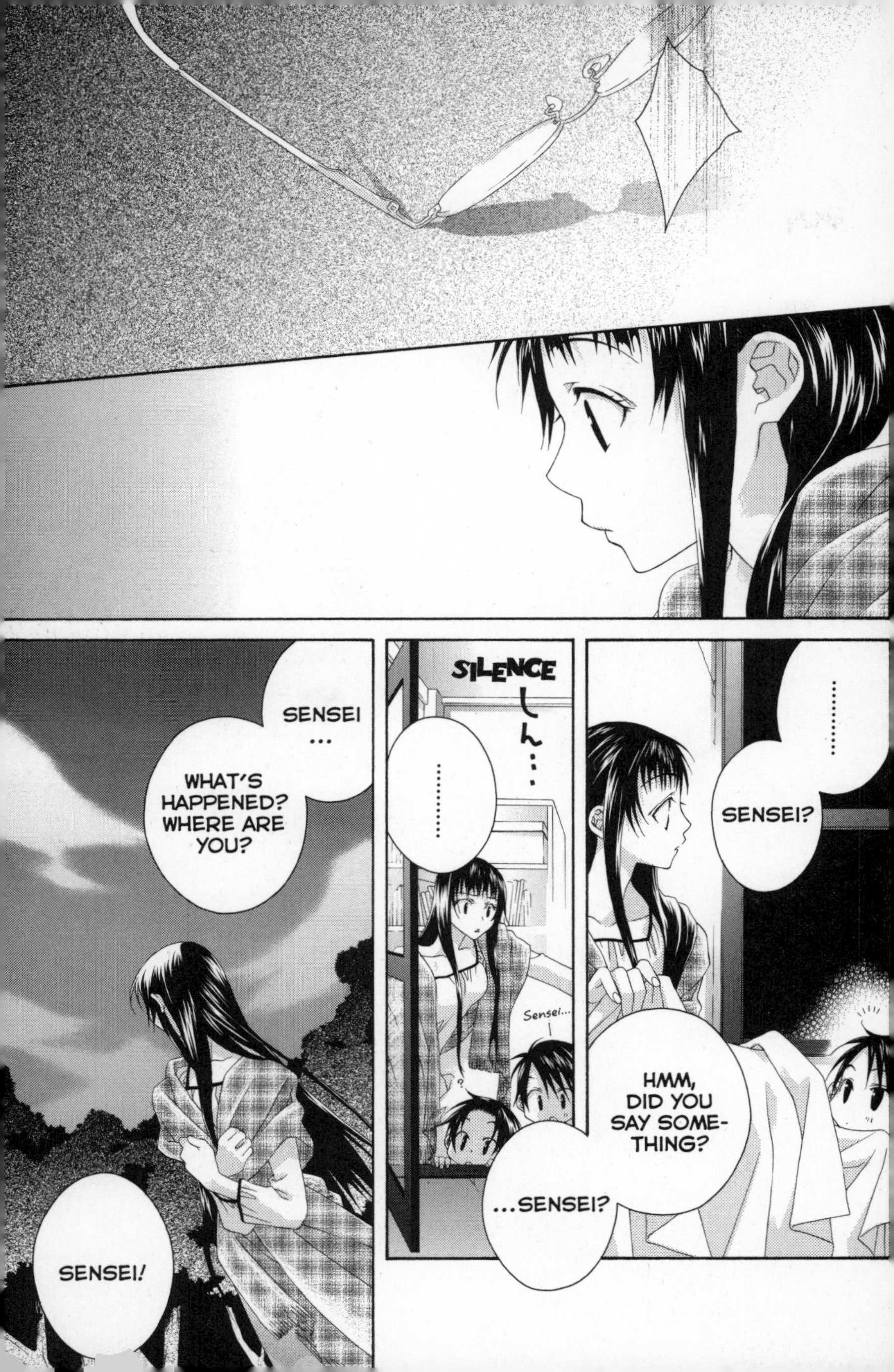

......
SENSEI?
HMM, DID YOU SAY SOME-THING?
SILENCE
しん…
....
Sensei...
...SENSEI?
SENSEI ...
WHAT'S HAPPENED? WHERE ARE YOU?
SENSEI!

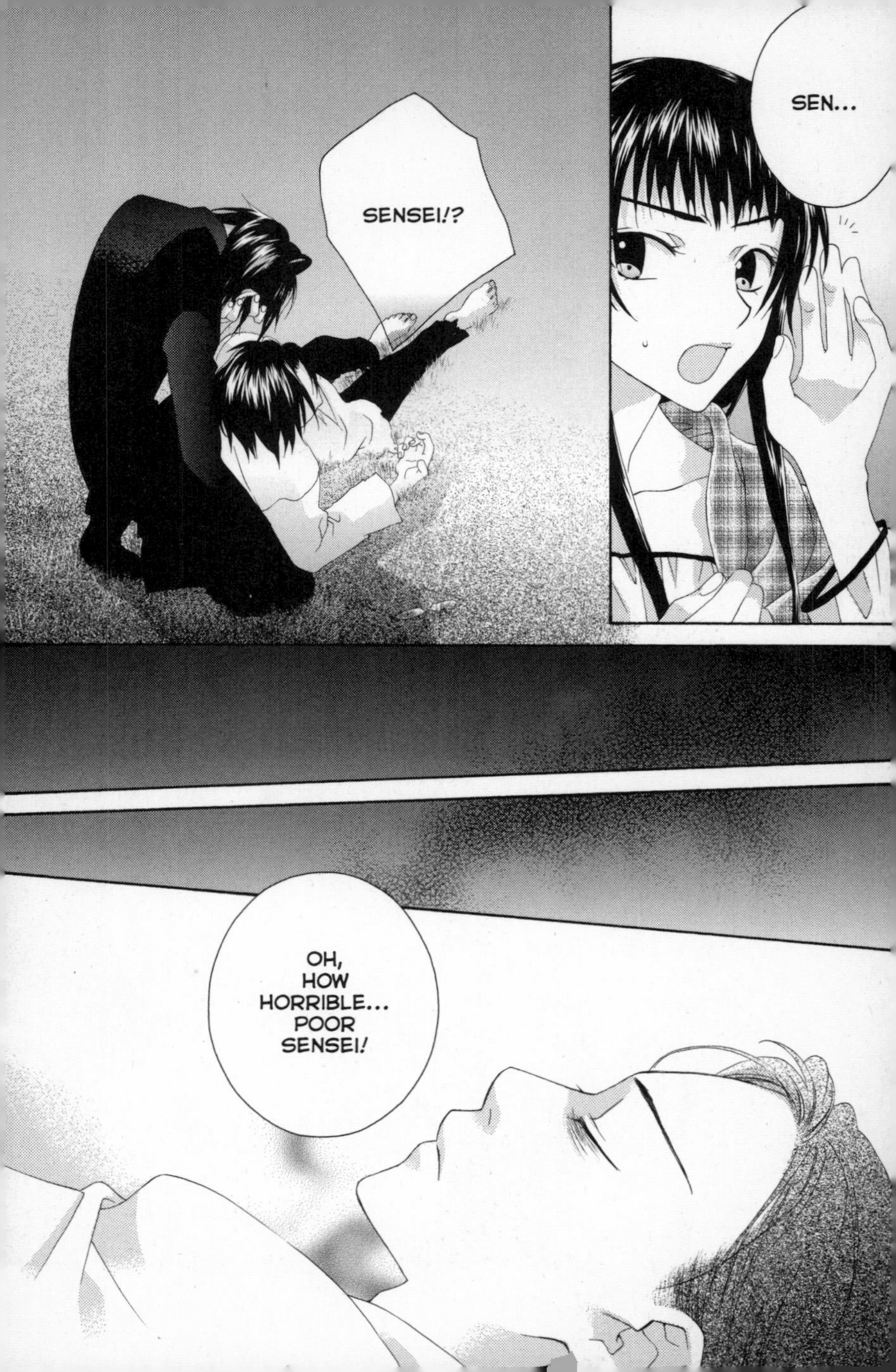
SEN...
SENSEI!?
OH, HOW HORRIBLE... POOR SENSEI!

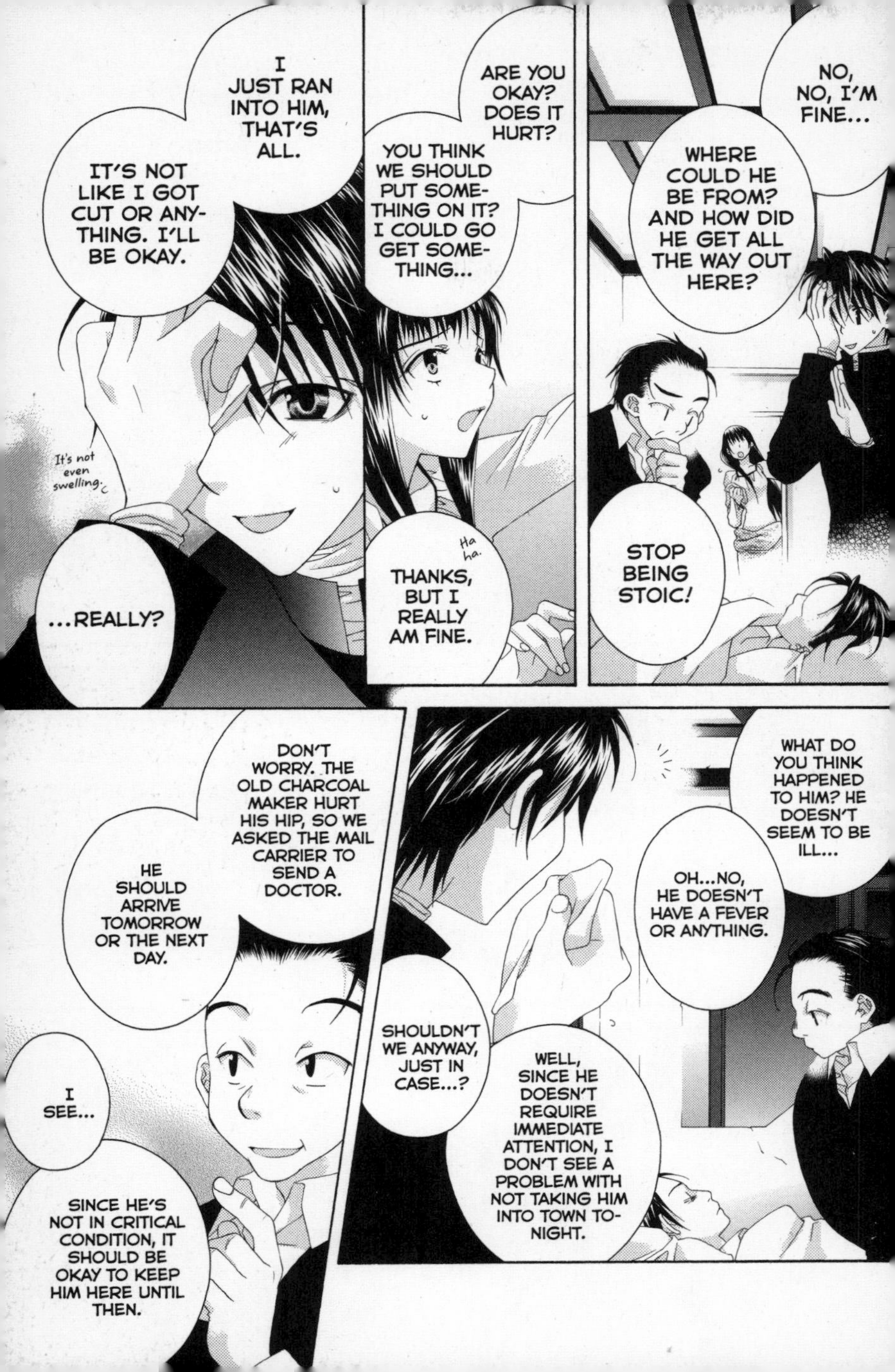
NO, NO, I'M FINE...
WHERE COULD HE BE FROM? AND HOW DID HE GET ALL THE WAY OUT HERE?
STOP BEING STOIC!
ARE YOU OKAY? DOES IT HURT?
YOU THINK WE SHOULD PUT SOMETHING ON IT? I COULD GO GET SOMETHING...
Ha ha.
THANKS, BUT I REALLY AM FINE.
I JUST RAN INTO HIM, THAT'S ALL.
IT'S NOT LIKE I GOT CUT OR ANYTHING. I'LL BE OKAY.
It's not even swelling.
...REALLY?
WHAT DO YOU THINK HAPPENED TO HIM? HE DOESN'T SEEM TO BE ILL...
OH...NO, HE DOESN'T HAVE A FEVER OR ANYTHING.
WELL, SINCE HE DOESN'T REQUIRE IMMEDIATE ATTENTION, I DON'T SEE A PROBLEM WITH NOT TAKING HIM INTO TOWN TONIGHT.
SHOULDN'T WE ANYWAY, JUST IN CASE...?
DON'T WORRY. THE OLD CHARCOAL MAKER HURT HIS HIP, SO WE ASKED THE MAIL CARRIER TO SEND A DOCTOR.
HE SHOULD ARRIVE TOMORROW OR THE NEXT DAY.
I SEE...
SINCE HE'S NOT IN CRITICAL CONDITION, IT SHOULD BE OKAY TO KEEP HIM HERE UNTIL THEN.

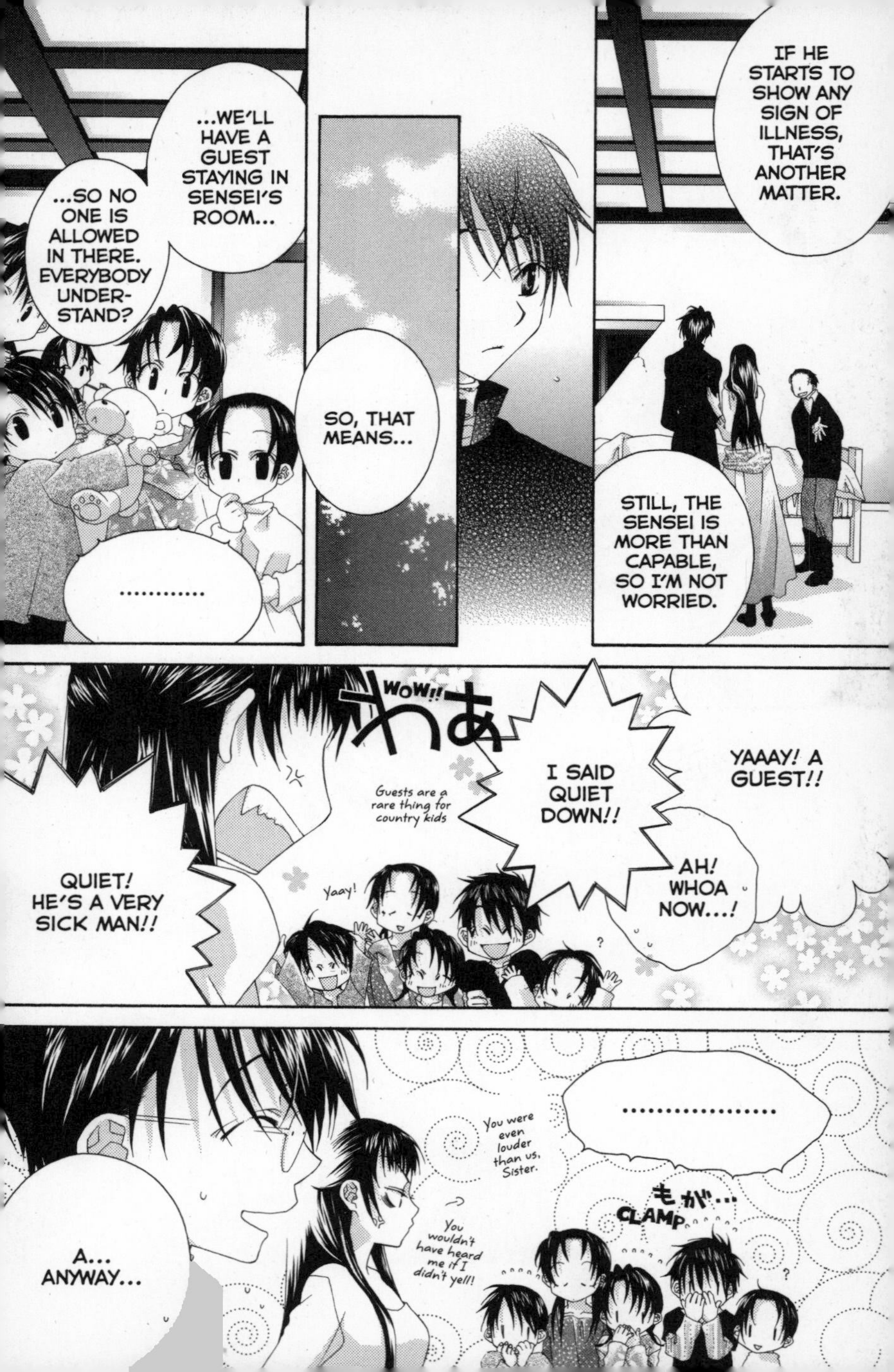
IF HE STARTS TO SHOW ANY SIGN OF ILLNESS, THAT'S ANOTHER MATTER.
STILL, THE SENSEI IS MORE THAN CAPABLE, SO I'M NOT WORRIED.
SO, THAT MEANS...
...WE'LL HAVE A GUEST STAYING IN SENSEI'S ROOM...
...SO NO ONE IS ALLOWED IN THERE. EVERYBODY UNDER-STAND?
....
YAAAY! A GUEST!!
AH! WHOA NOW...!
I SAID QUIET DOWN!!
WOW!!
わあ
Guests are a rare thing for country kids
Yaay!
QUIET! HE'S A VERY SICK MAN!!
....
You were even louder than us, Sister.
もが...
CLAMP
You wouldn't have heard me if I didn't yell!
A... ANYWAY...

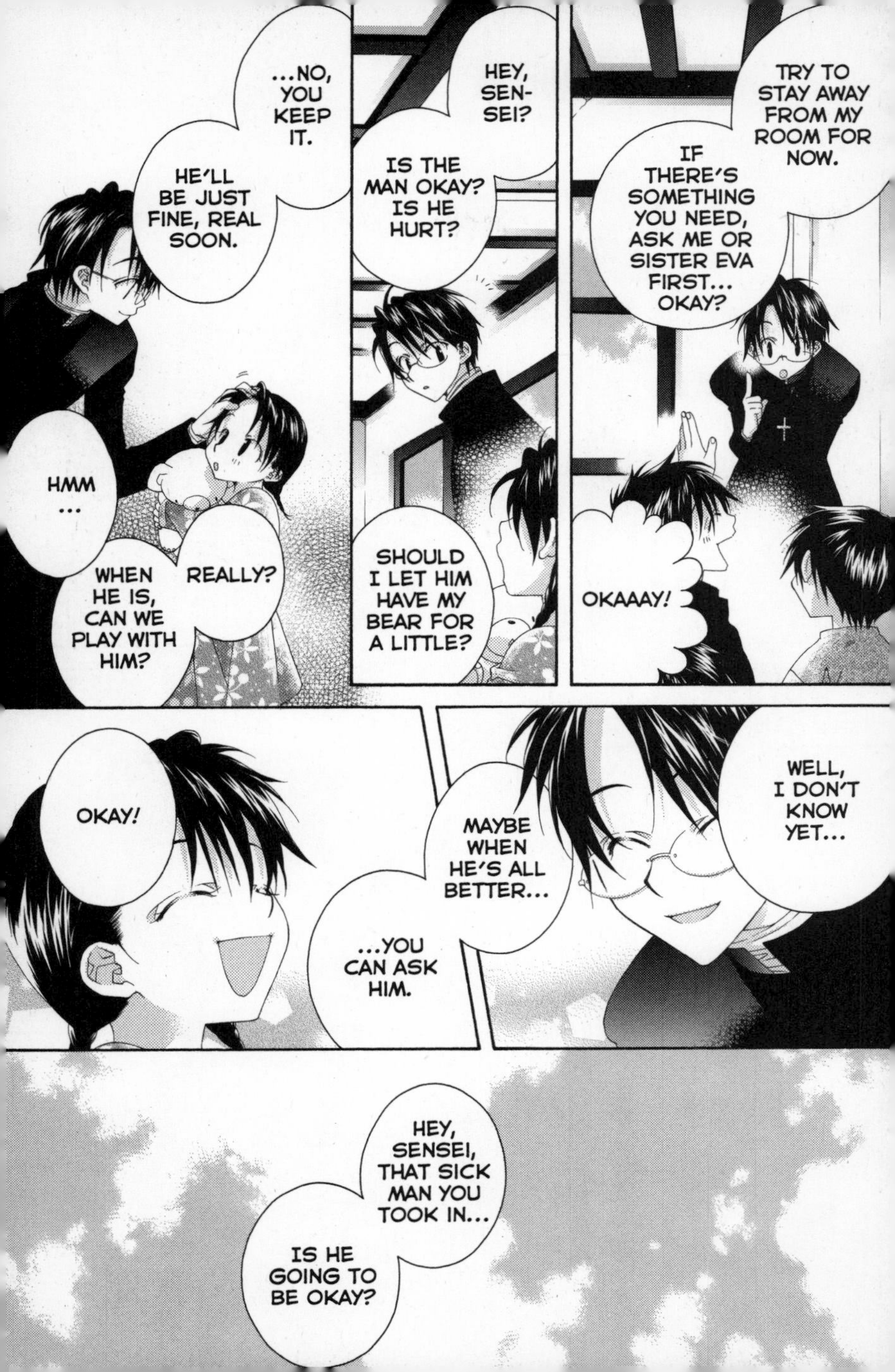
TRY TO STAY AWAY FROM MY ROOM FOR NOW.
IF THERE'S SOMETHING YOU NEED, ASK ME OR SISTER EVA FIRST... OKAY?
OKAAAY!
HEY, SEN-SEI?
IS THE MAN OKAY? IS HE HURT?
SHOULD I LET HIM HAVE MY BEAR FOR A LITTLE?
...NO, YOU KEEP IT.
HE'LL BE JUST FINE, REAL SOON.
REALLY?
WHEN HE IS, CAN WE PLAY WITH HIM?
HMM ...
WELL, I DON'T KNOW YET...
MAYBE WHEN HE'S ALL BETTER...
...YOU CAN ASK HIM.
OKAY!
HEY, SENSEI, THAT SICK MAN YOU TOOK IN...
IS HE GOING TO BE OKAY?

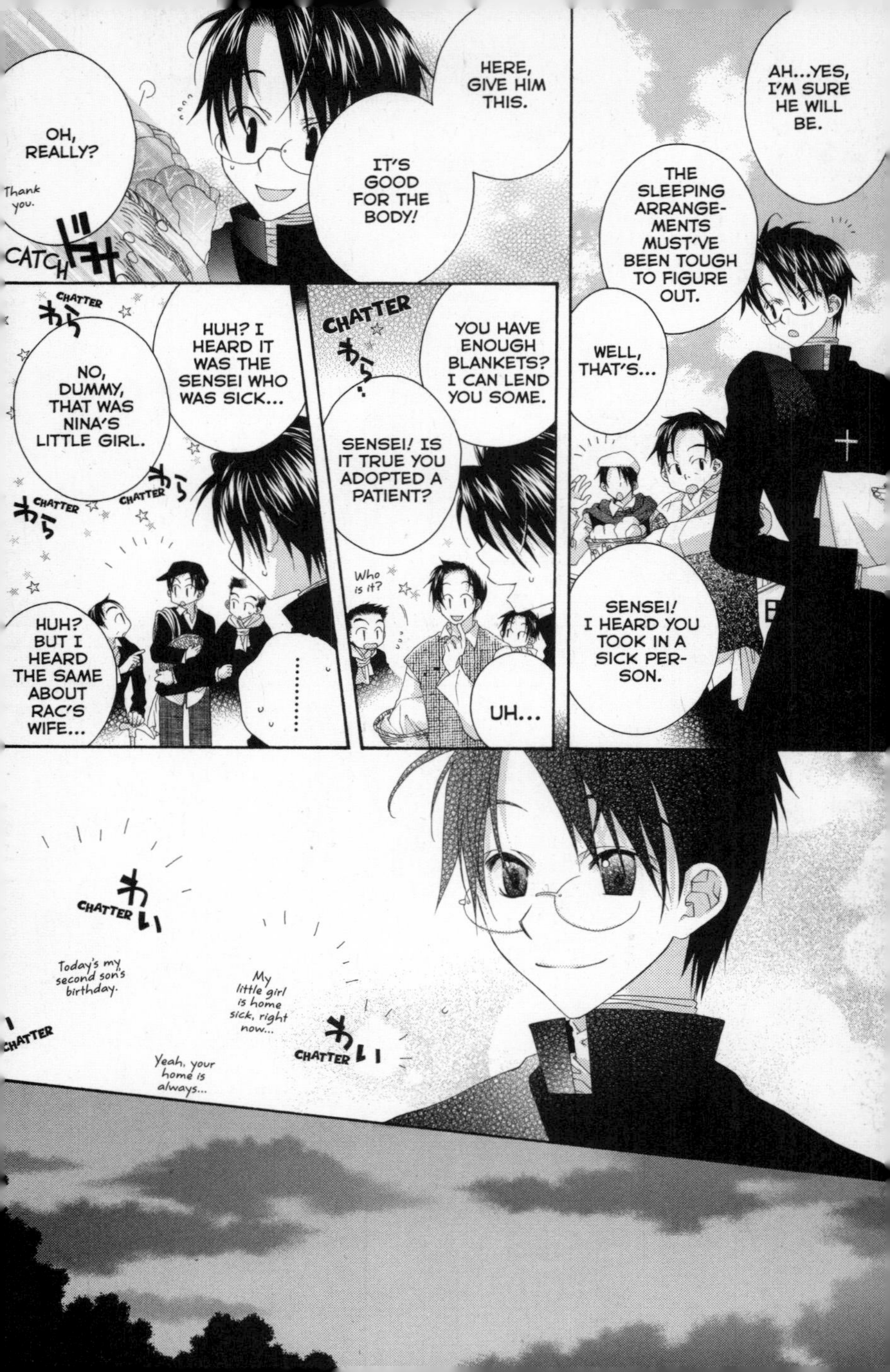

AH...YES, I'M SURE HE WILL BE.
THE SLEEPING ARRANGE-MENTS MUST'VE BEEN TOUGH TO FIGURE OUT.
WELL, THAT'S...
SENSEI! I HEARD YOU TOOK IN A SICK PER-SON.
HERE, GIVE HIM THIS.
IT'S GOOD FOR THE BODY!
OH, REALLY?
Thank you.
CATCH
CHATTER わら
YOU HAVE ENOUGH BLANKETS? I CAN LEND YOU SOME.
SENSEI! IS IT TRUE YOU ADOPTED A PATIENT?
Who is it?
UH...
HUH? I HEARD IT WAS THE SENSEI WHO WAS SICK...
CHATTER わら
NO, DUMMY, THAT WAS NINA'S LITTLE GIRL.
CHATTER わら
CHATTER わら
HUH? BUT I HEARD THE SAME ABOUT RAC'S WIFE...
......
CHATTER わい
My little girl is home sick, right now...
Today's my second son's birthday.
CHATTER わい
CHATTER
Yeah, your home is always...

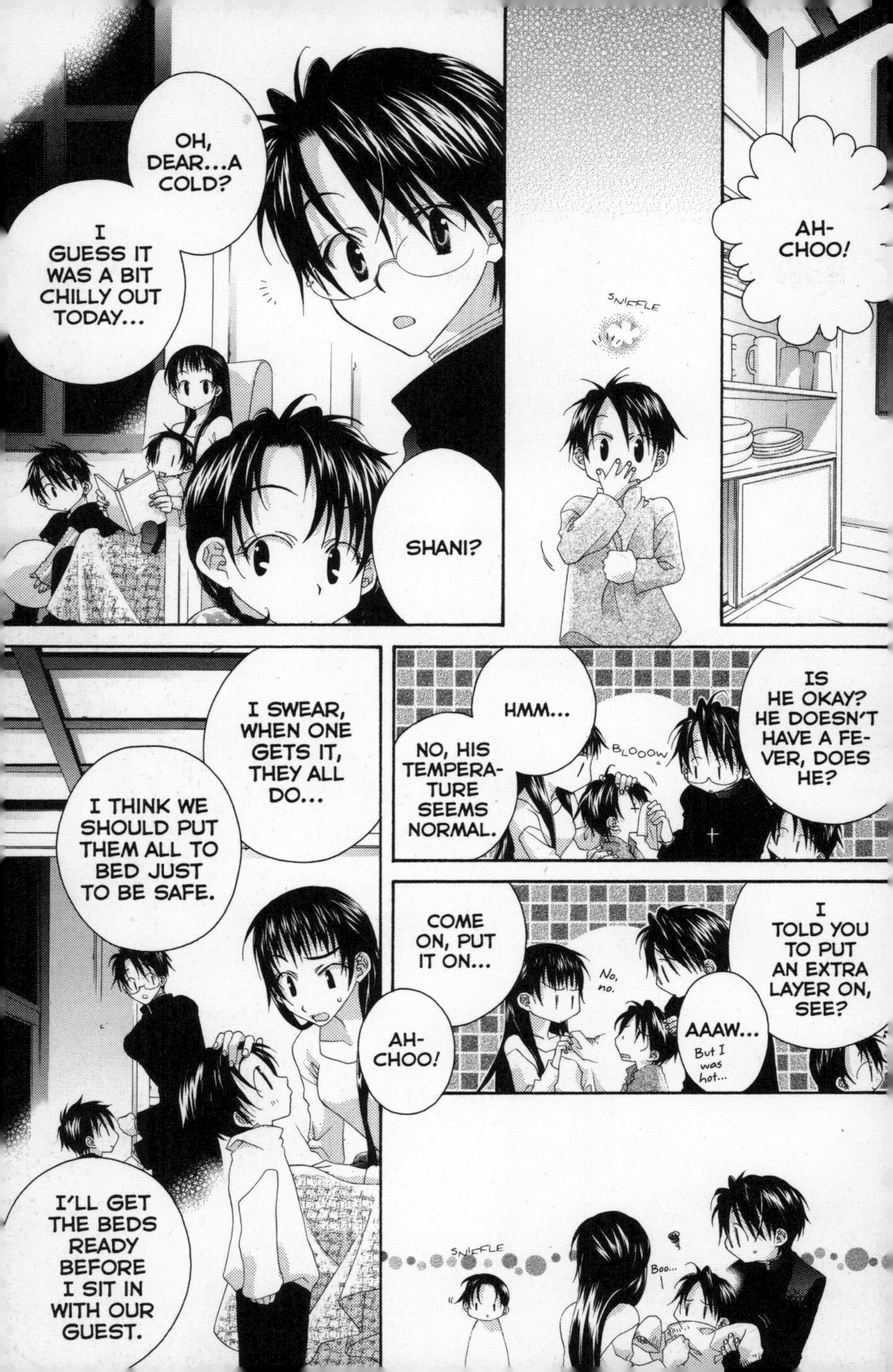
AH-CHOO!
SNIFFLE
OH, DEAR...A COLD?
I GUESS IT WAS A BIT CHILLY OUT TODAY...
SHANI?
IS HE OKAY? HE DOESN'T HAVE A FE-VER, DOES HE?
BLOOOW
HMM...
NO, HIS TEMPERA-TURE SEEMS NORMAL.
I TOLD YOU TO PUT AN EXTRA LAYER ON, SEE?
AAAW...
But I was hot...
No, no.
COME ON, PUT IT ON...
AH-CHOO!
Boo...
SNIFFLE
I SWEAR, WHEN ONE GETS IT, THEY ALL DO...
I THINK WE SHOULD PUT THEM ALL TO BED JUST TO BE SAFE.
I'LL GET THE BEDS READY BEFORE I SIT IN WITH OUR GUEST.

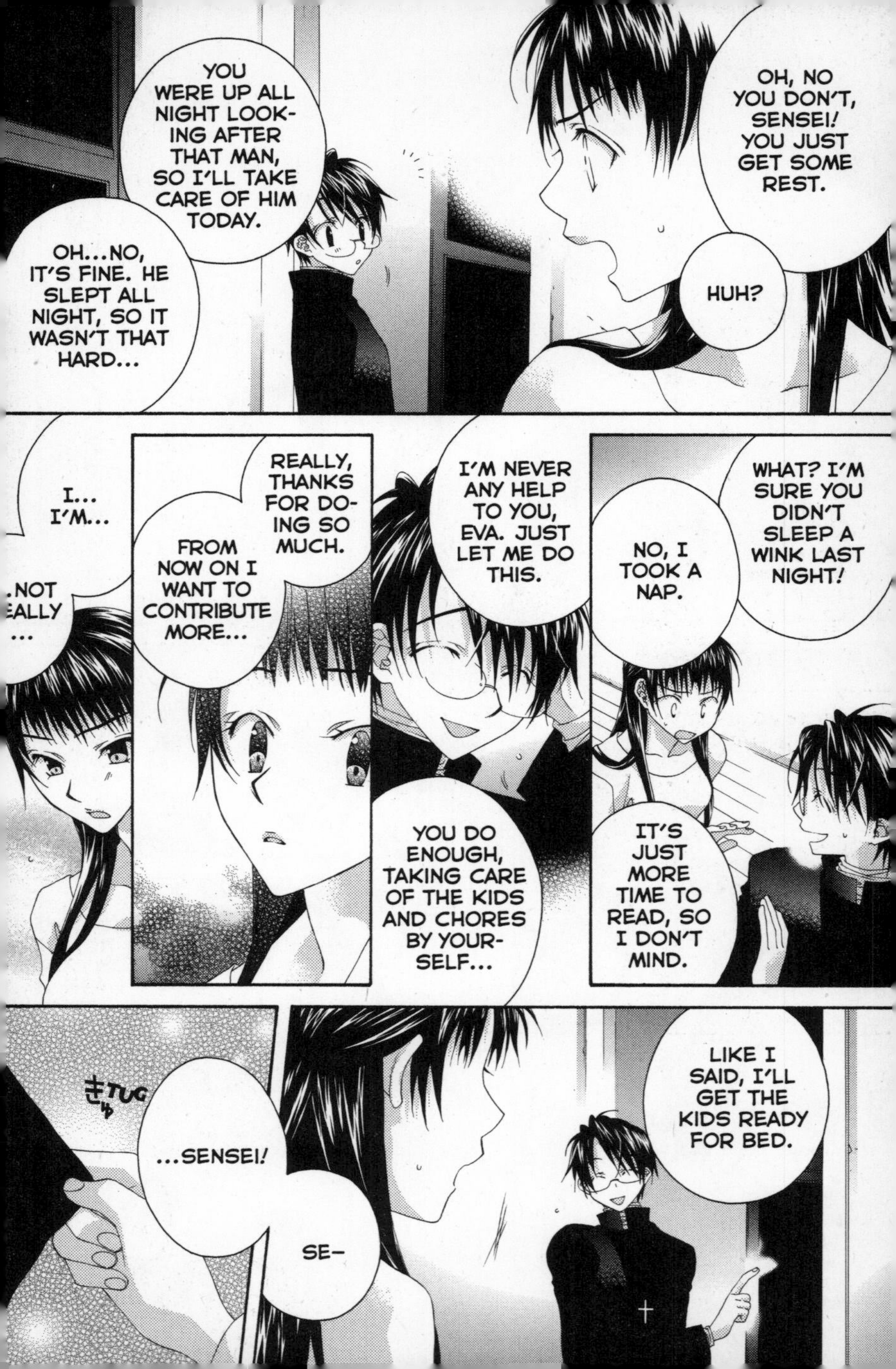
OH, NO YOU DON'T, SENSEI! YOU JUST GET SOME REST.
HUH?
YOU WERE UP ALL NIGHT LOOKING AFTER THAT MAN, SO I'LL TAKE CARE OF HIM TODAY.
OH...NO, IT'S FINE. HE SLEPT ALL NIGHT, SO IT WASN'T THAT HARD...
WHAT? I'M SURE YOU DIDN'T SLEEP A WINK LAST NIGHT!
NO, I TOOK A NAP.
IT'S JUST MORE TIME TO READ, SO I DON'T MIND.
I'M NEVER ANY HELP TO YOU, EVA. JUST LET ME DO THIS.
YOU DO ENOUGH, TAKING CARE OF THE KIDS AND CHORES BY YOURSELF...
REALLY, THANKS FOR DOING SO MUCH.
FROM NOW ON I WANT TO CONTRIBUTE MORE...
I... I'M...
.NOT EALLY ...
LIKE I SAID, I'LL GET THE KIDS READY FOR BED.
きゅ TUG
...SENSEI!
SE-

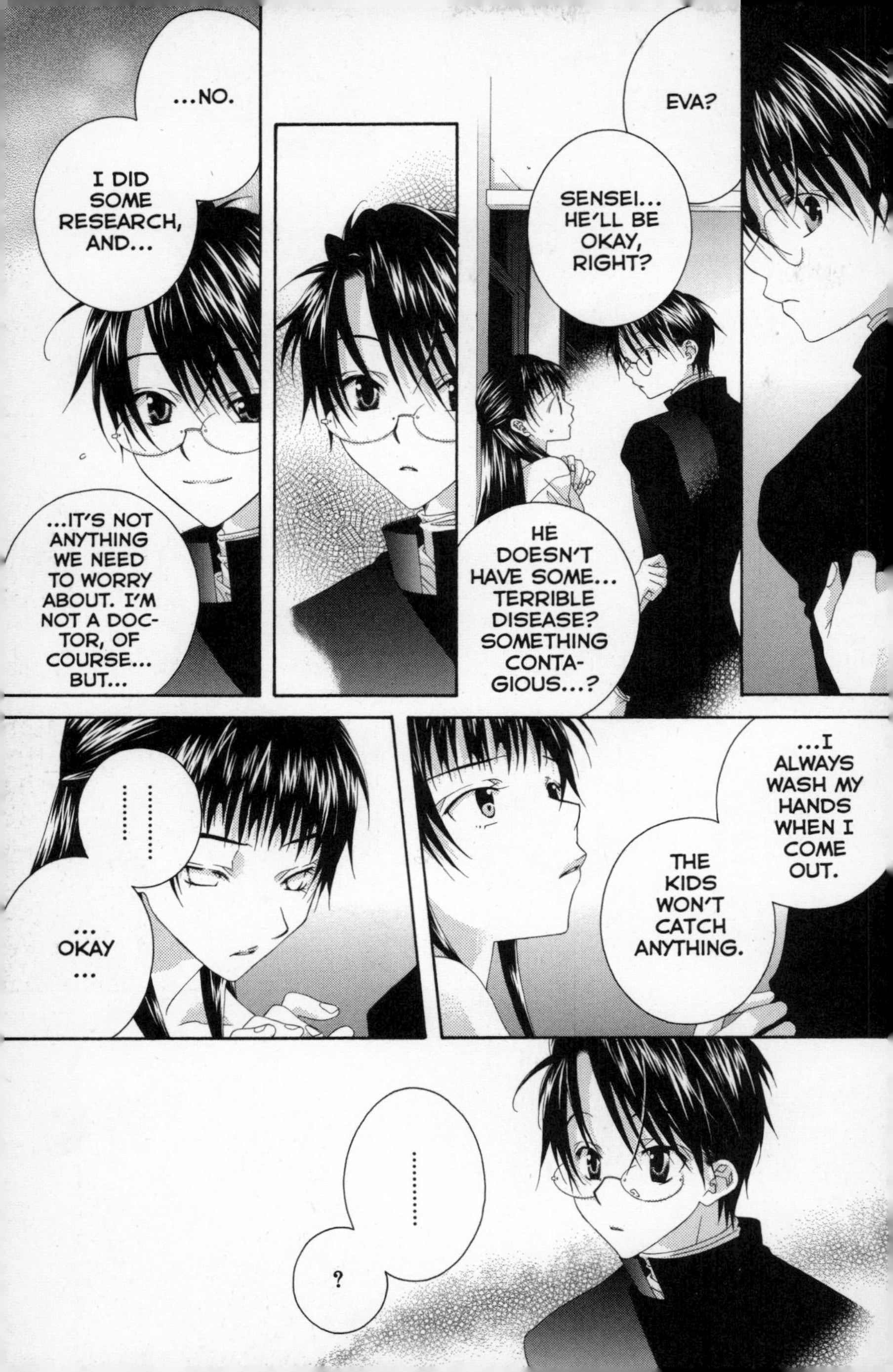
EVA?
SENSEI... HE'LL BE OKAY, RIGHT?
HE DOESN'T HAVE SOME... TERRIBLE DISEASE? SOMETHING CONTA-GIOUS...?
...NO.
I DID SOME RESEARCH, AND...
...IT'S NOT ANYTHING WE NEED TO WORRY ABOUT. I'M NOT A DOC-TOR, OF COURSE... BUT...
...I ALWAYS WASH MY HANDS WHEN I COME OUT.
THE KIDS WON'T CATCH ANYTHING.
......
...OKAY...
......
?

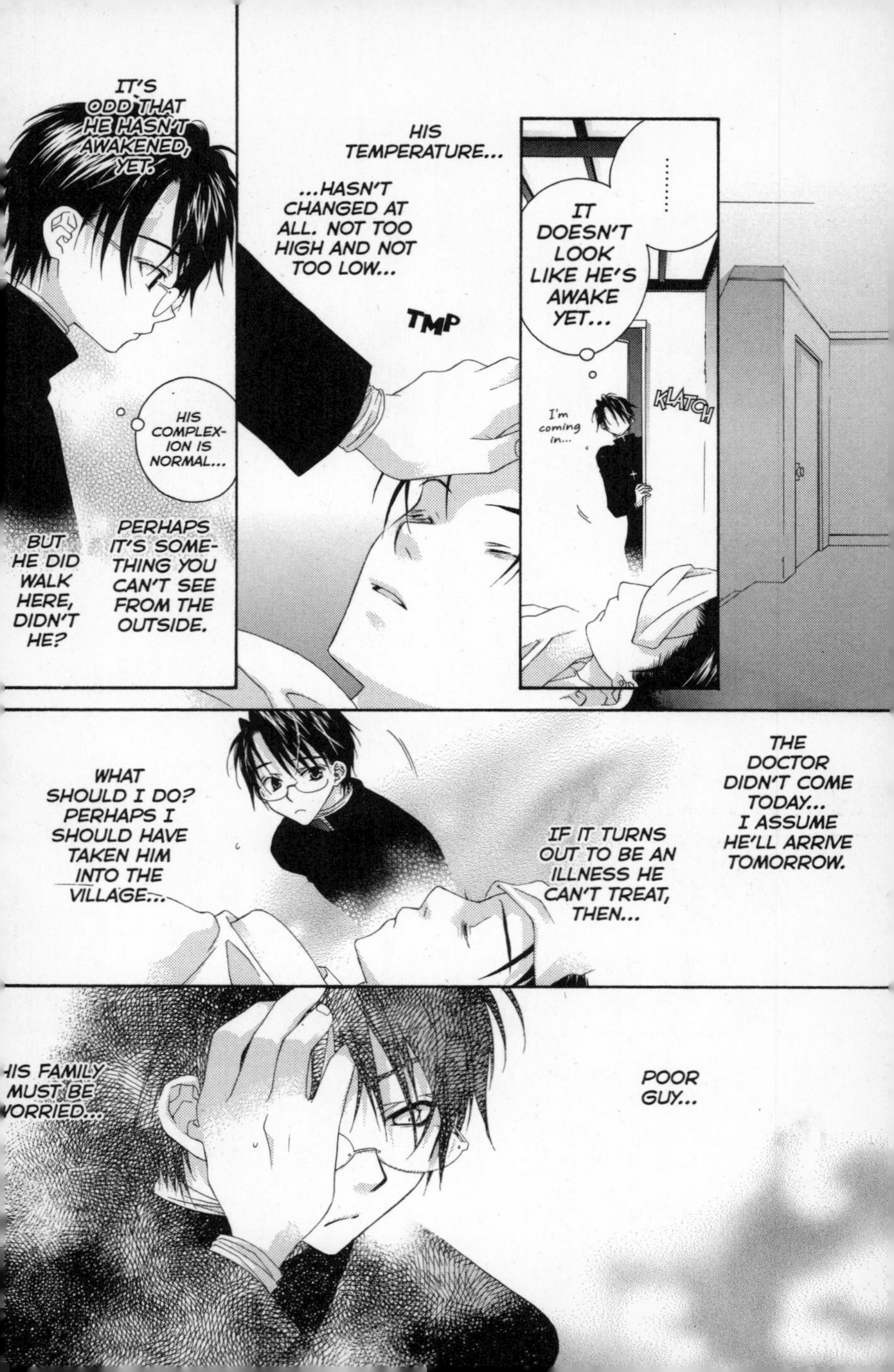
......
IT DOESN'T LOOK LIKE HE'S AWAKE YET...
KLATCH
I'm coming in...
HIS TEMPERATURE...
...HASN'T CHANGED AT ALL. NOT TOO HIGH AND NOT TOO LOW...
TMP
IT'S ODD THAT HE HASN'T AWAKENED, YET.
HIS COMPLEXION IS NORMAL...
PERHAPS IT'S SOMETHING YOU CAN'T SEE FROM THE OUTSIDE.
BUT HE DID WALK HERE, DIDN'T HE?
THE DOCTOR DIDN'T COME TODAY... I ASSUME HE'LL ARRIVE TOMORROW.
IF IT TURNS OUT TO BE AN ILLNESS HE CAN'T TREAT, THEN...
WHAT SHOULD I DO? PERHAPS I SHOULD HAVE TAKEN HIM INTO THE VILLAGE...
POOR GUY...
HIS FAMILY MUST BE WORRIED...

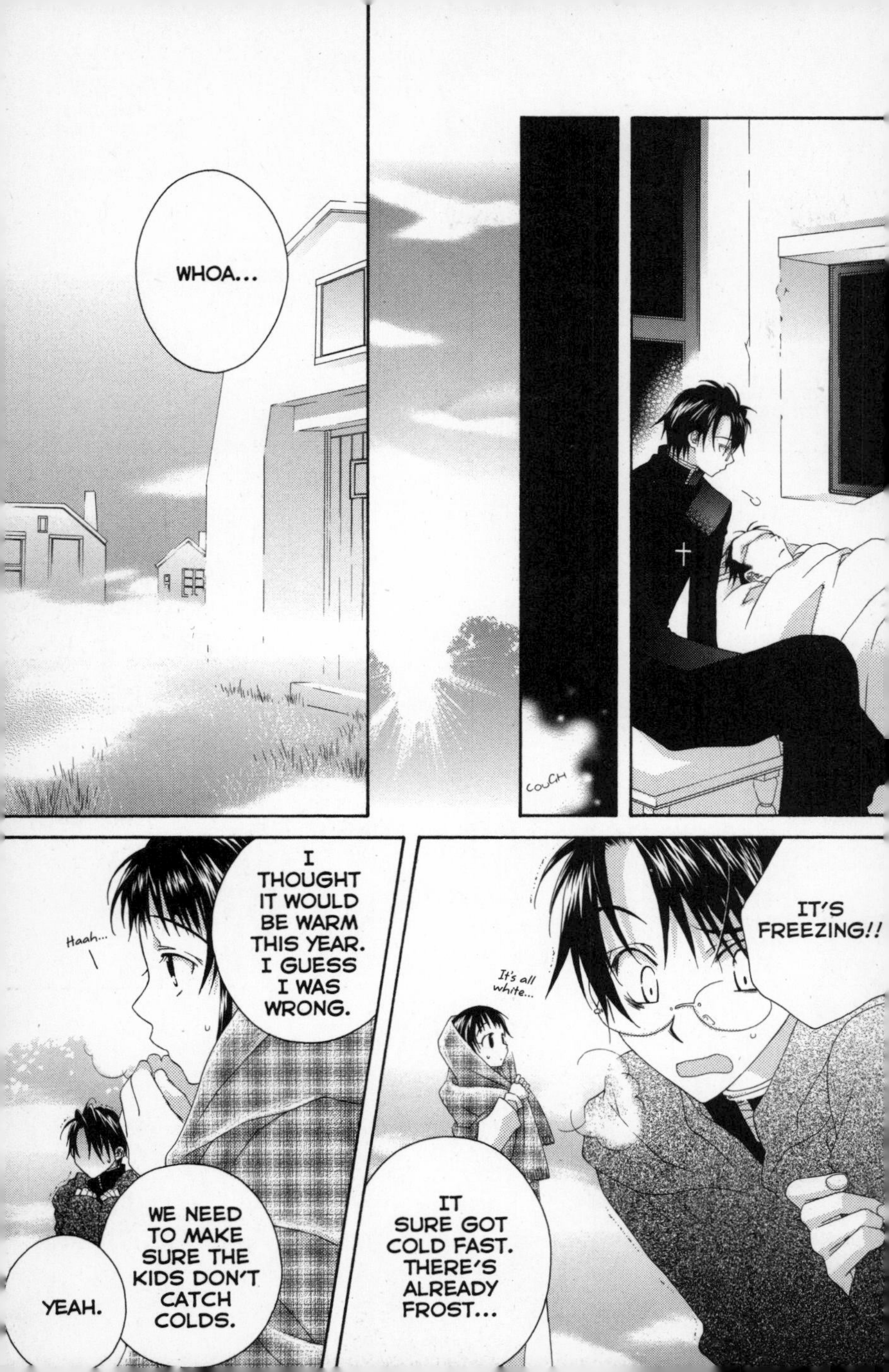
COUGH
WHOA...
IT'S FREEZING!!
It's all white...
IT SURE GOT COLD FAST. THERE'S ALREADY FROST...
I THOUGHT IT WOULD BE WARM THIS YEAR. I GUESS I WAS WRONG.
Haah...
WE NEED TO MAKE SURE THE KIDS DON'T CATCH COLDS.
YEAH.

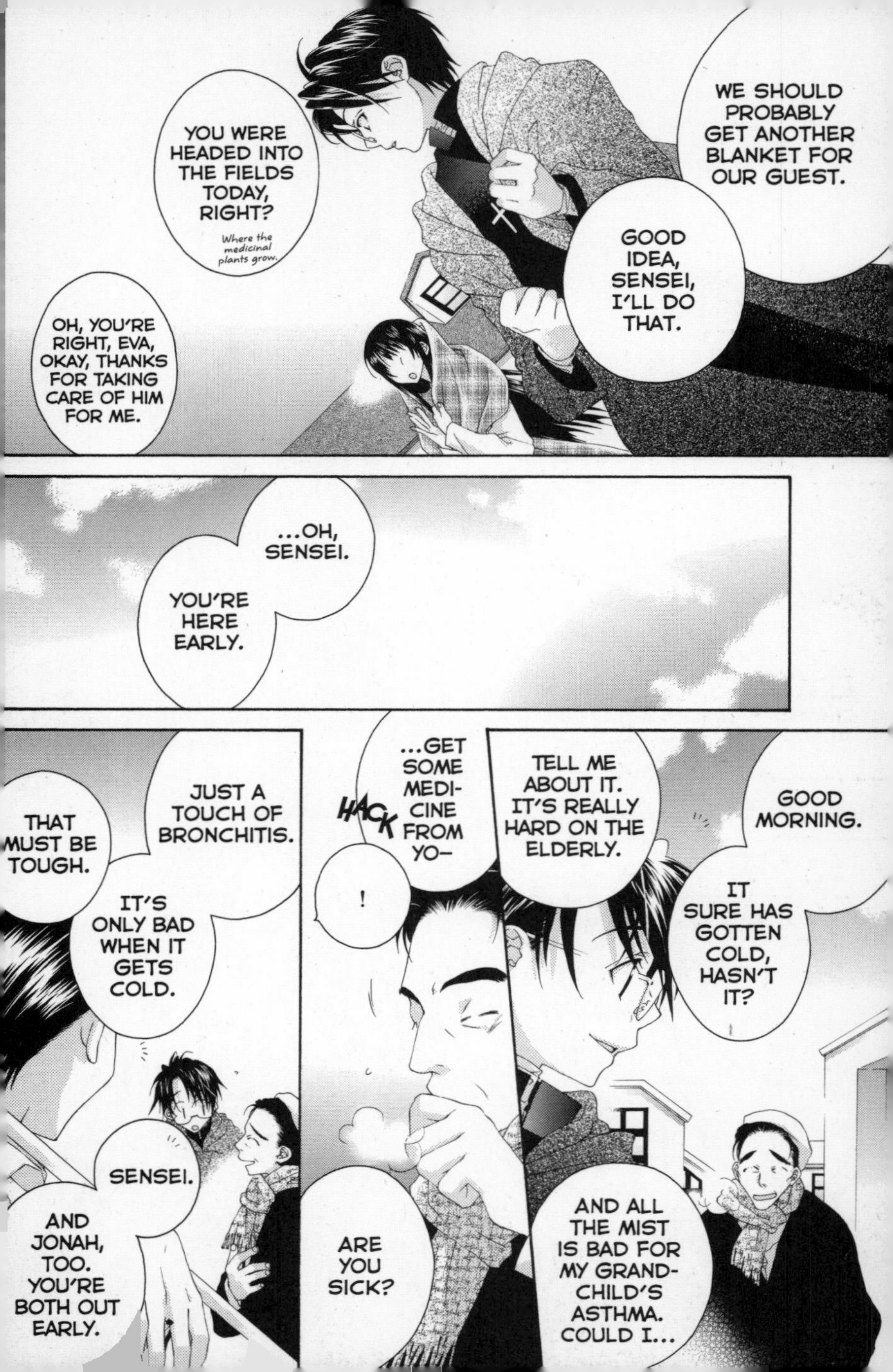
WE SHOULD PROBABLY GET ANOTHER BLANKET FOR OUR GUEST.
GOOD IDEA, SENSEI, I'LL DO THAT.
YOU WERE HEADED INTO THE FIELDS TODAY, RIGHT?
Where the medicinal plants grow.
OH, YOU'RE RIGHT, EVA, OKAY, THANKS FOR TAKING CARE OF HIM FOR ME.
...OH, SENSEI.
YOU'RE HERE EARLY.
GOOD MORNING.
IT SURE HAS GOTTEN COLD, HASN'T IT?
TELL ME ABOUT IT. IT'S REALLY HARD ON THE ELDERLY.
AND ALL THE MIST IS BAD FOR MY GRAND-CHILD'S ASTHMA. COULD I...
...GET SOME MEDI-CINE FROM YO-
HACK
!
ARE YOU SICK?
JUST A TOUCH OF BRONCHITIS.
THAT MUST BE TOUGH.
IT'S ONLY BAD WHEN IT GETS COLD.
SENSEI.
AND JONAH, TOO. YOU'RE BOTH OUT EARLY.

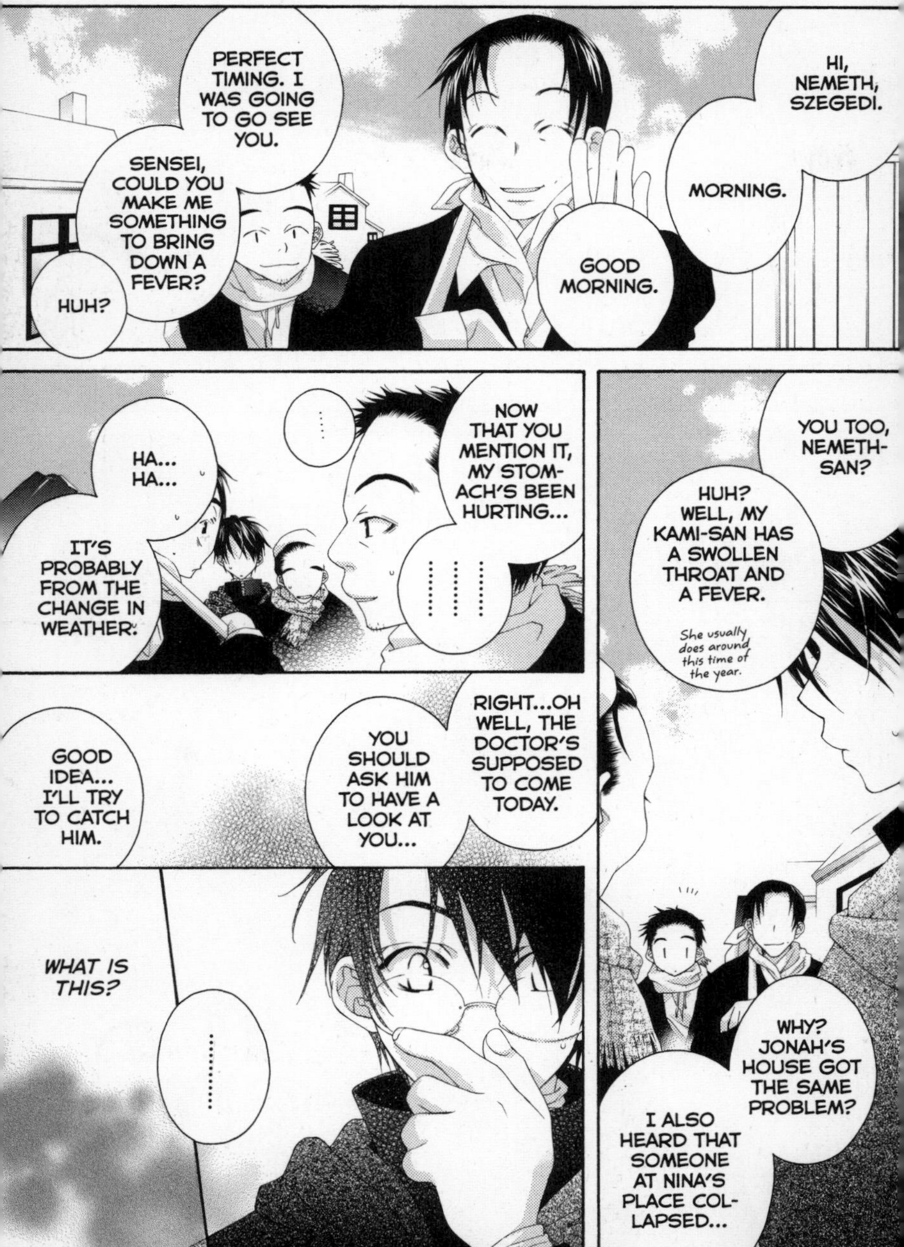
HI, NEMETH, SZEGEDI.
MORNING.
GOOD MORNING.
PERFECT TIMING. I WAS GOING TO GO SEE YOU.
SENSEI, COULD YOU MAKE ME SOMETHING TO BRING DOWN A FEVER?
HUH?
YOU TOO, NEMETH-SAN?
HUH? WELL, MY KAMI-SAN HAS A SWOLLEN THROAT AND A FEVER.
She usually does around this time of the year.
NOW THAT YOU MENTION IT, MY STOM-ACH'S BEEN HURTING...
...
......
HA... HA...
IT'S PROBABLY FROM THE CHANGE IN WEATHER.
RIGHT...OH WELL, THE DOCTOR'S SUPPOSED TO COME TODAY.
YOU SHOULD ASK HIM TO HAVE A LOOK AT YOU...
GOOD IDEA... I'LL TRY TO CATCH HIM.
WHY? JONAH'S HOUSE GOT THE SAME PROBLEM?
I ALSO HEARD THAT SOMEONE AT NINA'S PLACE COL-LAPSED...
....
WHAT IS THIS?

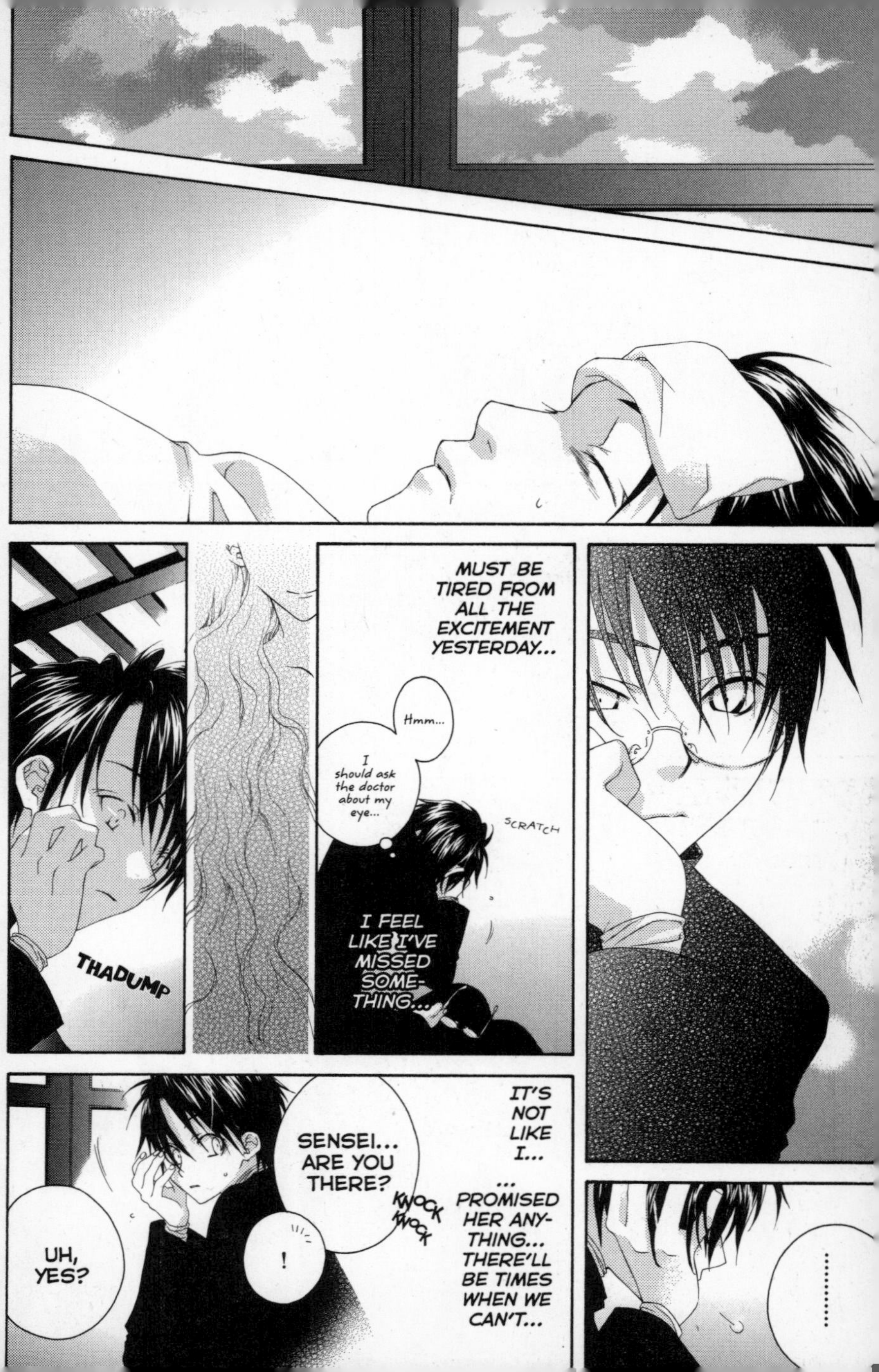
MUST BE TIRED FROM ALL THE EXCITEMENT YESTERDAY...
Hmm...
I should ask the doctor about my eye...
SCRATCH
I FEEL LIKE I'VE MISSED SOME-THING...
THADUMP
......
IT'S NOT LIKE I...
... PROMISED HER ANY-THING... THERE'LL BE TIMES WHEN WE CAN'T...
SENSEI... ARE YOU THERE?
KNOCK KNOCK
!
UH, YES?

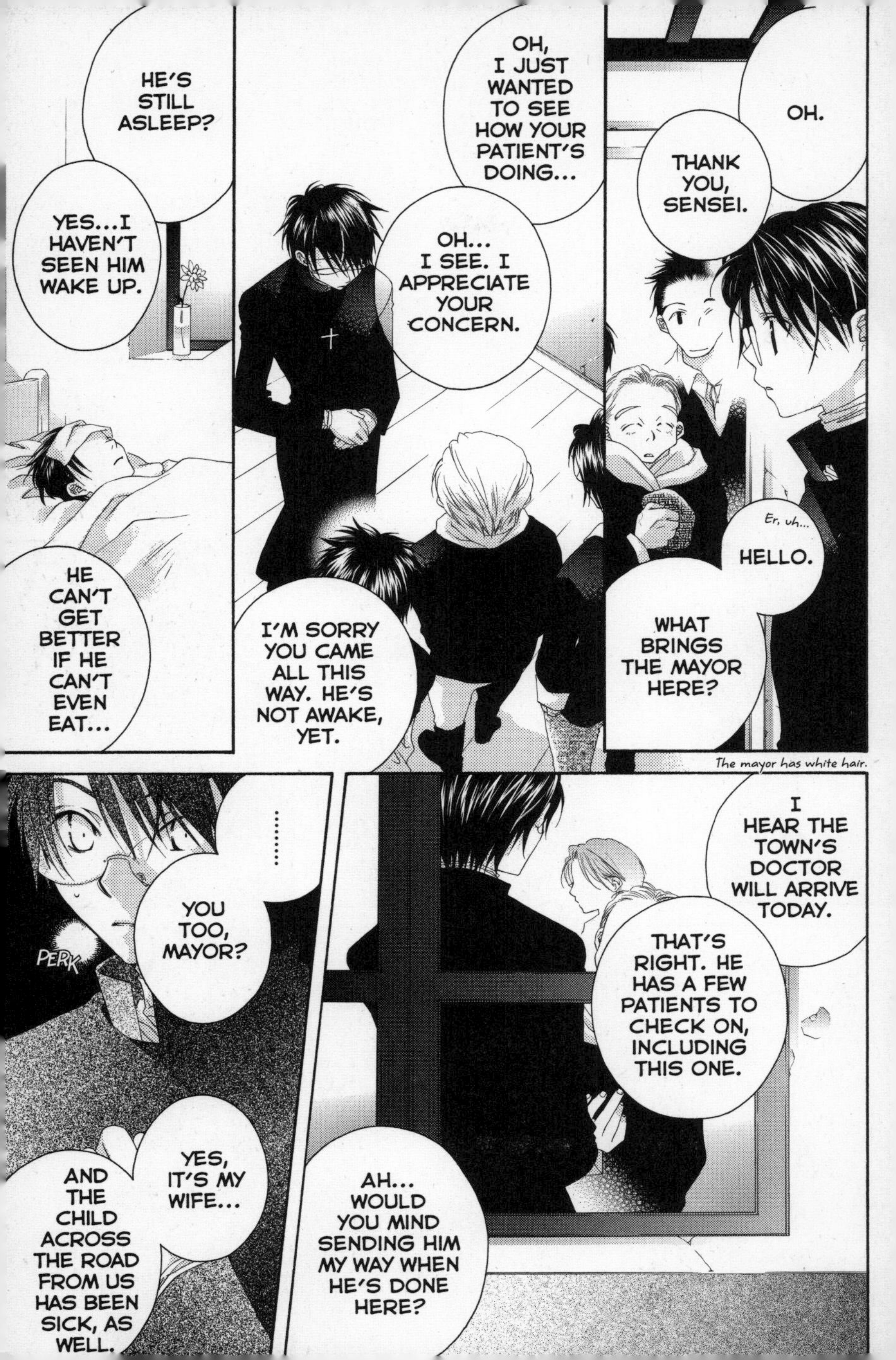
OH.
THANK YOU, SENSEI.
Er, uh...
HELLO.
WHAT BRINGS THE MAYOR HERE?
The mayor has white hair.
OH, I JUST WANTED TO SEE HOW YOUR PATIENT'S DOING...
OH... I SEE. I APPRECIATE YOUR CONCERN.
I'M SORRY YOU CAME ALL THIS WAY. HE'S NOT AWAKE, YET.
HE'S STILL ASLEEP?
YES...I HAVEN'T SEEN HIM WAKE UP.
HE CAN'T GET BETTER IF HE CAN'T EVEN EAT...
I HEAR THE TOWN'S DOCTOR WILL ARRIVE TODAY.
THAT'S RIGHT. HE HAS A FEW PATIENTS TO CHECK ON, INCLUDING THIS ONE.
AH... WOULD YOU MIND SENDING HIM MY WAY WHEN HE'S DONE HERE?
......
PERK
YOU TOO, MAYOR?
YES, IT'S MY WIFE...
AND THE CHILD ACROSS THE ROAD FROM US HAS BEEN SICK, AS WELL.

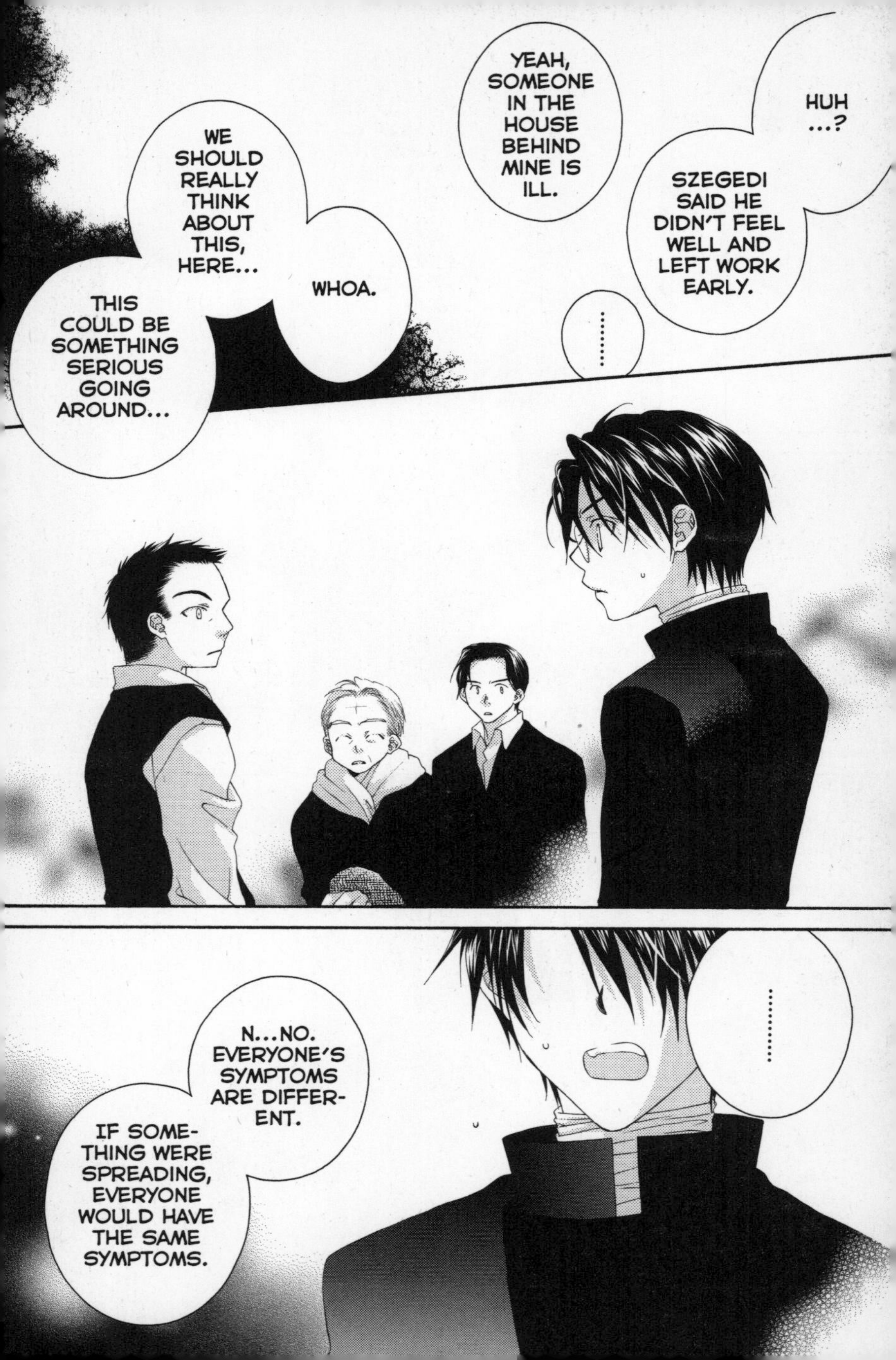
HUH ...?
SZEGEDI SAID HE DIDN'T FEEL WELL AND LEFT WORK EARLY.
YEAH, SOMEONE IN THE HOUSE BEHIND MINE IS ILL.
......
WHOA.
WE SHOULD REALLY THINK ABOUT THIS, HERE...
THIS COULD BE SOMETHING SERIOUS GOING AROUND...
....
N...NO. EVERYONE'S SYMPTOMS ARE DIFFER-ENT.
IF SOME-THING WERE SPREADING, EVERYONE WOULD HAVE THE SAME SYMPTOMS.

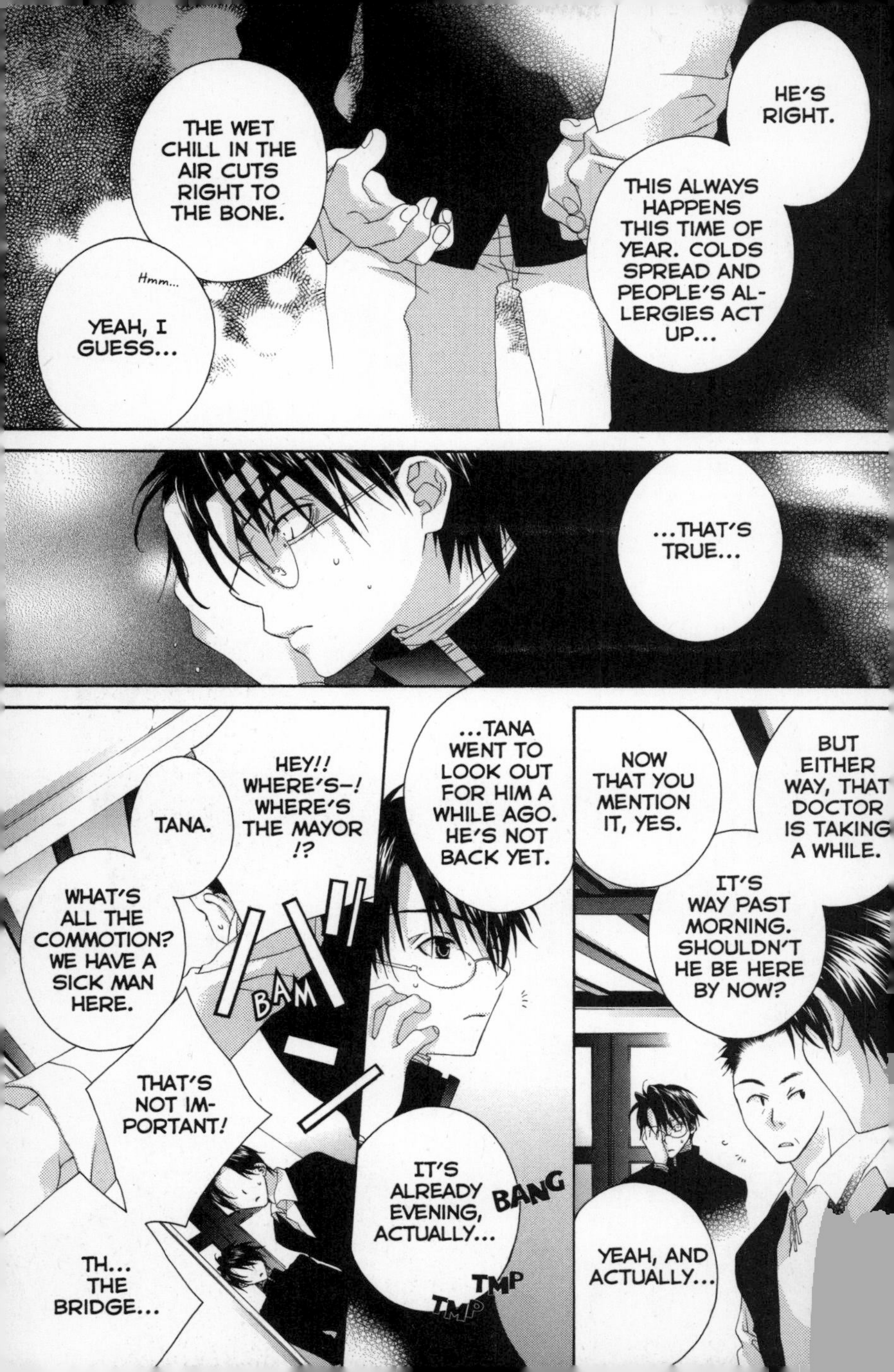

THE WET CHILL IN THE AIR CUTS RIGHT TO THE BONE.
HE'S RIGHT.
THIS ALWAYS HAPPENS THIS TIME OF YEAR. COLDS SPREAD AND PEOPLE'S ALLERGIES ACT UP...
Hmm...
YEAH, I GUESS...
...THAT'S TRUE...
BUT EITHER WAY, THAT DOCTOR IS TAKING A WHILE.
NOW THAT YOU MENTION IT, YES.
IT'S WAY PAST MORNING. SHOULDN'T HE BE HERE BY NOW?
YEAH, AND ACTUALLY...
...TANA WENT TO LOOK OUT FOR HIM A WHILE AGO. HE'S NOT BACK YET.
IT'S ALREADY EVENING, ACTUALLY...
BANG
TMP TMP
HEY!! WHERE'S—! WHERE'S THE MAYOR!?
TANA.
BAM
WHAT'S ALL THE COMMOTION? WE HAVE A SICK MAN HERE.
THAT'S NOT IMPORTANT!
TH... THE BRIDGE...

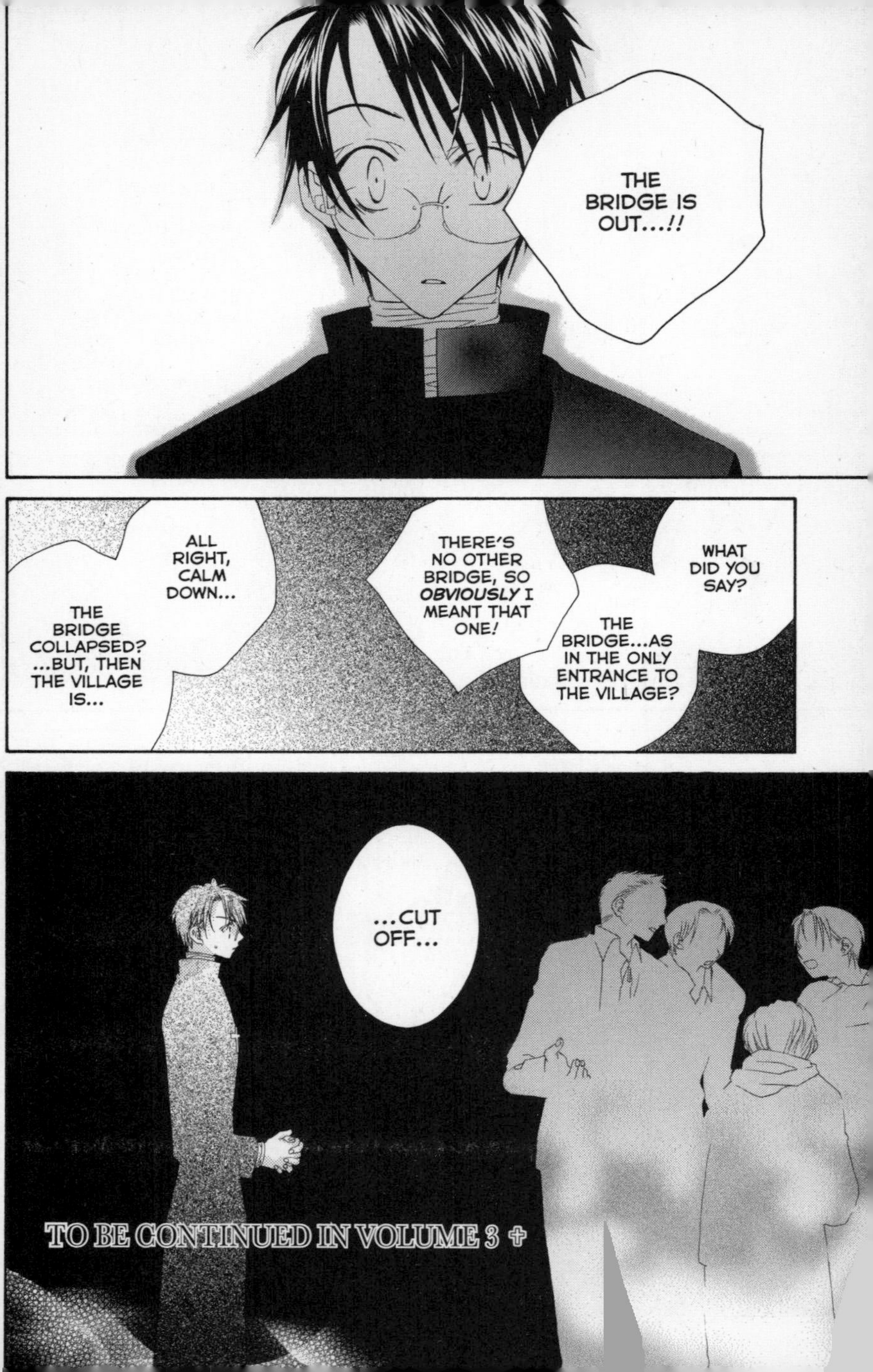
THE BRIDGE IS OUT...!!
WHAT DID YOU SAY?
THE BRIDGE...AS IN THE ONLY ENTRANCE TO THE VILLAGE?
THERE'S NO OTHER BRIDGE, SO *OBVIOUSLY* I MEANT THAT ONE!
ALL RIGHT, CALM DOWN...
THE BRIDGE COLLAPSED? ...BUT, THEN THE VILLAGE IS...
...CUT OFF...
TO BE CONTINUED IN VOLUME 3

Afterword

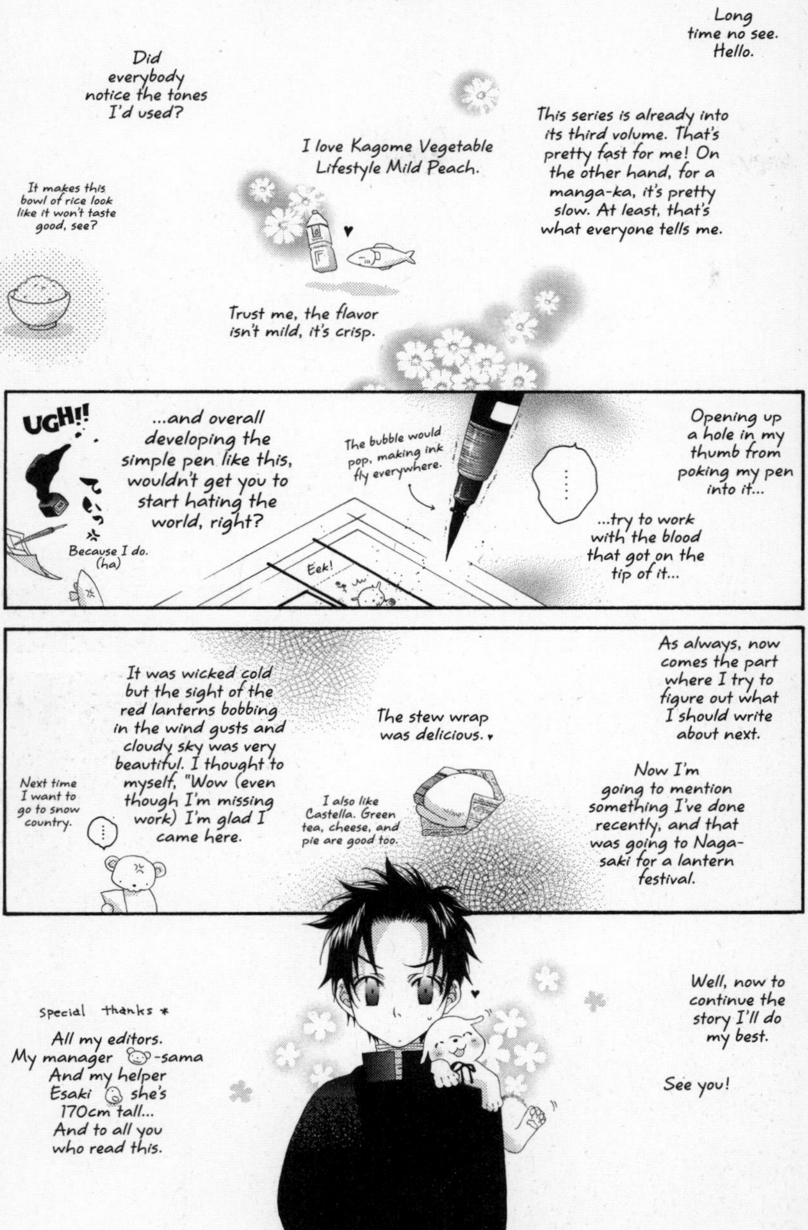
Long time no see. Hello.
This series is already into its third volume. That's pretty fast for me! On the other hand, for a manga-ka, it's pretty slow. At least, that's what everyone tells me.
I love Kagome Vegetable Lifestyle Mild Peach.
Trust me, the flavor isn't mild, it's crisp.
Did everybody notice the tones I'd used?
It makes this bowl of rice look like it won't taste good, see?
Opening up a hole in my thumb from poking my pen into it...
...try to work with the blood that got on the tip of it...
The bubble would pop, making ink fly everywhere.
Eek!
...and overall developing the simple pen like this, wouldn't get you to start hating the world, right?
UGH!!
Because I do. (ha)
As always, now comes the part where I try to figure out what I should write about next.
Now I'm going to mention something I've done recently, and that was going to Naga-saki for a lantern festival.
The stew wrap was delicious.
I also like Castella. Green tea, cheese, and pie are good too.
It was wicked cold but the sight of the red lanterns bobbing in the wind gusts and cloudy sky was very beautiful. I thought to myself, "Wow (even though I'm missing work) I'm glad I came here.
Next time I want to go to snow country.
Well, now to continue the story I'll do my best.
See you!
Special thanks *
All my editors.
My manager -sama
And my helper
Esaki she's 170cm tall...
And to all you who read this.

Translator's Notes

Pg. 11 – the ocean and folklore

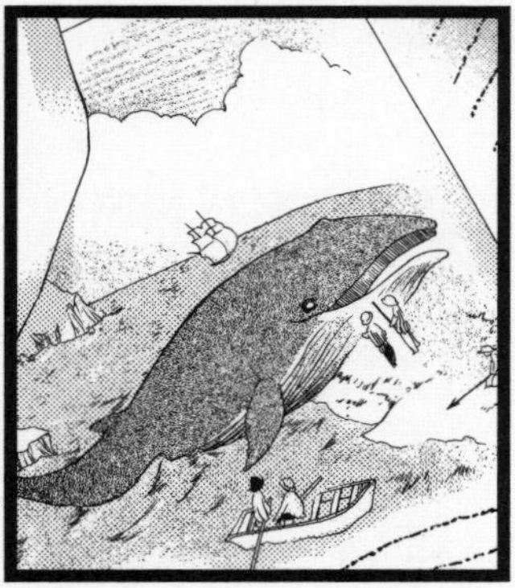

Because Japan is an island country, the ocean is an integral part of its folklore. Such famous tales include "Urashima Taro" and the Creation Story of Japan, itself. All children grow up learning about the ocean through these stories, so it is very shocking to find someone who doesn't know the basics, like Taki here.

Pg. 122 – stuttering chicken

In Japanese, chickens make a "ko ko ko" sound. This is also the first syllable of the word "hello" (konnichiwa). So when Amaria was stuttering and repeating just the first part of "konnichiwa" she sounded like a chicken.

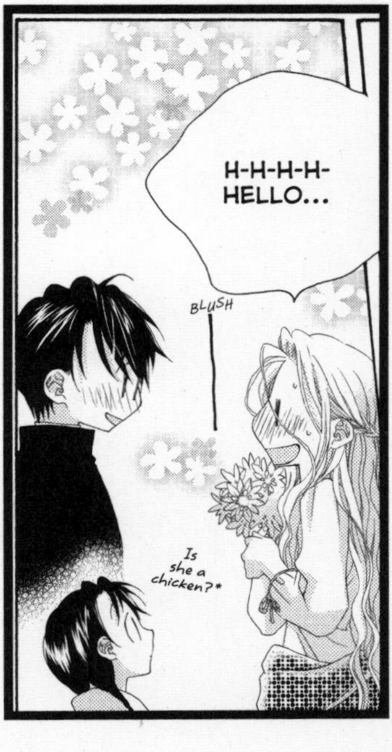
H-H-H-H-
HELLO...
BLUSH
Is she a chicken?*

BONUS TALK

THE COLOR OF WATER, THE BLUE OF THE SEA

It seems Shikimi's fretting and worrying have finally boiled over enough that he's decided to put a stop to it. But things don't always change as easily as we think they will. Since being impatient won't do anything about it either, it's better to just stay calm.

Since I drew the Church to be very deep in the mountains, the ocean's supposed to feel like a really distant illusion.

...Sometimes...the characters' right and left hands suddenly get flip-flopped but...let's try not to notice that, shall we...? Please don't even think about it.

THE FOREST AT NIGHT IS BEAUTIFUL

This title was decided rather quickly for me.

It was mentioned in this radio commercial for a new picture book that was on sale that I barely paid attention to. And yet, even though it's quite a simple phrase, for whatever reason it really stuck in my ears. I wrote it down wondering if I might ever have a chance to use it, so I guess that's really paid off.

The girls in the story have suddenly increased and the Sensei we see now is so different outwardly -- and inside, too -- that it feels like a completely different manga.
This is the first time I've ever had to draw an ordinary flirtatious couple...
It's not so bad having all this lovey-doveyness.

◀◀ AMARIA
About
20 years old.

Type O or B blood.
Aren't her bangs just begging to have something done about them?
She's a little spontaneous, but more direct than Shikimi.

◀ EVA
I think she's about one year or so older than Amaria.
Type A blood.
She's the female version of Taki...
A person who was raised in an environment where she had to be on top of things.
Eva is Amaria's childhood friend.

Oh crap, all the "Bonus Talk" took up only one page. And I could only think of one four-panel funny I could draw.
I could always fill this space with some illustration or something, but since the reader would only glance at it for a second and be done, I've decided to do a Bonus Bonus Talk.

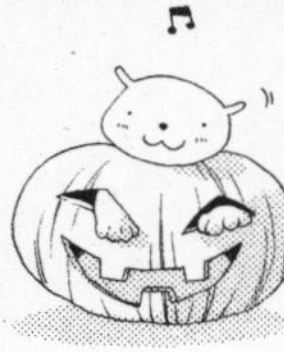

Halloween = The night before All Saints Day.

All Saints Day = Pretty much like "Obon"...I think

ABOUT THE NAMES

Lazlo's actual nickname is "Lazly" but since it makes her sound weak, she went for "Laz."
Doesn't "Lazly" sound like "Lassie" though?
"Agi" is actually the nickname for "Agnes." But I think "Agi" sounds cuter.
As for Taki's last name "Juhas": it reminded me of chocolate wafers. Doesn't it sound tastier?
Grey simply came from his eye color which is a blue-grey. Though that's not to say I didn't put any love into it...eh?
I'm sure people who know will know about Shikimi's deal. It's a poison. His birthday is March 19th.

ABOUT THE DOG

It's scary how quickly she's become brighter.
Compared to when she first showed up, it was as though she was a stuffed animal only. It's almost tempting to think that something's only **wearing** her as a costume.

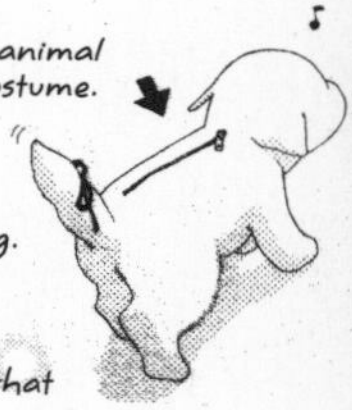

LIKES AND DISLIKES

This manga has few eating scenes. Not to say I've got anything against eating.
Since Taki grew up so poor he doesn't categorize foods between likes and dislikes. He'd eat even a monster if he could... But that also just seems to be his nature. I wonder...
For some reason I really imagine Shikimi to have such a hatred for carrots that they make him vomit.
And Laz probably likes to drink. Even though she most likely can't hold her liquor.

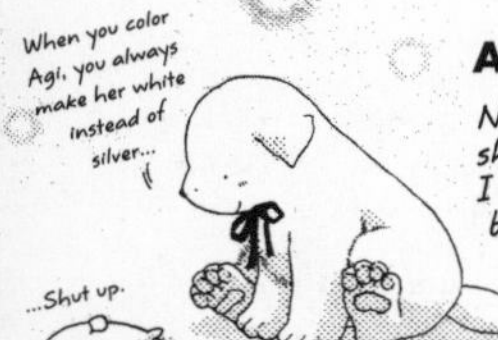
When you color Agi, you always make her white instead of silver...
...Shut up.

ABOUT THE COLORS

Now for the colors. All the characters are supposed to have different shades of skin color but...only very subtly...
I have a poor sense when it comes to colors but when there are a lot of blacks it has a relatively settled and orderly feel to it, so I love this cast of black-suited characters. I also like drawing flowers. Even though they're all (?) guys.

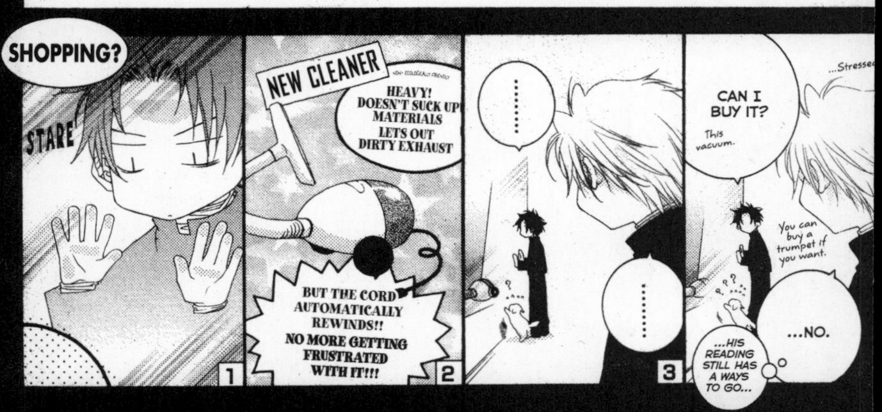
SHOPPING?
STARE
1
NEW CLEANER
NOW ECOLOGICALLY FRIENDLY
HEAVY! DOESN'T SUCK UP MATERIALS LETS OUT DIRTY EXHAUST
BUT THE CORD AUTOMATICALLY REWINDS!! NO MORE GETTING FRUSTRATED WITH IT!!!
2
......
?
......
3
...Stresse
CAN I BUY IT?
This vacuum.
You can buy a trumpet if you want.
...NO.
...HIS READING STILL HAS A WAYS TO GO...

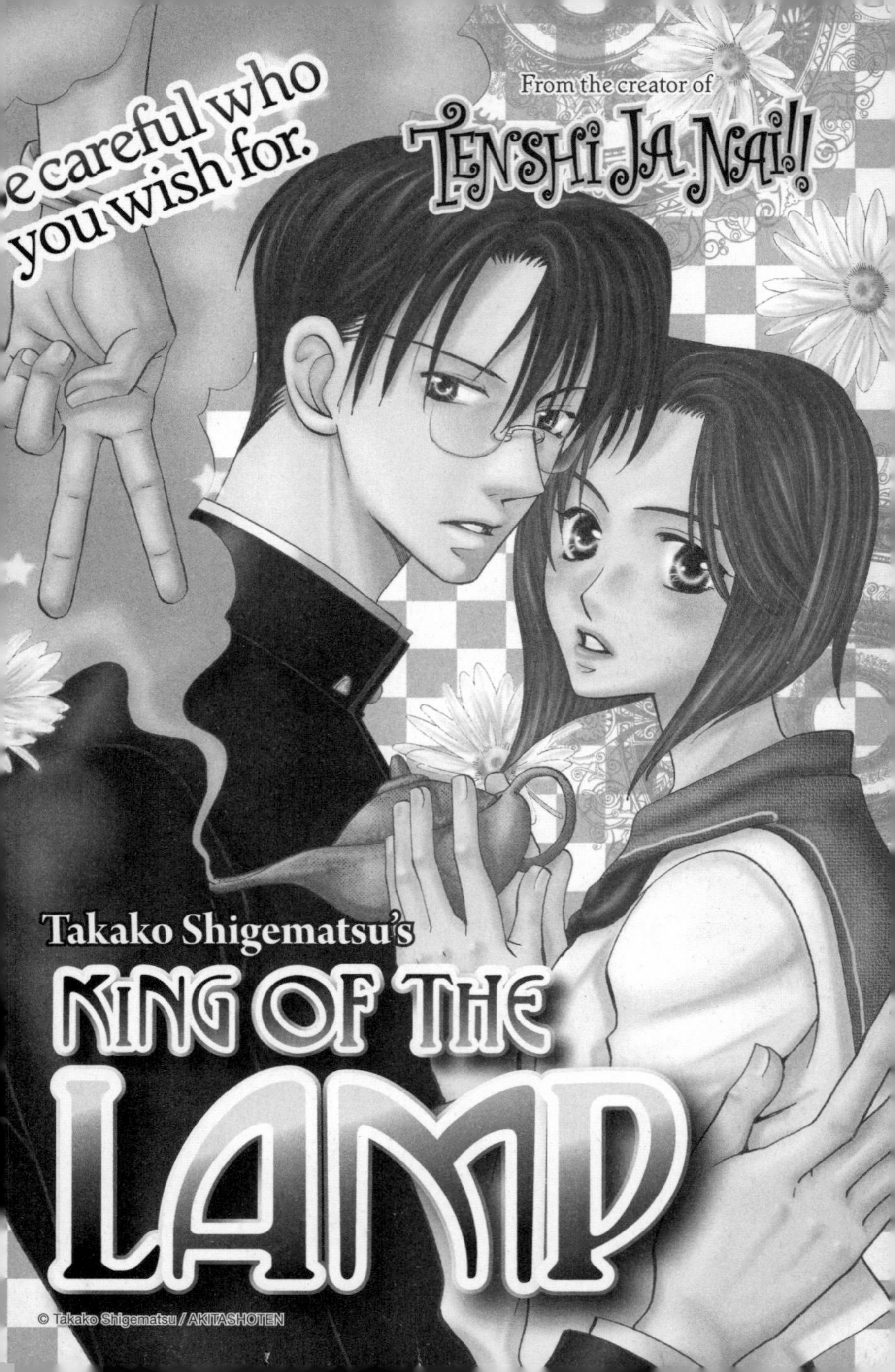
e careful who
you wish for.
From the creator of
TENSHI JA NAI!!
Takako Shigematsu's
KING OF THE
LAMP
© Takako Shigematsu / AKITASHOTEN

Reading. 'Riting. 'Rithmetic.

Romance.

LOVE MASTER A

by Kyoko Hashimoto

They finally
built a better
boyfriend.

A.I. REVOLUTION

by Yuu Asami